Peter Brook is regarded as one of the most important and influential directors today. In this fascinating study, Albert Hunt and Geoffrey Reeves chronicle Brook's development beginning with his earliest productions and concluding with some of his most recent and innovative work. As Associate Director to Peter Brook on a number of important productions, Geoffrey Reeves was able to observe at first hand many of the director's rehearsal and performance methods. Both Reeves and Hunt are established directors themselves and can offer special insight into Brook's techniques.

The book traces the director's work from the Birmingham Repertory Theatre to the Royal Shakespeare Company, the establishment of his own company and theatre at the Bouffes du Nord in Paris, and the creation of his unique theatrical style. Reeves and Hunt also focus on Brook outside the theatre including the film version of his *Mahabharata* and work for the opera house.

The book will be of interest to theatre practitioners, students and scholars as well as to the general reader. It includes a chronology of Brook's theatre career and is illustrated with photographs from key productions.

DIRECTORS IN PERSPECTIVE

General editor: Christopher Innes

Peter Brook

What characterises modern theatre above all is continual stylistic innovation, in which theory and presentation have combined to create a wealth of new forms – naturalism, expressionism, epic theatre, and so forth – in a way that has made directors the leading figures rather than dramatists. To a greater extent than is perhaps generally realised, it has been directors who have provided dramatic models for playwrights, though of course there are many different variations in this relationship. In some cases a dramatist's themes challenge a director to create new performance conditions (Stanislavski and Chekhov), or a dramatist turns director to formulate an appropriate style for his work (Brecht); alternatively a director writes plays to correspond with his theory (Artaud), or creates communal scripts out of exploratory work with actors (Chaikin, Grotowski). Some directors are identified with a single theory (Craig), others gave definitive shape to a range of styles (Reinhardt); the work of some has an ideological basis (Stein), while others work more pragmatically (Bergman).

Generally speaking, those directors who have contributed to what is distinctly 'modern' in today's theatre stand in much the same relationship to the dramatic texts they work with, as composers do to librettists in opera. However, since theatrical performance is the most ephemeral of the arts and the only easily reproducible element is the text, critical attention has tended to focus on the playwright. This series is designed to redress the balance by providing an overview of selected directors' stage work: those who helped to formulate modern theories of drama. Their key productions have been reconstructed from prompt-books, revues, scene-designs, photographs, diaries, correspondence and – where these productions are contemporary – documented by first-hand description, interviews with the director, and so forth. Apart from its intrinsic interest, this record allows a critical perspective, testing ideas against practical problems and achievements. In each case, too, the director's work is set in context by indicating the source of his ideas and their influence, the organisation of his acting company, and his relationship to the theatrical or political establishment, so to bring out wider issues: the way theatre both reflects and influences assumptions about the nature of man and his social role.

Christopher Innes

Peter Brook

BY ALBERT HUNT AND GEOFFREY REEVES

PUBLISHED BY THE PRESS SYNDICATE OF THE UNIVERSITY OF CAMBRIDGE
The Pitt Building, Trumpington Street, Cambridge, United Kingdom

CAMBRIDGE UNIVERSITY PRESS
The Edinburgh Building, Cambridge CB2 2RU, UK   http://www.cup.cam.ac.uk
40 West 20th Street, New York, NY 10011–4211, USA   http://www.cup.org
10 Stamford Road, Oakleigh, Melbourne 3166, Australia
Ruiz de Alarcón 13, 28014 Madrid, Spain

First published 1995
Reprinted 1999

Printed in the United Kingdom at the University Press, Cambridge

A catalogue record for this book is available from the British Library

Library of Congress Cataloguing in Publication data
Hunt, Albert.
Peter Brook / by Albert Hunt and Geoffrey Reeves.
    p.   cm. – (Directors in perspective)
Includes bibliographical references and index.
ISBN 0 521 22662 7 (hardback) ISBN 0 521 29605 6 (paperback)
1. Brook, Peter – Criticism and interpretation.
I. Reeves, Geoffrey.   II. Title.   III. Series.
PN2598 B69H86   1995
792'.0233'092–dc20 94-27333 CIP

ISBN 0 521 22662 7 hardback
ISBN 0 521 29605 6 paperback

SE

Contents

Illustrations

Chronology

	Colombe	Anouilh and Cannan	New, London
1953			
	Faust	Gounod	Metropolitan, New York
	Venice Preserv'd	Otway	Lyric, Hammersmith
	The Little Hut	Roussin/ Mitford	Coronet, New York
1954			
	The Dark is Light Enough	Fry	Aldwych, London
	Both Ends Meet	Macrae	Apollo, London
	The House of Flowers	Capote/Arlen	Alvin, New York
1955			
	The Lark	Anouilh/Fry	Lyric, Hammersmith
	Titus Andronicus	Shakespeare	Stratford-upon-Avon, and Stoll, London, 1956
	Hamlet	Shakespeare	Phoenix, London and Moscow
1956			
	The Power and the Glory	Greene/Cannan and Bost	Phoenix, London
	The Family Reunion	Eliot	Phoenix, London
	A View from the Bridge	Miller	Comedy, London
	La Chatte sur un toit brûlant	Williams/ Obey	Antoine, Paris
1957			
	Eugene Onegin	Tchaikovsky	Metropolitan, New York
	The Tempest	Shakespeare	Stratford-upon-Avon and Drury Lane, London
1958			
	Vu du pont	Miller/Aymé	Antoine, Paris
	The Visit	Dürrenmatt/ Valency	English provinces, Lynn Fontanne, New York, and Royalty, London, 1960
	Irma La Douce	Breffort/More, Heneker and Norman	Lyric, London and Plymouth, New York
1959			
	The Fighting Cock	Anouilh/Hill	ANTA, New York
1960			
	Le Balcon	Genet	Gymnase, Paris
1962			
	King Lear	Shakespeare	Stratford-upon-Avon, Aldwych, London, European tour and New York

1963

The Physicists	Dürrenmatt/ Kirkup	Aldwych, London
The Tempest	Shakespeare	Stratford-upon-Avon
The Perils of Scobie Prilt	More and Norman	New, Oxford
La Danse de Sergent Musgrave	Arden/Pons	Athénée, Paris
Le Vicaire	Hochhuth	Athénée, Paris

1964

Theatre of Cruelty		LAMDA, London
The Screens: Part One	Genet/ Frechtman	Donmar, London
The Marat/Sade	Weiss/Mitchell	Aldwych, London, and Martin Beck, New York, 1966
The Physicists	Dürrenmatt/ Kirkup	Martin Beck, New York

1965

The Investigation	Weiss	Aldwych, London

1966

US	collective	Aldwych, London

1968

Oedipus	Seneca/Hughes	Old Vic, London
The Tempest	after Shakespeare	Round House, London

1970

A Midsummer Night's Dream	Shakespeare	Stratford-upon-Avon, Aldwych, London and world tour 1971 and 1972
The Bee Man of Orme	after Stockton	Mobilier National, Paris

1971

Orghast	Hughes	Persepolis

1973

Kaspar	Handke	Mobilier National and suburbs, Paris

1972/3

African trip including *Conference of the Birds* in Niger, Nigeria and Dahomey
American trip including *Conference of the Birds* in California, Colorado, Minnesota and New York

1974

Timon d'Athènes	Shakespeare/ Carrière	Bouffes du Nord, Paris

1975

Les Ik	Turnbull/ Cannan and Higgins	Bouffes du Nord, Paris
Conference of the Birds		Bouffes du Nord, Paris
Timon d'Athènes		Bouffes du Nord, Paris

1976			
	The Ik		Round House, London, United States and Europe
1977			
	Ubu	Jarry	Bouffes du Nord, Paris
1978			
	Ubu		Young Vic, London, and Latin America
	Mesure pour Mesure	Shakespeare/ Carrière	Bouffes du Nord, Paris
	Antony and Cleopatra	Shakespeare	Stratford-upon-Avon and Aldwych, London, 1979
1979			
	Mesure pour Mesure		Europe
	Conference of the Birds	Attar/Hughes and Carrière	Avignon and Bouffes du Nord, Paris
1980			
	L'Os, The Ik, Ubu, Conference of the Birds		Australia and New York
	L'Os, Conference of the Birds		Bouffes du Nord, Paris
1981			
	La Cérisaie	Chekhov/Brook and Carrière and Vavrova	Bouffes du Nord, Paris
	La Tragédie de Carmen	Bizet/Mérimée/ Meilhac/Halévy/ Constant/ Carrière/Brook	Bouffes du Nord, Paris
1982			
	Carmen		New York
	Carmen		Bouffes du Nord, Paris
1983			
	La Cérisaie	Chekhov/ Lavrova/ Carrière	Bouffes du Nord, Paris
	Chin Chin	Billetdoux	Théâtre Montparnasse, Paris
1985			
	Le Mahabharata	Carrière/Brook	Avignon, Bouffes du Nord, Paris, and Europe
1986			
	Carmen		Japan
1987			
	The Mahabharata		Zurich, Los Angeles and Brooklyn

1988

The Cherry Orchard	Chekhov/ Lavrova/Brook	Brooklyn
The Mahabharata	Carrière/Brook	Glasgow, Australia and Japan

1989

Woza Albert!	Simon	Bouffes du Nord, Paris

1990

La Tempête	Shakespeare/ Carrière	Bouffes du Nord, Paris, and Glasgow

1992

Impressions de Pélleas	Debussy/ Maeterlinck/ Constant/Brook	Bouffes du Nord, Paris, and Europe 1993

1993

L'Homme Qui	Brook/Carrière Sacks	Bouffes du Nord, Paris, and Europe

Film and television work

1944	*A Sentimental Journey* (film)
1952	*The Beggar's Opera* (film)
1953	*Box for One* (television)
	King Lear (television)
1955	*The Birthday Present* (television)
	Report from Moscow (television)
1957	*Heaven and Earth* (television)
1960	*Moderato Cantabile* (film)
1963	*The Lord of the Flies* (film)
1966	*Zero* in trilogy *Red, White and Zero* (film)
1967	*The Marat/Sade* (film)
1968	*Tell Me Lies* (film)
1971	*King Lear* (film)
1979	*Meeting with Remarkable Men* (film)
1979	*Mesure pour Mesure* (television)
1983	*Carmen* (television)
1989	*Mahabharata* (film & television)

Preface

This is an account of Peter Brook's theatre work. In order to minimise the necessary documentation it assumes that the reader has access to three other books:

Peter Brook, *The Empty Space* (Harmondsworth: Penguin, 1968), a revised version of the four Granada lectures he gave in 1965.

Peter Brook, *The Shifting Point* (London: Methuen, 1988), a collection of articles written and interviews given between 1946 and 1987.

David Williams, *Peter Brook: A Theatrical Casebook* (London: Methuen, 1988; updated 1992), a collection of reviews and articles about Brook's work from 1962 to 1991.

Brook's and others' comments are only quoted at length if they do not appear in any of these three books.

Although an attempt is made to trace a path through the work, as Brook has over eighty productions to his credit, it is not possible to deal with each in any detail: a weighty book could be written on the fifteen Shakespeare ones alone.

This book is a collaboration: it is the joint work of the authors. However, as we value highly the personal response, certain passages have been contributed solely in the voice of one of the authors; such passages are marked AH or GR.

Acknowledgements

This book was commissioned when the *Mahabharata* was only a gleam in Brook's eye. We should therefore pay tribute to the great patience of Christopher Innes, the quiet midwife of a book fifteen years in the making. We are also grateful to Sally Jacobs, for her informative interview, and to Martin Esslin and Patricia Ryan, who contributed much raw material, to Jim Carmody and Larry Maslon, who read the early chapters and steered us in the right direction, and to Catherine Burroughs and Helena Pope, who read the text at twice its present length and greatly helped us to achieve its present form.

AH/GR

Prologue

I'm living all my life in the theatre. I made my cash there and have proved my ability to live in the competitive world through one form, the theatre. Now I want to know what it is, and to know what it is is to know what it could be.

Peter Brook, a month before leaving for Africa in December 1972

This book tells the story of a search. The search began, in public at least, when a seventeen-year-old Peter Brook directed a production of Christopher Marlowe's *Dr Faustus* at the Torch Theatre, London, in 1942. The production was scarcely noticed and has long since been forgotten. But, after a handful of other productions, in London and at the Birmingham Rep, Brook stepped on to the national stage in 1946 with a production of *Love's Labour's Lost* at the Shakespeare Memorial Theatre in Stratford-upon-Avon. Since then he has only been out of the public eye when he has chosen to pursue his search in remote areas of the world. He has always returned to put his findings on display, in Paris, London, New York and, more recently, in Glasgow.

The precise object of the search is hard to define. In the early days, the search had a strictly limited, practical objective. During a brief stay as an undergraduate at Magdalen College, Oxford, while the Second World War was on, Brook and some friends had succeeded in raising enough money to make a full-length film of Laurence Sterne's *A Sentimental Journey*. Brook was, apparently, seized with a passion for film-making. But the British Film Industry was then an entirely closed monopoly: there was no possible way for an unknown outsider to be given the opportunity to direct films. (It was not until the late 1950s that a new generation of directors succeeded in penetrating the closed world of British film-making – and they got in, interestingly enough, on the back of a successful piece of theatre, John Osborne's *Look Back in Anger*.) A decade earlier, Brook, faced with the impenetrability of British cinema, found himself also faced with openings in the theatre. He eagerly seized them and found, in a very short time, that he had launched himself on a glitteringly successful career.

It would scarcely be an exaggeration to say that in those early days in the theatre what he was searching for was a passport into film-making. He got it in 1952 when he directed John Gray's *The Beggar's Opera*, for Herbert Wilcox and Laurence Olivier, with a cast that included (as well as Olivier) Stanley Holloway, Dorothy Tutin, Hugh Griffith and Laurence Naismith. The scriptwriters were Denis Cannan and Christopher Fry, both of whom figured largely in Brook's theatre work. If this eighteenth century costume drama had been as successful at the box office as Tony Richardson's version of the eighteenth century novel *Tom Jones* was to be nine years later, Brook's search might have taken off in a different direction. Fortunately for the theatre, the film was a flop. But he was to continue to make films throughout his career – *Moderato Cantabile* in France in 1960, *Lord of the Flies* in 1963, the year after one of his greatest successes in the theatre, *King Lear*, and the year before his theatre career itself took off in a different direction. Since 1970, when he formed his Centre International de Créations Théâtrales (C.I.C.T.) in Paris, Brook seems to have regarded the filming of the theatre work, developed in the Centre, as a part of his on-going projects. He filmed three versions of *Carmen* and spent much of 1989 making a filmed version of *The Mahabharata*, which was markedly different in style from the epic he has created in the theatre. (But virtually all his film-making since *Lord of the Flies* has been dependent on his theatre work. Films like *King Lear* and *The Marat/Sade* derived directly from stage productions.)

If, however, he began working in theatre largely because the offers of work were there (and in the hope that theatre might give him a passport into film) he quickly found that he was enjoying the success his theatre work brought him. In 1972, a few weeks before taking a group of international actors on an 'experimental' trip through remote African villages, he looked back on the process that had taken him to that particular point in his search:

> Of course I am delighted if a play I do is successful. I like playing the game of the commercial theatre, of going into the box office and asking what the advance is and so forth, but that's the fringe. It's totally unimportant and in no way connected with my real work. Fundamentally all the work I've done has been like an airplane circling to land. It has been spiralling and dealing with one question only: what is the nature of theatre? I've worked in every form – West End farces, TV, comedies, musicals – I've worked just to explore the field. But exploring the field doesn't mean going on in the same way, for that would mean being locked into an eternal adolescence. Circling the field eventually narrows and now I am coming closer to the point of landing.

What Brook seemed to be searching for primarily in those early years of exploring the field was variety of experience. He was like a magpie, apparently snapping up anything that came his way. As he flitted between *Measure for Measure, The Little Hut, Salome* and *Irma la Douce*, between Stratford-upon-Avon, the West End, Paris and Broadway – not to speak of a year as Director of Productions at the Royal Opera House, Covent Garden, a title he invented for himself – he gives the impression of being driven by an insatiable curiosity. But it is not until the 1960s that he begins to show a more overt curiosity about the nature of what he is doing. Articles start appearing, mainly in the recently launched magazine, *Encore* (which refers to itself as the 'Voice of Vital Theatre'), in which Brook begins to speculate about the nature and purpose of theatre. These speculations are summed up in his book *The Empty Space*, published in 1968, in which he tells us that his search is for a 'less deadly, but as yet largely undefined, theatre'. But by 1968 he was already nearing the end of what for many people would have been regarded as a second career.

In *The Empty Space*, Brook wrote:

Anyone interested in processes in the natural world would be very rewarded by a study of theatre conditions. His discoveries would be far more applicable to general society than the study of bees or ants. Under the magnifying glass he would see a group of people living all the time according to precise, shared but unnamed standards. He would see that in any community a theatre has no particular function – or a unique one.

If we put a magnifying glass on the 'theatre conditions' Brook has worked in, we can see the way in which he himself has changed them. His theatre work falls into three distinct phases.

In the first phase, from 1946 to 1963, he worked in the commercial theatre. In Britain, this normally meant three or four weeks' rehearsal with a maximum of forty hours a week. In the United States, this rehearsal period would be followed by weeks of playing in places like Boston and Philadelphia, during which time the production was often changed in the light of the audiences' responses.

In Britain, productions usually toured the provinces for two to four weeks before they reached London, but there were very few radical changes during the tour. Rewrites were minimal and actors were hardly ever fired, as happened in the States.

In Paris, there might be five weeks' rehearsal, but there would be no pre-opening tour. Only at the Memorial Theatre in Stratford-upon-Avon would there be more rehearsal time, perhaps five or six weeks, but during the rehearsal period actors on contract to what became the Royal Shakespeare Company (RSC) would be performing in other plays while they rehearsed. Actors would be lost to matinées. It was only towards the end of this first phase of his career that Brook had enough power to demand longer rehearsal periods. The success of his RSC production of *King Lear* in 1962 put him in a particularly strong position.

The second phase of Brook's work can be said to have started at the beginning of 1964, after he persuaded Peter Hall, Artistic Director of the Royal Shakespeare Company, to give him three months for research with a specially selected group of ten actors. This phase lasted until 1970. During this period he worked only for the large subsidised theatres: the RSC and the National. His rehearsal periods at the RSC were now anywhere between six and eight weeks. *US* was given four months. The National gave him ten weeks' rehearsal time for *Oedipus*. The six years between 1964 and 1970 were to be decisive in changing Brook's relationship with theatre production.

In 1964, he was able, following his period of research, to form the nucleus of an acting group in the RSC. But throughout the 1960s he was still forced to make compromises, particularly concerning casting. During the first phase of his work, Brook himself had helped to make the director a more powerful figure in the theatre. But by 1964 new authority figures had emerged. The Artistic Directors, both at the RSC and the National could, and did, have a say in what went on the stage.

The third phase of Brook's career began in 1970 (after a false start in 1968). Brook had decided to acquire control of his own means of production. Backed by a million-dollar subsidy for a three-year programme, from the Ford Foundation and others, he set up his Centre International de Créations Théâtrales in Paris, and has made this his base ever since. In the last twenty years he has only made one foray into a theatre not under his control: in 1978, when he returned briefly to the RSC to direct *Antony and Cleopatra*.

The existence of the Centre in Paris (which acquired its own theatre, the Bouffes du Nord in 1974) has given Brook virtually complete freedom to 'experiment', as he sees it, in his attempt to answer the basic question of 'what the theatre is and . . . what it could be'. He has been able to gather round him a permanent group of collaborators and performers from several continents. The rhythm of his working life is no longer built around the demands of first nights: he juggles with a number of projects that sometimes seem to disappear only to reappear in a different context. He takes his flock to remote places in search of new experiences – but from time to time they make acclaimed appearances on world stages – in quarries in Avignon and Adelaide, in theatres in Brooklyn and Glasgow (redesigned at huge cost to look as decayed as the Bouffes).

This last phase of his work, though, and the freedom it has given him to follow his deepest instincts, sheds a questioning light on the earlier stages of his search. What precisely has he been looking for? A search for a 'less deadly' theatre seems modest enough. But it has taken him into obscure regions of experience. 'The work is about something more than theatre style', Brook told his group in 1973, after a night in which they performed three different improvised versions of *The Conference of the Birds* in Brooklyn – a marathon effort which pointed the way to the even more marathon all-night versions of *The Mahabharata* twelve years later. Brook went on:

It's about revealing truth – and there's no way of dividing truth up into 'spiritual' or 'funny' truth: there's only one truth. All this has been opened up for us by doing a work like the *Birds*; it took us perhaps a year of reading to realise that understanding this book necessitated serving it, getting inside it, grasping it. In coming to grips with this reality, one comes to grips with a work which is about theatre and about life: it has to become true in a theatre, and yet it is about something far beyond theatre, something within each one of us.

So Brook's search for a 'less deadly' theatre leads him to what he perceives as 'truth', of which there is only one. As we follow him in his search, we shall attempt to put a magnifying glass on the nature of this 'truth' which he believes his work reveals. We hope that our discoveries will, in Peter Brook's words, be 'far more applicable to general society than the study of bees or ants'.

1   Playing the field: 1946–56

To the young people who form a large section of Peter Brook's following in the late 1980s and early 1990s, the first eighteen years of his career must seem like pre-history. Even the list of plays he produced between Jean Cocteau's *The Infernal Machine* in 1945 and *King Lear* in 1962 contains titles that seem to belong to a bygone age. (What on earth was *Both Ends Meet* in 1954? It was a play by a comedian, Arthur Macrae, about a man who hates the Inland Revenue. He won't marry his fiancée, because the two of them get better tax concessions as 'separate units', and he won't sleep with her without getting married. Audiences were, according to one witness, 'briefly and brightly entertained'.)

Shakespeare, of course, was ever-present, but often in the form of plays that were considered at the time as slightly off the beaten track: *Love's Labour's Lost* (1946), *Measure for Measure* (1950), *The Winter's Tale* (1951); above all *Titus Andronicus* (1955), which had normally been regarded as unstageable. When Brook did tackle one of the recognised 'greats' (*Hamlet*, also in 1955) the production was seen as generally disappointing.

Brook also directed plays by modern writers, both British and European, who were regarded as 'significant' after the war. There were productions of Cocteau, Sartre, Anouilh – the latter translated by a British writer who had been heralded for bringing 'poetry' back into the British drama: Christopher Fry. Another Anouilh translator was Denis Cannan, who at one time was critically hailed as a latter-day Shaw on the strength of the anti-war satire *Captain Carvallo* and a political farce called *Misery Me*, but who turned into a typical merchant of mid-century doom and gloom. (Brook had also produced a version of Dostoevsky's *Brothers Karamazov*, written by Alec Guinness, in 1946.)

It could be argued that Brook – who, from the beginning, acquired a reputation for being 'successful', and who, as the decades rolled by, had an increasing say in the choice of plays he produced – was simply taking the best that was available; from the United States, for example, he took Arthur Miller and Tennessee Williams. Jean-Paul Sartre's *Huis clos* (entitled *Vicious Circle* in English), seems a suitably lugubrious follow-up to *Karamazov* in 1946: its central image of three incompatible people, locked forever into a hell with Second Empire decor, belongs to the Peter Brook landscape. But why, in 1947, did he choose to stage two comparatively minor Sartre plays, *Men Without Shadows* (*Morts sans sepulchres*) and *The Respectable Prostitute* (*La P* . . . . . .

1 *Love's Labour's Lost*, Stratford-upon-Avon, 1946–7

respectueuse). According to contemporary reviewers, *Men Without Shadows* consisted largely of a display on stage of Gestapo tortures, though Brook was said to have handled these with 'ingenuity'; perhaps the problem of handling violence on stage was already beginning to intrigue him.

Mr Peter Brook has arranged his animals to every possible advantage in their squalid cage and has lavished formidable ingenuity on the stage delights of the Gestapo.

Stephen Potter, *The New Statesman*

The continuing sight of physical beastliness is nauseating, except presumably for sadists, and impedes any of the emotions likely to be stirred by imaginative art . . . the blood-bath presented with excessive slowness in Peter Brook's otherwise vivid direction has dulled one's eagerness to listen.

Ivor Brown, *The Observer*

Presenting murder, rape, torture and sadism, it achieves as much aesthetic effect as a street accident.

Harold Hobson, *The Sunday Times*

The Respectable Prostitute (the title was mistranslated, the adjective means 'respectful' or 'colluding') satirised, from a safe distance, American attitudes to blacks in the Deep South. Both plays had that hint of the scandalous that has always attracted Brook, and Rita Hayworth came to the first night. Sartre was very fashionable. Existentialism was the prevailing, and highly dramatic, philosophy of post-war western Europe, and it is not surprising that an inquisitive young man would be drawn to the plays of one of its major proponents, however weak dramaturgically they might be. Brook played the texts not as philosophical debates (as they had been staged in Paris) but as dramatic situations: so that *Huis clos* became almost twice as long on the stage, the audience being made to *sense* the destructive frictions of the characters' relationships long before the announcement is made, in the last minute, that 'Hell is other people'. Brook was certainly not interested in the plays for any political reason: Sartre was a Marxist actively engaged in a daily debate about the society he lived in, who saw his philosophy as having a direct bearing on the life of that society. *Morts sans sépulchres* dealt with events not two years old. Brook's sense of the dramatic was very different, but by the time Sartre had improved his dramatic craft and arrived at his major texts (*Le Diable et le bon Dieu, Les Séquestrés d'Altona*) Brook, the endless conqueror of new mountains, had moved on. He was not tempted by them at all.

His choice, in 1951, of John Whiting's very English comedy *A Penny for a Song* seems, in retrospect, slightly bizarre. Brook, apparently, played charming games with this play about an English eccentric waiting for the arrival of Bonaparte. But Whiting was, potentially, the first major English playwright to appear since the war, and two exceptionally meaty plays, *Saint's Day* and *Marching Song*, still remain neglected. Brook productions could have put both of them on the theatrical map. When *Saint's Day* won a new play competition and was staged at the Arts Theatre Club in 1951 to howls of outrage from the critics, Brook (together with Tyrone Guthrie and other theatrical notables whose championing of new material was always more obvious in print than in their stage work) wrote defending the choice and praising the extraordinary talent displayed by the author. But Brook never staged that play; and, more importantly, when Whiting's major work *Marching Song* came along in 1953, he did not stage that either; he and Olivier (who also later expressed a regret that he had not played the leading part) were busy celebrating the coronation with their fiasco of a film of *The Beggar's Opera*.

Brook's encounters with British authors seem equally perverse. He chose to stage an adaptation of a pre-war novel by Graham Greene, *The Power and the Glory* (Cannan was one of the adapters), rather than a new Greene play. Perhaps this particular choice was made by Paul Scofield. Greene's novel about a whiskey priest on the run from the police in an atheist, pre-war Mexico, gave Scofield a success as the priest. He needed one. His *Hamlet*, in the same season (at the Phoenix in 1955/6), had been seen as lacking in inspiration. Perversely, as usual, the most successful production of the three-play season was Brook's staging of T. S. Eliot's turgid retelling of the Eumenides myth *The Family Reunion*. This was ironic as Greene's *The Living Room* had received an inadequate production redeemed only by a powerful performance by Eric Portman: the play had many resonances of Eliot's piece but without either the creaking form or the self-conscious dramatic verse. A Brook production at this point might have made Greene into a more important dramatist than he became; after all, this was the decade when he was interested enough in the theatre to write several original plays.

Some of Brook's choices were undoubtedly dictated by his own taste for pushing back the frontiers of the acceptable. The notorious homosexual kiss in Arthur Miller's *A View from the Bridge*, to which the Lord Chamberlain objected in 1956, offered the kind of *frisson* Brook liked to be associated with. And Tennessee Williams's *Cat on a Hot Tin Roof*, which Brook produced in Paris in a translation by André Obey, was also one of the more 'scandalous' plays of the fifties. Because of the objections of the Assistant Comptroller of the Royal Household, both the Miller and the Williams plays (together with the negligible *Tea and Sympathy*, a potboiler which showed the seduction of a teenager by a married woman – a theme clearly designed to subvert what remained of the English Empire), were staged at the Comedy Theatre under the umbrella of the New Watergate Theatre Club. It was necessary to pay five shillings to join before tickets could be bought. Miller's portentous play, complete with a lawyer chorus-figure explaining what the dumb hero could not articulate for himself, hardly seemed worthy of the scandal that surrounded it (Marilyn Monroe, the current Mrs Miller, appeared at the first night and caused much more of a stir than the long awaited man-kissing-man moment on the stage). Williams's *Cat*, a far more explosive and well-written piece, received an inadequate and lightweight staging from Peter Hall, but of course Brook had already done the play in Paris – brilliantly, with Jeanne Moreau; he did not want to do it again.

There are, though, some titles which seem to deviate completely from what, looking back, we would tend to see as the narrative line of Brook's search. Leaving aside the unlikely Macrae farce, we find in 1958 a Brook production of a popular musical, *Irma la Douce*. It tells the unlikely story of a French prostitute who is rescued from her profession by a highly moral law student, who is then forced to impersonate a rich protector whose money will keep her from her other customers. The production was apparently fast, light and very funny. According to Kenneth Tynan, it invaded 'a realm of pure fantasy' and achieved 'magic'.

It is worth remembering, as we accompany Brook in his never-ending search, that in *The Empty Space* he also wrote the following sentence: 'I came to the theatre myself for sensual and often irresponsible reasons.' Of course in

Paris, where he chose to live, the sensual and the scandalous are regarded as being traits of the mind.

A major problem in putting a magnifying glass on the early years of Peter Brook's work in the theatre is that we are almost entirely dependent for information on rare and distant personal memories, or on the written witnesses – the theatre critics of the time. And the witnesses, particularly in the early years, tend to tell us more about themselves and their attitudes than they do about the productions they are trying to describe.

Long-forgotten names crawl out of the memory holes. The language they use is redolent of must and old paper.

Avonian Stratford, blamed of recent years for humdrummery, attempts fanfares and has already been no less blamed for their flourish.

This is how Ivor Brown, of *The Observer*, opens his review of Brook's 1947 *Romeo and Juliet*. T. C. Worsley, in *The New Statesman*, wrote of *Measure for Measure*, which Brook produced in 1950:

It is not a very easy play to make sense of for a modern audience; the climate of the play, is lust . . . a lust accepted as all-pervading in an age much rougher, rawer, cruder, more violent, natural and more loose than in our late day we can easily imagine.

2   *Romeo and Juliet*, Stratford-upon-Avon, 1947

Ivor Brown and T. C. Worsley may fairly be taken as spokesmen for the intelligent middle-class audience which might be expected to take an interest in whatever was new in English theatre. Ivor Brown occupied the theatre column in what was regarded as a liberal-minded Sunday newspaper. T. C. Worsley wrote for a self-proclaimed left-wing weekly. In the first half of *The New Statesman*, the editors and contributors proclaimed the need for a radical change in society if the end of civilisation was to be delayed. But in the second half of the paper, its arts contributors wrote as if nothing had changed since the heyday of Bloomsbury. T. C. Worsley fitted comfortably into the second half.

Ivor Brown's review of *Romeo and Juliet* unconsciously summed up the values that ruled English theatre in the years immediately following the end of the Second World War. Brown wrote:

Peter Brook, the young producer who started with much achievement on his side, has made a gallant mess of things for once. He claimed . . . to have studied the play exceeding long and hard . . . in the end he has entirely missed the point . . . Let him read less next time and trust in common sense the more.

Ivor Brown had no doubt at all what 'the point' was:

This play, one must, at risk of platitude, advise him, is one of the finest helpings of verbal noise in a language and literature notably rich in such aural provender. Here is lyric love indeed, and, if the poetry is slurred, if the matchless wedding of melody and moonshine be dissolved, then the horrified listener may contemplate a leap into the Avon, now torrential.

Fortunately, Brown added:

the riparian [i.e. by a river] dining-rooms are open again, and so comfortably victualled as to deflect the suicidal impulse.

A year earlier, Brook had been in the ruins of Hamburg, where Ivor Brown's fellow-Britons had helped to create the first man-made firestorm. In a garret, Brook had seen a production of *Crime and Punishment*. An actor, sitting in a chair 'touching our knees', had begun, very quietly, to tell a story. Later, Brook was to write that 'by sheer necessity, all problems of theatre style at a clap of the hands vanished . . .'.

The Stratford-upon-Avon of Ivor Brown belonged on a different planet. The ruined cities, the gas ovens at Auschwitz and Treblinka, the lampshades made from human skin at Buchenwald (up the hill from Weimar, which still stages its own Shakespeare festival) might never have existed for those playgoers now able, once again, to enjoy the pleasures of the 'riparian dining-rooms'. Intellectuals the world over were trying to comprehend the enormity of what had happened. But no hint of intellectual curiosity should be allowed to impinge on the 'helpings of verbal noise' in *Romeo and Juliet*.

As T. C. Worsley saw it, 'our late day' lacked the violence necessary for an

3   *Measure for Measure*, Stratford-upon-Avon, 1950

understanding of *Measure for Measure*. But Mr Brook did right to bring 'all this' forward, to make us 'not merely accept' the climate of lust 'but enjoy it . . . Mr George Rose's Pompey was 'brilliantly impertinent' (at one point he was dragged rapidly across the stage and down a trap at the end of rope); and Mr Brook had been 'as successful in this sense with the clothes and settings as he has with the crowd-scenes'. He had 'taken hints from the Flemish, and Breughel, in particular, to touch in the barbarous edges'. And the prison scenes, especially, had got back 'beyond our usual Dickensian or eighteenth-century stage prisons to the wheels, the fires, the ships and the racks of a still cruder epoch'. And at the centre of the production was 'Mr John Gielgud' with his 'perfection of speaking and absolute assurance'.

Both Ivor Brown and T. C. Worsley felt a similar 'absolute assurance' in passing judgements about Brook's handling of Shakespeare – as Brook himself commented in an article in *Orpheus* in 1948:

Indeed, in England, far too large a proportion of intelligent playgoers know their Shakespeare too well. They are no longer capable of going to the theatre with the willingness to suspend disbelief which any naive spectator can bring. They go coldly, as specialists, to listen to the over-familiar lines, and to watch the actor's treatment of them.

Yet faced in 1954 with a new poetic drama, Christopher Fry's *The Dark is Light Enough*, these critics thrashed around like drowning men.

Lines like Christopher Fry's were unlikely ever to become over-familiar.

> At the one place of experience
> Where we're most at mercy, and where
> The decision will alter us to the end of our days,
> Our destination is fixed:
> We're elected into love.

Both Brown and Worsley could recognise poetry when they heard it. But although they had been absolutely sure about the nature of Shakespeare's verse, the meaning of Christopher Fry's eluded them.

Fry himself had labelled the drama a 'Winter comedy'. Seizing on this, Brown suggested that perhaps a 'Winter comedy' was 'entitled to some fog'. Not to be explicit, he said, was the artistic fashion of the time, and Fry conformed to this.

Brown was at home, however, with the central protagonist, 'an elderly Austrian Countess who is engulfed in the Austro-Hungarian war of 1848–9 . . . and sees her castle-salon and swarming-ground of chattering philosophers over-run by soldiery . . .'. Brown continued:

Amid these alarums the Countess dwindles sweetly to her end, discoursing a witty pacifism and summing up the frailties of her family and of mankind. If this passing of a great lady be like 'the end of an old song' certainly it could not be more beautifully sung than by Dame Edith Evans. She does, in fact, fade away with the music on her lips, like the dying fall of the willow-hen's song now to be heard in our copses.

With one simile, Brown whisks us back to the safety of the English countryside. Worsley is unwilling to give up the struggle so easily.

The date is 1848 and we are in Austro-Hungary at the moment when the Hungarian part of the Empire is fighting for its independence. Passions run dangerously high. But out of her extreme charity – but not quite without priggishness, with an ironically detached charm that it is a triumph for her creator to have caught – the Countess . . . shelters a deserter . . . and refuses to give him up when the colonel of a Hungarian regiment . . . demands his surrender. This firm and well-drawn outline has carried us to the end of an admirable first act.

The outline was so firm and solid, wrote Worsley, that it had 'roused expectations which reasonably demand to be satisfied'. Mr Fry denied Mr Worsley that satisfaction:

The deserter, Richard Gettner, is the first husband of the Countess's daughter . . . and he for a moment tries to regain her. Her second husband had been captured by a Hungarian patrol and offered in exchange for Gettner – an offer which the Countess brings herself to refuse: 'No man is mine to give you'.

But none of this, said Worsley, made the same kind of sense as the first-act sense.

Mr Fry has moved onto another level and leaves us fumbling behind with our rather obvious questions. Who, for instance, exactly is Gettner? Why did he join the Hungarians and why did he desert them? Why did the Countess let her daughter marry him? There are answers to these and other questions to be found in the text but they are not answers which satisfy us, at least on the level of our asking. There is, I am convinced, another level of asking on which Mr Fry does answer. One feels that overwhelmingly in the texture. But I am equally convinced that Mr Fry has not succeeded in showing us the way to that level and making it real for us.

Readers must have found Worsley's review as incomprehensible as Worsley found Fry's play. But in the context of the confidence with which the witnesses pigeon-holed Shakespeare, Worsley's struggle to read meaning into a modern verse-play that seems to defy description can only suggest an approach to theatre that was woefully inadequate. His aesthetic of a theatre of clarity and beauty hardly made him any more capable than Christopher Fry of responding to the violence of the world around him. (By comparison Sartre's plays, although bogged down in Ibsenite dramaturgy, had the qualities of documentary films by offering to deal with the Europe of the 1940s.) Worsley concluded that

finally it all depends on Dame Edith Evans and the spell-binding magic of voice and movement which she exerts. With Dame Edith at its centre, catching every glint and gleam of the beautifully modulated verse, *The Dark is Light Enough* is an experience that no one will want to miss.

What is surprising is that, in such a context, Peter Brook was able to hang on to his intellectual curiosity. He must at least have been aware of the temptation simply to deliver the moonshine.

Two years later when Brook produced T. S. Eliot's *The Family Reunion*, as the last play of his season with Paul Scofield at the Phoenix, Worsley suddenly felt on safe ground again. Eliot, like Shakespeare, wrote texts that became well known in the study. Worsley clearly knew the Eliot text very well. He knew it so well that he did not feel it necessary to remind his *New Statesman* readers that it was a reworking of the Orestes myth. Instead, he offered them a dissertation about the relationship of poetry to action in drama. He concluded that for much of the time in Eliot's play, the poetry was irrelevant. But when it was not, it had dramatic life – as in 'a truly beautiful poetic speech' made by the Mother. Mr Brook had missed many of the jokes, but 'that apart, he has staged it imaginatively and sympathetically and with as much clarity as the text allows'.

Worsley did not search *The Family Reunion*, as he had searched *The Dark is Light Enough*, for hidden meanings. He had read the play and knew what was what. As he knew what was what when he saw Brook's production of *Titus*

Andronicus the previous year – although on that occasion he did feel it necessary to give his readers a run-down on the plot.

Worsley saw the production of *Titus* as an example of the welcome willingness of 'our Theatre' to tackle 'the great Unstageable and the great Unstaged'. Nevertheless, *Titus* has 'no moral centre . . . and no poetic centre either'. There were, however, 'flashes and gleams of beauty in the language more than is generally realised. . . . Mr Brook only began to find his way as a director in the second part of the play, where his atmospheric and art-nouveau set opened out into a flaring red study and we were in the world of the German expressionist cinema of the Twenties.' These scenes were the only ones that worked as scenes. On the other hand, 'Sir Laurence Olivier brought all his immense resources to the part of Titus'.

There was a suggestion here – as there was in many of the early reviews – that the 'acting' was somehow separate from the 'direction'. It is hard to realise that Brook, who has spent most of his life exploring with actors, was seen, in the early days, as a master of visuals: in the fifties he often designed his productions, as well as contributing *musique concrète* to *Titus*. But when Brook arrived on the scene, the concept of a director who shaped *all* the elements of theatre, including the acting, was still a comparative novelty in England, at least to the established actors and critics.

G. R. writes:

It's difficult reading Worsley and Brown to realise that the productions of the Fry and Eliot plays were vibrant and unmissable. What made them unmissable was certainly not the projection of English middle-class literary values, nor the apparent nostalgia for the quality of a life now swept away by war. What seemed to have escaped the notice of these dodo-like chroniclers was the fact that Brook was using the plays as a pretext to explore the tensions and issues that were alive at the time. If the *Hamlet* was dismal, then the Fry and the Eliot were full of life. Both Paul Scofield and James Donald powerfully suggested civilised beings who were only too well aware of the savagery both outside the gates and inside themselves.

In retrospect we can wonder why he didn't use the better opportunities that Whiting or Greene might have afforded him to explore the problems of contemporary life: both wrote scripts that articulated this theme more immediately in a contemporary way, not obliquely through the Austro-Hungarian War – Fry's placing of his subject in that era was decidedly not for Brechtian reasons. The Eliot play was written before the Second World War; and in 1950s London anything from the thirties seemed almost prehistoric. Brook's production came one month after *Look Back in Anger* had opened at the Royal Court.

However stilted and stillborn the quality of the material, the performances of the Fry and Eliot in the theatre were spellbinding because of the engagement of the actors, who gnawed away at the inner tensions and conflicts and so provided a stage reality that gripped the audience, an action that it was impossible to take the eyes away from.

This use of material as pretext – the mining of its inner tensions for a truth often unintended by the author – was to become more pronounced in the work of the sixties (when

4   *Titus Andronicus*, the final scene, Stratford-upon-Avon, 1955

Brook would talk of the existence of a 'secret play' beneath the text – and encourage the actors to burrow for it).

The comparative failure of the *Hamlet* raises another question: why has Brook been more successful in animating (with the two notable exceptions of *King Lear* and *A Midsummer Night's Dream*) what are regarded as the lesser plays of Shakespeare?

There was one critic who appeared on the scene, at roughly the same time as Peter Brook, who was to challenge the insularity and philistinism of the older generation. Kenneth Tynan was two years younger than Brook, and followed him to Oxford University. Like Brook, he was eager to challenge establishment conventions. If Brook was the *enfant terrible* of directors, Tynan became the *enfant terrible* of critics. He challenged head-on Ivor Brown's view of *Romeo and Juliet*.

There is an elderly group of critics which insists that Mr Brook is not nearly old enough to appreciate *Romeo*: to them I would say (and I hope rudely) that they are not nearly young enough.

Brown had described Brook's set as 'a vast, cold, blue cyclorama, with fragmentary scenery in front', which suggested that the play was happening among 'air-raid ruins'. (So the war had not gone completely unnoticed in Stratford-upon-Avon, at least not by Brook.) 'Torrid', was how Kenneth Tynan described the atmosphere of the play:

the streets crackle underfoot with aridity: it is very warm indeed. Canopies, loosely pendant from the flies, are a necessary shield against this daze of heat.

Tynan described Brook's *Measure for Measure* as 'a perfect marriage of shrill imagination and sober experience', but his review of *Titus* was flip and studied – it tried to be as shocking as the play; and unlike the older literary critics he avoided any discussion of the fact that Brook had cut what some considered to be the best lines in a patchy early work of Shakespeare. But, looking back, we can see that Tynan at least knew where Brook was going. '*Titus*', he wrote, 'didn't show the "pity" of tragedy. *Titus* reminds us that it is also a harsh way of saying harsh things.' And Tynan – as if he could see seven years ahead – compared Titus with Lear: 'Lear himself has nothing more splendid than

> "For now I stand as one upon a rock,
> Environ'd by a wilderness of sea".'

Tynan left us with a picture of Olivier as Titus that was sharp and physical, and that hinted at the qualities Brook was to look for in actors:

Titus enters, not as a beaming hero, but as a battered veteran, stubborn and shambling, long past caring about the people's cheers. A hundred campaigns have tanned his heart to leather, and from the crackling of that heart there issues a terrible music, not untinged by madness. One hears great cries, which, like all of this actor's best effects, seem to have been dredged up from an ocean-bed of fatigue. One recognised, though one had never heard it before, the noise made in its last extremity by the cornered human soul.

Tynan brought to English theatre criticism an ability to describe what he had seen on stage, instead of referring to words on a page. But in 1955 his was a lone voice in the English critical establishment. And it is in the context of that establishment – and of its Paris and New York counterparts – that Brook's work in these early years needs to be seen.

Why did Brook spend time on plays like *The Dark is Light Enough?* What made him decide to go to war with the traditions of opera by spending much of 1948 and 1949 as a director at Covent Garden? (That particular experiment came to an end after the critical assault on his production of *Salome* with Salvador Dali's decor.) What place does a 'salacious' French comedy, like Roussin's *The Little Hut*, have in the story of Brook's search for a 'less deadly' theatre?

It would be easy, looking back, to find rational and schematised answers to these and similar questions. So, from the outset Brook has shown a particular concern about how Shakespearian verse should be spoken. Christopher Fry is the best-known and most successful English post-war dramatist to use verse in the theatre. Moreover, his verse is flamboyant and demands to be spoken like verse. What could be more natural when a new Fry becomes available than that Brook should want to try it out – particularly since Dame Edith Evans is available too? And having tried out Christopher Fry, what more natural than that Brook would then also want to try out a verse-drama by T. S. Eliot, whose approach to poetry in the theatre was at the other extreme from that of Fry? (Eliot believed that the verse should, as far as possible, be left to go unnoticed. It should, for the most part, sound like ordinary drawing-room comedy dialogue, but the carefully hidden rhythms would work on the audience's subconscious.) Brook's decision to stage *The Family Reunion* two years after his production of *The Dark is Light Enough* could be made to fit into the rational story-line of the search.

But to impose such a structure on Brook's early career is to do violence to three driving forces that have always been at the centre of his work.

First, Brook has always thought of himself as empirical in method, metaphysical in thought. He has always, and repeatedly, insisted that he is not one of those directors who maps out a plan at the beginning of rehearsals, and then keeps to it. He feels his way through a production, making discoveries together with actors, designers, musicians. As we shall see, this approach is not, in practice, as open-ended as it sounds. But it makes more sense to see Brook's early career in terms of Brook making the most of what comes to hand rather than working his way through a carefully thought-out plan.

Secondly, Brook has always been driven by a voracious curiosity. 'What if?' is, for him, a central question, together with 'How?' *How* can an actor speak a well-known line of Shakespeare in such a way that people in the audience feel they have heard it for the first time? *How* can singers in grand opera be incorporated into the dramatic action? Covent Garden invites him to direct opera; his eagerness to try everything available makes him seize the opportunity.

Thirdly, and perhaps most importantly at this stage in his career, Brook has always had a strong awareness of what is realistically possible. He has sometimes pushed the boundaries of the possible so far back that he has seemed to be living out a fantasy – as when he took his international group to invent a performance at Persepolis as part of a festival paid for by the Shah of Persia. But even there he stayed inside the boundaries. Persian actors had to be accommodated, performances had to be prepared for specific occasions – the situation at least partly dictated the choice of material.

Brook's realism was strongly in evidence during the first eighteen years of his career. He knew what was possible given the theatre conditions of the time, and he had an instinct for what he could make work and what would be successful.

He knew, for instance, that in the huge theatres he was forced to work in he needed stars. Only they were *big* enough to make the big parts work; and so he used them quite consciously. His early productions are studded with star names. And, increasingly, the stars wanted to be in a Brook play, because a Brook play virtually guaranteed success. (Only one Brook production was ever closed on the first Saturday night, *The Perils of Scobie Prilt* in Oxford in 1963.) The stars and Brook fed on each other. *Titus* had Anthony Quayle as well as Sir Laurence; *and* Alan Webb; *and* Vivien Leigh. With some stars – John Gielgud, in particular – Brook discovered he had an affinity. Others found he could be trusted, warily, to get the best out of them. When it came to a crunch between the material and the stars, Brook was capable, on occasion, of treating the material less than reverently; for example, in the affair of the Lunts vs. Friedrich Dürrenmatt.

Brook's realism also showed itself, surprisingly, in a willingness to tone down material that he thought would not be acceptable to London and New York audiences. When in 1950 he staged André Roussin's *The Little Hut*, in a translation by Nancy Mitford, at the Lyric in London, he shifted the emphasis. This story of a wife who finds herself on a desert island, alone with her husband and her lover, had that whiff of scandal about it that has always appealed to Brook's mischievous desire to outrage. But Brook's realism told him that the London audience would not tolerate the same *kind* of moral shock that had been acceptable in Paris. The Paris production had told the story from the point of view of the husband – he was sophisticated, worldly, describing the accommodation he came to with his wife and her lover with an amused superiority. In Brook's London version, the wife became the central figure. She was the one who watched with amusement as the lover, rather than the husband, took up the conventional moral position.

Jean Anouilh's *L'Invitation au Château* became, in Christopher Fry's hands, *Rings Round the Moon*, and was described in the programme as 'a charade'. The action takes place at the turn of the century in the winter-garden of a château before, during and after a sumptuous ball. It opposes youth and age, wealth and poverty, nobility and servants, beauty and drabness. One of a pair of twins, a would-be playwright (Horace in Anouilh, Hugo in Fry), stage-manages an experiment about love, using a ballet dancer to enchant his brother. Ivor Brown, in *The Observer*, thought it one of Brook's 'less exhibition-ist productions' and called it a 'variety entertainment', most of which he had already forgotten. T. C. Worsley, in *The New Statesman*, perceived it as a fairy tale:

Elegant, ironic, immensely mannered, it performs a skilful intricate figure-skating over the most highly polished of self-conscious surfaces, keeping just on the right side, if it does indeed always do that, of a certain kind of twentyish French chic.

He had read the French text and pointed out that typical Anouilh lines – like 'La mort est franche, la mort est nette. C'est imbécile. Mais je lui tire mon chapeau. Elle sait ce qu'elle veut.' – had been cut. But as he believed this kind of simple profundity was sentimental and the style needed for it to be 'not in our tradition' he did not seem to mind too much. He thought Brook 'kept the top spinning gaily and prettily' and that it was 'a very enjoyable evening'. Kenneth Tynan, betraying no knowledge of the original text, said it was a

complete wedding-cake: it has been traced with an icing-gun on gossamer. It is a testimony to the cunning of the set and the lighting that, though there is no change of scene, there was

5   *Ring Round the Moon*, The Globe Theatre, 1950

a round of applause every time the curtain rose. Brook's fireworks display (in the literal sense) at the end of the play is a superb bonne-bouche; a dewdrop, you might say, from the lion's mane.

Brook, in an introduction to Fry's published text, indicated an awareness of the different styles. After relating how he walked out of the Paris production because the performance was 'uninspired', he said he was 'in a fever for a copy of the script' as he had discerned an 'enchanting mood' hidden in it and Christian Bérard had remarked that it was a great chance for a designer. Brook then dealt with the problem of finding a text:

This matter of adaptation is one of our greatest nightmares. Although Shakespeare is almost improved in German, and Chekhov is wonderful in French, our language is somehow as insular as our people, and it fights viciously against translators. Every season, plays successful abroad fail in London, their flops have a monotonous regularity, and although the cause is at times the producer or the cast, mostly it is the change of language. When a play is written in a realistic style, the problem is acute but not insuperable. But Anouilh is a stylist, he has a manner and a way of phrasing in which much of his charm lies. To translate Anouilh is no matter of matching chat with chat: it demands re-creation, a reshaping of ideas into phrases that have an English elegance and grace. Christopher Fry seemed the ideal person for the job.

The key word is 'charm'; this quality has to be rendered into English with 'elegance' and 'grace'. If done successfully then a flop is avoided. Clearly this is the theatre of the 'higher escapism', as Ivor Brown characterised it, designed to bury all heads in the silver sands of fancy – a welcome relief from the boring slogans of the general election which was taking place, the first since the end of the war. Well, Anouilh may not be a Genet or a Beckett, but it is hardly 'charm' which kept him in the forefront of French theatre for thirty years; and 'charm' is not the subject of the many critical works. They tend to concern themselves with how Anouilh creates a serious meaning within the theatre by using the theatre itself: they talk about the contradictions, the use of conventions, the creation of a mythology, the following of Pirandello into the *teatro nel teatro*.

Is it 'elegance' that makes Anouilh's first line 'And last night, the same thing?' become Fry's 'And how about last night, Joshua? Did the same thing happen?' The reference to Calliope survives the channel, but gets an explanation – 'a classical character' – for those who might be lost. But Iphigenia becomes St Pancras and de Medici is lost to the explanatory 'a patron of the arts'. References to Salome and Eurydice go. The Grande Dame in the wheel-chair – played as an English eccentric by that past-mistress of the lunatic, Margaret Rutherford – had an entire new scene written for her so she could get laughs like:

MME DESMORTES: Where have you been?
CAPULET: You said the list was in the left-hand bottom drawer, madam, but it was the right-hand drawer.

MME DESMORTES: That's just another way of looking at it.

Almost a quarter of Anouilh's text was cut, which is understandable as spoken French moves faster than English, but the material that was cut was hardly as enchanting as Brook suggests in his foreword.

DIANA: You're nothing but an old Jew with too much money . . . Old Jew!
You think you're invincible. You're all the same: drunk with pride
when you've got four sous in your pocket.
MESSERCHMANN: [sweetly] Four sous Four sous! Now, you're going too far.

Charming stuff. Fry appears to have colluded in suppressing all of Anouilh's text that might have punctured the balloon of escapist entertainment. He and Brook also changed the dramaturgy. Paul Scofield had a great success playing the twins, brash Hugo and timid Frédéric providing a great opportunity for virtuosity. Hugo has the first scene with the butler. He departs and Frédéric immediately appears, requiring a total transformation by the actor without the aid of costume. (*Exit Hugo. Enter Frédéric. It is the same actor.*) The brother has been mentioned in the first dialogue. The immediate return of the same body might confuse an audience, but Joshua identifies the character so we know whom we are watching. Perhaps Scofield's distinctive gravelly sound made Brook nervous, for Fry gives the butler a speech about rhododendrons between the exit and the entrance. This enabled Brook to stage the old music-hall gag of one character continuing to talk while the other exits and immediately returns from the other side of the stage. It usually gets a laugh, sometimes applause if a large distance has obviously been covered, but it does not introduce the idea of the double in quite the clean metaphysical way that Anouilh requires.

The next year, 1951, Brook staged another Anouilh play, *Colombe*, this time adapted by Denis Cannan. The opening scene showed startling changes from the original. Julien and his young wife, Colombe, go to the theatre where Julien's mother is a leading actress. Julien has been called up for military service, and has to leave his wife in the hands of his mother. Back stage, Julien and Colombe meet his mother's dresser, Mme Georges. In the Paris version, Julien is a sullen creature who ignores Colombe. Colombe sits passively in her mother-in-law's dressing room, while Georges talks earthily – about varicose veins, pains in the backside, someone's legs who have been cut off by a machine. In Cannan's version, Julien and Colombe are still in love with each other after two years of marriage. Colombe is active and vivacious. All George's references to physical decay have gone.

Harold Hobson, the theatre critic of *The Sunday Times* (who sometimes carried his devotion to the French theatre to the edge of self-parody), wrote:

6   *Colombe*, The New Theatre, 1951

All these changes were made, I gathered from conversation with Peter Brook, because it was thought that the English public would misunderstand the frank and physical language of the French original.

Tynan described the London version as 'emasculated' and 'played all out for prettiness and sniggers'. T. C. Worsley referred to

M Anouilh's little love stories, which he handles so adroitly as to fool many people into taking them seriously as a Philosophy of Life.

It was generally felt that Brook had failed to unite the tragedy with the comedy. But he had generalised the realistic text by removing the concrete references and had taken every opportunity for farcical playing in the scene of back-stage life in a Parisian theatre of the 1900s. And by casting the genial Yvonne Arnaud as the great actress he ensured that the audience would not take it too seriously. As Worsley remarked:

She never persuaded me for a moment that she would icily trample on a son's heart and mock his poverty. The part as written seems to be a gallon of vinegar, but Miss Arnaud is a champagne actress and it is ridiculous to ask her to be an old horror.

7   *Penny for a Song*, The Haymarket, 1951

Brook himself, rather self-servingly, argued in another of his comments on the difference between the English and the French:

> Word for word the French and English *Colombes* vary: idea for idea they are just about the same. Anouilh's aim is to speak through comedy: to woo his audience into swallowing his bitter pill. Cannan's aim has been equally to divert, so that even those most on their guard against the wickedness of cynical and pessimistic Frenchmen can be seduced into forgetting their suspicions in laughter and tears.

Brook's use of the word 'idea' dates the play – there were not many ideas around in the London theatre of 1951. It is far from certain how seriously Brook took himself, at this stage, as a purveyor of ideas. Four years later he produced *The Lark*, Anouilh's version of the story of St Joan (in a translation by Christopher Fry) rather than Shaw's *St Joan*. Shaw's play was heavier on ideas, but was an established classic; *The Lark* gave Brook an opportunity for a dazzling *coup de théâtre* – it ended with Joan crowning the Dauphin.

It was a *coup de théâtre* which also offered a climax to *Colombe*: a scene from the Great Play of Paris in 1900 is staged from behind, 'with all the absurdities of the contemporary stage devices exposed to our view', stated T. C. Worsley. Brook must have found *that* a rich and concrete idea.

'Ideas' may not have mattered much to Brook in versions of plays by Anouilh, a master craftsman offering watered-down Sartre for the middle classes, who replaced existentialism and commitment with a chic cynicism. But seven years later, we find Brook producing, for audiences in London and New York, a European play that was, very definitely, a play of ideas. The play was Dürrenmatt's *The Visit*, and the story of Brook's involvement with this play and, in 1963, with the same dramatist's *The Physicists*, demands closer examination.

GR writes:

Just because Brook had more control over his work than the other jobbing directors in the English theatre of the fifties should not make us believe that he could completely choose at will. The pressures of play production, particularly in a commercial structure, are strong and many. Plays may be delayed for a star or two, but not often; and very rarely for a director. Playwrights, producers and agents are impatient; options are expensive to keep up and will not be renewed indefinitely. In the world of the London theatre before 1956 one has to ask: what were the choices open to a director? Terence Rattigan, N. C. Hunter, Enid Bagnold? Apart from the case of Whiting, Brook seems to have got his hands on the best available. And his example of not repeating his successful productions in various theatres around the world might well be copied by others who seem more concerned with financial, rather than artistic gains.

2 Wanderings in the alien corn: Dürrenmatt

By the time Brook opened *The Visit* (under the title *Time and Again*) at the Theatre Royal, Brighton, on 24 December 1957, the theatre climate in England had changed dramatically, at least on the surface. The change is usually associated with the first night of John Osborne's *Look Back in Anger*, which opened at the Royal Court on 8 May 1956. The play was received grumpily by the older critics, but Kenneth Tynan nailed his flag to the mast:

I agree that *Look Back in Anger* is likely to remain a minority taste. What matters, however, is the size of the minority. I estimate it at 6,733,000, which is the number of people in this country between the ages of twenty and thirty. . . . It is the best young play of its decade.

('I've never heard such damn nonsense in my life', said Ted Willis, originator of the popular TV series *Dixon of Dock Green*. 'This is what a small section of young people were thinking, but it certainly isn't what six-and-a-quarter million of our younger generation were thinking.')

What Tynan responded to was John Osborne's tone, reflected in the outpouring of his anti-hero, Jimmy Porter:

There aren't any good, brave causes left. If the big bang does come, and we all get killed off, it won't be in aid of the old-fashioned grand design. It'll just be for the Brave New Nothing-Very-Much-Thank-You. About as pointless and inglorious as stepping in front of a bus.

Ironically, the young playgoers who responded to Osborne did so because 1956 was the year when many of them began to discover 'good, brave causes'. The year 1956 saw the beginnings of the campaign against the H-bomb (Hiroshima and Nagasaki had left British public opinion remarkably unconcerned for more than a decade). It was also the year of the Hungarian Revolution and the Suez War. The first seemed to offer a new 'good, brave cause' – the possibility of socialism without Stalin. (It was crushed by Russian tanks.) The second seemed to be the last gasp of a dying imperialism. Both political and cultural events brought together people who had seen themselves as isolated individuals.

Osborne's success attracted a new generation of playwrights to the Royal Court. Until he saw *Look Back in Anger*, Arnold Wesker had never thought of writing for the theatre. He was soon hailed as one of a new breed of working-class writers. In Stratford East, Joan Littlewood had been working in obscurity for several years. Brendan Behan's *The Quare Fellow*, which opened in the same month as *Look Back in Anger*, was the first play ever produced by Littlewood's Theatre Workshop to be transferred to the West End. Soon Littlewood was to unearth a young writer from Salford, Shelagh Delaney. The song of the willow-hen in English copses seemed to have been displaced by music-hall songs and bright trad jazz.

A theatre magazine, *Encore*, had been launched in 1955 without attracting much attention. Now it became a forum for the writers and directors who had suddenly arrived in the theatre. In 1954, Tynan had written that there was nothing in the London theatre 'that one dares discuss with an intelligent man for more than five minutes'. After 1956, everyone seemed to be trying to get into the discussion. Soon, Brook was to use *Encore* as a platform for his own rapidly evolving ideas.

But there was nothing in the list of Brook's productions in 1956 and 1957 (before that provincial opening of *The Visit*) to suggest that Brook had been in any way touched by this 'revolution'. He did play his part in flouting the Lord Chamberlain with the homosexual kiss in *A View From the Bridge*, but his other productions in those two years consisted of *The Power and the Glory* and *The Family Reunion* (part of his Scofield season), the French version of *Cat on a Hot Tin Roof* and Tchaikovsky's *Eugene Onegin* in New York. He also had his first shot at *The Tempest* at Stratford-upon-Avon. In choosing to work on a play by Dürrenmatt, though, he was entering new territory. For Dürrenmatt had been strongly influenced by one of the twentieth century's major dramatists – Bertolt Brecht. Zurich, where Dürrenmatt lived, had, in the forties, seen the first production of four of Brecht's major plays – *Mother Courage, The Good Woman of Setzuan, Galileo* and *Puntilla* – and Brecht had made his way back to East Berlin from the United States by way of Switzerland in 1948.

Both of the Dürrenmatt plays Brook directed – *The Visit* in 1957 and *The Physicists* seven years later – had been written with Brecht's revolutionary approach to theatre form in mind. Brook's handling of Dürrenmatt's plays demands particular attention, because critics were later to use the word 'Brechtian' to describe some of Brook's productions. Brecht himself had written of the 'alienation effect' he was looking for from his actors. 'Alienation' became a buzz-word in some British theatre circles in the sixties, the second visit of the Berliner Ensemble to London in 1964 having more effect on the theatrical community than the first in 1956. If Brook saw them then he seems not to have been particularly influenced by what he saw – he only began to refer to Brecht as an influence in the sixties – and when the Ensemble asked him to direct a production in Berlin he declined. His excursions into the Brechtian world proved to be diversions. Brecht's conviction that the theatre could be used to show how society might be changed meant little to Brook,

8 *The Tempest*, Stratford-upon-Avon, 1957

whose cultural frame of reference was very different from that of Brecht. His lack of curiosity about Brecht fundamentally affected the way he staged the Dürrenmatt plays.

GR writes:

The first visit of the Berliner Ensemble to London was in the summer of 1956, a week after Brecht died. One of the last things Brecht wrote was the exhortation for the company notice-board urging them to play 'lightly and quickly' as the English were well known for their dread of Teutonic heaviness. Although two of the three plays they brought were the finest examples of Brecht's work – his own productions of *Mother Courage* and *The Caucasian Chalk Circle* – the visit attracted little attention in the theatre community. John Osborne may have lobbed a hand grenade into the content of drawing-room comedy but he had done nothing yet to attack its form. When George Devine produced *The Good Woman of Setzuan* at the Royal Court the following month it had sets by Teo Otto and music by Paul Dessau, but it appeared, thanks to Peggy Ashcroft, to be third-rate Ibsen and left most of the audience nostalgically longing for Terence Rattigan. It wasn't until the Berliner returned in 1964, with five productions at the Old Vic, that they made any impact. By then there was an audience curious to see what Epic really meant on the stage, after having endured various productions either written or directed, according to the critics, in a Brechtian manner. The height of these had been the infamous and subversive play by Robert Bolt, *A Man for All Seasons*.

9   *The Visit*, The Royalty Theatre, 1960

The English theatre 'revolution' of 1956 had brought politics back into the theatre, and *The Visit* was unquestionably a political play. It should have slotted easily into the new theatre scene. What it did not slot into was a London theatre: no house could be found for it because of the technical complexities of the set. It went on one of the longest pre-London tours ever in British theatre. After the Brighton opening in December 1957, it played, mostly in two-week runs, at Blackpool, Stratford-upon-Avon, Dublin and Edinburgh. It eventually reached Newcastle, and closed there on 15 March 1958.

10   *The Tempest*, Stratford-upon-Avon, 1963

Then it surfaced in New York on 6 May. It finally reached London in June 1960. Ironically, as Tynan pointed out, it was housed in a newly opened commercial theatre, The Royalty (ironically, because *The Visit* deals with the power of money). The 'new' theatre replaced an old one; at a time when many large old theatres were being torn down to make way for office blocks, the local council (the LCC of beloved memory) insisted that a performance space be kept. The old Stoll was one of the few auditoriums capable of housing opera: the Royalty had a cinemascope-shaped proscenium (best coped with by Brook in the scenes at a railway station) but the stage was remote from the audience. Six months after *The Visit* closed it became a cinema.

A. Alvarez, who had replaced T. C. Worsley as *The New Statesman* theatre critic, gave a concise summary of the play on its belated arrival in London:

> *The Visit* is a myth made modern. Gullen is a small town turned into a wasteland because of an unacknowledged and unexpiated crime. Its industries stand idle and its citizens are rotted with poverty. The crime was the betrayal of a young girl, Clara, who has been one of those wild natural Ibsenesque creatures, bitched by the town's false morality. A local lad had made her pregnant, denied it and brought false witnesses to prove him right. The town then threw her out. When the play begins, she returns infinitely wealthy. The local magistrate is now her butler, the false witnesses, who she has blinded, follow her like performing animals; she owns all the local industries. She offers to bring the town back to life, but on condition that they kill her seducer. Flushed with righteous indignation the citizens refuse. But the idea of wealth is as corrupting as the idea of respectability. They begin to live on it; they buy on credit. Inevitably, perfect greed casteth out both fear and love. The scapegoat is democratically voted to death and slaughtered.

It is worth noting that, although the play takes the form of a ruthless Brechtian parable, Alvarez's own references are to Ibsen and the New Testament. Tynan saw it as a 'lacerating assault on greed', but also as a 'satire on bourgeois democracy' – the citizens vote to kill the hero: 'The verdict is at once monstrously unjust and entirely democratic'. In New York, Walter Kerr, in *The Herald Tribune*, said the play was 'as hard as the nails that wait in the wings all night' – the nails, presumably, being those of the coffin which was waiting for the victim. Brooks Atkinson, of *The New York Times*, noted that 'it attracted the audience of *My Fair Lady* as well as *Long Day's Journey*', a reference to Eugene O'Neill's marathon play which had just had its first performance in America.

The reason why the play attracted the audience of *My Fair Lady* was that Brook had followed his normal realistic practice of building what might be a controversial production around stars. In this case the stars were the legendary Lunts: Alfred Lunt and Lynn Fontanne. They had starred in Terence Rattigan's *Love in Idleness*, Noel Coward's *Quadrille* and countless other popular successes. Brook had no problems finding a house for *The Visit* in New York: the Lunts had been brought back to open the new Lunt–Fontanne Theatre.

The witnesses were almost unanimous in their praise of the Lunts: 'magnificent', 'commanding elegance', 'amazing vitality', 'ravishing'. Kenneth Tynan, who first caught up with the production in New York, wrote:

Miss Fontanne plays the pure capitalist with blood-curdling aplomb, and Mr Lunt as her sacrifice makes much use of his defeated shoulders, his beseeching hands, and the operatic bleat of his voice. . . .

When the show reached London, Tynan was even more fulsome:

the noise he emits when terror makes him vomit is as naked an expression of anguish as anything we have heard since Olivier's Oedipus. . . . A large question haunts the mind when this savage unnerving play is over; at what point does economic necessity turn democracy into an unworkable hoax?

There was similar widespread praise for Brook's production. Walter Kerr wrote:

Something of the appalling fascination that seeps through the playhouse is due to director Peter Brook's manipulation of abandoned figures in constantly constricting space. The idle, silky, subtly threatening movement of presumably innocent townsfolk as they halt their man's escape by night, the terror of a line of stubborn backs blocking his every turn, the infinitely slow and quiet encircling that ends in a most discreet murder – all are images of insinuating power.

According to Kenneth Tynan, 'The style of Peter Brook's production is low-keyed and surgically precise, exactly matching the grotesque gallows poetry in which the play abounds'. Alvarez added that, in Peter Brook, Dürrenmatt had 'a producer who matches him power for power, dramatic invention for dramatic invention'. 'Brook', he adds, 'is one of the few producers who can be stylish without stylising the play to death. He imposes an extraordinary complexity of movement and detail on his cast, but uses it to force the action forward instead of merely using it to fill in while nothing much is happening.'

The general opinion was that Brook had made the return of the Lunts to 'serious' theatre into a resounding success. Not surprisingly Brook himself wrote in flattering language about Alfred Lunt. Directing him, Brook affirmed, was 'a revelation'.

You can't imagine the countless tiny details that Alfred puts into a performance. This may sound like finicky acting, but those painstaking details make up an enormous conception. It is like one of Seurat's pointillist paintings. Each little dot is not art, but the whole is magnificent.

In a scene in which he points a gun at Claire and then sits, with his back to the audience, listening to a long speech she makes,

He found a way by using his back to make the audience known how he felt at that moment: and she was inspired in raising her finger to him as he raises his gun.

Years later, Brook returned to the theme in *The Empty Space*:

I did a play with that perfectionist Alfred Lunt. In the first act, we had a scene sitting on a bench. In rehearsal, he suggested as a piece of natural business, taking off his shoe and rubbing his foot. Then he added shaking the shoe to empty it before putting it back on again. One day when we were on tour in Boston, I walked past his dressing room. The door was ajar. He was preparing for the performance, but I could see that he was looking out for me. He beckoned excitedly. I went into the dressing room, he closed the door, asked me to sit down. 'There's something I want to try tonight', he said. 'But only if you agree. I went for a walk on Boston Common this afternoon and found these.' He held out his palm. It contained two tiny pebbles. 'That scene where I shake out my shoes', he continued, 'It's always worried me that nothing falls out. So I thought I'd try putting the pebbles in. Then when I shake it, you'd see them drop – and you'd hear the sound. What do you think?' I said it was an excellent idea and his face lit up. He looked delightedly at the two little stones, back to me, then suddenly his expression changed. He studied the stones again for a long anxious moment. 'You don't think it would be better with one?'

This episode in the everyday story of theatre folk is not without a certain folksy charm. But it is not easy to see precisely what connection it has with what Dürrenmatt wrote.

In Dürrenmatt's play, Claire has only one arm and one leg. Dürrenmatt described her as 'snobbish and monumentally vulgar'. In West German productions of the play, actresses had stressed Claire's grossness, coarseness and physical deformity. Brook said, 'I felt that to play her as a dazzling, impersonal beauty would be more vivid and effective . . .' So, presumably, did Lynn Fontanne.

Dürrenmatt had conceived of Claire as 'a spitting, biting, ugly and hard old witch'. 'Well', said Brook, 'we only played her twenty per cent witch. Lynn thought Claire was mad, so in order to give her some balance, she added the qualities of tenderness, grace and style.' She also restored the missing limbs.

But if Dürrenmatt had made Claire a grotesque, rather than a dazzling, impersonal beauty, he must have done so for a purpose. In answer to critics who suggested that Claire represented the United States bringing the Marshall Plan to western Europe, Dürrenmatt said she was 'just what she is supposed to be – the richest woman in the world'. Riches are conventionally associated with glamour. Claire is rich *and* deformed. She does not seduce the townspeople with beauty, grace and style. She seduces them with money. By making Claire a grotesque, Dürrenmatt was able to show the townspeople as acting from naked greed, unalloyed by any 'human' response to physical charm. Brook clearly thought there was little theatrical mileage to be had in the West End and on Broadway by letting Lynn Fontanne be grotesque: that kind of shock would not be useful.

In Dürrenmatt's play, the false witnesses who followed Claire had been castrated. The image said, quite clearly, 'Rich people cut your balls off'. Brook castrated the castration. He made the false witnesses blind. The image of blindness shifts the emphasis from power to perception.

In Dürrenmatt's play, Ill (renamed Schill in the English translation) is a figure out of black farce. He is caught in the workings of a social machine he has helped to construct. Once the switch has been thrown, there is nothing he can do to stop the relentness progress towards his own destruction. His plight is ridiculous, and his end, when it comes, is deliberately and absurdly theatrical. His ritual murder is carried out behind a scarlet front curtain that was, in Germany, flown into a gilded, rococo proscenium. (Brook thought 'a Gothic hall with hanging lamps in a dark and somber mood would be more appropriate'.)

Dürrenmatt set up a mock tragic ending. But Brook's translator, Maurice Valency, chose to see the play in a very different way. The theme, he said, was 'medieval and Christian'. It was built round the text, 'Money is the root of all evil'. In the course of the action 'the city grows daily more evil; the man grows progressively purer and better, until in his despair he attains the possible height of human goodness. So the outlines of tragedy in the Christian sense are rounded out.' So a play which showed people farcically trying to cover the workings of naked greed with the trappings of tragedy became, in translation, an example of the tragic form Dürrenmatt was mocking.

Once the decision had been taken to turn Ill into the suffering, sacrificial figure of Schill, Dürrenmatt's play had to be reshaped to fit the new form. 'I wanted the audience', said Brook, 'to feel that Claire and Schill were two comprehensible human beings whose actions were real and motivated'. This meant 'dramatising their human traits'. Schill had to be played 'with the utmost realism, torn by the conflicts of the common man'. ('He looked delightedly at the two little stones . . . then suddenly his expression changed. . . . "You don't think it would be better with one?"') Although the play 'transcends the limits of domestic drama', Valency said, the characters are 'rather minutely observed, the most realistic details are explored and expressed' (give or take an arm and a leg).

Sometimes, however, Dürrenmatt seemed to have observed them inaccurately. Brook wrote: 'Dürrenmatt thought the priest ought to be a physically big, heavy man who had a worldly heartiness: but on the tour I realised this didn't work, so in New York I used William Swansea, who is short and slight, quiet and serious, and whose performance was remarkable for its understanding'. (Brook did not say what happened to the 'big heavy' actor who never made it to Broadway – was it the quality of his acting, or a significant difference between New World and Swiss heartiness that made it 'not work'?) There was a schoolmaster, too, for whom Dürrenmatt had carelessly omitted to provide 'motivation'. Throughout the play this schoolmaster has gone along with the townspeople. But, suddenly, towards the end, he publicly denounces Schill's murder (Brook described this as a 'breakdown').

I tried it different ways. On the English tour, we tried the final speech as a total denunciation, but in New York it was the expression of a man without moral courage, who finally did not dare to act upon his convictions. We also changed his age. In England, Peter Woodthorpe, who's still in his twenties, played him as an old man with a grey wig; but in New York he played him his own age – young, energetic and passionate – so his confrontation with Claire and his stubbornness in resisting the arguments of the other citizens became perfect expressions of the intransigence of youth.

Ah – the intransigence of youth – we were, after all, in the decade of the angry young man. The fact that Dürrenmatt's schoolmaster was an established figure in the town, mouthing (too late) high-flown moral sentiments, and becoming absurdly irrelevant in the context of the machinery of naked greed, did not fit into the context Brook had created. (Walter Benjamin once commented that Brecht's 'crude thinking' could often be expressed in the form of popular proverbs. The saying 'Fine words butter no parsnips' might have been of more help to an actor than a search for reasons for the character's 'breakdown').

Brook's explanation for the changes he made was simple and dogmatic. 'Out-and-out expressionism has very little meaning for Anglo-Saxon audiences.' 'Dürrenmatt', he said, 'also put a heavy layer of farce and cabaret humour into the play. These and the grotesque we had to take out.' For the Anglo-Saxon audience. But what had happened to Brook's empirical search, his openness before a text, his willingness to try anything out?

Well – that was still there. Up to a point.

In Stratford, we introduced a completely new version of the play, with much less text and much more action. Lynn went on trembling, but came off convinced that the new version was better than the old.

Having decided that he wanted Claire and Schill to be 'comprehensible human beings' he searched empirically with the Lunts for the details that would make them more real. And when they found something together, the Lunts would say to him, 'You've done something good, let's save it'. (Brook obviously found it completely natural that the Lunts should tell him that *he* had done the 'something good'; they clearly belonged to the 'I am putty in your hands' type of actor.)

In his comments on Dürrenmatt's script, Brook seemed to equate 'epic theatre' with 'expressionism' (although Brecht had seen his theatre as a reaction *against* expressionism) and regarded this as being fundamentally alien to English and American audiences – he talked darkly of 'different cultural traditions'. In fact both London and New York had seen a certain amount of expressionist experiment; what Brook presumably means is that it was not part of the average, as opposed to the 'serious', theatregoer's language. His comments on the audience always implies finding one large enough to sustain a reasonable run, maybe not years but certainly months. While this desire to reach a public has never led him to exploit the musical jackpot in the way certain of his colleagues at the RSC have done, it has always kept his work in the market-place; Brook never followed Grotowski down the path of only playing for a selected few.

Dürrenmatt said:

I do not understand why Broadway is so realistic and naturalistic when the greatest figures in American literature and American films were masters of fantasy and the grotesque. Mark Twain, like Aristophanes and Swift, satirised politics and democracy: his stories are written in every conceivable style, including surrealism. If modern literature can do it, why can't the stage?

In one of the scenes of *The Visit* Dürrenmatt asked for the couple on a seat to be surrounded by actors holding branches. Brook took this out. His main stylistic coup (repeated several times) was to have a long line of people at the station watching trains go by. The choric movement, aided by a dynamic soundtrack, made the audience believe in the passing of the train. But when Dürrenmatt talked of, and asked for, style he was after something else: he was following Brecht in inviting the audience to perceive the world in a different way. Brook was reinforcing things as they were. His total rejection of the style of Dürrenmatt's play led him into serious structural difficulties. In searching for the details of individual motivation, Brook muddied the motivation that governed the actions of the townspeople, which is what the play is about.

The farcical and grotesque elements in *The Visit* were not put there because Dürrenmatt was working in a Germanic, as distinct from an Anglo-Saxon, context. They were there because Dürrenmatt was saying that the workings of what Tynan called 'economic necessity' in a context of 'bourgeois morality' *are* farcical and grotesque. That is how Dürrenmatt saw his 'fantasy'.

He set up a structure that showed the machinery at work. When Claire first offers the townspeople wealth in return for committing an act of communal murder, they reject the offer, appalled. What kind of people does Claire think they are? But, gradually, the idea of wealth begins to seduce them. Dürrenmatt shows the process of seduction in the second act.

Brook wrote:

I found the second act the most difficult to direct. Act I was sheer story-telling, and all we had to do with Act III was to trim it so it would move more quickly and more starkly to its conclusion. However, in the second act, Schill starts out by being self-satisfied and ends up by being submissive and it is necessary to show this slow and subtle development; but many of the scenes are repetitious and all are on the same tone and are predictable. Also there were too many scenes on the balcony that added nothing to the play. I asked Maurice Valency to write a big scene for the Lunts in order to bring the principals on, but we finally dropped it. We tried another scene in which Claire visited a tailor to order the funeral clothes, and for which Dürrenmatt wrote her a monologue. That, too, we dropped. Finally we solved it by judicious cutting.

At least one witness, Gordon Rogoff (who reviewed the New York production for *Encore*), found the cutting anything but judicious.

Even while surrendering to the visceral impact of the play, we couldn't help thinking that a fine cutting comb had been working on Dürrenmatt. Arguments seemed to be missing . . .; the second-act desertion of Schill by the town occurred too quickly. We realised that we were being asked to accept certain motivations and behaviour almost by definition. A barber had been thinning hair; the impression of a full head of hair remained, but important strands were missing.

In Dürrenmatt's second act, a citizen comes to Schill's shop to buy a pair of new shoes on credit. Then another citizen comes to buy a pair of new shoes. Then another, and another, all of them buying on credit. All Schill can do is sell them shoes, knowing that he can only possibly be paid after he has been murdered.

These are, presumably, the scenes that Brook found repetitious. But they demonstrate the process of corruption, as well as evoking Brecht's tendency to repeat patterns in an ironical way. And they work in a style that Hollywood comedians, like Laurel and Hardy and the Marx Brothers, have taught us to enjoy. In Laurel and Hardy's *The Music Box*, for example, the two comedians are trying to push a piano up a flight of steps. The piano keeps sliding back to the bottom of the steps. Each time it happens you say, 'It can't happen again', but you know it is going to, and when it does you are reduced again to laughter.

As Brook saw it, the second act was about Schill's inner feelings. He started out 'by being self-satisfied and ended up being submissive'. How could this 'slow and subtle development' be shown? But as Dürrenmatt had originally written it, the second act was about how the citizens were corrupted by greed. When the piano evades your grasp and slides down the steps, all you can do is watch it go. When the citizens start to buy shoes on credit, all Schill can do is sell them shoes – on credit.

Schill's plight is funny because he is caught in a paradox. The comedy works through the repetition. And the repetition demonstrates the process. 'Everyone may not like this play', wrote Brook, 'because it shows so vividly that people will do absolutely anything for money'.

Gordon Rogoff said:

We are told reliably that Mr Dürrenmatt agreed to all the changes suggested by his Anglo-American collaborators. . . . We can almost visualise the business transaction as directed by Mr Brook. The lights are dim . . . . A mass of extras hover in the shady background, occasionally bringing on materials needed for the action: a pair of scissors, a cheque book, pens and pencils. The script of the play is down stage centre, limp if not quite lifeless. On one side stand the management . . . on the other the huge imposing figure of the Swiss play-wright, now wearing dark glasses. A faint echo of Beethoven's setting of Schiller's 'Ode to Joy' can be heard on the off-stage tape-recorder. The management hands a cheque over the script to the playwright. The playwright, never looking down at the script, gently takes the cheque, places it in his pocket, nods, clicks his heels and begins to move away . . . we suddenly notice that he is wearing a sleek, black, shiny pair of new shoes. The lights fade. Beethoven can't be heard anymore. Curtain.

At the newly opened Royalty in London, *The Visit* was booked in for eight weeks. It ran for twenty. Brook's production of *The Visit* was a major milestone in his career. It helps us to see more clearly what he was about.

Since his arrival on the scene, he had frequently threatened to disturb the placid surface of British theatre. He had been seen as an *enfant terrible*, and he did, in some ways, resemble an urchin throwing pebbles into a still pool. But – if we leave aside his tilts at opera – his challenge to the insularity and philistin-ism of British theatre had mainly been seen in his productions of Shakespeare. *The Visit* was the first modern play Brook had produced which questioned, in its form as well as its content, the dominant assumptions of the theatre in which Brook worked – even if he clearly felt the need to refashion that form considerably. At that time hardly anyone in the English theatre, neither practi-tioners nor audience, even knew who Brecht was, let alone understood epic theatre.

Brecht had been developing his concept of epic theatre since the late twen-ties, not as an abstract theory but as a working method. At the same time, Brecht had seen himself as a Marxist. (He once said that when he first read Marx, he recognised that here was a man who would understand his plays.) Brecht was attracted to Marx because of Marx's belief in dialectics – the fruitful collision of contradictions – and because of Marx's materialist interpretation of history. Brecht himself worked through contradictions – the contradiction, for example, between a character's words and his actions. And he recognised, as his friend, Walter Benjamin, pointed out, that Marx's materialism made him a satirist – an element in his work which his disciples have usually overlooked.

Marx believed that history had been shaped by the clash of economic inter-ests between opposing classes. Whether or not this version of history is 'true' is less important, in the present discussion, than the fact that it gave Marx a way of interpreting past and contemporary events. He looked at the way heroic figures in history had behaved and asked: 'But what were they *really* after?' His philosophy enabled him to confront familiar historical events in a fresh and sceptical way.

It was precisely this approach that Brecht brought to the theatre. He wanted his audience to look sceptically at the behaviour of familiar stage heroes, and this led him towards irony. When he contemplated producing *Romeo and Juliet*, for example, he wrote two rehearsal scenes. The actors were to see the scenes as taking place immediately before the love scene on the balcony. Romeo has been to a party. Before the party, he has declared his undying love for Rosaline. But at the party he sees and falls in love with Juliet.

In the first of Brecht's two rehearsal scenes, Romeo is ordering an old tenant farmer off his land. Romeo needs to sell the land, he tells the old farmer, because he needs the money to buy a present for Rosaline. You can not just jilt a girl and leave her without giving her a present. When the old man points out that his family will be left to starve, Romeo accuses him of having no finer feeling, of having forgotten what it was like to be young.

In the second scene, Juliet is talking to her servant girl. The girl is in love with a soldier, but she has a rival. She must keep a date with the soldier. Juliet encourages her – she must put on her best stockings. But as the girl is ready to leave, Romeo appears over the garden wall. How can Juliet speak to him? If her parents hear no movement in her room, might they not be suspicious and come to see what is the matter. The girl must walk up and down the room making a noise, even though she will miss her date.

Throughout the balcony scene – 'the matchless wedding of melody and moonshine' – the old man will stand under the balcony, chewing straw and spitting it out of his mouth, and the girl will walk up and down shaking a bowl full of dishes.

Brecht, unlike Brook, never produced *Romeo and Juliet*. His rehearsal scenes were a joke. But they were intended to make us see the lovers as two rich, spoilt, mooning adolescents whose 'tragic' sufferings are self-indulgent, over-dramatised and ultimately absurd. And the rehearsal scenes were, in themselves, very funny.

When Brecht talked about an audience watching with 'detached alienation', he meant that they would see through the pretensions of the tragic heroes. They would see through them and laugh. Far from being unmoved, they would find their laughter liberating – they would see their own oppressors in a less reverent light, and would, hopefully, be encouraged to resist them.

Such a form of theatre is, potentially, deeply subversive. Dürrenmatt himself was strongly aware of this:

Our task today is to demonstrate freedom. The tyrants of this planet are not moved by the works of poets. They yawn at a poets's lamentations. . . . Tyrants fear only one thing: a writer's mockery.

Mussolini recognised the subversive implications of a similar form of popular art when he banned the Marx Brothers' *Duck Soup* (a film in which Groucho played a dictator). The Marx Brothers came out of American vaudeville. Yet Brook wrote of *The Visit*:

The play is written in epic and fabulous terms: the productions of the play in Germany and France differ vastly from those in England and America because of the different cultural and theatrical traditions in each country. So I did not try for a detached alienation from the audience, I wanted to tell the story in heightened human terms.

In other words, Brook wanted to bring the play back inside the framework of a form of theatre that Brecht had tried to demolish.

Brook was to revisit Dürrenmatt two-and-a-half years after *The Visit* finally reached London, and almost immediately after the famous production, in 1962, of *King Lear* (which some critics saw as 'Brechtian'). *The Physicists* opened at The Aldwych in January 1963. This is how Kenneth Tynan described the play.

The setting is a madhouse de luxe in Switzerland run by a hunchbacked female psychiatrist, whose prize patients are three nuclear physicists. One of them, who thinks he is Einstein, has strangled his nurse just before the play begins. . . . Another, a soi-disant Newton, has done the same a few months earlier; and the third, to whom King Solomon appears in visions, follows suit at the end of the first act.

It teasingly emerges that neither Newton nor Einstein is mad: they are the rival hirelings of the Great Powers, feigning insanity in order to abduct their fellow-prisoner, who has invented, during his incarnation, a machine for universal destruction. They have been cursed with perceptive nurses, who had to be killed because they knew too much.

Their prospective victim, the votary of life-loving Solomon, turns out to be saner than either of them; he is a scientific genius who has preferred to immure himself in a mental home rather than expose the human race to the consequences of his discoveries. . . .

He wins them over to his pacifist point of view: but no sooner have they sworn amity than power mania in another human form . . . bursts in to enslave them. They retire to their cells confirmed once more in their respective fantasies, this time for life.

Tynan hides the identity of the 'human form' who seizes power – he compares the play to a Hitchcock movie, and so observes the convention of not giving away the ending. But it is, in fact, the 'hunchbacked female psychiatrist' who seizes Möbius's secret: 'You have taken refuge in a prison you have built for yourselves. Solomon thought through you. He acted through you. And now he destroys you. Through me. . . . Everything that can be thought is thought at some time or other, either now or in the future.'

In the London production, the Fräulein Doktor was played by Irene Worth. Unlike Lynn Fontanne, she was left with her deformity. For most of the play she showed a gentle, perplexed understanding, mixed with what seemed to be 'real' bewilderment when the Solomon-worshipping Möbius strangled his nurse: 'Möbius, how could you do it? You have killed my best nurse, my sweetest nurse.' (She had herself engineered the murder.) But she played the scene in which she seized power with a strong sense of the melodramatic. Dürrenmatt himself was surprised to find a British actress performing more demonstratively than her German counterpart: 'In one of the best German productions . . .

the mad lady doctor made her revelations at the end sitting quietly on the sofa, using very little voice and emphasis. That gave it a marvellously mad effect.'

Brook produced the play, both in London and in New York (a year later with a different cast), as a thriller and with a strong sense of the dramatic: the thug-like attendants produce a steel curtain to incarcerate the patients as the Doktor takes over; at the end, after she has shown her hand, and the three know they are going to be imprisoned as 'mad' for the rest of their lives, Brook gave Newton a monumental pause before he began the speech 'I am Isaac Newton'. Tynan described the play as 'conceived and carried out like a chess problem'. But he added that

beneath the Arctic cap of the argument there simmers a passionate concern for human sur-vival, and this wedding of logic and charity prompts me to hail the piece as Dürrenmatt's finest work.

Dürrenmatt said that what prompted him to write the play was 'not politics at all':

I was interested in working out a situation, a situation that takes the worst possible turn, and also the workings of chance, which always fascinate me. In this case, everything turns on the physicist who wants to escape into a lunatic asylum having chosen the worst possi-ble lunatic asylum to hide in; and on that choice, which is pure chance, the fate of the world may hang.

Dürrenmatt also said he had tried to write a modern version of *Oedipus*, based on

a chain of events in which the hero goes to great lengths to avoid a disaster he fears, and everything he does to prevent the disaster does in fact make it inevitable.

In his battle of wits with the Sphinx, Oedipus shows himself to be a man of superior intelligence. But the more he uses his intelligence, the more certainly it leads him to the conclusion he most wants to avert.

I am much concerned with logic and how its consequent application leads us into more and more difficult paradoxes. I would call my own theatre 'a theatre of paradox', because it is precisely the paradoxical results of strict logic that interest me. I am concerned with logical thought in its strictest applications, so strict that it sets up its own internal contradictions.

But with a theatre of contradictions, we are once again back with Brecht.

At the beginning of the play, all three physicists behave as if they were mad. Later, each of them affirms his sanity. But then they all solemnly decide that they will return to their feigned madness, for the good of humanity. But each of them has strangled a nurse. Their actions contradict their words. They solemnly drink to the memories of the nurses they themselves have murdered. The text calls on the actors to demonstrate this contradiction. Instead, the British actors in the London production, tried to iron out the contradictions.

AH writes:

To my mind, the performance worked well enough on a level of naturalism, but lacked a dimension. The actors failed at the level of comic irony. They said, 'We're not really mad, we were only pretending' – and they asked us to believe them, to share their convictions. 'Poor men: they had to strangle their nurses. Such reasonable men, too.' We sympathise with their predicament, as the actors asked us to do.

I thought the actors should have found a way of asking us to question, through mockery, the way they behaved. Brook himself said he agreed with this – he wrote to me saying that this is what he himself had wanted; he had had my notice copied and had sent the copies to the cast. I remember thinking, 'Well, Brook *is* the director, why didn't he tell the actors what was required?' At that time I had no idea of the tortured processes that were involved in the staging of a Brook production, or of the ingrained habits of traditional British actors.

Brook had, increasingly, been using Brecht as a point of reference. But he had shown no real curiosity about Brecht's working methods in his productions of the Dürrenmatt plays, and when, in 1964, he came to stage Peter Weiss's *The Marat/Sade*, a play that could not have been written if Brecht's theatre had never been invented, he was to tilt the balance of the play firmly away from Brecht.

Apparently Brook never thought of Brecht as offering, for him personally, an alternative to the deadly theatre, the category in *The Empty Space* he most despised. Eventually, he came to argue that Brecht had done for acting what Gordon Craig had done for stage design. Craig had stripped stage design of its non-essentials; Brecht had done much the same thing for acting. Faced with character roles, actors felt they had to 'do it all', to fill in all the details in order to create rounded characters. This was all very well, said Brook, in naturalistic plays. But in Shakespeare the 'reality' of the characters was more complex. If actors spent all their time on naturalistic details, they had no time left to explore the richer reality. Brecht offered them a way of stripping away what was unnecessary. Brook's interpretation of Brecht was a long way from Brecht's attempt to create a theatre form that would lay bare the workings of society. He says, in his *Encore* review of *The Connection*, that 'There is so much of Brecht's work that I admire, so much of his work with which I totally disagree'; for him 'alienation' is Brecht's invention of a device of 'quite incredible power'. He never mentions the political possibilities; we might assume this is the part he totally disagrees with.

Brook's lack of curiosity about Brecht left British theatre the poorer. The 'revolution' of 1956 had led to the reintroduction of political subject-matter into British theatre. But there was little interest in the revolutionary *forms* of theatre that groups in the Soviet Union and Germany had been trying to develop in the twenties and thirties. The work of a whole generation was virtually forgotten.

Joan Littlewood, through her collaborator, Ewan McColl, had been aware of the work of the political theatre groups in Germany, which had been destroyed under Hitler. Now working at Stratford East, she had tried to extend their ideas in an English context, by drawing on English popular theatre traditions. Her Theatre Workshop productions of Elizabethan plays won acclaim at international festivals abroad, but were ignored in Britain. It was as if she were working somewhere in the wings of British theatre.

However, Brook was very definitely centre stage by the time of his Dürrenmatt productions. He was in a position to help give the new British theatre a sense of direction. Political playwrights like John Arden were struggling to create a theatre language. Brecht had begun to forge one. If Brook had allowed his curiosity to take him where Dürrenmatt's texts were inviting him to go, Brecht might have become a living force in British theatre, instead of being regarded as the author of a few solemn plays that belong in a theatre museum.

But Brook had his own directions to follow. He marked them out in his 1962 production of *King Lear,* which can now be seen as a landmark, not only in Brook's career, but in post-war British theatre.

3   Climbing the mountain: *King Lear*

We need to look to Shakespeare. Everything remarkable in Brecht, Beckett, Artaud, is in Shakespeare. For an idea to stick it is not enough to state it: it must be burnt into our memories. Hamlet is such an idea.

Peter Brook

I am more easily bored by Shakespeare and have suffered more ghastly evenings with Shakespeare than with any other dramatist I know.

Peter Brook

In an article in *Encore* in 1960, Brook asked:

Is there nothing in the revolution that took place in painting fifty years ago that applies to our own crisis today? Do we know where we stand in relation to the real and unreal, the face of life and its hidden streams, the abstract and the concrete, the story and the ritual? What are 'facts' today? Are they *concrete*, like prices and hours of work – or *abstract*, like violence and loneliness? And are we sure that in relation to twentieth-century living, the great abstractions – speed, strain, space, frenzy, energy, brutality – aren't more concrete, more immediately likely to affect our lives than the so-called concrete issues? Mustn't we relate this to the actor and the ritual of acting to find the pattern of the theatre we need?

It seems strange, in this century of Auschwitz and Hiroshima, to think of 'violence' as abstract. But what Brook had in mind was the abstraction of modern painting.

I'm interested in why the theatre today, in its search for popular forms, ignores the fact that in painting the most popular form in the world today has become abstract. Why did the Picasso show fill the Tate with all manner of people who would not go to the Royal Academy?

Brook returned to the Picasso analogy in a 1963 essay in a book about the RSC, *The Crucial Years*, where he writes of looking

beyond an outer liveliness to an inner one. Outer splendour can be exciting, but has little relation with modern life: on the inside lie themes and issues, rituals and conflicts, which are as valid as ever. Any time the Shakespearian meaning is caught it is 'real' and so contemporary.

In writing about Shakespeare, Brook uses the word 'reality' in almost a mystical sense. It relates to an ultimate truth. But when he talks about the process of putting together a Shakespeare production, he brings us down to earth with a bump.

For example, he told his audience in a discussion, organised by *Encore* in the spring of 1963, how, immediately after the war, the new director at Stratford-

44

upon-Avon, Sir Barry Jackson, had instituted a 'giant reform'. The reform of saying that in the future each play would have not less than four weeks' rehearsal ('which was a revolution in those days') and that each play would have a different director:

and he threw us all loose on the plays with a general blanket encouragement to do what we wanted. Well now, the result was that the director very rapidly discovered that he could not trust his cast. . . .

Four weeks of rehearsal time was simply not long enough for getting plays with fifty people on stage 'to any boil . . .'. The directors found that

the middle of the company, those key parts where all the real sense of Shakespeare is eventually held, was inevitably in the hands of the middle-aged, not-so-good actors, who were only there in the middling parts at Stratford because they hadn't made it anywhere else. And so the directors, I think all of us in different ways, took the same essentially pessimistic view of saying, 'Here's an area where we know that whatever we do, broadly speaking, this is the result we're going to get. Here [gesture of top level] is an area which, if we're fortunate enough to have an outstanding talent in a leading part, may be open to something different; and here [gesture of lower level] is this possibility in the smaller parts, through the opportunities that all the big scenes give the director of making an interpretation by arranging all the scenes which deal with crowds differently. Here [lower level] we have a freedom; here in the middle we have to counterbalance the conventional brought by the actor with something external, with the costumes, with the scenery; and here [top level] we can go and spend our four weeks working very intimately with three people, trying in this way to squeeze the ends of what we're doing into something which will take on an overall coherence.'

This realistic account of the theatre conditions Brook worked in at Stratford-upon-Avon throws a different light on those early Shakespeare productions. When the witnesses defined Brook as a director with a strong visual sense, they were responding to the rearranged crowd scenes, or to the costumes and scenery behind which he tried to hide the conventional acting. And when they praised the star performers, as if their performances had nothing to do with the director, the witnesses were clearly unaware that it was with them that the director had worked 'very intimately' for four weeks.

Brook's 1950 production of *Measure for Measure* showed the method in action. Brook, wrote Tynan, had permitted himself only one 'trick':

the grisly parade of cripples and deformities which Pompey introduces into that leprous Viennese gaol. Last of all appears 'Wild Half-Can' who stabb'd pots: a very aged man, naked except for a rag coat, twitching his head from side to side, and walking poker-stiff, bolt upright on his bare heels, with his toes turned up. All the ghastly comedy of the prison scenes were summed up in this horridly funny piece of invention.

Brook was clearly exercising his freedom with the 'lower level'; and at the top he had the 'astounding talent' of John Gielgud, who had, at the beginning, a sense of Angelo, a lot of shapes, impressions, faces, facts of him not yet in clear shape. And I'm therefore open to discover, although if someone were to ask me, I'd say, 'Of course, he's in a wild temper here, that's my impression'. And I'd be certain that when I start rehearsing this . . . that's going to be changed, so I'm not hooked at all to that idea. And I then start doing that with John, who, because he would have the same feeling, takes this line in which Angelo is clearly in a fury, and would suddenly try it not moving. . . . He would have just that smell of something and, doing it motionless, suddenly a line that's apparently a loud, passionate and flamboyant line, will suddenly *isolate*, and at that second, if he is suddenly sensed right, you get a clue to Angelo. Suddenly, Angelo appears for a moment, and because of that you see him as he could be twenty lines after in a different light. So then either you or John or both seize on it and say, 'Ah, but were that true, then we could start quite differently in the following scene'. It's a form of impressionism.

Gielgud, for his part, saw *Measure for Measure* as a key moment in his long career. Years later, after playing Oedipus in Brook's 1968 production, he said:

I am determined not to vary in performance. I don't think I do any more. I'm proud of myself because ever since *Measure for Measure* at Stratford in 1950, I started to discipline myself and not experiment as I always used to do.

The sages in the riparian dining-rooms at Stratford-upon-Avon, who saw Gielgud as holding the production together, would probably have been surprised to learn that the *enfant terrible* had taught this most-controlled of British actors self-discipline.

Brook says he worked well with Gielgud because they were both 'empirical' in their approach. He comments:

All sorts of roads lead to Rome, and. . . . The method of the director working everything out ahead of time and then giving it to the actor is . . . a perfectly sound method if the director is absolutely right. If I had the capacity, which is alien to my whole nature, to sit at home and think out a play, not only completely, which anyone can do, but absolutely unerringly rightly, then there is no reason why this shouldn't happen. But in fact what happens is that directors who use that as a method think wrongly, and they cling to what they have thought out, because otherwise their authority is challenged. . . .

In a well-known passage in *The Empty Space*, Brook describes how he arrived for his first ever rehearsal at Stratford-upon-Avon with 'a fat prompt book under my arm'. But when he began to rehearse the first scene, he found that the forty actors he was trying to move according to his thought-out plan were creating their own patterns and their own rhythms.

It was a moment of panic; I think looking back, that my whole future work hung in the balance. Then, I walked away from my book in amongst the actors, and I have never looked at a written plan since.

Brook makes the gesture of moving 'in amongst the actors' sound very much like a declaration of complete openness. But we must not forget that he also came to see actors in terms of lower level, middle level and top level. With John at the top he could 'improvise': they could say to the lower orders, 'Go here, go there, no, that's not worth trying' while together they teased out a meaning. And people who have worked closely with Brook – or who have watched him at work – are aware that the 'openness' has its own boundaries.

GR writes:

When Brook says, I threw away the blocking, it means that he throws away one blocking, which has been worked out and prepared in his head while reading the text, in order to move to the next stage, because of what he sees and relates to when the actors speak the lines and move. He's only taking away *this* to get to *that*. He's not going in and saying, 'As the spirit moves me'. There's an enormous amount of preparation. And he's still moving inside an over-all concept. In his head, I think he's always working towards a dimly perceived shape, as a sculptor works his material into a form.

The structure of *Measure for Measure* found its form in a *coup de théâtre* in the final act. Tynan wrote:

Brook's triumph, however, is in the fifth act: a scene of such coincidences and lengthy impossibilities, such forced reconciliations and incredible cruelties, that most producers flog it through at breakneck speed towards the welcome curtain. Fully aware of the tension his flawless timing has created, Brook here has the affrontery to sit down and let it ride: into the dreadful act he inserts half a dozen long pauses, working up to a new miracle of tension Shakespeare knew nothing about. The thirty-five seconds of dead silence which elapse before Isabella decides to make her plea for Angelo's life were a long prickly moment of doubt which had every heart in the theatre scudding.

AH writes:

But why were the hearts scudding? Brook has always insisted that every *performance* of Shakespeare should be presented as if the audience were seeing the play for the first time. And in building the sculpture of *Measure for Measure* towards this pause, Brook was behaving as if the audience would not know what was coming next. This was the moment when the play touched 'reality'. According to Brook, 'The device became a voodoo pole – a silence in which the abstract notion of mercy became concrete for that moment to those present'.

But the realist in Brook must also have known that the word would rapidly get round the playgoers of 1950 that in this final act of *Measure* there was this very dramatic pause. A sceptical non-witness may be forgiven for wondering if the celebrated pause didn't, in the end, become a nightly game between Barbara Jefford and the audience. Barbara Jefford had been told to hold the pause until the audience could stand no more. The pause at first lasted thirty-five seconds. It reportedly grew to two minutes. Did the collective consciousness of the audience collude with the actress to help her break the record? Did someone stand off stage with a stop-watch?

'Two minutes exactly tonight, Barbara.'
'Only two minutes? Are you sure you started the stop-watch at the right time?'

Could this be what Brook meant by a 'secret play', the play within the play, the actors working on an inner meaning known only to them? (The observers were generally agreed that the pause was about thirty-five seconds.)

11   *King Lear*, Stratford-upon-Avon, 1962

In his review of *Measure for Measure*, Tynan had written that Brook would soon be 'at the height of his powers'. But it was to be another twelve years, and five Shakespearian productions later, before he reached the climax of even this first stage of his career, with his 1962 production of *King Lear*.

The set was open: two vast rectangular flats, the backcloth and stage all painted in a subtle whitish, chalky grey – geometrical straight lines only broken by dangling squares and triangles of painted metal (for the palace) and three corroded metal thunder sheets (for the storm).

The play looked like a series of medieval tableaux. The lighting was bright, blinding white, even during the storm. The costumes were ornamented leather, both supple and heavy; for the nobles there were long capes, cloaks, skirts; for the servants and men-at-arms a uniform of smock-frocks and mantles of coarse cloth: their colour predominantly brown, the texture rough, giving an impression of barbaric plainness. The furniture was of natural, rough-hewn wood, the props of rusty metal.

The actors entered while the house lights were still up, and at the end of each act the action continued for a while after they came back up; at the interval the servants went about their business of putting the furniture straight while newly blinded Gloucester slowly groped his way off stage; and at the end Edgar dragged off the body of his brother. The pace was slow and full of pauses. It was very static for most of the time, so the bursts of action, like Lear and his knights overturning the tables, became explosive. The speaking was extremely clear, sometimes loud but never ranting.

Torches had no flames, wounds drew no blood. Gloucester sat on stage listening to the off-stage battle suggested by the clangour of rattling shields. Edmund and Edgar fought in slow-motion, looking like figures from an Eisenstein film. Corpses were continually dragged very slowly across the stage.

Not all the witnesses approved. The old writers of light, literacy essays had, for the most part, disappeared, but some members of the new generation of critics, now edging towards middle age themselves, were not entirely happy with the production.

Alan Brien, who had been Tynan's contemporary at Oxford, wrote in *Theatre Arts* that it was a 'diminished' Lear:

The gruff, grizzled, north-country Lear of Paul Scofield is no Lord's anointed majesty, whose authority is divinely approved.

But he added, however, that at certain moments ('In the warmth of his sympathy for the Fool, in his affection for his swaggering soldiers . . . and especially in that slow determined struggle back to sanity') Paul Scofield had 'achieved what had seemed impossible – the creation of a contemporary out of a symbol'. He concluded, 'This may be a partisan and partial version of *King Lear*, but it remains the first to speak direct to a modern audience'.

According to Irving Wardle (*Plays and Players*) the production offered the critic 'a bewildering choice of angles'. It could be seen as 'an objective reappraisal of the tragedy', or 'as Shakespeare's most Eastern play: the link it establishes between poverty and spiritual progress is much closer to Buddhism than Christianity'. The production underlined this in decor and costume ('both reminiscent of the Chinese theatre'), and in 'the impersonality of the acting'. But, 'What one missed was a continuous dramatic line'. The general level of Scofield's performance was 'bleakly negative – it leaves an impression more of determination to avoid clichés than of any positive expressive intent'.

When the production reached New York, several leading American critics were even more hostile. John Chapman (*Daily News*) objected to the 'bare stage. . . . It puts a strain on me to have to imagine where I am.' 'Monotony overtakes Mr Brook's staging all too frequently', wrote Walter Kerr in the *New York Herald Tribune*, adding graciously that 'possibly because the company has been performing it for so long that incidental breaths for emphasis became overnight stops'. Susan Sontag found what she saw 'rather dull – I can't see what is gained by going against the emotional climaxes of the play'. She complained of 'the desire to make explicit and to underplay which must have led Brook, in one of the most curious choices of the production, to keep the stage fully lit and bare during the storm scenes'. Harold Clurman, commenting that 'The calm irony of Brecht is not intended as negation but as a purification of the spirit which might lead to the understanding required for action', went on to write 'But Shakespeare is not Brecht. Shakespeare's immense force, his overwhelming lyric might, the volcanic life that fires his every scene and speech, are not to be conveyed in the reasoned, shrivelled and bleached terms of Peter Brook's staging, impressive though they be . . . and then, one does not attempt to describe the Himalayas by likening them to the Catskills' – after which Clurman remarked, with double-edged praise, 'Peter Brook is to be congratulated on a *Lear* made to the measure of our day and the circumstance of modern theatre'.

Brook himself came to believe that the 'austerity' of the production was not right for the United States. The best audience lay 'between Budapest and Moscow', as he had discovered with the tour of *Titus Andronicus*:

These audiences brought with them three things: a love for the play itself, real hunger for a contact with foreigners, and, above all, an experience of life in Europe in the last years that enabled them to come directly to the play's painful themes. The quality of the attention that this audience brought expressed itself in silence and concentration, a feeling in the house that affected the actors as though a brilliant light were turned on their work. As a result, the most obscure passages were illuminated, they were played with a complexity of meaning and a fine use of the English language that few of the audience could follow, but which all could sense.

In Philadelphia the audience understood English, but was composed 'largely of people who were not interested in the play, people who had come for all the conventional reasons. . .'. Eventually, their impresario took the play to the Lincoln Center in New York,

a giant auditorium where the acoustics were bad and the audience resented its poor contact with the stage . . . the actors, responding to the given conditions, had no choice: they faced the front, spoke loudly and quite rightly threw away all that had become precious in their work.

Over thirty years later, it is difficult to remember how directors saw *Lear* before Brook. The production was one of those theatre events that change people's perceptions of received material. 'Lay him to rest, the royal Lear with whom generations of star actors have made us familiar', wrote Kenneth Tynan when he first saw Brook's production. Brook laid him to rest. (Although the previous Stratford Lear had hardly been any more royal: Charles Laughton, who only came into his own in the second half of the play, had been thought too plebian to rule Albion; 'Lear as common man' was the headline in *The Times*.)

Brook made two significant textual changes which brought *King Lear* inside the boundaries of his over-all concept. In the versions we agree to accept as Shakespeare's, there are two moments when the author relents. After Gloucester has been blinded, kindly servants lead him away, criticising the behaviour of his tormentors. And, at the end of the play, Gloucester's bastard son, Edmund, who has played a major part in bringing about the catastrophe, makes a speech in which he repents and tries to repair some of the damage. Brook removed this speech. And, after having Gloucester blinded in a bright light by a Cornwall wearing golden-pointed spurs, Brook brought the house lights up. Brook's assistant producer, Charles Marowitz (who wrote a *Lear Log* about 'salient' parts of the rehearsal process) describes the scene:

Gloucester is covered with a tattered rag and shoved off in the direction of Dover. Servants, clearing the stage, collide with the confused blind man and rudely shove him aside. . . . The house lights remove all possibility of aesthetic shelter, and the act of blinding is seen in a colder light than would otherwise be possible.

According to Marowitz, Brook saw *Lear* 'mainly as a play about sight and blindness'. Brook presented the play in a permanently bright light – like the light that is never turned off in a political prisoner's cell. In the storm scene, he borrowed a convention from Chinese opera. In a classic Chinese opera scene, two actors stage a carefully choreographed sword fight. They play it in bright light – but, by their actions, it is quite clear that they are fighting in pitch darkness. In the same way, Edgar led the blinded Gloucester up a steep hill, on a flat, bare stage.

The year he produced *Lear*, Brook told an audience at the Oxford University Dramatic Society:

I am absolutely incapable of solving a production other than through the scenery. The set is a summing-up of everything that one has felt and studied in a production. . . . I worked on the set of *Lear* for about a year.

(But Brook later told A. C. H. Smith, who wrote *Orghast at Persepolis*, that he had thrown out most of the *Lear* set just before the first night; for him there would be no contradiction in this – one works by discarding what one has found.)

Tynan's first impression was of a 'Flat white setting, combining Brecht and oriental theatre, against which ponderous abstract objects dangle'. More than one critic referred to Brecht, but, according to both Marowitz and Brook himself, the world of this *Lear* is the world of Beckett's *Endgame*. Marowitz writes of what he calls 'the germinal scene':

Fable. A blind man, resolved to die, is led up a steep mountainside by one he takes to be a naked lunatic. The steep mountainside is, in reality, a flat field; the naked lunatic his son. Arriving at what he takes to be the topmost point, the blind man leaps into what he takes to be a fathomless chasm, and falls in a faint two feet from where he stood. His son, now disguised as a passing peasant, revives the blind man, wards off the treachery of a would-be assassin and leads him to temporary safety, but not before he has had a wild encounter with a distracted king dressed in weeds and nettles.

Marowitz comments:

The plot is as Beckettian as anything out of *Molloy* or *Malone Dies*; the scene a metaphysical farce which ridicules life, death, sanity and illusion. Although Beckett has never used such a plot, the production certainly seemed at times to be a vivid dramatisation of Beckett's own universe: an isolated and forbidding landscape, a lack of empathy, a slow continuum of action, or non-action, focusing on futility, exhaustion and cruelty.

Tynan said he still could not understand why Edgar did not reveal himself to his blind father after the leap – why he suddenly became a passing peasant. The question itself seems farcical in a world of 'metaphysical farce'. Yet Marowitz and Brook themselves walked around Kensington Pond solemnly trying to find a rational centre for Edgar, so Marowitz tells us:

In terms of the text, Poor Tom has more definition (and more scenes) then the original character of Edgar. Where is the consistency in this transformation, and if it is deliberately inconsistent, how can one perform it without forfeiting either Edgar or Poor Tom?

In spite of their intellectual commitment to the absurd, both Marowitz and Brook brought a post-Stanislavski concern with inner motivation to the work with the actors. Marowitz searches for a 'subtextual reason' to set the tone of the opening scene. There is usually a sense of boring inwards in Brook's work, of peeling the onion, of stripping away, the search for the essential reality. So sometimes he may arrive at the same point as Beckett, an image so striking it burns into the consciousness; but he never plays the absurdist comedian or demonstrates in order to explain the motivation of a particular action.

Brook says he was strongly influenced by a passage in *Shakespeare Our Contemporary* (which had not then been published in English) by the Polish professor, Jan Kott. (He had become friends with Kott when *Titus Andronicus* had played in Warsaw.) Kott wrote:

Tragedy is the theatre of priests, grotesque is the theatre of clowns. . . . When the established values have been overthrown, and there is no appeal to God, Nature or History from the tortures inflicted by the cruel world, the clown becomes the central figure in the theatre.

Scofield did not play Lear as a clown. But he was closer to the clown than to the traditional figure of the Lord's anointed in majesty. Brook says that Shakespeare produces images that burn themselves into the imagination over the centuries. Brook's Lear, as played by Scofield, changed the image.

And this is what made the production such a surprising and revelatory experience in 1962. This picture we had all carried round with us from our schooldays was that of a king who divides up his kingdom unwisely, but who is then punished, beyond reason, by two of his daughters, who are monsters, and by their wicked husbands.

In Brook's production, Lear becomes, in Tynan's words, 'an edgy, capricious old man, difficult to live with'. He gives up his kingdom and his responsibilities, but he expects to hang on to his privileges. In a key scene, early in the play, he arrives with his knights, back from hunting, at Goneril's castle, expecting supper. Traditionally, Goneril is presented as showing base ingratitude when she complains about his behaviour. But in Brook's production, Lear gives her every reason to complain. He overturns the dinner-table in a fit of rage and his action becomes the signal for an outbreak of violence from his knights – they hurl drinks and plates, kick over chairs and wreck the room. Marowitz describes how, in an early rehearsal, the actors playing the knights, egged on by Brook, went beserk:

the stage exploded and sent shrapnel flying in a dozen different directions. Tankards whizzed through the air hitting actors and rocketing into the laps of the stage managers below; set pieces were smashed over up-ended bits of furniture and a chandelier above the rehearsal stage was splintered into a thousand pieces which came raining down on the full company. . . . The stage manager spoke very soberly to the actors about artistic control and deportment. Brook smiled like an oriental Cheshire cat. . . .

The simple shift in attitude to Lear reverberates through the play as the rusted metal objects (which are in fact thunder machines) reverberate in the storm scenes. Goneril and Regan also acquire human dimensions. In *The Empty Space*, Brook describes how, during a lecture, he encountered a woman who had neither seen nor read *King Lear*. He gave her Goneril's first speech to read aloud:

Sir, I love you more than words can wield the matter;
Dearer than eyesight, space and liberty;
Beyond that can be valued, rich or rare;
No less than life, with grace, health, beauty, honour;
A love that makes breath poor, and speech unable;
Beyond all manner of so much I love you.

The woman, says Brook, read it very simply, 'and the speech itself emerged full of eloquence and charm'. Brook then explained that it was supposed to be the speech of a 'a wicked woman' and suggested her reading every word for hypocrisy. She tried to do so, and the audience witnessed a hard unnatural wrestling with the simple music of the words when the woman sought to act to this definition. In his production, Brook tried to recapture 'the simple music'.

The shift in attitude also affected other characters. Kent becomes a coarse-spoken bully, a crude hanger-on; the Fool's jests become barbed truths; above all, Gloucester is no longer simply Lear's understudy.

Gloucester is an old politician, in the shiftiest sense of the word, a man who has, in his time, been a lecher; his bastard son, Edmund, is now a figure to be understood rather than hated. Brook strips away our reasons for pitying both Lear and Gloucester and then turns his bright light on the horror and the meaninglessness of their suffering. In doing so, he creates his own images that burn into the memory. Gloucester sits, sightless, staring out at the audience, while a battle clangs off stage. The mad Lear and the blind Gloucester huddle together for comfort in the bright light of the bare stage. Albany sums up the play's attitude when he hears that Regan and Goneril are dead:

> This judgement of the heavens that makes us tremble
> Touches us not with pity.

He is not moralising: simply stating what Brook has turned into a self-evident fact.

Marowitz's account of Brook's rehearsal process – while not as detailed as David Selbourne's description of *The Making of A Midsummer Night's Dream* – gives us glimpses of Brook's working method. He brings his overall concept to the rehearsal process, but his way of arriving at the realisation of that concept is, says Marowitz, 'relentlessly experimental'. Marowitz quotes Brook offering a romantic vision of the artist starting work (far removed from his other, often expressed, analogy of the scientist doing research in his particular field):

My analogy is with modern painting. A modern painter begins to work with only an instinct and a vague sense of direction. He puts a splotch of red paint on to the canvas and only after it is on does he decide it might be a good idea to add a little green, to make a vertical line here or a horizontal line there. It's the same with rehearsals. What is achieved determines what is to follow, and you can't go about things as if you knew all the answers. New answers are constantly presenting themselves, posing new problems, reversing old solutions, substituting new ones.

Yet most people who have worked with Brook would argue that he starts with something more than a 'vague sense of direction'. He clearly pointed Scofield towards a conception of Lear; but, having done the pointing, he would work on a trial-and-error basis with Scofield until, together, they found the 'right solution' – i.e., the one Brook finds right.

For some of the actors in *Lear*, Brook asked Marowitz to devise improvisations. Both of them felt that Alec McCowen was handling the 'ethereal' character of the Fool in too organised a way. Marowitz invented a scene for him with Cordelia. It takes place while she is preparing herself for the play's opening ceremony. 'An easy, banteringly affectionate, thoroughly credible relationship was built up between the two characters. The Fool tried out some new material on Cordelia. He teased her about her royal suitors.' The second improvisation was of the scene immediately after Cordelia has been rejected by her father and married off to the King of France. The Fool 'quickly realises that he is about to lose his only friend in the palace, the only one with whom he can afford the luxury of a private life'. The pathos was there, but the scene ended 'amiably and lightly' – in a British fashion, thought the American Marowitz. It turned out to be useful, though, because

It became clear that the character of the actress playing Cordelia was radically different from the Acting-Self she adopted for the role. The problem now is to get the actress in control of her own reality in such a way that it begins to nourish the character.

But it is at points like this that other questions being to break in.

What does Marowitz mean by 'her own reality?' A central part of the actress's reality is that she is being paid, for a time, to play her role in a way that will satisfy a particularly demanding director. But Marowitz is clearly not thinking of *that* kind of reality – the reality of the power relationship between director and actress. Marowitz is referring to some kind of 'inner reality' which he (and Brook) claim the right to explore. But to explore for what purpose? In order to achieve a more 'truthful' performance of Cordelia – that is, a more convincing deception? In the bare light that Brook sheds on his empty stage, the process goes round and round and ends up – on the empty stage. For it is difficult to see in what way Brook's *Lear* leads us to a better understanding of our human plight. It leads us to a *different* understanding of a well-known play – and this sense of a different understanding gives us pleasure and delight, even while it is telling us that our predicament is one of pointless despair. This was, perhaps, grasped by the Soviet director who had to explain the virtues of this production in a climate in which only the optimism of social-realism was normally approved. 'So far as I was concerned', wrote Kozintsev when *Lear* was taken to Moscow in 1964, 'Peter Brook and Paul Scofield were talking not so much about the powerlessness of man, but about the power of art'. Or at least about the power of theatre as practised by Peter Brook.

For behind Brook the searcher for 'truth', and Brook the abstract painter, is Brook the practical craftsman. And in Marowitz's *Lear Log*, as the first night approaches and we reach the first run-through, it is Brook the practitioner who asserts himself. He tells the cast, 'We've spent all our time structuring individual scenes and have necessarily lost sight of the whole. Now we must begin looking at one scene in relation to the next.' So far so generalised – but now comes the realist:

And you must all beware of the 'Law of Falling Inflections'. Each time you make a downward inflection the rhythm of a speech comes to a halt. What is happening now is you are ending your last speeches with a downward inflection and so the play comes to a halt after every scene. You must keep the ball in the air being passed from one to the next without a fumble.

Marowitz refers to this as 'an overall theory of continuity'. But it is in fact hard, practical realistic advice by the Brook who knows how to make a play work on stage.

Marowitz ends his account of the work on *King Lear* with a paragraph which sums up, with unconscious irony, Brook's absorption with his own thought-processes. With the first performance only six hours away, Brook asks the company to give 'an easy, underplayed rendering of the play, so as to conserve their energies for the evening performance'. 'The result', writes Marowitz, 'was astonishing.' Actors were suddenly giving 'scaled-down, unfussingly true performances':

> Basic relationships, so long obscured during erratic rehearsals, suddenly became crystal clear. A host of textual misconceptions loomed large on the stage like elusive bacteria suddenly caught on a microscope-plate. Those performances which were organically rooted and internally based were revealed in a bright, non-Shakespearian clarity. Those which lacked foundation from the first emerged as the loosely knit sketches they were.

Surprisingly, says Marowitz, the entire performance was audible from every part of the house. Even Scofield (who at the dress rehearsal had hurled his hunting-cloak at a photographer whose camera had been clicking during Lear's speeches) could be heard over the thunderous clamour of the storm scenes. Brook, says Marowitz, was 'hypnotised by the effect'.

But not, apparently, hypnotised into silence. 'You see how little you really need to capture the reality', he said to Marowitz. 'If only theatre audiences listened to plays with the same intensity as concert audiences listen to Oistrakh, the performance of a play would be so much richer. But the level of concentration in the theatre is terribly low; there's always coughing, muttering, crinkling and shifting about. But in a concert hall there is a taut silence; everyone is listening for *and* perceiving subtleties. You see this level of acting . . .' – Brook pointed, says Marowitz, to the stage where modern-dress actors were moving easily through the Hovel scene – 'in thirty years this is the way all Shakespeare will be played'.

There is no record of Scofield throwing a hunting-cloak at Brook; nor of the number of subtleties Brook's muttering caused Marowitz to miss.

4   Crucifixion in Paris: *Serjeant Musgrave's Dance*

This is not a nihilistic play. . . . Nor does it advocate bloody revolution. I have endeavoured to write about the violence that is so evident in the world, and to do so through a story that is partly wish fulfilment.

> John Arden, Introduction to the published text of *Serjeant Musgrave's Dance* (1960)

John Arden's remarkable play *Serjeant Musgrave's Dance* can be taken amongst many other meanings as an illustration of how true theatre comes into being. Musgrave faces a crowd in a market place on an improvised stage and he attempts to communicate as forcibly as possible his sense of the horror and futility of war. The demonstration that he improvises is like a genuine piece of popular theatre; his props are machine guns, flags and a uniformed skeleton that he hauls aloft. When this does not succeed in transmitting his complete message to the crowd, his desperate energy drives him to find still further means of expression, and, in a flash of inspiration, he begins a rhythmic stamping, out of which develops a savage dance and chant. *Serjeant Musgrave's Dance* is a demonstration of how a violent need to project a meaning can suddenly call into existence a wild unpredictable form.

> Peter Brook, *The Empty Space*

I have found in my own tentative experiments that audiences (and particularly critics) find it hard to make the completely simple response to the story that is the necessary preliminary to appreciating the meaning of the play.

> John Arden, 'Telling a true tale', *Encore* (May/June 1960)

At the end of the 1962 season, Brook's production of *King Lear* was a mighty triumph at Stratford, and later at the Aldwych and abroad. Yet, in retrospect, *Lear* was the climax and ending of a period in his work. What was beginning was first seen in public in January 1964, at the little *Lamda* theatre in London. . . .

> A. C. H. Smith, *Orghast at Persepolis*

'In retrospect' that is how the 1962 *Lear* production appears. Yet 1963 was a prolific year for Brook. His film *Lord of the Flies* appeared. He produced *The Physicists* in London and his second version of *The Tempest* in Stratford-upon-Avon. And he had what was virtually the only total failure of his career: a sci-fi musical, *The Perils of Scobie Prilt*, which opened at the New Theatre, Oxford, on Wednesday 13 June (three days after Harold Macmillan asked Lord Denning to enquire into John Profumo's afternoons) and was closed by the management three days later (on the pretext that the slipped disc suffered on the first night by the star, Nyree Dawn Porter, made it impossible to continue). Brook said, presumably in a reference to the then recent Cuban Missile Crisis, 'What with the end of the world being so close . . . either you read the Bible or you read science fiction'. The play sent up everyone from Sexton Blake to Dr No, with a plot which the *Oxford Times* found unoriginal and ill conceived. A scientist who has invented a black box capable of robotising humans was chased across glaciers and deserts by 'our spy' and 'their spy'. It ended with the launching of a rocket on stage.

Brook rounded off the year with two productions at the Athénée in Paris. The second of these was Rolf Hochhuth's *Le Vicaire* (*The Representative*), which was then sweeping across Europe. It belonged to the world of scandal – although this time political – that Brook had always enjoyed flirting with: the play alleges that Pope Pius XII failed to rescue the Jews from the Nazis in the Second World War. However, Hochhuth was more journalist than dramatist; although he had a nose for the big story (he went on to portray Churchill as a ruthless murderer in *Soldiers*) his technique never matched his themes. *The Representative* is a sprawling piece whose main interest lies in the stage directions and notes, rather than in the clumsy naturalistic scenes which usually decline into debate unredeemed even by traces of Shavian wit. Hochhuth deliberately wrote the play for the best possible motives: he had a cause, a political view on history, and he wanted it aired to best effect. The accusation had been made before in print but to minor effect compared with the stink caused when state theatres across Europe put on stage a pope more concerned with position and property than the fate of people. Unfortunately, Hochhuth did not even possess Sartre's limited powers of dramatisation. German audiences lapped up the four hours of journalistic debate. In other countries the script was cut: Clifford Williams, Brook's recent collaborator on *The Tempest*, staged the play by cutting half the scenes but playing the rest intact (this was the common solution to the problem of length, although it still lasted over three hours). Brook, who could recognise essentially undramatic material when he saw it whatever the scandalous nature of its content, did differently. He played every scene, but cut absolutely to the bone. He removed all the turgid naturalism, simply concentrating on the arguments with no pretext of credible characterisation, and he had the stage directions (which contained a wealth of background material) incorporated into a narrative which linked the scenes. So it became a clear presentation of data, shocking in content but unemotional in tone; it lasted two hours. Brook argued, as he did later with Weiss's *The Investigation* when he insisted on having it read, not acted, at the Aldwych, that certain material was so horrific that it was wrong for actors to derive pleasure from performing it. Others who staged *The Representative* 'properly' only found themselves on the slope that led to the Holocaust as TV soap opera.

But before *The Representative* came a version of John Arden's *Serjeant Musgrave's Dance*. Brook had previously worked on texts by such distinguished British writers as John Whiting, Christopher Fry and T. S. Eliot. But Arden was one of the new writers who had emerged in the Royal Court 'revolution'. For the first and only time in his career Brook was to engage himself with a major work of 'new' English drama. He produced it in French.

Serjeant Musgrave's Dance was first produced at the Royal Court in London in October 1959. The established critics greeted it with derision – 'another dreadful ordeal' one of them wrote. This critical response produced a violent reaction from the play's supporters, many of whom were also supporters of the growing peace movement. The violence of their reaction must have been appreciated by Arden, who wrote, in his introduction to the published text:

Complete pacifism is a very hard doctrine: and if this play appears to advocate it with perhaps some timidity, it is probably because I am naturally a timid man – and also because I know that if I am hit I very easily hit back.

Arden's supporters hit back so successfully that by the time Brook staged his Paris production, *Serjeant Musgrave's Dance* was already being described as a modern classic – it was soon to become a set text in schools for students of English literature.

Arden himself was not slow to take part in the controversy which surrounded the original production. In the introduction to the published text, in articles in *Encore* and in more than one interview, Arden made his intentions in writing the play very clear. But Brook has never been a director who would allow a writer's intentions to affect his own vision of the play. He had a very particular vision of *Serjeant Musgrave's Dance* which led him quite simply to ignore what Arden and the play were saying.

Arden's play is about four army deserters – Musgrave, Attercliffe, Hurst and Sparky – who have turned their backs on a colonial war. Arden says:

One of the things that set the play off was an incident in Cyprus. A soldier's wife was shot in the street by terrorists, and according to newspaper reports . . . some soldiers ran wild at night and people were killed in the rounding-up. The atrocity which sparks off Musgrave's revolt . . . is roughly similar.

Cyprus was, in the fifties, a British protectorate – the British army was keeping the peace. In Arden's play, the British army is also keeping the peace in a British protectorate, only for Queen Victoria – a century earlier. A British soldier, Billy Hicks, has been shot in the back on his way home from the opera. The troops have been ordered out in search of the killers. Civilians have been rounded up, thirty-eight of them have been injured, and five people – one young woman and four men – have been killed.

The incident leads Musgrave and his men to desert. And when they run away they take with them the skeleton of Billy Hicks. They take it back to the coal-mining town in the north of England where he came from, and put it on display at a public meeting in the market-place. They hope the demonstration will turn the town's population against the war.

The first two acts of Arden's play are taken up with the installation of Musgrave and his men in the town. In the third act, the stage becomes the platform of a 'recruiting meeting' and the audience in the theatre are treated as townspeople. Musgrave and his men demonstrate their weapons, then the skeleton of Billy Hicks, draped in a scarlet uniform, is hauled up a lamppost, while Hurst 'beats frantically on his drum' and Musgrave 'begins to dance, waving his rifle, his face contorted with demoniac fury'. After the dance, Musgrave proposes turning the guns on the representatives of authority in the town – the Parson, the Mayor and the Constable. Five people had died following the death of Billy Hicks, 'Therefore, for five of them we multiply out, and we find it five-and-twenty'. Musgrave invites the town's colliers, who are on strike, to join him in shooting the twenty-five people, and he holds them at gunpoint. But before he can carry out his threat, the Dragoons arrive and the town is saved. Beer is handed out and Dragoons and colliers dance in a circle, while the only two surviving deserters, Musgrave and Attercliffe, wait to be hanged.

The initial hostility of the critics of the original production was based on their attitude to Musgrave himself. As decent liberals, they picked up quickly that Musgrave was a Serjeant who had turned against war, and a colonial war at that. Well, we on the arts pages were all against colonial wars, weren't we? Musgrave was clearly a man to be admired. They identified with him in the first two acts. And then, in the third act, he suddenly, as they saw it, turned out to be a madman. He wanted to shoot people! What on earth was Arden suggesting – that people who were against war were mad? Arden argued that he had never imagined people would identify with Musgrave, that he had written a story: 'The action is the argument'. Brook disposed of such arguments in his own visionary way. He made Musgrave into Jesus.

Both the authors of this book saw Brook's Paris *Musgrave*. We saw it independently of each other and reviewed it in two different journals. It was only when we began working on this book that we went back and compared notes. We also became aware that the response of a French critic, Françoise Koubilsky, was similar to our own.

What struck all of us in the first place was the set. GR wrote, in *Encore*:

The set is the most hideous example of modern art: against a large curved cyclorama painted dirty neutral are two flats, one tall and thin, the other shorter and almost the width of the stage. The latter divides into three unequal parts where necessary, the joints being runny rather than straight lines. Pipes stick out at various places. The final effect is one of irrelevance. . . . In fact, the set nullifies any attempt at a precise historical setting, which seems a pity.

Françoise Koubilsky, in *Théâtre Populaire*, saw 'great darkish jagged slabs embellished with monstrous pipes made of twisted metal'. AH, in *Scope*, saw the dominant colour as 'grey-green':

In the opening scene, the soldiers are dressed in blue-grey overcoats, and what dominates the stage is a huge slab of grey-green, on which Sparky stands, which could, I suppose, represent the canal bank, but which is there in fact to create an immediate generalised effect. This grey-green slab is present throughout the play. In the churchyard scene, for instance, it breaks up to give a vague, semi-abstract impression of tombstones (but the colours the play is built around are black, white and red).

To be more precise, the play is built around the colours black, white, red and green – but the green is the green of spring and of apples, not the dirty 'neutral' green of Brook's set.

Arden had made it clear that what he called the 'primary colours' were central to his conception. He wanted to draw on what he called 'the bedrock of English poetry' – the traditional ballads. In the ballads, the colours were 'primary', and in *Musgrave*

Black is for death and for the coal mines. Red is for murder and for the soldier's coat the collier puts on to escape his black. Blue is for the sky and for the sea that parts true love. Green fields are speckled with bright flowers. The seasons are clearly defined. White winter, green spring, golden summer, red autumn.

Arden's search for primary colours had, in fact, dictated the 'historical setting'. He had thought of his Serjeant in red, and this had led him to 'one of those Crimean Serjeants, who fought with rifle in one hand and Bible in the other'.

Colours dictated the place and the season. The deserters come to a black coal-mining town, but they arrive in winter; the town is cut off by snow. The Dragoons are able to reach the town because there has been a thaw, the first sign of a green spring. The play ends with the image of a green apple. By ignoring the primary colours, Brook took not only the historical setting but the meaning out of the play. Instead of making the play concrete and Brechtian he made it abstract and metaphysical. Although the programme had several reproductions of Lowry, the stage never had any of their clarity of form. Where Arden demanded precision and sharpness of outline, Brook gave us images of dissolution, abstract shapes of indefinable menace (like the strange iron circle that hung over Musgrave), an overall sense of madmen moving through a dream.

Arden's Serjeant is Bible black – 'the straightest Serjeant on the line'. He lives by the rule book. The phrase 'It's not material' is one of the phrases he lives by. But the accidents Musgrave describes as 'not material' destroy the plan he has worked out by what he calls 'the Logic of God'. 'The action is the argument', Arden says, and the action shows us a man who has been seized by an idea and who will drive the idea through in a straight line no matter what accidents scribble across it. But the accidents defeat Musgrave: they are indeed 'material'. This is what the action of the play is about. Brook's translator did not find a French equivalent for 'It's not material'. (He also did not find the French equivalent for the fragment of song, 'Here we sit like birds in the wilderness . . .'. It was replaced by the meaningless phrase, 'Nous sommes deux oiseaux', uttered in a sing-song voice.) Arden's language, rooted in popular proverbial speech, with images from the Bible and ballads, was replaced by a discursive form of French, which sounded as if it belonged to Camus or Sartre and the theatre of discussion. And the absence of precise verbal and visual imagery made nonsense of the play's ending.

In Arden's play, the circle of violence and non-violence, which Musgrave has tried to break by the straight line of his logic, is reformed, visually, on the stage as the Bargee (called, significantly, Crooked Joe) hands out beer. The Dragoons and the colliers form the circle and dance, to the Bargee's song, 'Finnegan begin agen. . .'. But the play does not end there. It ends with Attercliffe and Musgrave waiting to be hanged. Attercliffe, we have been told in an earlier scene, joined the army because his wife had run off with a green-grocer, who looked like a rat, but who sold good green apples: 'He fed the people and he fed my wife'. Musgrave, says Attercliffe, has been trying to end war by its own rules – 'You can't cure the pox by further whoring'. Attercliffe ends the play with a song about 'blood-red roses' and an apple:

> I plucked a blood-red rose-flower down
> And gave it to my dear.
> I set my foot across the sea
> And she never wept a tear . . .

The soldier, 'the blood-red rose', comes home and finds her eating an apple. She tells him:

> Your blood-red rose is withered and gone
> And fallen on the floor:
> And he who brought the apple down
> Shall be my darling dear.
>
> For the apple holds a seed will grow
> In live and lengthy joy
> To raise a flourishing tree of fruit
> For ever and a day.

Attercliffe is given the last words in the play:

They're going to hang us up a length higher nor most apple-trees grow, Serjeant. D'you reckon we can start an orchard?

GR described in his review what Brook did to this final scene:

Brook has rejected Arden's suggestion to fly in a prison grille for a simple transition to the epilogue, and he has done so for a specific purpose. After the failure of Musgrave and the arrival of the Dragoons, the Bargee starts signing 'Michael Finnegan' and the dance beings;

as it grows, the lights dim, while the rostra is hoisted up and Musgrave stands stage centre, arms outstretched, crucified (this seems to me a monstrous trick); the dance slows to a halt while the prison scene is played, but there is always enough light to see the arranged Tableau around the men; then at the end the dance begins again. . . . It is here that Brook is betrayed by the longing for *les grands gestes.*

Brook, in fact, simply reversed the meaning of Arden's fable. Instead of offering Arden's timid advocacy of a non-violent approach to the ending of the war (an approach, incidentally, which Arden was to reject later in his career) Brook put *Musgrave* firmly back into the slough of post-war pessimism in which he himself felt most at home. Arden's play said, 'Well, the old way hasn't worked. Perhaps we should reach for something new, however tentatively.' Brook's production said, 'It's no good. Nothing will ever change. The good is crucified while men dance round the foot of the cross. All we can do is celebrate our despair with style.'

To be fair to Brook, he probably was not even aware of what he had done to Arden's play. Confronted with the text, he had, like Musgrave, been violated by an idea. Françoise Koubilsky described the idea as follows:

Peter Brook dreams of a theatre of 'pure behaviour', freed from the ascendancy of time, characters and action. And because the image of the dance seemed to him the be-all and end-all of *Serjeant Musgrave's Dance*, he conceived his production as a sort of fantastic choreography, which reduced Arden's play to the outline of an infernal ballet in which lurid red puppets, grey phantoms, well-to-do shadows intercross, grope for each other, find each other, push each other away, draw together, separate, find each other again, lose each other. . . .

Brook had been writing for some time about a theatre of 'pure behaviour':

I want to see characters behaving out of character in the lies, inconsistency and total confusion of daily life. I want to see outer realism as something in endless flux with barriers and boundaries that come and go – people and situations forming and re-forming before my eyes. . . .

But in his 1961 article, Brook referred to a new prophet, Artaud. Artaud, as Brook read him, had asked for a theatre that went beyond words. In striving to communicate directly, through gestures and dance, Artaud's Theatre of Cruelty would be driven towards desperate cries, sounds trying to articulate themselves. In the very title of Arden's play, Brook saw the birth of such a theatre. Musgrave, having tried to communicate his message using the props of 'popular theatre', realises he has failed, after which 'his desperate energy drives him to find still further means of expression, and, in a flash of inspiration, he begins a rhythmic stamping, out of which develops a savage dance and chant'. *Serjeant Musgrave's Dance*, Brook concludes, demonstrates 'how a violent need to project a meaning can suddenly call into existence a wild and unpredictable form'.

Now there is very little in Arden's text to suggest that this is what happens. Musgrave says at the end of the first act:

I'm in this town to change all soldier's duties. My prayer is: keep my mind clear so I can weigh Judgement against the Mercy and Judgement against the Blood, and make this Dance as terrible as You have put it into my brain. The Word alone is terrible: the Deed must be worse. But I know it is Your Logic, and You will provide.

'Keep my mind clear' does not sound like a prayer for Artaudian frenzy. And the song he sings to accompany his dance, as the white skeleton dressed in the red tunic is hauled up the lamppost, is precise and articulate:

> Up he goes and no one knows
> Who it was that rose him
> But white and red
> He waves his head
> He sits upon your back
> And you'll never never lose him
> Up he goes and no one knows
> How to bring him downwards.

And Musgrave's Logic – twenty-five deaths for five – may be 'wild-wood mad', but it does not consist of an inarticulate cry.

Brook's production of *Musgrave* became oddly schizophrenic. Maurice Pons' translation gave us a script in which the issues of war and violence were discussed in Anouilh's *Antigone*. But at the same time, Brook gave us a choreography in which blurred figures were 'in endless flux' and a Christ-like Serjeant, taken out of any historical context, called into existence a 'wild and unpredictable form', spoke in tongues like a Pentecostal and was crucified while the world shuffled on.

The Parisians remained unimpressed. Françoise Spira, the brave director of Théâtre Vivant, was forced to give away free tickets in order to find an audience (although her public could hardly have been prepared for abstracted Arden by the previous productions: comedies by Audiberti and Hugh Mills (*Pas de pique-nique à Calcutta*)).

At the end of his review of Brook's *Musgrave*, AH suggested that what Brook really needed was a permanent group he could work with over a longer period. Brook was, in fact, on the point of returning to London to do just that. The RSC had given him the money to work with a group of twelve actors on an experimental basis. The show he eventually produced with them, and which was to signal a new and productive phase in Brook's attempts to escape from 'the deadly theatre', was to be called the Theatre of Cruelty.

5   The embracing of Artaud: the Theatre of Cruelty

The theatre must give us everything that is in crime, love, war or sadness if it is to recover its necessity.

> Artaud, *The Theatre and its Double*

It is to the lasting credit of Peter Hall and the Royal Shakespeare Company that it was understood from the start that this work required total subsidy.

> Marowitz, 'Notes on the Theatre of Cruelty'

Either we restore all the arts to a central attitude and necessity, finding an analogy between a gesture made in painting and the theatre and a gesture made by lava in a volcanic explosion, or we must stop painting, babbling, writing or doing whatever it is we do.

> Artaud, *The Theatre and its Double*

An in-group definition of Theatre of Cruelty was twelve actors working for twelve pounds a week.

> Marowitz, 'Notes on the Theatre of Cruelty'

Brook needed a theatre of his own, but he was not to get it until 1974. He was returning to London to work, for the first time in his life, on research rather than rehearsal, with a group of hand-picked actors. The group had been picked by Charles Marowitz – or so Marowitz claims.

Marowitz was the expatriate American who had been Brook's assistant director on *King Lear*. He ran his own experimental theatre in London, called In-Stage, and years later he was to imply that he was the one who first set Brook on his experimental way. He wrote, of Brook:

He'd seen the things I'd been doing in my theatre, which was experimental work different from what he had done before. This was in the mid-sixties, when Peter was basically the kind of director who would be directing the Lunts in a new Dürrenmatt play or Rex Harrison in an Anouilh play – he wasn't into the kind of thing he's doing now. This was the first foray into experimental work, and it was from there that he went further and further.

In fact, Brook had used improvisations three years before, when he was rehearsing Genet's *Le Balcon* in Paris in 1960 – although he had not found long evenings of obscene jokes particularly helpful (probably because the *grande dame* at the centre of the show, Marie Bell, regarded improvisation on the level of charades, an attitude very widespread in the acting profession at the time; Bill Gaskill had a similar response from Olivier when he used such methods on *The Recruiting Officer* at the National in 1963). Brook had for some time been showing increased disenchantment with the conveyor-belt of four week`s rehearsal. What had changed by 1963 was that the success of his work had given him a better bargaining position. Peter Hall, when he took charge of the RSC in 1960, had asked Brook and one of the grand old men of French theatre, Michel Saint-Denis, to become his associate directors. It was two years before Brook worked for the new regime – he was busy making two films. His first productions for Hall were *King Lear* and *The Physicists*, but he also asked for time, money and people for a research project. Hall agreed to finance ten weeks' work (he got most of the money from the Gulbenkian Foundation). Brook would be free to experiment. The work was not expected to lead to a public performance.

Martin Esslin has another version of how Brook arrived at his first real experiment. According to Esslin (who had been asked to become the RSC's first dramaturg, but was stopped from doing so by his contract with the BBC) Brook told Hall that he wanted to produce Jean Genet's *The Screens*. It had been staged in Berlin, at the Schlosspark, in June 1961, but not in Paris, being banned because of the Algerian War. Hall said that the Lord Chamberlain would also ban it in England. Brook said that did not matter much, because the RSC had already presented a season of plays in a theatre club, the Arts, which was beyond the censor's reach. The real problem was that the company did not have any actors capable of performing the play. Then, as Esslin tells it, Brook suggested that if he could spend some time training a group of actors, he might put together some scenes from *The Screens* and invite the Lord Chamberlain to a private performance. The Lord Chamberlain might well be persuaded to allow the play to be produced; and Hall wanted it to get a large, and public, production.

The story has an authentic Brook feel about it, and the fact that Esslin says Hall gave Brook the money for ten actors, whereas Marowitz, who picked them, says there were twelve, does not necessarily make Esslin's story apocryphal. In fact there were only ten actors: Mary Allen, Jonathan Burn, Richard Dare, Freda Dowie, Rob Inglis, Glenda Jackson, Alexis Kanner, Leon Lissek, Robert Lloyd and Susan Williamson.

What was important was that the artistic director of the RSC had asserted the Company's right to spend money on theatre research. Nothing like that had ever happened in the mainstream of British theatre before. (Brecht, of course, had been given his own theatre in the ruins of East Berlin more than a decade earlier, but public money for the theatre was not a debatable issue on the Continent.) The improved situation was not to last for long: when the National Theatre established its own Studio for research in the late eighties it was always careful to point out that its work was entirely funded by private money, thus saving its subsidy for the production of Ayckbourn's oeuvre.

In 1959 Brook has given *Encore* readers a polemical report from the West-

End front, both blaming the system and the practitioners for its appalling state and even calling for someone to follow Brecht's example.

Why then is the theatre so bad? Because, let's face it, it is on a catastrophically low level: weak, watery, repetitive, drab and silly. Why are there no plays that reflect the excitement, the movement, the change, the conflict, the tragedy, the misery, the hope and the emancipation of the highly dramatic moment of world's history in which we live? Why are we given the choice between colour and poetry in the classics, or drab prose in contemporary drama? Why has no one followed on Brecht's track? Why are our actors lazy and passionless? Why do so few of them do more than two hours a day? Why do so few of them think theatre, dream theatre, fight for theatre, above all practise theatre in the spare time at their disposal? Why is the talent in this country – and the goodwill – frittered away in a mixture of ineffectual grumbling and deep complacency? I think that to find the causes one must not look for individual villains or a race of villains: I think the villain is deeply buried in the system: it lies in laws that operate at almost all levels. . . .

For England destroys artists. This is a peculiar property of our social system. In England the edge (and what else matters?) is rapidly knocked off an artist – not by a concerted and wicked policy of the *them* – but by the artist's best friends. Social snobbery in England takes many forms, infinite in their variety, subtle in their invisibility, powerful in the illusion of total freedom they seem to give. No one presses the artist to do anything – all they do is to create a climate in which he only too readily will castrate himself. . . .

He complained that the yardstick of 'Full or empty seats' had became 'a sort of artistic standard', that 'a good show should *pay its way . . .*', and asserted 'The theatre that covers its costs is the true theatre with its edge knocked off'. The answer was subsidised theatre:

National theatres, many of them, of different shapes and sizes would be part of the answer. Of course, we won't ever get one – because the Government will never spend the money. Anyway it would be such a cumbersome organisation, inevitably in the wrong hands, bound to pass through so many ghastly years of teething troubles, that it would not affect the scene as far ahead as we can look. No I think we should clamour for the big National Theatre, as a thorn in the flesh of successive governments, but actually hope for something more realistic. I would like to see a start made – and the principle established – with one tiny theatre with a hundred seats, even fifty seats, *and subsidised to the hilt*. By this I mean that the subsidy should cover all that such a theatre could lose even if every seat were empty at every performance. If we think of a small theatre this would still be a reasonable sum, one that a rich television company, a mineral-water manufacturer, or even a government department could furnish. This subsidy would then be a *total subsidy*. It will be run by a director and a new sort of committee. This committee will applaud the director if he announces that he has lost every penny – he is entitled to do this. It will chase him with furies, however, if he has failed to keep his theatre alive. It will hound him if his theatre becomes consistently groupy or cliquey, if it seems to belong too much to one type of person, to one set of experiments. Its appeal must be that it can *dare completely*: that it can *dare* offer any author with a completely uncommercial idea, a stage *immediately*. It would be an actor's studio of writers, it would be our avant-garde.

Brook was wrong about the National Theatre never coming, but he was right about the money – they never gave enough; like other projects of the period, by the time the buildings were in place there was little money for running them. Brook enjoyed great freedom in England in the sixties in what now looks like a golden age; already by the eighties artistic directors were nostalgically looking back on the time when plays could be rehearsed for more than five weeks. The National Theatre that England finally saw was not a place that Brook would work in: the only time he would work there was when it was still housed in a Victorian building. Not for him the custom-built concrete spaces on the South Bank.

'Peter was interested in experimental work, and I was interested in Artaud', says Marowitz; but in fact Brook had been interested in Artaud since picking up the Grove Press edition of *The Theatre and its Double* in New York in 1959 (he had been rehearsing Rex Harrison in Anouilh's *l'Hurluberlu* so it must have seemed like an oasis in the desert). Within the year he was passing large chunks of it on to *Encore* readers in his article 'Search for a hunger'. Brook had described Artaud as 'this visionary, undoubtedly mad'; Artaud had, in fact, been kept in a French mental hospital from 1937 until a few months before his death in 1948. Brook declared that Artaud 'wrote more sense than anyone else about theatre in our time'.

One of the things Artaud wrote was that theatre must

swoop down upon a crowd of spectators with all the awesome horror of the plague, the Black Death of the Middle Ages, with all its shattering impact, creating a complete upheaval, physical, mental and moral, among the population it struck.

He also wrote:

We must believe in a sense of life renewed by the theatre. . . . Furthermore, when we speak of life, it must be understood that we are not referring to life as we know it from the surface of fact, but to that fragile, fluctuating centre which forms never reach.

In 1932, Artaud had invented the term 'Theatre of Cruelty'. In a letter to the editor of the *Nouvelle Revue Française*, he explained that in using the word 'Cruelty' he was not referring exclusively to sadism or bloodshed or horror. He wanted

. . . to return to the etymological origins of language, which always evoked a concrete notion through abstract concepts. . . . Essentially, cruelty means strictness, diligence and implacable resolution, irreversible and absolute determination.

Artaud was also looking for a theatre in which 'the director becomes author – that is to say, creator'.

Brook codenamed his research project *Theatre of Cruelty*.

The task of recruiting a group of actors capable of taking the first tentative steps along the road towards a theatre which would swoop down on spectators with 'all the awesome horror of the plague' might well have been daunting. It was necessary, Marowitz wrote, 'to devise a completely new audition technique'. Marowitz (as he tells it) set briskly to work. The actor was, first of all, asked to reel off 'his two-minute set-piece in his own way, without suggestions or interference'. But then he was confronted by the Artaudian bombshell: he was given a new character and a new situation and asked to play these 'still retaining the text of his original speech'. If, for example, he had prepared Hamlet's 'To be or not to be . . .', he might be asked to perform that speech as if he were Romeo in the balcony scene.

The idea of asking an actor to perform a speech about suicide as if it were an exercise in seduction was in line with good Artaudian principles. In his first Theatre of Cruelty manifesto, Artaud had pledged himself to adapt Shakespearian and other Elizabethan plays 'without taking account of text'. Brook, on the other hand, in the 1961 article in which he paid homage to Artaud, wrote, 'I believe in the word in classical drama, because the word was their tool'.

Having learned that the *meaning* of a Shakespearian text was irrelevant to the exercise he was engaged in, the actor negotiating the Marowitz audition was then, logically enough, given a piece of nonsense-text.

There is no discernible character or situation. The actor makes of it whatever he can, but he is obliged to use the given words. (This enabled us to discover how the actor, on the most elementary level, coped with language – where his natural instincts led him. It is like a Rorschach test with words instead of ink-blots.)

The actor was also asked to play with and 'develop a bridge between' unrelated objects: a toy shovel, a briefcase, a shoe-horn, a telephone directory, a plant. Then there were 'discontinuous improvisation' exercises:

An actor performing a simple, recognisable action (digging, golfing, wall-papering, exercising) enters. The others choose actions which relate to that actor's choice and a scene (with words) develops. A enters digging with a shovel; B mimes a pneumatic drill; C grabs a wheelbarrow; D becomes a works-supervisor checking his stopwatch. Then a new actor enters performing a completely unrelated action (making lyrical knee-bends), the other actors adapt to the new action as quickly as possible.

These collective hour-long auditions were, apparently, exhaustive enough to enable Marowitz confidently to select a group of actors with the qualities needed to create, in Artaud's words, 'a world ephemeral but true, a world in contact with reality'. Out of fifty actors auditioned, Marowitz says he chose twelve. The average age was twenty-four – only one was over thirty, most were just over twenty. When Marowitz presented the chosen twelve to Brook, Brook (according to Marowitz) queried only one of of them, a woman. Her name was Glenda Jackson.

Her agent had arranged for her to go along, and she was asked to bring her own prepared material. She took along an edited version of a Dorothy Parker short story. Brook asked her to 'do it as though you're a woman in a home'. She performed it as a woman in a straitjacket. She did not hear any more from Brook for about four weeks. Then she was invited to go back for an an audition in which actors worked in groups of six. After that she still did not hear anything for some time. She was told later that it was 'a toss up between her and somebody else'.

The designer Sally Jacobs also remembers being interviewed by Brook. She had been very impressed by *King Lear* and when she heard that Brook was recruiting people for an experimental workshop she wrote and said she would like to work with him. She was invited for an interview and took along a portfolio of work. Brook talked to her and looked at the work and said he would contact her later. She thought that was the end of that. And then she was suddenly asked to turn up for the first workshop. She was to work with Brook for many years. She says that what she really learned from the Theatre of Cruelty workshops was how to cut rough paper into masks with eye-holes so that the holes did not give the mask a character.

More than a quarter of a century later, it is hard to judge precisely how completely new Marowitz's audition techniques were. His account of them was published in his 'Notes on the Theatre of Cruelty', which appeared, almost three years later, in the *Tulane Drama Review* (Winter 1966). By then *The Marat/Sade* had appeared on Broadway, and *US* at the Aldwych. The account was quickly read by teachers in drama schools, and it became commonplace for students seeking entry into the schools to be asked to take part in collective auditions, to be given unrelated objects to play with, to be involved in discontinuous improvisation exercises. Yesterday's completely new technique becomes today's cliché.

Because he distrusted the actors' training, Marowitz

felt the need to start from scratch, to plunge the whole company into elementary Method exercises before totally demolishing the Stanislavsky ethic. . . . Stanislavsky was the grammar out of which we were going to build a completely different syntax and I wanted the basis to be sound before shifting it.

Brook disagreed.

When the actors arrived at the small church hall for their first day's work on what Marowitz called 'the swirling waters of Artaudian theory', Brook gave each actor something to bang with and something to bang on.

In his 1960 *Encore* article, Brook quoted Artaud's assertion that 'the theatre must give us everything that is in crime, war or madness. . .'. But what had seized Brook about Artaud, on the practical level to which Brook has always returned, was Artaud's belief in a language of theatre that went beyond words.

In 1922, Artaud had seen a group of Cambodian dancers at a Colonial Exhibition in Marseilles. Nine years later, he saw the Balinese theatre perform at a Colonial Exhibition in Paris. In both cases, Artaud was strongly affected by the fact that communication was by movement and gesture rather than by words. The performers used a vocabulary of hieroglyphs, according to J. L. Styan,

whereby the turning of the eyes or the raising of a finger could magically evoke a music, a 'poetry' of its own, with sound and motion flowing rhythmically into one another.

Brook had come to share Artaud's dissatisfaction with a theatre based on words. The word, he said, was the tool of the classical dramatists, but today words did not communicate, did not express much, failed abysmally to define.

Such is the complete breakdown of the word that I can't make the simple statement that all great theatre is religious with the faintest hope of communicating clearly what I mean.

Brook realised, however, along with Artaud, that the displacement of the supremacy of the word in drama inevitably led to the displacement of other elements which were generally accepted as the stuff of theatre. Brook quoted Artaud again:

I am well aware that the language of gestures and postures, dance and music is less capable of analysing a character, revealing a man's thought or elucidating states of consciousness clearly and precisely than is a verbal language, but whoever said the theatre was created to analyse a character, to resolve the conflicts of love and duty, to wrestle with all the problems of a topical and psychological nature that monopolise our contemporary stage?

Brook was looking for a form of theatre that would not depend on anecdote or character, or on verbal messages, but which would communicate *directly* to an audience through a combination of all its elements – sound, gesture, the visual relationship between actors and objects. And so he began his search for a new theatre language, not by using words to explain to the actors what the project was about, but by inviting them to explore basically simple sounds.

Marowitz describes what happened. The actors, he says, were

asked to explore the range of their *instrument* (the sound the thin end of a ladle made on a tin can; the sound the tin made against the floor, muted with one palm, held suspended, in two hands, tucked inside a sweater, rapped with the knuckle instead of the ladle, with the forehead instead of the knuckle, the elbow instead of the forehead . . .). Once the range of the instrument had been explored, a series of rhythms were rapped out. Some of these were varied while others remained the same; some were accelerated while others were slowed down; there were combinations of twos and threes; dialogues between broomhandles and empty crates; scenes from *Romeo and Juliet* played out between metallic tinkles and bass percussions; mob violence with soap crates and pitch battles with tennis rackets.

Eventually, says Marowitz, *rhythm* 'got redefined in exact, physical terms'. And soon, 'the same attitudes the actors had taken to their objects was applied to their voices and bodies'.

There was, however, a fundamental difference between the actors being given objects to make sounds with, and exercises through which they could explore their voices and bodies. In the context of the work, the objects to make sounds with were simply that – objects to make sounds with. They held no other meanings. But the voice and movement exercises described by Marowitz already held their own socially agreed meanings.

Exercise: You come back to your apartment after a hard day's work. Enter, take off your coat, hang it up, pour yourself a drink and sit down at the table. On the table is a letter which you suddenly notice. You put down the drink, open the letter and begin to read. The contents of the letter are entirely up to you; the only condition is that it contains news which puts you into a highly emotional state of one sort or another. Express this state using only a sound and a movement.

Example: Scene – *A* wants to break off a long-standing affair with his girlfriend *B*. He now realises he does not love her, and it would be lunacy to marry. *B*, however, has become help-lessly attached to *A* and cannot bear the idea of parting. She tries desperately to maintain the relationship.

In his 1960 *Encore* article, Brook had written:

If I had a drama school, the work would begin very far from character, situation, thought or behaviour. We would not try to conjure up past *anecdotes* of our lives. . . . We would search deeper. . . . Then we would begin to study how to sit, how to stand, how to raise one arm.

But the exercises described by Marowitz begin precisely from character, situation, thought and behaviour. Not only that, but the characters and situations offered are of a mind-boggling banality, and belong to a social milieu that is both limited and limiting. Artaud had at least been ridiculous on a grand scale. In his *Spurt of Blood* (1927) human limbs fell on the stage and the wrist of God was bitten by a whore. And in his original *Theatre of Cruelty* (1935), Artaud offered a version of Shelley's *Les Cenci*, played in the round, with flashing lights and music that came at the audience from all directions. But what would the man who wanted theatre to swoop down like a plague have made of exercises that place us firmly in the world of apartments, before-dinner drinks, clinging girlfriends looking for marriage, would-be artists turning their backs on the family business. One can only conclude that Marowitz had succeeded in getting the Method school's version of Stanislavsky back on the agenda – with the already stated intention, of course, of 'demolishing the Stanislavsky ethic'.

Marowitz was to write, in *Confessions of a Counterfeit Critic*, that, whereas during the production of *King Lear* he had done little except 'act as a kind of background-intelligence, a sharp-toothed little jaybird picking holes at everything and everyone', during the work on the Theatre of Cruelty he 'became aware of the balance shifting'.

The group was given improvisational exercises, acting-tests, games, a whole slew of theatrical inventions which I had worked up over five years' training with my own experimental group. This was relatively new territory for Brook – although he was thoroughly *au fait* with its theory – and I felt, presumptuous as it may sound, that even he was learning about techniques never encountered before.

One of those techniques was, presumably, the one Marowitz applied to the situation of the sensitive man trying to get rid of his over-fond girlfriend. After the scene had been played, the actor and the actress were asked to divide their own contribution to the scene into three units, and give a line-title to each unit. The scene was then replayed, using only the line-titles for dialogue. The actor and the actress were than asked to choose only one representative word from each line-title, and the scene was replayed a second time using only the chosen words. Then, and only then, Marowitz stressed, 'the actor could choose a sound which accurately reflected the main quality of his scene and play the scene for a final time, using variations of that sound. The playing in sound invariably prompted a non-naturalistic use of movement. . .?'

Marowitz lays out for us in detail the way the scene between reluctant boy and clinging girlfriend worked.

Scene breakdown in terms of line-titles: first replay
BOY: (1)   I want to break off this affair.
         (2)   I want to be as kind as possible.
         (3)   I won't be persuaded to change my mind.
GIRL: (1)   I want to keep my hold on A.
         (2)   I want to be reasonable with him so as to make him change his mind.
         (3)   I refuse to be hurt.

Second replay: essential words
BOY: Break
         Kind
         Won't
GIRL: Keep
         Reason
         Refuse

Third replay: sounds
BOY: Ey-ayeOoghn
GIRL: Eey-zoohz

Marowitz notes that the sounds were 'fluid and free, merely *based* on the vowels and consonants of the essential words'.

AH writes:

'Ey-ayeOoghn' and 'Eey-zoohz'?

What were actors, directors, stage management, or the caretaker at the church hall to make of *that*? What were they *supposed* to make of it? What were these sounds, arrived at by such a laboured process, supposed to communicate?

Little by little, Marowitz wrote, they (the directors) insinuated the idea that 'the voice could produce sounds other than grammatical combinations of the alphabet, and that the body, set free, could begin to enunciate a language which went beyond text, beyond subtext, beyond psychological implication. . .'. And that these sounds and moves could '*communicate feelings and ideas*'.

Feelings and ideas? 'Ey-ayeOoghn – Eey-zoohz?'

The situation set up in the exercise came straight out of soap opera. Any competent *Coronation Street* scriptwriter could have moved the heart of the nation with a scene like that. You could have played it any number of ways: as two actors out of *Brief Encounter* – the understated phrases, the long pauses, the surface control hiding a turmoil of hidden emotion. 'Ey-ayeOoghn – Eey-zoohz'! Or as Cary Grant trying in vain to get rid of a self-possessed Katharine Hepburn. Or as Tony Curtis pretending to be Cary Grant ditching Marilyn Monroe. Shakespeare could have shown the inner tempests with what Marowitz calls 'murky' soliloquies. Brecht could have interrupted the action with a song: 'Hear now what the girl thought but did not say'. But *first* to improvise it, *then* to rewrite it in cable-ese, *then* to select single words out of the cables, and *then* to make sounds out of the vowels and consonants of the selected words – in a search for the theatre of the awesome plague – is to behave like the academics in Book 3 of Swift's *Gulliver's Travels*, who experimented with putting blind people to work sorting out different coloured threads.

What were the sounds supposed to communicate that couldn't be communicated in straightforward dialogue? Some depths of sexual anguish previously unheard by man? Or woman? Describing the other exercise – the one in which you go back to your apartment after a hard day's work, take off your coat, pour yourself a drink and open a letter – Marowitz says that the sounds made by the actors in response to the letters had the 'resonance of wounded animals; of prehistoric creatures being slain by atomic weapons'. For whom did the sounds have these resonances? Did someone on his way home, after a hard day's work, drop into the church hall, take off his coat, sit down, hear a cry and say, 'That sounds like a prehistoric creature being slain by an atomic weapon'?

The movements which arose from this exercise, says Marowitz, were 'stark and unpredictable. . . . Facial expressions, under the pressure of extended sounds, began to resemble Javanese masks and Zen sculpture'. Then, he adds, with disarming candour,

But once the actors realised what we were after, some of them began to select an arbitrary sound or movement effective in itself but unrelated to the emotional state growing out of the exercise. Very quickly, frighteningly quickly, actors became as glib with non-naturalistic sounds and movements as they were with stock dramatic clichés.

But if the sounds and movements had to relate to the emotional state growing out of the exercise, and the exercise itself was rooted in dramatic cliché, how could the actors be expected to transcend the clichés?

Brook seems at some time to have suggested to Marowitz moving beyond Method-school situations. Two years earlier, he had seen an actress at Marowitz's In-Stage playing, in short discontinuous scenes, all the characters in another, male character's life: his 'wife, sweetheart, charlady, male-employer, secretary, mother. . .'. Afterwards, Brook had said that it would be 'fascinating to see *Hamlet* played that way, reshuffled like a deck of familiar cards'. So Marowitz spliced up *Hamlet* into a twenty-minute collage.

One of the conditions of the project was that Brook would not be required to prepare a public performance. But Brook had always recognised the need for work to be shown to an audience: until that happened the circle of communication was inevitably incomplete. After eight weeks, they put together a programme representing the diversity of their work, and offered it as 'work in progress' to what was expected to be a largely professional audience at the brand new theatre at The London Academy of Music and Dramatic Art (LAMDA). This was an empty space, if not quite a black box, as there was a tiered section designed for spectators and a flat one designed for performers. Brook put seats for the audience on the stage area, and strewed the action across the tiers.

The programme was played, with variations, for five weeks. It consisted of two sketches by Paul Ableman, using nonsense text; two versions of Artaud's *Spurt of Blood*, one as he wrote it and one using only sounds and paintings; a wordless dramatisation of a short story by Robbe-Grillet; two collages by Brook; three scenes from Genet's *The Screens* (which were soon dropped and replaced by a short Arden–D'Arcy play, *Ars Longa, Vita Brevis*); short pieces by Ray Bradbury and Cyril Connolly; the collage *Hamlet*; and two 'free' scenes. One of these consisted of improvisations supervised by Marowitz, sometimes using suggestions thrown out by the audience; the other usually took the form of discussion, in which Brook and Marowitz questioned the audience's motives in coming. Sometimes Brook conducted a rehearsal, of, say, a scene from *Richard III*.

They both hoped that the audience would not think of the programme as a 'show'; but in this, as Marowitz later acknowledged, they deluded themselves. Anything offered by Brook would inevitably arouse critical interest, particularly when it was called *Theatre of Cruelty*. They believed that because they had told the audience that it was work-in-progress then the audience would know how to watch it, that they would be able to discriminate between that and a real performance. This delusion also extended to the choice of title. Brook complained afterwards:

The title for the LAMDA season was much misunderstood, although the work itself was presented with a quotation from Artaud which established absolutely precisely his extraordinary definition of cruelty as being a form of self-discipline, and therefore cruelty meant cruelty to oneself. That notwithstanding, for years and years after that, question after question would be put to one towards an apparently avowed taste for sadistic material, sadistic relationships with an audience, with actors and so on and so forth.

However, to call something Theatre of Cruelty at a time when Artaud was hardly in currency – Peter Hall had never encountered him until Brook gave him a copy of *The Theatre and its Double* – and not to expect that words would carry their normal meaning does seem slightly naïve. Brook could hardly assume that an audience would go to LAMDA with a sophisticated understanding of Artaud's ideas. In addition Brook was to follow the Theatre of Cruelty with a major production in which he made the Marquis de Sade the central figure. Brook seemed surprised that audiences did not immediately throw off their preconceptions:

Audience habits are difficult to break, and sometimes amusing to explore. At the end of one performance *God Save the Queen* was played but the tape was looped so that no sooner was the anthem completed than it began again. The interesting thing was that it took two complete rounds before the audience realised they were being fooled. The second time through they thought that it was a terrible mistake and they weren't going to embarrass us by drawing attention to it. When the third time came around they began to move towards the door very painfully, fighting against an umbilical cord that told them to stand still.

But this experiment would seem to belong more to a Footlights Revue than to Artaud. Much in the 'show' had this tone and was clearly intended simply to amuse – like the reading of a list of cuts the Lord Chamberlain had ordered in *The Screens*. It seems as if Brook the showman kept popping out from behind Brook the scientist, instinctively realising that even a professional audience might be bewildered by some of the material and therefore, since part of his contract with them was to provide entertainment, the seriousness of the evening should be leavened with a few gags. A familiarity with Artaud might indeed have encouraged exaggerated expectations, for Artaud had also written:

Cruelty is, above all, lucid, a kind of rigid directness, a submission to necessity. There is no Cruelty without consciousness, without a kind of applied consciousness. It is this which gives to each act of life its bloodcolour, its cruel nuance, because it is understood that Life is always the Death of someone. . . . That erotic Desire is Cruelty, because it burns of necessity; Death is Cruelty, the Resurrection is Cruelty, Transfiguration is Cruelty.

Anyone going to LAMDA in the hope of experiencing the Cruelty of erotic Desire must have felt badly let down by the opening sketch. A theatre manager, who is giving Artaud an audition, asks him to sit on a chair. Artaud runs, jumps and crawls towards the chair, while the manager watches him, perplexed. Finally, Artaud says, 'Well, if it's realism you want, adieu!' and leaves.

The sketch had actually been adapted from a story Jean-Louis Barrault had told about Artaud. According to Barrault, Artaud, as a young actor, had been rehearsing the part of Charlemagne for the experimental French director, Dullin. Artaud had approached the throne on all fours, and Dullin had suggested that perhaps the performance was too stylised, at which Artaud had reared up and shouted, 'Oh, if it's realism you're after! Well then!' The original story at least had historical interest. It had, typically, been adapted into revue.

A short playlet, performed by masked actors, using only cries and screams, simply confirmed the dramatic limitations of cries and screams. As Tom Milne wrote in *Encore*:

Artaud talked glibly enough about the oriental theatre from a nodding acquaintance with it, and anybody who has watched even part of a Kabuki or Noh play, for instance, is liable to fall prey to the same enthusiasms. But one should not forget, not only the years of training which go into the making of an oriental actor, but also the fact that every stylised sound and gesture has an exact meaning which is known to the audience. If your audience doesn't know what your sounds are intended to communicate . . . then you might as well present a simple melodrama in which the words are only shortened for simple emotions.

Audiences did not seem to know how to take the two versions of *The Spurt of Blood*. Artaud's script seemed dated and laughable. Two lovers screaming 'I love you' hysterically at various pitches, a priest, a fat nurse, an apocalyptic appearance by a monstrous hand, a storm, a downpour of dismembered limbs, a frog, a beetle, three scorpions, Jacobean-tragedy-like deaths for all at the end. It all happened in three minutes, after which it was performed again, accompanied by wordless sounds and action paintings. Most audiences found it ridiculous rather than awesome.

Clive Barker, who had acted for Joan Littlewood before becoming a teacher, described what he saw:

The Spurt of Blood is a montage of physical objects and processes which are intended in isolation or in juxtaposition to make a demand on the audience and to elicit a response. How it should be realised we have not been told. I can imagine him (unreasonably perhaps) asking for the utter physical reproduction of the stimuli. I can even imagine him agreeing (reluctantly) to presenting the natural objects not in the condition described and letting the imagination of the audience be stimulated by the association.

I cannot by any stretch of my imagination fancy his agreeing to the placid, tasteful, meaningless 'theatre of illusion' representationalism that the play got at LAMDA.

Take one line. The narrator gives the line: 'Enter a knight in medieval armour followed by a wet-nurse, her breasts in her hands'.

The physical effect of a man in one of the suits of the Black Prince – ornate to the point of sensuality – followed by a big girl cupping in her hands a pair of great steaming tits, milk dribbling from the nipples, must be almost overwhelming in its immediacy and power.

I can see this scene as I have described it. I can see it performed by a man in a polished steel breastplate draped in cold acid silks followed by a girl decorated with a pair of crudely painted bladders, filled with water. It might be obscene in execution but the ritual quality and associations would stimulate me.

What we saw was a man in standard Old Vic imitation armour followed by a girl, inexplicably in pseudo fourteenth-century costume, cupping her empty hands eighteen inches in front of her. The contradiction between words and images depressed me beyond words.
. . .

Marowitz's *Hamlet* had more substance. Marowitz himself wrote that 'Of all the discontinuity exercises, this had the firmest foundation . . .'. It also had the advantage of words written by Shakespeare, even if these were 'radically rearranged'.

Marowitz juxtaposed lines, dropped or blended characters, rearranged sequences, and presented fragments 'which appeared like subliminal flashes out of Hamlet life'. Unfortunately the oblique style was carried to a point where the end-product was meaningless to anyone who did not know the original and know it well. (It became a cabaret turn for audiences reeling from the reverential four-hour version currently offered by the RSC.) If you did know the original, the twenty minutes offered you an entertaining gloss on Shakespeare's play designed to demonstrate concretely that Hamlet wants to be like Fortinbras; that every time Hamlet tries to kill Claudius somebody else dies; and that Hamlet himself is very funny (the collage brought out his broad humour, as in, for example, the stress on 'Count-ry matters'). Hamlet swung out on a rope over the audience.

Tom Milne wrote:

I doubt whether the technique is of any general application, unlike the reinterpretation of classical plays by Brecht, or Planchon, or Jerzy Grotowski, where the result is a play which exists in its own right, different from the original, but not dependent on an audience's knowledge of the original. What use, then, was the *Hamlet* experiment?

In the context of the research project, though, it made sense: it pushed the discontinuity exercises further than fragments from the life of an out-of-work writer could have done.

Marowitz described the response to the whole evening:

No one had seen anything quite like that in London, a show based on a happening score. There were areas of it which were random every night – the first night, for instance, was just an improvised talk between Peter and me. It wasn't really thought of as a show: it was a nutty little programme of surrealist vaudeville. It created a lot of interest but at the same time a lot of antagonism, particularly from the senior members of the RSC, who felt that this was just child's play. People running around with paper bags on their heads and screaming was so much the antithesis of Shakespearian production: the well-rendered line, wearing the costume, and all that stuff. The irony is that five or six years later even the squarest of the RSC directors were taking on our exercises and our warm-ups and so forth.

The main achievement with the actors seemed to be in getting them to move very physically, clearly something they were not used to in the early sixties, although some practitioners were critical of what was being attempted. Clive Barker wrote:

We were first of all treated to a montage of grunts and animal noises from a company of actors wearing masks. This would work and be very exciting but for two things: the animal makes his noises using chest resonance – the British drama schools teach head resonance –

and secondly the British actor is not taught the superbly controlled and relaxed movement of , say, the Chinese National Theatre, nor does he possess the natural primitive quality of , say, the African dancers. In its place he substitutes the inhibited control of P. T. classes.

There is a theatrical language that goes beyond the theatre of talk and ideas – I would go so far as to say that the vital basic language of theatre is not dependent upon either words or intellectual ideas. The reverse is true. (The realisation of this fact is the root of Rudolf Laban's exploration of movement.)

It is a physical language that communicates through rhythms. In *The Significance of Movement* Laban's theory is that 'rhythm seems to be a language apart and rhythmic language conveys meaning without words. The modern European races seem now to be totally lacking in the intelligence capable of grasping the meaning underlying rhythmic movements.'

We hit the trouble when we attempt to follow the instructions without the training. The natural rhythms of communication flow through the breathing. If we practise restricting breath-control methods and force the voice to be made in the head, instead of in the chest, we restrict the directness with which we can communicate nuances and subtlety of meaning in our conversation and vocal means of expression.

If we teach control of movement before we break down the movement inhibitions of our actors then we serve to perpetuate a muted range of movement expression. There is much more that could be said on this subject but this should serve to indicate the point at which experiment fails to realise its intentions. I would rather have seen one actor standing still making a noise like a real cow, than eight or nine rushing around making noises like phoney bulls.

I am not criticising the performance, which was what I would have expected from actors trained in our Dramatic Academies, but the direction which sought to use this, instead of destroying it, in the cause of its stated intention.

Brook was clearly aware of the limitations of his work with abstract sounds. He did not return to it until he got to Paris and had months, not weeks, for preparation – and a classical Japanese actor to work with.

The whole research project might, in fact, have been written off as a self-indulgent exercise going nowhere, but for one piece of pure theatre invented by Brook. It related, as Tom Milne pointed out, to one of Artaud's visions that Brook had not quoted. In a manifesto for the Théâtre Alfred Jarry, Artaud had written:

The theatre must present this ephemeral world, truthful but only tangential to reality. It must be *this* world, or else the theatre will have no hold on us.

So far so generalised – but Artaud had then gone on to offer an example far removed from monstrous wrists spurting blood. Artaud wrote:

There is nothing more puerile, and at the same time more sinister, more terrifying, than the spectacle of a police manoeuvre. A society reveals itself in such a *mise-en-scène*, which reflects the ease with which it disposes of its people's life and liberty. As the police prepare a raid it is almost like a ballet. Policemen come and go. The air is rent by shrill whistles. A kind of painful solemnity emanates from every movement. Gradually the circle narrows. Movements which at first seemed aimless can now be seen to have a purpose: their pivot, the point they were aiming at, appears. It is a nondescript sort of house. Suddenly the door opens and a file of women troops out, like a herd of cattle on the way to the slaughterhouse. The plot thickens. The trap has not been set for some shady gang of crooks but simply for a few women.

Never has such a beautiful *mise-en-scène* been crowned by such a denouement. The whole operation is really a show, and it epitomises our ideal theatre. This anguish, this sense of guilt, this triumph, this relief – these are the thoughts and feelings with which the audience must leave our theatre. They will be shaken and upset by the inner dynamism of the spectacle, a dynamism which springs from the troubles and preoccupations of their own lives.

Artaud sees a police raid on a brothel as an elaborate piece of theatre. It is a dramatic ritual which holds its own disturbing meanings. His 'ideal theatre' would communicate these meanings, would disturb in a similar way.

The year before Brook's project, 1963, had been rich in public spectacles. There had been what came to be called the Profumo Scandal: the British War Minister, John Profumo, had been exposed as having had an affair with Christine Keeler, who also claimed to have had an affair with a Soviet diplomat. There had been the theatre of Profumo lying to the House of Commons; of Profumo confessing his lie; of Stephen Ward, the osteopath and artist who had introduced Christine Keeler to Profumo, being put on trial for living on immoral earnings and committing suicide while the jury were out deciding the verdict. There were bit parts for Keeler's friend, Mandy Rice-Davies, and Profumo's wife, Valerie Hobson, who was a real actress and film star. Out-of-work writers and nice boys trying to ditch their girlfriends gently could hardly hope to compete with the public drama. But one other event, in the United States, did. President Kennedy was shot on television, and his alleged assassin was also shot on television, and the grief of his wife was displayed on television like a scene from the latest soap opera. It was out of some of these pieces of 'this ephemeral world' that Brook shaped an image which summed up the point he had arrived at in his theatrical search.

AH:

Brook talks about images that burn into the memory. This is how I remembered the image twenty years later.

The performers were working on the steeply raked side of the theatre, where spectators normally sat. High at the top of one of the stairways that led down between the seats, Glenda Jackson appeared. She was *physically* distanced.

She was wearing – as I remember it – the conventional costume of a high-class whore: tight black dress, black stockings, high-heeled shoes. She stood for Christine Keeler.

Then, still distanced by space and height, she began to strip. She didn't do a 'strip', the kind of act you might have seen in naughty music halls or strip clubs. Clothes were simply taken off. Presently Glenda Jackson was totally naked..

When she was naked, her body turned into an object on display. The clothes had made her available: the naked body was just that – a naked body, cold neutral.

She came, was led – by whom? – from her height, down the steps, down to the floor of the theatre, still naked, less distanced physically, still an object. She was put in a public bath. When she stepped out of the bath, the naked body was reclothed, in a shapeless blue-grey garment. Clumsy shoes. Thick stockings. All the overt sexual appeal previously given her by the conventional sexy clothes was systematically erased. She was turned into a female prisoner in front of our eyes. She knelt by the public bath. The bath was a coffin. The coffin was borne away.

I associated the coffin with the death of Stephen Ward. That was what I remembered twenty years later. Reading Marowitz and Tom Milne brought back other details.

There was a judge reciting over her at the top of the stairs. There were distinguished gentlemen courting her for fun and flagellation. The same distinguished gentlemen offered their condolences as she knelt by the coffin.

Marowitz writes that Brook created the text from a collage of cuttings about Christine Keeler and Jackie Kennedy. How? All Glenda Jackson could say is that 'Peter creates a climate where things evolve'.

The Jackie Kennedy connection never struck me at all, and when Harold Hobson referred to it in his *Sunday Times* column I thought he was indulging in a search for meanings. But Clive Barker describes how, at the interval, he 'was asked by someone connected with the experiment if I had "got" the identification with Jackie Kennedy. Eight other people with me hadn't "got" it either.'

So the coffin at the end belonged to John Kennedy and not Stephen Ward. Unless it belonged to both.

What stayed with me for twenty years was the image of the performer and her *neutrality*. It was as if Brook had found a person who was willing to turn herself into an object and who had the discipline to do so. Traditionally, British performers got themselves and their personalities in the way of what they were presenting. The workings of the market made them want to call attention to themselves.

Some years later, a young actor who worked with Brook on *Oedipus* at the National described how difficult it was to achieve the kind of impersonal performance that Brook demanded. You were conscious that *this* production would end in a few weeks, that you would be looking for a new contract with a different director. You were always wondering whether some manager or agent was in the audience. If so, were you being *noticed*? There was always the temptation to do something that called attention to *yourself*.

In this Theatre of Cruelty image, Glenda Jackson achieved impersonality in the most personal of situations. In doing so, she demonstrated where Brook was going.

In his *Encore* articles, Brook had called for abstraction. He was looking for performers who could present visual images, almost devoid of narrative content, through their bodies and their gestures.

The image created by Glenda Jackson wasn't entirely devoid of content. It consciously evoked Christine Keeler and her imprisonment. But telling the story of Keeler wasn't Brook's main concern. He was looking for an image and he found one. Later, he described to me how he had once visited a film exhibition in Paris. The room, he said, was filled with TV monitors. And on every monitor the same film was being shown. It was a conventional thriller. All Brook saw was a man taking out a gun and shooting another man. He had no idea of the context, because he wasn't watching the story in *time*: he simply saw one image taken from it. But the image, he said, had a powerful effect in its own right.

At the time of the Theatre of Cruelty experiments, Brook was looking for images that could *exist*, in their own right, on the stage. He'd written, with respect to Gelber's *The Connection*, about a scene in which a character had put an LP jazz record on and simply allowed it to play. Why, asked Brook, were we perfectly willing to sit in a friend's house and listen to an LP, yet felt uncomfortable at being asked to sit and listen to an LP in a theatre? Because, he answered, we were looking for story, for character. Why couldn't actors simply *be* on the stage, like marks in an abstract painting?' How could they show *being* in change? Glenda Jackson showed precisely that. But the image didn't work in isolation. It didn't explore a character or tell a story; but it did depend on shared associations, on a common consciousness. The disturbing public meanings were there.

However, the tone of the evening at LAMDA was mainly comic, and comfortably comic at that, not anarchic or subversive. Artaud's intention in conceiving his Theatre of Cruelty was a social one: he wanted to overturn society – his was a revolutionary aim. Brook's intention in his Theatre of Cruelty was to develop techniques and train actors which would enable him to produce *The Screens*. Of course, Genet also wanted to overturn society. Brook never produced the whole play publicly. Even if he had, would it have changed society? And would that have been his aim in presenting it?

When the LAMDA season ended the group went to work on *The Screens*, which by then had been translated and submitted to and, as predicted, rejected by the Lord Chamberlain. But he was invited to one of the two performances given privately in the Donmar Rehearsal Rooms of the first part of the play. Brook felt that the first twelve scenes contained all the guts of the work, and that the remaining two-and-a-half hours were only endless variations.

At one end of the vast converted warehouse, tiers of rough planking were crowded with chairs for the spectators; the other was dotted with tall white screens on castors. Stagehands in white-cowled, Arab-style robes, hidden behind the screens, rolled them silently into place; in front of a screen painted with a single palm, Said, the young Algerian hero, entered, dressed like a doll or a character from a child's picture-book in green trousers, red jacket, tan shoes, white shirt, mauve tie, pink cap. The screens glided swiftly and silently about the stage, sometimes blank, sometimes decorated with vestigial suggestions of scenery, sometimes painted by the characters themselves to represent an object or an emotion.

The Screens is a cartoon history of Algeria. The colonialists and the military were deliberately presented as crude caricatures (Sir Harold had a false nose, rabbit teeth and chattered like an imbecile; Blankensee had a padded belly). There was a gigantic dummy covered with medals and ribbons and a huge glove which Sir Harold left in the fields to keep law and order in his absence. The rebels presented their victories in the shape of crudely childish drawings. The faces of the Europeans – 'an Academician, a Soldier, a Vamp with her cigarette-holder, a News Photographer, a Widow, a Judge, a Banker, a Little Girl wearing a communion dress, and a General' – peered from the top of a screen, behind cut-out figures painted to represent period costume, like coconuts on a shy.

The Theatre of Cruelty

Brook's friend, the Russian film director Grigori Kozintsev, sa

> Many places . . . were acted with truly scorched throats. Frenzy, hoarse gabbling, bursts of complete incomprehensibility, howls, and now and then barking; hysteria and the grotesque; the actors themselves painted red spots on the white screens; fantastic stuffed birds, ritual rhythms, masks. It was n distinguish Artaud's ideas.

And the audience invited to the performances were also impressed. Martin Esslin thought it was 'tremendous'.

> In one of the last scenes the peasants set fire to the colonialists' houses by painting the fire with red paint on white screens; after the performance the audience rushed to grab these – they were some of the best action paintings you have ever seen.

Tom Milne, in *Encore*, thought it

> . . . effortlessly achieved the quality of cruelty so obstinately absent from the LAMDA experiments. . . .
> One is left with series of shattering images: as two Colonialists chat cosily about the aesthetics and economics of their plantations, Arab terrorists creep stealthily in to draw tiny flames on the screens behind them; then more Arabs, more flames, until the action seems to dissolve in a sheet of fire. Or when the 'La Marseillaise' of the revolution, Kadidja, calls evil to her: and the Arabs come, swiftly drawing their murders, their rapes, their fear, until her screens are covered with scrawled images of evil. The result is electrifying: naked hatred is present on the stage. In both cases we are presented with an image apparently derived out of fantasy but which, like Picasso's *Guernica*, is a poetic distillation which contains a truth more bright than reality.

The Lord Chamberlain was not impressed and said almost at once the RSC could not do *The Screens*, even with cuts, as it was an insult to the French nation (he cited the scene of soldiers smelling farts of the dying man as if it were the air of France) and that it was extremely obscene (the brothel scenes were far too explicit). So that left Brook with a group of highly trained actors and no play to perform. Martin Esslin relates what happened next:

> One week after the rejection of *The Screens*, a German agent sent me the script of *The Marat/Sade*. I read the play and rang up Brook and told him this was the play he had been looking for. I had it translated by a colleague in the BBC literally overnight and the RSC bought the rights the next day, thereby beating Tynan, who had gone to Berlin to see it for the National, by a nose.

AH:

> Why didn't the RSC stage *The Screens* as a private club performance? Was it because Brook had already given up the idea before the script of *The Marat/Sade* arrived?

6   The thing itself: *The Marat/Sade*

The Second World War presented a mirror to the human condition which blinded anyone who looked into it. For it tens of millions were killed in concentration camps out of the inexorable agonies and contradictions of super-states founded upon the always insoluble contradictions of injustice, one was then obliged also to see that no matter how crippled and perverted an image of man was the society he had created, it was none the less his creation . . . and if society was so murderous, then who could ignore the most hideous of questions about his own nature?

What the liberal cannot bear to admit is that hatred beneath the skin of a society so unjust that the amount of collective violence buried in the people is perhaps incapable of being contained, and therefore if one wants a better world one does well to hold one's breath, for a worse world is bound to come first . . . .

Norman Mailer, The White Negro

Between 1797 and 1811, the Director of the Charenton Asylum, Monsieur de Coulmier, established regular theatrical entertainments in his clinic as part of the therapeutic treatment of his patients. De Sade, an inmate of Charenton from 1803 until his death in 1814, wrote and directed many of these entertainments, and it became fashionable in Paris to visit the asylum, as much to watch the louche antics of the lunatics as to watch the performance. These facts are the starting point of Peter Weiss's play.

Aldwych Theatre Programme

Albert Hunt placed these quotations at the head of his review in *Peace News* of the new play directed by Peter Brook which opened at the Aldwych on 20 August 1964. The play was to run at the Aldwych for three months, during which time the billboards outside the theatre offered prospective customers the choice of:

The Persecution and Assassination of Marat
as Performed by the Inmates of the Asylum of Charenton
under the Direction of the Marquis de Sade
by Peter Weiss
and
EH!
by Henry Livings

Charles Marowitz:

When Peter Weiss's play *The Marat/Sade* came along, it was the natural conclusion of the [LAMDA] Group's work; a play which could not have been contemplated before the Group's existence and which now, after the work on Artaud and Genet, could not be ignored. The play even contained certain features from our first Theatre of Cruelty pro-

84

gramme: Marat's bath tub was mystically related to Christine Keeler's in *The Public Bath*; the guillotine imagery to Brook's collage-play. Weiss acknowledged Artaud as his mentor, Artaud had played Marat in a film for Abel Gance, sounds and 'happenings' were embedded in the play in a way that had been integral to the group's thinking from the start.

Weiss's play pretends to re-create a performance at Charenton in 1808, played in the bathhouse of the asylum, and telling the story of the assassination of Marat by Charlotte Corday. Corday, Marat and all the other characters in the performance are played by inmates.

Weiss's script is built around a philosophical debate between Sade and Marat. Put very crudely, Marat believes that society can be changed by violent revolution; Sade believes that change can only come about if individuals use their unrestricted imaginations to unlock the 'cells of the inner self'. The 'inner self' Sade describes is one which can invent images of unspeakable cruelty. Weiss offers these positions as two poles of a contradiction:

> Our play's chief aim has been
> To take to bits great propositions and their opposites,
> See how they work and let them fight it out
> To point some light on our eternal doubt.
> Marat and I both advocated force
> But in debate each took a different course.
> Both wanted changes, but his views and mine
> On using power never could combine.
> On the one side, he who thinks our lives
> Can be improved by axes and by knives,
> Or he who, submerged in the imagination,
> Seeking a personal annihilation.

The play's first production in Berlin had been centred on this debate. Sally Jacobs:

Peter saw *The Marat/Sade* in Berlin. He said he could see in it what he wanted to do, although it wasn't there in that production at all, which was very static. He said that when the curtain went up there was this stunning image of the people of Charenton sitting in tiers of seats around a small acting area the size of a postage stamp. The image was stunning but you were stuck with it, there was nowhere to go. He wanted to do exactly the opposite: he wanted to be able to use the whole stage and to have the inmates of Charenton always present but on the perimeter, so that they could come and go and form into great set pieces. He wanted to make a completely free space in which any of this would erupt but could at the same time have the tremendous focus, when it was necessary, for the duologues.

Brook's decision to have an acting area into which all of the inmates could move at will directly affected his approach to the play. His rehearsals did not begin with the text but as a workshop on madness. He said:

My first approach was to have the actor do anything he could think of, in a wild way. The next step was by conversation and through improvisation to get each person to remember –

but of course he had seen, he had lived with, he had had in his family one, two, three very close, intimate cases of madness, and as he began to talk about them he began to illustrate them. And so, in fact, he was then, as an actor, beginning to live them with his body; and in talking about four or five different cases, and then showing it, and then perhaps playing it out, he began to find that one of them corresponded more to himself than another. And in this way he began to discover something of his own possible madness.

Brook was looking for kinetic images of insanity. Glenda Jackson later said that 'we were all convinced that we were going loony'. Brook talked to his brother, a psychologist; he went himself to visit asylums in England and France. He gave the cast books by Sade, Artaud and Ezra Pound, articles on madness, pictures by Breughel, Goya and Hogarth. After six weeks they saw two films, one shot at a performance given by inmates in a French asylum, the other made by Jean Rouch in Nigeria depicting a savage ritual played out in a state of extreme madness.

After the immersion in madness the actors faced enormous technical problems when confronted with the demand that they should play their parts as deranged characters. Brook said:

The play is about madness as it was in 1808 – before drugs, before treatment, when a different social attitude to the insane made them behave differently, and so on. For this the actor had no outside model – he looked at faces in Goya not as models to imitate but as prods to encourage his confidence in following the stronger and more worrying of his inner impulses. He had to allow himself to serve these voices completely; and in parting from outside models, he was taking greater risks. He had to cultivate an act of possession.

Meanwhile Sally Jacobs was working on the problems thrown up by Brook's concept of the set:

He had right from the beginning the idea that there should be a swimming pool, or pools, in the floor; he thought of having little gangways around open pools, but I came up with the idea of having small baths sunk into the floor which were covered with duckboards, so it could be a floor when necessary. We then had terrible practical problems of how to sink all those baths into the floor of the old Aldwych stage. I kept going round the stage and looking at what was there and nothing was in the right place. Then one day they were doing work on the revolve and there in front of me I saw the baths. The revolve was like a pie: you take it off in sections, and there between the girders were these triangular holes. So we built the baths in a circle in the revolve, and had some others down stage where the old orchestra pit used to be (it had been built over as a stage extension when the RSC took over the Aldwych). From that circle the rest of the set fell into place. As the idea was that the inmates were locked in for the performance unable to get out I put benches all around the extreme edges of the set , so the inmates could either sit there or be down in the baths when they were not involved in the action.

Brook was later to talk to Albert Hunt about how, during the rehearsal process of *The Marat/Sade*, he first faced the violence inside himself, then tried to get the actors to face the violence inside themselves, so that in the end they could force the audience to face its own violence. Sally Jacobs found it difficult to believe that Brook had any violence inside himself to face. Over the many years she worked with Brook she knew him as a man who always came back in the end to practicalities – how to make something work as theatre.

When we saw the set for the first time, at the technical rehearsal, Peter did what no other director I've ever worked with has done. He went to the back of the stalls and asked a few actors to go up and show him what the stage was about. Stand up stage, let me see you, now go into a down-stage bath, get right in (he wanted to see how much of their bodies stuck out). Can you duck down? How do you get out? Go into an up-stage bath, close the lid, what happens if you stick your hand through. I just loved him for that, because if you can imagine the frustration of being a designer with a director who doesn't actually know how to use what's there: to see him actually exploring for himself what I knew was there so he could make the most use of it.

What that set gave him was a real place, with real doors, with real lids over the baths, real benches, and which was all finished and designed in the conventional way, delivered, as a design has to be, before rehearsals start; but he knew within that, because we had blocked it in the model, he had everything he needed on stage to be able to work *with* the actors, to *improvise* with them, with those objects, how to build up and disperse the set pieces using only what was on stage. We started on the completely realistic premise that we could only have things in the set which would appear as if the inmates had made them up for this performance. We thought of a lot before rehearsals began – old brooms, cabbages, newspapers, towels, pots and pans – but it developed from there: the actors invented some things, such as the quartet developing puppets from old scrubbing brushes.

What his method of working dictated was that there has to be a strong design decision taken early on, you must commit to the way you're going to do it, but it has to be the kind of design which allows for growth.

The set Sally Jacobs gave Peter Brook allowed him to stage what Marowitz, with some justification, described as 'a spectacular and breathtaking production – perhaps the boldest we are to see this half-century'.

The vast bathhouse, with walls and ceiling of dirty clay-coloured tiles, had a bleached-out look; the walls dwarfed the human figures; here and there were pieces of pipe and water jets; the red and blue of France were the only colours. The centre of the raked stage comprised a complete circle of triangular duck-boards, hinged on the outer edge so that they could be lifted to enable the inmates to get down into the baths underneath; great visual play was made with these in the set pieces, often the inmates were inside them, sometimes hidden, sometimes with just their heads showing.

The stage was uniformly lit: there was no curtain, no auditorium black-out. No props were used but Marat's hip-bath and the usual paraphernalia of a bathhouse. Aged and obese, Sade sat on one side of the stage supervising the performance, assisted by a stage-manager who acted as Narrator. On the other side sat Marat in his hip-bath, in the manner of the David painting. Coulmier, with his wife and daughter, all formally dressed (he with a red sash), sat in a box by the side of the stage; after welcoming the audience he only intervened when the show got out of hand, usually when a seditious speech was made.

The mad inmates made a striking entrance; shepherded by nuns and male nurses, they represented, in their off-white straitjackets, a terrifyingly convincing bedlam, partly through make-up (grey faces, scarred skulls, suppurating wounds, elongated and distorted heads, electrified hair) and partly through the most carefully sustained delineation of insanity on the part of all the actors: one talked to herself with her hands held aloft, another stared fiercely at the audience, another suffered involuntary spasms, another continually slavered from mouth to chin, another played with an imaginary child. It looked like a chamber of horrors.

Black, white and grey were the predominant colours: the inmates wore uniforms of stained off-white, the guards and nuns were grey and white. Sade had a white shirt, Marat white bandages under a white sheet. Corday's hat and dress were white. The bath was black, Coulmier and family wore black, the Herald's hat was black.

The central event was the assassination of Marat by Charlotte Corday, which she did, on her third visit to him, in slow motion. The verbal action, conducted by Sade and consisting of frenzied speeches and debates between Marat and himself, was repeatedly interrupted by the lunatics acting out the events of the revolution in tableaux and mimes. There were musical history lessons, given by four patients in clown make-up, and surrealist episodes out of Marat's past.

The acting style was physically strenuous, but simple, consisting of attitudes and postures. Most of the cast were syphilitics, spastics, catatonics, schizophrenics, paranoiacs, manic depressives. None of them, except Marat, was able consistently to remember the script, or keep within Sade's scenic scheme, so they needed continual prompting.

Sade declaimed his long speeches with a painful clenched sing-song deliberateness; Marat was swathed in wet cloths and encased throughout the action in a portable metal bath tub. Even in the midst of the most passionate declamation he stared straight ahead as though he were already dead. Corday was a girl with sleeping sickness who periodically went blank, forgetting her lines, and lay down on stage to be awakened by Sade. Duperret, her lover, was played by a lanky stiff-haired patient, an erotomaniac, who constantly broke out of his role of gentleman and lover and lunged lustfully towards Corday, so that he finally had to be put in a straitjacket. Simone, Marat's mistress, was played by an almost wholly disabled patient who could barely speak and was limited to jerky idiot movements as she changed Marat's dressings. Other figures looked like characters from Breughel, Bosch and Goya.

The music was clangorous, featuring cymbals, bells and organ. The wooden platforms were used as drums to be struck by whatever the actors could find to hand. Catatonic musicians in boxes above the stage contributed chamber music, cabaret background and eerie sound effects, as well as accompanying the Brechtian songs that kept interrupting the action. A dance of white sheets prepared a nightmare for Marat, and while the Marquis de Sade sensuously arranged for the plunge of a dagger, an orchestrated stageful of collaborators beat out rhythms with wooden spoons against their knees, their ankles, their thighs.

There was a mass guillotining sequence, in which some inmates made metallic rasping noises, banging together parts of the set and poured buckets of paint (representing blood – red, blue and black, depending upon the victim's pedigree) down drains, while other madmen gleefully jumped into a pit in the centre of the stage, leaving their heads piled above stage level, next to the guillotine. The King was a dummy with cabbage head and carrot nose. After he had been guillotined, the inmates fought over and ate the carrot and torn-off pieces of cabbage.

When Corday had to whip Sade she used her hair, sometimes holding it in her hand, sometimes letting it hang freely; she would lovingly caress his bare shoulders with it and lash him as she flicked her head; inmates' whistling accompanied the strokes building to a climax as Sade collapsed on the phrase 'the severed genitals of men'.

At the end of the play the madmen got out of control, attacked the guards, raped the nuns, trampled the fallen and murdered the helpless, until a stage-manager, in her everyday twentieth-century clothes, walked on to the stage and blew a whistle, at which point all the actors stopped acting and turned and looked at the audience. They moved down stage and as the audience began to applaud, the actors started clapping back at them, sometimes in rhythm, in a hostile manner.

The play became an immediate sensation in London. The critics were enthusiastic about the production, though many of them had reservations about the play. Bernard Levin wrote, in *The Daily Mail*, 'It is without doubt one of the half-dozen most amazing achievements in *mise-en-scène* that the English theatre has seen in my lifetime'. *The Times* described it more modestly as 'the most ambitious example of the theatre of cruelty yet to appear', while B. A. Young, of the *Financial Times*, wrote of Peter Brook's 'fantastic richness of kinky invention'. Stephen Vinaver, in *Encore*, wrote of Brook transforming the play into

a theatrical image of violence. The naked forces at play among the inmates performing seems suddenly the focal point of the play and its justification. The great thing is that the company doesn't seem to 'play' insanity: in this production after the first few minutes, insanity takes hold and becomes the norm.

Few of the London critics discussed the political implications of the production, but when Brook took the show to New York in January 1966 it provoked a much more considered reaction. Brook once said that in theatre there was always a time when a combination of circumstances made a production right. This combination of circumstances arose with *The Marat/Sade* when it went to New York.

Two factors radically affected the production and its reception. The first related to the casting.

One of the reasons why Marat's position had seemed so weak in the London production was that Marat had been played by an actor unsuited to the part. Clive Revil had made an excellent narrator in *Irma la Douce* and later became a comic stalwart of Broadway. But the role of a radical politician with an itchy skin, played by a paranoid, was not exactly his cup of tea. Fortunately for the production, he declared himself unavailable for New York. Ian Richardson, who had played the Herald in London, took over Marat. Michael Williams moved from Kokol to the Herald.

Richardson brought much more weight to Marat than Revil had been able to do. He presented the arguments with much more conviction and redressed some of the imbalance that had been evident in the first production, although the fact that the play was set in an atmosphere in which lunacy was the norm always tilted the scales against reasoned argument.

The second reason why the performance reached a peak in New York that it had not reached in London was that the audience – and the city they lived in – was ready for the production. For three months the actors lived at the centre of an enormous energy that came from the audience's response – so much so, that, one afternoon towards the end of an exhausting run (the show was played eight times a week, whereas it had been given in repertory in London), Patrick Magee suddenly clasped his heart in the middle of the second act and staggered from the stage. Michael Williams and the rest of the cast so naturally provided the remainder of Sade's text that the audience assumed Sade's physical collapse was a part of the play.

What made the audience particularly responsive was the growing unease about the Vietnam War. The audiences applied references about Napoleon and the wars after the French Revolution to the Vietnam War. The play, Brook said, struck a nerve in a way it never had in London. In New York, he felt, the play was needed. Though Brook had already embarked on the journey that was to result in US before he left, the American response was to reinforce Brook's determination to make a play that confronted the Vietnam War.

That the play struck a chord in New York is undoubtedly true, as the many considered reviews confirm. The critics in the United States have much more space than their British counterparts and they made good use of their advantage. They were much more involved than most of the British critics with what the play was saying.

Wilfred Sheed, in *The Commonweal*, saw it as

undercut all the way through by matching ironies, which then proceed to undercut each other. Marat is a character in the mind of the Marquis . . . but . . . the part has been given to one of the asylum's paranoid patients . . . Marat's radicalism and the actor's paranoia periodically intertwine so that you can't always be sure which is talking. . . .

The audience gradually becomes implicated in this confusion. The night I was there people began to applaud their favourite ideas, only to waver when they realised that the avowed lunatics on the stage were clapping even louder. . . . The uncertainty reached a screaming crescendo at the end when the lunatics . . . solemnly applauded the audience: de Sade and Weiss have obliterated all distinctions – the monkeys are outside the bars, the visitors inside.

Harold Clurman, a veteran of pre-war American radical theatre, said it was 'a particularly German political play' and that he left the theatre 'unmoved':

It is true that when Coulmier intervenes – after Roux has shouted 'Once and for all the idea of glorious victories won by the glorious army must be wiped out. Neither side is glorious' – with the admonition 'This is outright pacifism. At this very moment our soldiers are laying down their lives for the freedom of the world and of our world', the audience applauds (and how delighted many of us are that it does) in recognition of the attack upon a contemporary parallel. Still . . . *Marat/Sade* converts all our political and intellectual concern into display, an artful fun house, a magnificent toy.

Robert Brustein, in *The New Republic*, argued that Weiss had never allowed his protagonists to 'engage each other fully'. He wrote:

There are divisions in the play which leave one with a divided response to it. As a political animal committed to revolutionary change, Weiss is naturally attracted to the Epic theatre as a medium of ironic disengagement, and he employs Brechtian conventions in order to indict the bourgeois spectator, and to awaken him intellectually to the social implications of the action. As an anarchistic theatre poet, however, Weiss is more attracted by the cruelty techniques of Artaud – fits, paroxysms, trances, hallucinations – and he is always tempted to subordinate coherent action to sensational spectacle, using language as a medium of incantation rather than of sense. Weiss is a master of both theatrical traditions, but is less masterly combining them. What results is a double exposure with blurred edges in which the theatre of cruelty accounts for the stronger image. Sade's most important speech – a melancholy diatribe about the withering of individual man under the mechanical uniformity of the State – is delivered while he is being whipped by Corday; and since gesture is more arresting in this play than language, the flagellation distracts rather than illuminates. Weiss's conceptual intellect is strong and his visual imagination fertile, but these qualities are still disjunct in him, so that we are left with a scattering of sharp impressions but an artistic experience that fails to fuse.

Peter Brook has understandably elected to emphasise the Artaudian features of the play, and the results are stunning, brutal, galvanic. The effects are always controlled and almost always organised towards ironic purposes. Brook has chosen to subdue Weiss's cruelties with the result that these cruelties are all the more harrowing and derisive (the text calls for

Corday to scourge Sade with a whip but the production has her lash him with her hair; the text calls for a belly to be pierced and arms and legs to be sawn off but the production offers a comic execution charade, climaxed with the pouring of blood from a bucket – red for people, blue for the King, white for Marat. All elements account for an evening that makes us remember whey we go to the theatre, and makes us want to return.

AH writes:

Twenty-five years on, with the Gulf War replacing the Vietnam War as the current American Nightmare, I find the reaction of the American critics to the New York production enthralling. Virtually all of them discuss, in a deeply engaged way, the ferment of ideas raised by the play. Susan Sontag, in particular, argues that the production works at more than a literary level, that ideas are communicated to us directly, in a physical way. Yet, astonishingly, there is almost no mention at all of the actors who enable the production to communicate so directly. In particular, very little attention is paid to the role of the actor who played Sade, Patrick Magee.

Looking back on my own instant review of *The Marat/Sade*, in a weekly that championed the cause of 'non-violent resistance', I find that I concentrated on the images: on Sally Jacobs's set; on the images created by the performers; on the image of the director of the asylum and his wife and daughter, there, like us, to enjoy the antics of the madmen; on the image of the Herald in blue, who assured us in soothing tones and rhymed couplets that terror was a thing of the past, while we saw terror in front of our eyes, as warders struggled to control the inmates. I was particularly impressed by the final image, in which the lunatic army began to march from the back of the stage towards the audience, then suddenly went berserk. This image, I wrote, took me straight back to an essay by Norman Mailer (*The White Negro*) in which Mailer had argued that the Second World War presented a mirror to the human condition 'which blinded anyone who looked into it'. For, said Mailer, if tens of millions were killed in concentration camps, 'out of the inexorable agonies and contradictions of super-states founded upon the always insoluble contradictions of injustice', we were forced to accept that no matter how crippled and perverted an image of man was the society he had created, it was nevertheless his creation. And if society was murderous, then 'who could ignore the most hideous of questions about his own nature?' What the liberal could not bear to admit, wrote Mailer, was the hatred beneath the skin of a society so unjust that 'the amount of collective violence buried in the people is perhaps incapable of being contained'. The *Marat/Sade*, I concluded, showed us a society in which the violence was 'incapable of being contained'. It offered no solutions, but it confronted us 'with an inescapable sense of the violence inside ourselves, and the links between this and a murderous society'.

Yes, well – I still think that was Brook's intention. But I also think – looking back from the early 90s – that his own unwillingness to accept the possible usefulness of political action, and his failure to recognise that this is in itself a political attitude, affected the production more profoundly than I realised at the time.

I notice that in my lengthy review I paid a suitable tribute to Glenda Jackson, who had struck me so much in the Theatre of Cruelty performance as being the kind of actor Brook was looking for, one who could 'be' on stage. In *The Marat/Sade* she 'was' a girl with sleeping sickness, 'playing' Charlotte Corday; her performance remains in my mind as one of those 'burnt-in' images Brook tries to create.

But I, too, made no reference at all to Patrick Magee. I don't think I'd met Brook when I first saw *The Marat/Sade*, so I failed to realise that Magee wasn't simply playing Sade – he was playing Brook as well. I only discovered this on the night Brook talked to me about the need to be aware of the violence inside oneself.

It was during the rehearsals for *US*, on which a team of us were working with Brook, in the summer of 1966. Late one afternoon, someone came into the rehearsal room and said that Verwoerd, the leader of white South Africa, had been stabbed. Adrian Mitchell and I did an impromptu dance – Mitchell had scripted Brook's version of *The Marat/Sade* and was writing the songs for *US*.

That night in the pub, Brook cornered me and asked me why we had celebrated the stabbing of Verwoerd. I said it wasn't every day you had something to celebrate and that a bit of celebration never came amiss. But Brook said that violence always had to be taken seriously, and then began talking about *The Marat/Sade* (we were to see the black-and-white rushes of the film version that night).

Brook said he was aware of the violence and cruelty inside himself (this was the remark that surprised Sally Jacobs when I told her about it twenty-five years later – she said that there was no violence in Peter, that he even hated competitive sports). Brook said that it was because he was so strongly aware of his own violence that he tried to confront it in his theatre. When directing *The Marat/Sade* (and *US*) he set up working situations in which the performers would have to confront the violence inside themselves. The performance then had to go to a stage further. By presenting the violence in themselves to an audience, the performers could make the spectators confront their own violence. Brook didn't expect the theatre to change people through one performance, but if the performance could plant the seeds for a change of consciousness in one individual, then the performance, and all the processes leading up to it, would have been worthwhile.

In this context, the role of Magee in *The Marat/Sade* takes on an added dimension. For Sade in the play is a theatre director. He is also a man whose name is associated with the inflicting of cruelty – he has given his name to what is commonly perceived as a sexual perversion. If Brook as director had wanted Magee as actor to confront the violence in himself, Brook couldn't have given him a more extreme character to play with. Moreover, in the play, Sade's relationship to the inmates is a mirror image of Brook's relationship to an acting group. And Brook had pushed his group, not to 'act' as inmates, but to 'be' inmates – they had made startling progress with Brook in the direction of 'being' rather than 'acting' since the early days of the Theatre of Cruelty. They were able to create a closed world which powerfully suggested that this was the world as it really is. Extremes of madness became the norm. And Magee, playing Sade with extraordinary conviction, and giving descriptions of the ultimate in cruelty, was able to imply, 'This is what human nature is really like', with the further implication that 'There's nothing to be done except to let your violence run riot'. (At the end of Brook's filmed version, in which the actors destroy the set, Magee watches with an enigmatic smile on his face, as Brook watched the actors who played Lear's Knights when they demolished a chandelier in rehearsal.)

In the play, Marat – whose script we must presume Sade has written – is allowed to put forward some cogent arguments, which became really cogent when Marat was played by Ian Richardson in New York. But the arguments are swamped by the overwhelming sense of the futility of reasoned argument. What's the use of thinking when you have an itchy skin? asks the production (but the text could have said, What does an itchy skin matter as long as you can think?). Thinking in Marat's case leads to Stalinist totalitarianism, and the implication is that this was inevitable. A stoic fatalism hangs over the production – Brook's Marat succumbs to it. Corday doesn't kill this Marat – as Glenda Jackson moved the dagger uncertainly across Ian Richardson's naked chest, Richardson seized the dagger and pointed it at himself. The clowns poured black paint out of their bucket. It was as if Marat accepted that he was destined to die – as indeed the script said he was: Corday was to knock at the door three times, and the third time Marat would be killed. It was historically determined – there was no action he could take to avoid his death.

Just as there was no action the audience could take to avoid being accused of complicity at the end. As the inmates applauded the applauding audience, the image said, 'Look into your own hearts. What kind of people are you to enjoy this spectacle?'

But Brook was, of course, cheating. For the spectacle of mad inmates had been created by the actors and the director using their imagination and intelligence. Brook left this intelligence out of the equation. He often talked, in public discussions, about the difference between madmen and actors. The madman who thought he was Napoleon, he said, was diminished because he could never escape from being Napoleon. The actor, on the other hand, could escape from his role and go back into it at will. But Brook asked his actors, not to 'act' mad but to 'be' mad. He wanted the illusion of madness to be total, and it very nearly was – which helps to explain why the American critics forgot about the actors.

But, while performing, the actors needed to keep all their wits about them – as this statement by actor Bob Lloyd confirms:

Every night I had to do a run from the back, in a straitjacket, up to a bath-top that was lying on its side. It was quite a narrow ridge to run up and then jump off at the end, and it was dangerous to do if the bath-top wasn't being supported. And I'd look down a few lines before I had to do the run and I'd see this slobbering lunatic, John Harwood, with foam coming out of his mouth, rocking and moving, and yet on the same cue every night, for all those months, his right foot would come out and he would support the bath-top, spot on, and the person in front of him would move a hand round and support it from the other side, and that was it. . . . There was a safe framework, but it looked so dangerous in the theatre. I wouldn't have liked to have seen it – the film is a pale reflection.

What Bob Lloyd is saying is that there was a trained intelligence at work during every performance to create the illusion. But Brook wanted us to ignore the intelligence, to be swamped by illusion. Unlike Brecht, who believed that the mechanics of theatre should be revealed, Brook hid the real mechanics. He used Brechtian tricks, pretended to break the illusion. When Corday raised her knife to kill Marat, on her third and last visit, Brook interrupted the action, Brecht-style, to give us an agitprop history in song of the fifteen glorious years which saw the rise of Napoleon. But he never broke the illusion that what we were seeing was real madness. *The Marat/Sade* was such an overwhelming experience theatrically because the actors had sunk themselves deep in madness. They abolished the sense that they were very skilled actors pretending to be mad, so much so that when, at the end, we emerged from our trance and tried to applaud them for being so skilful, they said, 'How dare you take pleasure in the miseries of these people?' (But that was the cheat: we hadn't taken pleasure in the miseries, but in the skill and intelligence of everyone involved.)

One of the show's songs asks, 'What's the use of a revolution without general copulation?' An intelligent response might be, 'What has general copulation got to do with revolution?' But in the world of Charenton, intelligence counts for nothing. 'We want a revolution NOW!' sing the inmates. And of course they do – they are the wretched of the earth. But what they give us is a pretend riot. The pretence is so convincing that we are seduced into forgetting that it is a pretence, and that is part of a process that tells us to dispense with our minds because they can't help us anyway.

Brook said that what he wanted to do was to make us confront the violence in ourselves.

But what he actually asked us to do was to surrender to an illusion, to accept that the world he had created was the mirror image of our world, and that it was a world in which political action was futile.

The Marat/Sade extended the vocabulary of British theatre in a spectacular way. With the exception of Joan Littlewood (whose approach to theatre was radically different from Brook's, but who, like Brook, was always looking for ways of changing theatre) nobody but Brook could have conceived an idea as rich as that embodied in *The Marat/Sade*, let alone have brought it to fruition. More than a quarter of a century later, *The Marat/Sade* stands alongside Littlewood's *Oh, What a Lovely War* as one of the outstanding productions of post-war British theatre.

But it did little to establish the theatre as a place in which urgent issues could be experienced and confronted in what Brecht called a 'cheerful and militant' way. Yet Brook clearly believed that the theatre needed to confront urgent issues, and this belief led him to his next production, *US*.

One final point needs to be made about *The Marat/Sade*. One critic has suggested that Charenton could be seen as a place specifically intended for political prisoners. If this image were to be the starting point for a production, the play would be startlingly different.

Whether it would be as theatrically exciting is very doubtful. In any case, such a starting point, in English at any rate, has become almost unthinkable. The text Brook created with Adrian Mitchell has become the definitive English text. And the world of *The Marat/Sade* has become the world Peter Brook's imagination invented – and the world his skill as a theatre magician made concrete on the stage.

7 Zapping the conscience: *US*

The birth of *US* was allied to the reaction of a group of us who quite suddenly felt that Vietnam was more powerful, more acute, more insistent than any drama that already existed between covers. . . . The problem was – how can current events enter the theatre?

We were not interested in Theatre of Fact. We were interested in a theatre of confrontation. In current events, what confronts what, who confronts whom? In the case of Vietnam, it is reasonable to say that everyone is concerned, yet no one is concerned: if everyone could hold in his mind through one single day both the horror of Vietnam and the normal life he is leading, the tension between the two would be intolerable. Is it possible, then, we ask ourselves, to present for a moment to the spectator this contradiction?

US used a multitude of contradictory techniques to change direction and change levels. It aimed to put the incompatible side by side. . . . We aimed not at a kill, but at what bull-fighters call the moment of truth. The moment of truth was also our moment of drama, the one moment perhaps of tragedy, the one and only confrontation. This was when at the very end all pretences of play-acting ceased and actor and audience together paused, at a moment when they and Vietnam were looking one another in the face.

Peter Brook, Preface to the published account of *US*

In December 1965, Brook had a meeting with two collaborators. He was concerned about the Vietnam War, what people living in London could do about it, how an awareness of it affected their lives. 'If you say you care about Vietnam how does this affect the way you spend your day? I know an actress who rations her day out – so many hours for rehearsal, so many hours for writing to MPs or newspapers or demonstrating. Is this an adequate way of responding to what is happening in Vietnam? If not, what is?'

He referred to the central question of the *Bhagavad-Gita*: a warrior about to go into battle stops and says 'Should I fight?' Brook thought it easy enough to give, in the abstract, a negative answer but, as people were fighting in Vietnam, to utter moral precepts seemed a useless gesture. But the question was there and he wanted to confront it. He felt it had to be dealt with through his work, not outside it in endless discussions. So he wanted to create a show in which the question would be raised in terms of the war in Vietnam.

Brook felt that the show would have to be made in a new way. Reading the scripts submitted to the RSC made him feel that no individual playwright, working alone, was capable of handling such a theme on the epic scale he envisaged. Perhaps the conditions were not right, perhaps Shakespeare could only have emerged out of a situation in which theatre artisans, groups of actors and writers had already established a common language. The job was not to produce *King Lear* but to start on the work of forging a language, to help

96

prepare the groundwork out of which contemporary giants might emerge. The theatre ought to be able to speak about a subject as central as the Vietnam War; no play existed that was in any way adequate, therefore he would establish a situation in which people, including writers, could collaborate to write such a play.

By spring 1966, when he returned from being with *The Marat/Sade* in New York, Brook had assembled a team: the playwright Charles Wood, the two collaborators, Albert Hunt and Geoffrey Reeves, who became Associate Directors, and three people he had worked with on *The Marat/Sade* – the designer Sally Jacobs, the poet Adrian Mitchell and the composer Richard Peaslee (who was American).

Brook explained to the team what he thought the theatre could do. We were all of us saturated by newsreels, reports and television programmes. Horrors no longer had any effect on us. But in a theatre, in a ritualised situation, it might be possible for us to see the horrors in a fresh way. He did not expect the show to convert anybody. But possibly something in the show would plant a seed of change, so that when people were later confronted by situations, they might begin to react in a different way. If only one or two people were given the beginnings of change, the work would have been worthwhile. 'On some night in October, we have a meeting with an audience. It is that meeting that we must always keep in mind.' It is worth noting, however, that although he had every intention of producing a show, Brook, always the realist, negotiated with Peter Hall that the work would have the status of an experiment and therefore might not lead to a result that would be suitable for the stage of the Aldwych. It was agreed that there would be fourteen weeks for rehearsals, and that a decision would be taken after ten weeks as to whether there would be any public performances.

Research began on a wide range of materials: the history of Vietnam; Happenings; American pop music; LBJ's speeches; Mao's Little Red Book; Vietnamese folk-tales; and Fulbright's Senate Hearings on Vietnam and China, which produced some gems, like John Fairbank's 'Great nations on both sides are pursuing their alternative dreams' and this exchange:

SENATOR FULBRIGHT: None of us has an answer. I am afraid I do not.
GENERAL GRIFFITH: I am afraid I do not have.
SENATOR FULBRIGHT: None of us has an answer.

('You can stop killing people for a start', Adrian Mitchell was later to suggest in a poem.)

Charles Wood wrote a number of speeches that were very funny, but that were also full of a bitter irony (there was one in which Lyndon Johnson in the White House agonised about the bombing. 'No, I have not lost my leg', he said, 'but I'm in agony, agonising. . . . No, I have not lost my head').

He also picked up on a suggestion of Brook's, a man who thought he was Vietnam:

I think I'm Vietnam. Once knew a bloke thought he was Ghana. Knew another thought he was France. Couldn't speak a word until he caught the bug, then he rattled away like a green beret. We call them berries.

The discussion on Happenings and how to involve the audience physically led Albert Hunt to invent a ritualistic game with students at an art college in Bradford. Brook went to see it.

From the ceiling there hung a structure, built on two cross-pieces that would spin round if it were touched. Hanging from this structure were dummy bodies, tin cans that made noises, brightly coloured balloons, sheets of pink cellophane, rubber tyres. If anybody collided with these objects the whole structure whirled round and up and down in colour and movement. Through this constantly moving structure five players felt their way, having paper bags over their heads. Two carried blue flags, two carried red and one, wearing a bag decorated with the stars and stripes, carried a stick. The player with the stick hunted for the others. When he caught anybody, he raised his stick. A referee, wearing a frock coat and a black bowler, blew his whistle; everybody froze; the referee led the victim to the front of the stage; the lights went off, feed-back screamed through an amplifier, a girl shrieked – and when the lights came on, the victim, holding a flag, was lying dead at the front of the stage, and another player, pushed through a door at the back, had taken his place. The hunter never knew whether he had caught a red or a blue.

The paper bags found their way into rehearsal, and even into the first night (the game was later adapted to the Black Death and played in the Mobilier National in Paris), and the alternating sequences of noise and silence pointed towards an overall pattern.

By the time rehearsals began there was little actable material, apart from a few speeches from Charles Wood and a poem from Adrian Mitchell, although there were pages of ideas and a document about the war that had been extracted from the piles of research. Unfortunately, there was an early set-back, which was vitally to affect the final production: Charles Wood did not arrive at rehearsals. He flew off to Germany, for the filming of *How I Won the War*, expecting to be away for a week, but he was never to return. For a month the production had no playwright.

Brook intended to draw on the pool of actors he had built up with his work on the Theatre of Cruelty and *The Marat/Sade*, and he was able to recruit many of them. To his great disappointment Patrick Magee declared himself unavailable (although he was acting for the RSC, appearing with Paul Scofield in a comedy about two gay hairdressers, *Staircase*). This, too, affected the shape of the production, which became increasingly centred on Glenda Jackson.

Rehearsals started at the beginning of July.

Brook began by restating his belief in a theatre that could speak directly about contemporary issues. The theatre ought to have a voice that could be listened to seriously. The trouble was that people found it only too easy to dismiss what they had seen as just another theatrical success. He talked about the *The Marat/Sade*. The audience, particularly in London, had been able to avoid the play's political implications. If a man like Harold Wilson had seen it, he would have been able to take refuge in describing the play as theatrically exciting. Brook wanted to make a statement that a Wilson or a Johnson would not be able to shrug off in this way.

At the same time, we must be aware from the start that we were not trying to make a documentary about Vietnam. We were going to examine our own attitudes, to ask ourselves as totally as possible how the Vietnam War affected *us*. He talked about the image of the Buddhist monk who poured petrol over himself and burnt himself to death as a protest against the war. What could drive a man to such an action? How could we begin to understand the totality of his commitment?

Brook stressed that the actors were not going to write the play. He explained the working process: the actors would improvise on material which would be given, and a playwright would take and shape what the actors produced. He asked them to bring material of their own, which several did. He also asked the actors individually what they thought of the Vietnam War. In various ways, and with varying degrees of interest, they said it was terrible and ought to be stopped.

As there was no script, Brook set up situations that could be improvised. He encouraged the actors to try and communicate with each other in wordless rhythms. He worked with them on exercises from classic Chinese theatre.

A morning was spent reading the long document which outlined the history of the Vietnam War largely from the US point of view. The cast found it boring. Brook commented on the limitations of this form from his experience of giving a late-night reading of Weiss's *The Investigation*. It has been seriously done and Weiss had shaped his material dramatically, but Brook felt that all the reading had achieved, in the end, was to demonstrate to the audience that they, too, could come to accept atrocity as boring. For the first twenty minutes, he said, you were shocked; then you began to get bored; in the end you waited impatiently for the catalogue of horror to end. He could never communicate to an Aldwych audience in that way. But after the reading Brook began to explore ways of forging the documentary material into a theatrical language. He took one of LBJ's speeches and had an actor try it in different ways: as if approaching death, then as a bright and open young man, then as if written by Beckett. This gave some phrases great clarity and force, and provided a way of communicating directly through what was, intrinsically, undramatic material. Joe Chaikin, the American director, worked with the group for the first four weeks. He got the actors to explore American life through naturalistic improvisation, as well as working on popular myths of America – from Blueberry Pie in the Mid-West, to horror comics, advertisements and movies (John Wayne waited for a daughter to come home late at night. He ordered the boy who had brought her out of the house, and when the boy had left, snarled at the girl, 'There y'are. I told you he had no guts').

One actor turned himself into a creature called 'the Sinister Sponge'. His body swelled out, his head was thrown back, the veins on his huge neck stood out, his arms were taut and he uttered a long, wordless cry. The image was to appear twice in the final show – during a song called *Zappin' the 'Cong* and in an air raid.

What came to be called the Chinese document was also produced, which offered history from a Chinese and North Vietnamese point of view (at that time, North Vietnam was seen as being very close in its political position to China). It included a description of a triumphant road journey from Hanoi to Saigon by members of the Vietnamese resistance after the surrender of Japan – after which British troops arrived, disarmed the resistance and rearmed the Japanese while helping to reimpose French colonial rule. This narrative was worked on as if it were a poem, backed by Richard Peaslee's music.

Brook asked the actors to create the experience of Vietnamese peasants in a village being bombed. The actors crawled across the floor of Bourne and Hollingsworth's ballroom in various attitudes of pain. Some scrabbled at the floor, others dragged useless legs, yet others were blind. After some time, Brook stopped the exercise and began again. The actors created a Vietnamese village. They found work to do. The air raid started again. The actors dropped their work, and cowered on the ground, whimpering. When the raid was over, they began to crawl across the floor again. They searched and found images. In an attempt to avoid the need to create a 'real air raid', Brook tried framing the exercise between two screens, in a theatrical situation. He asked the actors to pretend that they were people from Vietnam who had come to a village to spread propaganda. They were trying to call the villagers to action against the Americans. Each actor was allowed to make just one point, through a gesture, about the air raid, in the time he took to cross from one screen to the other. The screens formed a little stage, maybe six feet across, and the actors crossed this in a line, one by one. They crawled, moved blindly, whimpered. But none of them could find the one clear gesture that could serve as a call to action. They were still too close to actors simulating 'real' wounds.

From all this work, Brook selected scenes, speeches, songs, images that he could collage together in such a way that a vivid picture of the confusions and complexities of the Vietnam War would, he hoped, be given in theatrical terms to the comfortable audience in the Aldwych. But the only material that was worked on with any degree of success was American. He felt there was a major problem when it came to dealing with a peasant culture when nobody in the company knew anything about peasants. He did not want the actors to imitate the Vietnamese badly.

A Vietnamese monk came to talk to the cast about the political attitudes of the Buddhists. He was a quiet gentle man, who looked as if he might cry at any moment; he talked about the tragedy of Vietnam, its suffering people, the horror of the bombing, and tried to explain why some Buddhists had been driven to burn themselves in protest. For a long time he was listened to in silence, as if the actors felt he was too fragile to be questioned. But eventually someone asked if he was not afraid that if the Americans withdrew the Vietcong would take over and persecute the Buddhists. He said nobody wanted the Americans to withdraw, only to fight the war more humanely, and let the Buddhists set up a popular government. But were not Buddhists against fighting? The monk said no, he was a monk and it was not the job of monks to fight. The soldiers would fight – that was their job. The actors suddenly became hostile, feeling the monk was not offering anything new, and they lost interest.

A Chinese man who knew about Chinese theatre came and watched the actors perform a Vietnamese legend – the Story of the Mosquito – which they did in simple mime. Chaing Lui began by correcting some basic errors. This, he said, is how the wife would cook rice, this is how she would sweep the hut, this is how the husband would say goodbye. He showed the actor playing the husband how to climb a mountain, how to depict the sunset. He showed the wife how to walk and bow.

For the actors, this was a most alarming experience. In the first place, Chaing Lui was fat and round and big, yet he danced lightly and gracefully every time he moved. He seemed to be able to leap gently into the air, almost float from one step to the next. The much less heavily built actors moved gawkily beside him. Even more disturbing for them was the precision he demanded and the way he obtained it. The actors had been working through free improvisation, searching for gestures inside themselves. Chaing Lui came and put their hands and feet into the correct position. Some of the actors complained that the method was restrictive, and in the afternoon, when they tried to repeat the exercise for other actors who had not been there, they found themselves unable to communicate. There had been too many gaps in their basic observation. They tried in pairs to imitate the scene from the Chinese theatre in which two people travel on a sampan; they found this extremely difficult. They tried to logically work out their relationship to the boat. For actors used to working inside a naturalistic framework, even a Chinese exercise was seen, instinctively, as a 'realistic' problem.

Meanwhile Sally Jacobs had been having problems with the set:

I just went on building bits and pieces for ever, and we never really liked any of it. None of it seemed right. It all came out of bits of barbed wire. There wasn't anything to get hold of, it was like a revue. You didn't know where you were supposed to be placing it except it was going to happen on a stage with all these bits and pieces from all these different elements that were being explored. You couldn't find a way of putting them on stage. Then I came up with this pop-art book *Dead Soldier*, which was very expressive of what the production was going to be about though it still didn't give us a set; it was such an amazing thing that we knew we should have it there somewhere. A friend said that all those countries in the world where there had been war year after year were like great big rubbish dumps: there was rubble, and stuff left over, and cultural bits and pieces, and burnt out husks of vehicles, aeroplane wings, old tanks – and maybe that's what the set should be. So then I made a whole pile of rubbish for the stage, of war-torn Vietnam (Lebanon would be the same thing), and we heaped it up into a pyramid; I converted it into a set so that it could be climbed up. I took the idea from pictures of the collections of bits and pieces of American planes that the Vietcong used to collect and display. In the middle was an aircraft wing, and there were old chairs and bits of furniture. It created the right atmosphere, pieces could be pulled out and used, and it provided circulation around it which gave us a dynamic for how to use the stage. I put it in the middle of the stage with a big bright chrome yellow surround, a really harsh difficult colour to look at. Then we got a jeep on stage; Chinese flags and silk banners. We could deal with things that came out of rehearsal improvisations, like the need for a tightrope. We hung the big pop-art soldier on the outside of the proscenium as a symbol. It was a thirty-six-foot puppet with arms and legs hanging down, one big hand was in a box. In the scene showing the escalation of the war it was winched down and then it became a great landscape on which the actors could climb. It was quite something when it started to move as, being out front, it was right on top of the audience. It looked dangerous and came down with a tremendous screeching sound effect. The puppet helped Peter find the next step forward as it was an object that focused all the material in a theatrical style. The fact that when I produced it we didn't know how we were going to use it was an example of how we worked together in those days: we fed off each other's sensibilities.

At the beginning of August Jerzy Grotowski, with one of his actors, Ryszard Cieslak, came to work with the company for two weeks. Brook believed that Grotowski was unique:

because no one else in the world, to my knowledge, not since Stanislavsky, has investigated the nature of acting, its phenomenon, its meaning, the nature and science of its mental–physical–emotional processes as deeply and completely as Grotowski.

Afterwards Brook refused to describe the work:

such work is only free if it is in confidence, and confidence depends on its confidences not being disclosed. And it is essentially non-verbal. To verbalise is to complete and even to destroy exercises that are clear and simple when indicated by a gesture and when executed by the mind and body as one. What did the work *do*? It gave each actor a series of shocks: the shock of confronting himself in the face of simple irrefutable challenges; the shock of catching sight of his own evasions, tricks and clichés; the shock of sensing something of his own vast and untrapped resources; the shock of being forced to question why he is an actor at all.

The first shock, though, came not to the actors but to the stage-manager. Grotowski took one look at the rehearsal-room floor and said it was filthy; he would not work unless it was clean enough 'to kiss'. There followed much scrubbing. The first session started two hours late. Cieslak went through a series of rigorous physical movements, including standing on one shoulder, and the company was invited to emulate. They found it extremely difficult.

The Monday after Grotowski left, Brook spoke to the company:

We are now entering the third stage of our work. In the first, you opened up as many fields as you could, ranged as widely through our knowledge and ignorance and images as you could. With Grotowski, you explored deeply and intensely a very focused, tight, personal area of commitment: your own bodily commitment as actors. Now, in the third stage, we shall broaden our scope again. But the intense personal exploration will continue. I know many of you found it painful. So I say that if anyone wants to pull out now, they can do so.

But no one wanted to leave.

Brook decided that burning was the central image of the play, and Grotowski's work had opened up possibilities for the actors to explore it now in Artaud's sense of burning oneself. Improvisations were done on the self-immolations of Buddhist monks and the Quaker, Norman Morrison.

Denis Cannan had now joined the team as playwright – he was to write the second half. The first part was going to be a collage of all that had been worked on in July. Cannan felt that we all '*want* extreme situations, that we yearn for invasion, apocalypse. Because they simplify our tangled lives . . .', and he suggested that the second half should be built round the image of an Englishman intending to burn himself on the steps of the American Embassy in Grosvenor Square. This idea was improvised, with Cannan himself stopping and questioning the actor in mid-scene as to his motives.

Two weeks after Grotowski's workshop, Brook selected half a dozen performers for a special day's work – they included Bob Lloyd and Glenda Jackson. In the morning, Brook asked them to find spaces for themselves and imagine themselves as nothing. Gradually, they were to develop senses, feelings, parts of the body. By the end of the morning's work, they were to have emerged as human beings.

In the afternoon, Brook asked the same actors to stand on wooden benches, the kind of forms people sit on in travelling theatres. Each actor was given a bench, and started at one end. The actors were asked to close their eyes and think about the Vietnam War. Whenever they reached the point where they were willing to give up one of the senses in order to stop the war, they were to take one step forward. When they were willing to commit suicide – as Norman Morrison had done – they could step off the bench. Six steps were allowed. Only one actor got to step five, most managed four.

In September Peter Hall and various associates of the RSC were shown a run-through of Act I and heard a reading of Act II. While feeling that 'all the material about the USA is richer, more complex, than the material from Vietnam' it was decided that the show would go on.

Almost every day the team met a different 'expert' on Vietnam, from journalists who knew the country well to historians who had never set foot there (and a cartoonist who had done a three-day tour and proclaimed that 'he had seen it all'). The most interesting of these visitors were asked to talk to the company, who were encouraged to adopt an investigative, rather than an aggressive, attitude in order to get the most out of the guests; some found this difficult to do.

Brook said that there should be a silence at the end which must be

like an open mouth, not a shut eye. I want you to think about silence, think about it in relation to our audience. They will come in, take their seats, and wait – with a sort of curious, expectant silence, waiting to see what we can unfold about a war and a political situation about which they have come to conclusions. Our job in this performance is to lead our audience – and ourselves – from one kind of silence to another: the silence of genuine concern, not just attentiveness, indignation, despair, impotence.

Brook's concern with making some kind of direct contact between actors and audience led to a dramatic decision about costumes.

Sally Jacobs:

The actors were portraying newsreel material, acting out real dialogue between politicians, playing famous people, being comic-strip characters. To find how they should be dressed so that they could do all these different things, I designed a series of slightly comic-strip Vietnamese pyjama-type (some more caricatured than others) basic athletic costumes that everyone could work in, adding bits when needed. This seemed like a marvellous solution to an impossible problem. But what happened when we put the costumes on was that we lost the connection between the actors and the audience: before the actors were speaking for us – because those actors looked like real people. Immediately we put them into costumes it turned into a costumed production, which had nothing to do with anything except the production. The costumes were all wrong, but we couldn't put our fingers on why. At the next rehearsal, which was not in costume, everything fell back into place again. So it became quite clear that we shouldn't have costumes. When Peter made the announcement everybody had a fit, because when you make a radical change like that everybody gets very insecure. . . . But it brought the whole thing back to life again. It was a very good decision.

When it was decided to go ahead with the show a script was sent to the Lord Chamberlain. When he had read it he promptly telephoned the Chairman of the Governors of the RSC, who was then on a fishing holiday in Scotland, to tell him that in his opinion it was 'bestial, anti-American and Communist'. He asked him to use his influence to stop the show. George Farmer flew to London and watched a run-through. With Hall and Brook he went to see the Lord Chamberlain at St James's Palace. As Brook told the story, the Lord Chamberlain was dressed in full regalia as he was going out to a dinner. He wanted to see Farmer alone and unsuccessfully tried to get him to leave the two directors in the antechamber. Farmer made it clear he was willing to stand by the production. Hall, said Brook, threatened to cancel the season at Stratford-upon-Avon. The Lord Chamberlain asked 'If the American Ambassador goes to the first night, will he walk out?' Brook said 'Not if he stays to the end'. Finally, faced with a united front, the Chamberlain said he would issue a licence for the play but that there would be cuts. There was to be much negotiation over these.

Towards the end of rehearsals, divisions over Cannan's second act, which had only been implicit at first, erupted into bitter dissent – on three occasions lasting through the night. It centred on a speech for Glenda Jackson in which she said of the violence of the war 'I want it to come here'. Several rebuttals were written, and even tried in a preview, but Brook finally refused to allow anything to undercut the dramatic impact of the speech, although he was prepared to try to find a context for it: by the use of the presence of the company on stage and the interpolation of a 'collision of dreams' sequence.

Fifteen minutes of the first act were cut between the last preview and the first night. There had always been trouble with the length of the show since the first assemblage of material for Act I had run well over two hours. The original script had three acts, the second consisting of forty minutes from the transcript of the Senate Hearings. This was cut and eight lines put in at the end of Act I (the whole act was given a reading one Sunday night for the RSC club, suitably sanitised by being made part of a double bill with John Barton's selection of Thucydides: the striking parallels between the two texts thereby proving that nothing had changed over two thousand years).

There were many technical problems with the set, mainly involving the operation of the dummy in its descent from the proscenium arch; the original costumes were thrown out; the attempt to juxtapose documentary film material, as well as live video, had to be abandoned as the internal paging system of the hotel next door continually interfered with the television monitors.

Act I took place on a stage empty at the start except for a pile of garbage in the middle, consisting of a large ladder, chairs, benches, a practice bar, paper bags etc. The collage dummy of the American soldier was suspended above it at the level of the proscenium arch. It had the structure of a musical revue. All of the text (and some of Adrian Mitchell's songs) was based on documentary material, much of it used verbatim.

At the beginning of the show the actors walked on, singing

> If you never spend your money
> You'll always have some cash
> If you stay cool
> You'll never turn to ash.

One actor, wrapped in a swathe of orange material, mimed burning himself: 'When we burn ourselves it is the only way we can speak'. Madame Ngu commented that nothing was served 'by allowing the export of newsreels which show in sordid detail these saffron barbecues in imported gasoline'.

A milk float was driven on. The history of Vietnam was presented as a series of tableaux vivants, using hand props, hats and flags, and with a tall thin actor personifying Vietnam. At the Geneva conference, after the French surrender at Dien Bien Phu, Vietnam was painted two colours, being divided at the waist. In the fighting that followed he became an action painting.

A Vietnamese poem, *The Lament of the Warrior's Wife*, was read, then six actors presented actuality from American soldiers:

Sometimes, someone has to make the decision to fire or not to fire on a village from which our troops are being fired on. I comment that it requires mature men.

By God, what this country needed was for Barry Goldwater to be elected in '64. I'll bet I'd be in Hanoi right now. Let China come in. Let them try. Barry would have had us in Peking if they'd tried.

Then came the song of the imaginative draft protester, Barry Bondhus of Big Lake Minnesota, who dumped 'Two full buckets of human excrement' on the files of the draft board. This was followed by a sequence called Torture School – 'We simulate V. C. interrogation conditions'. In the midst of images of violence – prisoners being kicked and beaten, their heads held under water – a journalist interviewed an officer:

How do you offset the damage to yourself?

Your belief. Your belief: you have to sincerely believe that in the long run you're helping this man. . . .

The soldiers started torturing again and, as the noise of screaming fans was heard, they sang the *Song of the Technical Language*:

> Zapping the 'cong back where they belong
> Hide your yellow asses when you hear my song
> All over the jungle up to old Haiphong
> I'm scrapping jelly petrol I've been zapping the 'cong.

Between the verses an actor playing a character from comic-strips, the Sinister Sponge, seized a girl and carried her up one side of the ladder only to be shot by an imaginary ray gun at the top. And men in battle were interviewed by journalists with microphones:

> What's war like, soldier?
> Hell.
> What's dying like, Major?
> Hell.

An English journalist agonised over the complexities of the situation he had found in Vietnam, which led to a reconstruction of one of the daily military briefings – 'the five o'clock follies':

ENGLISH JOURNALIST: Can you tell us why you persist in your refusal to give us any estimate of civilian casualties?

OFFICIAL: You've got to keep this war in proportion, Roger. Fewer people of all categories are killed here per day than we kill on the highways of the United States.

GERMAN JOURNALIST: May I suggest . . . the quickest way to get rid of Communists in Asia would be to drop them Cadillacs by parachute?

An actor mimed the death of Norman Morrison, who burnt himself on the steps of the Pentagon in Washington. Around the body there assembled a Quaker meeting. A letter an American housewife sent to the President was read. Then came the escalation sequence in which the gradual build-up of troops and material was dramatised with a refrain:

> We know what we're doing
> We know what we're doing it for
> We know what we're doing
> We ought to know
> We've done it before.

As it reached the bombing of Hanoi and Haiphong – US air-force jets criss-cross Hanoi . . . 72 tons . . . 750lb bombs in 25 minutes – with a great screeching noise the dummy slowly descended until it lay right across the width of the stage. The actors reacted as if they were caught in an air raid. The song of *Make and Break* was sung by two doctors in white coats while dealing with a procession of wounded people:

> Fill all the area with whirling metal
> 5,000 razor blades are slashing like rain
> Mr Hyde has a buddy called Jekyll
> Picks up the pieces and puts them together again.
>
> Want to be humane, but we're only human
> Off with the old skin, on with the new.
> We maim by night
> We heal by day,
> Just the same as you.

Between the verses were speeches from an artificial limb-maker from Spain and an American sergeant who spent all his spare time in a children's hospital.

Can you put your arms round my neck a bit tighter then I can carry two of you, because you are a heavy girl, is that your brother, hang on tightly then, ups a daisy ... yes kid you climb onto Uncle Hiram, he's taking you all to be fitted. One more and that's that I guess ... your hook thing is in my ear if you could put it through my epaulette . . . yes, I am a real soldier ...

The hospital was bombed. The dummy started to rise to a dreadful cacophony. Sudden silence. Mark sang 'What made you think you could fly' and sat down and lit a match. Two actors with paper bags over their heads were led on. They spoke a brief exchange from the Senate Hearings.

Now with respect to China itself ... is it your opinion, General, that we could subdue China by an all-out bombing attack against them?
Nuclear bombing?
Well, let us say first of all, conventional bombing.
In my opinion it would take nuclear bombs anyway.

On the first night, the act ended with all the actors with paper bags over their heads entering calling 'Help', climbing off the stage and trying to find their way to the stalls' exits. This was a vestige of the Bradford students' war game that had been played in rehearsal. It lasted only four days into the run before being cut; the actors had disliked doing it in the first place and found the response of the audience, which ranged from helpful pushes in the right direction to various remarks (most of them sarcastic), extremely dampening. It was replaced by the two paper-bagged actors being dragged off by their mic leads and the lights fading to a spot on Mark.

Act II was played on a bare stage. The dummy had gone and only the ladder remained, now up stage and surrounded by a little garbage. It consisted of the duologue between the man who wanted to burn himself on the steps of the American Embassy in London and the woman who finally admitted that she wanted the war to go on.

The act began with a sentimental song, *Rose of Saigon*, a pastiche of *La Vie en Rose*, followed by a fast aggressive, almost scat, version of Adrian Mitchell's poem *To whom it may concern*

> I was run over by the truth one day
> Ever since the accident I've walked this way
> So stick my legs in plaster
> Tell me lies about Vietnam.

After the song Mark sat down with a can of petrol, a box of matches and a letter. Glenda entered and watched him. After he had unscrewed the top of the can she darted forward and grabbed the matchbox and the letter. She began:

Do you suppose President Johnson or Mr Kosygin or Harold Wilson will ever even *see* this letter?

The papers will publish it.

And so began the dialogue on what could be done in the way of demonstration against the war, including holding liberal opinions about homosexuality and South Africa, marching for CND, contributing to charities, political affiliations, the example of Christ, belief in the afterlife, the reasonable nature of the Vietnam War.

The dialogue was interrupted by a dream sequence which presented a series of speeches from Mr Matsuda (who spent his life savings in putting an advertisement in *The Times* containing his ideas for world peace), Andy Warhol ('If you pay attention to it you're part of it. . . Boring, boring, boring'), John Cage (on the banning of his piece in which the butterfly is turned loose: 'I felt certain the butterfly made sounds. . . it didn't seem to me at all necessary that anyone should have to hear the sounds'), Timothy Leary ('through LSD each person will become his own Buddha, his own Einstein, his own Galileo') and LBJ (called the Prophet in the script as the Lord Chamberlain would not allow the portrayal of friendly heads of state on the stage. Mao would have been all right). He said:

Every night before I turn out the lights to sleep I ask myself this question: Have I done everything I can to unite the world? Have I done enough?

Then Mark talked about what was being done to the people and countryside of Vietnam. Glenda asked him what made him want to burn himself, and then asked what he saw when she said 'Jew' – he saw Auschwitz; to 'burning negro' he saw the KKK; to 'American' he saw people shopping, buying everything. They discussed racism. Glenda told the story of the kind Englishwoman in Spain who, by trying to help a seagull with a broken wing, had unwittingly caused twenty more to have their wings deliberately broken. Excerpts from the Fire Sermon of the Buddha were spoken by the actor who had 'burnt' at the beginning of the first act.

Everything is burning; what the eye sees is burning . . . it is burning with the fire of lust, the fire of anger, the fire of ignorance; it is burning with the sorrows of birth, decay, death, grief, lamentation, suffering, dejection and despair.

Then came a reasoned and reasonable defence of the American position from a quietly spoken liberal diplomat (written by Albert Hunt and based on a member of the Embassy staff in Grosvenor Square):

When you protest, you should realise that you are in fact protesting not against the war in Vietnam but against the whole concept of an orderly society.

(Adrian Mitchell said the speech almost turned him into an anarchist.)
   Glenda launched into a passionate speech:

So you end the war in Vietnam. Where's the next one? Thailand, Chile, Alabama? I WANT IT TO GET WORSE!! I want it to come HERE! . . . I would like to smell the explosion of frightened bowels over the English Sunday morning smell of gin and the roasting joint and hyacinths. I would like to see an English dog play on an English lawn with part of a burned hand. I would like to see a gas grenade go off at an English flower show, and nice English ladies crawling and swallowing each others' sick . . . I want it to go on. . . . Like lust it goes on because we want it. And as we lust, we suspect most of all those who shout loudest, 'No!'

Finally, one of the actors, Bob Lloyd, brought a small table with a box on it downstage centre. He was wearing gloves. He opened the box, he took out a butterfly and threw it into the air, then another, the third he held in one hand while with the other he took a lighter from his pocket and set it alight. He put down the lighter. Everything on the stage was still. The house lights came up.

The cast waited for the audience to leave.

The show got a mixed reception from the London critics. Although Brook was impressed by the quality of the silence at the end of the first night it was, in fact, broken by the voice of Kenneth Tynan, in the middle of the stalls, loudly enquiring 'Are you waiting for us, or are we waiting for you?' (And people like Arnold Wesker were anything but silent by the time they had reached the pub.)

The reviews were very varied, often revealing more about the critic than what actually occurred on the stage of the Aldwych.

Irving Wardle, in *The Times*, wrote

This event conforms to no existing theatrical category and lies outside the scope of conventional criticism. Detachment is finally broken down. I have never before experienced this so fully in a theatre.

B. A. Young, in *The Financial Times*, said

If I believed that *US* would bring the war in Vietnam to an honourable conclusion one minute sooner, it would get the loudest cheer from me that I have ever given. I believe in fact that it probably won't. The chief reason is that the appeal made in this remarkable production is directed exclusively at the emotions.

D. A. N. Jones, in *The New Statesman*, called the show

indecent by its very nature; you have to sit comfortably in the Aldwych stalls and enjoy clever acting, exhilarating verse, music, jokes – and all of it, in a sense, at the expense of the burning Vietnamese.

Bryan Magee, in *The Listener*, complained

During the interval I felt that my interest had been held by the medium, not the message. I returned to my seat expecting more of the same. But what happened was not merely unexpected, it developed into one of the major experiences of my life. Instead of carrying on in the same ingenuous or disingenuous way about the US in Vietnam, the actors turned their attention to us in the audience. . . . Suddenly, after the intellectual dishonesties of the first half, the production was saying something real. . . .It becomes the theatre of compassionate involvement.

Charles Marowitz, who by now had parted company with Brook, dismissed it:

One doesn't need a theatrical performance to explain we are all at an impasse . . . but if one has no overriding conviction to express on the Vietnam War other than the fact that it is horrible and insoluble, it is almost better to say nothing. Many reviewers have been subtly intimidated by the urgency of this subject and the unfamiliarity of the treatment which is nothing more than Living-Newspaper technique brought up to date. This has angered me and many like me who would like criticism to stare down the po-faced intensities of productions like *US* which, with the best intentions in the world, produce superficial flurries on incendiary subjects that can be justified neither on artistic nor ideological grounds.

And David Bulwer Lutyens wrote:

I regard *US* as criminal slander on the one power able to defend Western blood, race and culture from Asiatic degeneracy. . . . No artist can escape from the deep and innermost call of blood, and the whole tendency of the Aldwych is to disintegrate culture even further by adding to the fragmentation of values, by denying even the possibility of a Weltanschauung.

Jean-Paul Sartre viewed *US* philosophically:

A happening is real. . . . The problem really is: what happens to the performance insofar as it is an appeal to the free imagination of the spectator? Is not this spontaneous bringing of something into being by means that are more or less cruel the very opposite of theatre, or rather is it not the moment when the theatre destroys itself? Most of the happenings are a carefully thought-out exploitation of the cruelty that Artaud advocates. You have to go in your old clothes. And the public for happenings have reacted to their own torture.

Can we say that we have gone past the limits of the idea and the essence of the theatre? Peter Brook has tried to find a mixture, that is to say a compromise, that would contain happenings inside the limits of a play. This he has done recently in *US*. By itself this play has no meaning and we cannot call it a play . . . there is a succession of scenes, words and violent acts without any purpose other than to create the confusion which inspires the two themes: the first part is about the horror of the war in Vietnam, while the second is principally about the impotence of the Left.

The public are not asked to take part in the performance: they are kept at a distance, for the most part. They receive this mixture of broken sketches, interrupted at the moment where an illusion is about to be created, as a blow in the face. And at the end they find themselves before a real event, a real happening, which is renewed every evening.

For on the stage one of the actors opens a box of butterflies. They are taken out and a hand holding a lighter burns them in its flame. They are burnt alive. This is a happening because something really happens: something alive dies and dies suffering. Nevertheless it is not altogether a happening because the play ends and the spectator, sent back to his solitude, leaves with a confused despair made up of shock, fury and impotence. There has been no conclusion and after all what is there to conclude? It is true that the war in Vietnam is a crime. It is also true that the Left is quite incapable of doing anything. Has it anything to do with the theatre? I think it is really on the borderline where form is only an intermediary and where we can either say 'this is theatre' or 'this is not'. In any case we can say that if it is theatre, this situation is an excellent example of what we can call the crisis of the imaginary in the theatre.

Unfortunately Sartre did not see *US*; does that invalidate his argument, or is it because only a representation of the burning of the butterfly took place and not the real thing?

US was given fifty performances at the Aldwych in repertoire over six months. It was always full. Although the company worked internally to keep the show alive the form remained frozen. Nothing could be improvised, nothing could be changed without prior submission to the Lord Chamberlain. One day a postcard arrived from Saigon, from one of the friendly journalists who had come to rehearsal. That night an actor read it out during the American Briefing Session. When Peter Hall found out the next day, via the stage-manager's report, his wrath descended on the Associate Director who had permitted it.

The quality, and length, of the silence at the end of the show depended on the audience: sometimes there would be enthusiastic applause, but more often it was desultory and the audience departed awed and in silence. One night the butterfly did not burn: as Bob Lloyd took the lighter from his pocket a middle-aged woman climbed on to the stage from the front row and stopped him, saying 'You see, you can do something'. When she saw what he had in his hand she turned to her friend and said 'It's only paper'. They were two Quakers who had already seen the show once from the balcony; they had brought front-row seats so they could stop what they thought was an outrage from happening again. The company, especially Bob Lloyd, greatly admired the courage of the action.

AH writes:

When I contributed an essay to the published text of *US*, Brook said that it lacked my usual critical astringency. So twenty-five years later I'll try again.

I find it hard to separate the experience of working on *US* from the product. It was, in the end, a painful and somewhat disillusioning experience. I felt I'd been manipulated – which was certainly part, but not the whole, of the truth. Paradoxically, it's also an experience I've never regretted. To work with Brook is to learn a great deal, even if afterwards you have to reject some of what you've learned.

The absence of a recognised playwright affected Brook's method of working with the actors, and led him to bring in, at a late stage, a playwright of a different kind and generation: Denis Cannan. (Temperamentally, Cannan shared Brook's post-Second World War pessimism. He belonged to the cultural generation of which Sartre wrote, 'We have been taught to take evil seriously'.)

One small incident in the air-raid exercise suddenly called attention to the thinness of the work. At the start of the raids, the chair thrown as a signal nearly hit one of the actors. He reacted spontaneously, flinching instinctively from the *real* threatened pain. Then, when the chair missed, he became a Vietnamese villager again, simulating a wound.

If we were to find a language to communicate to other people, we must first be able to look honestly at ourselves. Throughout rehearsals, this proved to be very difficult. We, all of us – the actors included – had a number of easy responses to the material we were studying. How to get through these responses until we were confronted with what we *really* experienced?

The difficulty became clear when Brook began working on a torture scene. He used four actors, with the rest sitting round in a group watching. He asked those watching to give their immediate, spontaneous reactions to what they saw, first as if they were watching Americans carrying out the torture, and then as if they were the inhabitants of a bombed village watching an American airman being tortured. Most of the responses were expected, being conventional expressions of disgust. A few of the spectators were able to sympathise with the desire of the Vietnamese for some kind of revenge; none of them seemed to have any sympathy at all for the American position. In discussion afterwards, I asked a woman, who said she had been revolted by what she had seen, what she would do if she were an American officer in a village, whose men were being shot, and who was convinced that the Vietnamese in front of him knew who the killer was. Would the officer not have a primary responsibility to try and save the lines of his men? She replied honestly enough that she could not imagine herself as an American officer.

I felt that the situation needed exploring in this way; as it was the watchers were simply reacting in disgust to actions taken out of context. But what was perhaps more interesting was the zest with which those actions were performed. Both the torturers and the tortured played the game with a lot of imaginative vigour, simulating, realistically, blows to the windpipe and the testicles, with the victim groaning and screaming in agony. The tortures were sickeningly convincing, and most of us watched them with fascinated attention. What was revealed was the gap between what we pretend to feel, and disturbing impulses inside. Much later we played a version of the blindfold game the students at Bradford had invented. On that occasion, everybody threw themselves with great gusto into the business of frightening those who could not see – and afterwards everybody sat around again, telling each other how torture was disgusting.

And yet – the instinctive, disgusted response to torture was healthy and genuine. It is a long step from teasing somebody you know in rehearsal, to torturing a prisoner. But it was important for each one to confront the germs of cruelty in himself as a first step towards understanding.

In the early days, Brook seemed to be open to all the ideas that were on offer. Naturally, he didn't accept them all, but he did throw them into the discussion, which was virtually permanent, amongst the team creating the show. Brook himself set a pattern of almost incessant work. He – and we – would work with the actors from ten in the morning till six at night. Then we would meet to discuss the day's work and make suggestions for the next day's work. The meetings would frequently go on into the early hours. Then the next day the work with the actors would begin again at ten.

Very soon, though, I became conscious of a hierarchy. *We* were creating the show, not the actors. The actors were simply there to explore the material we produced. They rarely took part in any serious discussion about content. One or two of them voiced political commitments from time to time, notably Bob Lloyd. Henry Woolf (who had directed the first performance of a Pinter play) spread his own brand of mischievous anarchy occasionally. But it seemed to me that for the most part the actors saw the production as an opportunity to do some prestigious work. With Brook as director, they expected it to be unusual. Typical was the woman who told me her agent had told her to grab the opportunity, because of the experience – and because the Polish director, Grotowski, had been booked for a three-week workshop with the cast in the middle of the production period. 'He said I was lucky to be getting paid to work with Grotowski', she said.

Brook himself accepted the principle of hierarchy, though he himself was prepared to use it for mischievous purposes. When we went to the American Embassy to be talked to by a high official, Brook kept a very polite and solemn face while the official told us that, of course, in spite of what President Johnson said, people in the know didn't believe that the United States was fighting for democracy in South Vietnam. People in the know knew that there was no democracy there. They were fighting to prevent south-east Asia falling to Communism – he went on to expound the domino theory. Afterwards, Brook remarked that people in power always tried to let some people feel that they were privileged, and were being given inside information. But all that was happening was that one outer layer of secrecy was being removed, while other layers were being left in place. Brook was undoubtedly the man in power in the production of *US*, and there were times when I felt he was using the same technique.

Sometimes, enthusiasms would seize him. One night we were all invited to the flat of Sally Jacobs, the set designer. She had made a model of a huge American soldier, lying prone. He would be big enough to fill the stage: the features of his face and his arms and elbows and knees and feet were objects to climb over. He had a rocket for a penis.

Brook was very excited about the model. He said, 'I think we've found our set'. He gave instructions for the model to be built, and for some time he kept in mind, in his studio work, that the actors would be performing on a prone American soldier. But soon the material began to take over again. In the end, the soldier was suspended from the roof of the Aldwych over the stage. If you were sitting in the front stalls it looked very menacing; but if you were sitting in the back stalls you couldn't even see it, until it was lowered at the end of the first act. That was the only time it was eventually used in the whole show.

I was there the morning the decision to drop the costumes was announced. Brook suddenly stopped the rehearsal, asked the actors to notice what they were wearing and said 'That is what I want you to wear in the shows' – after which the rehearsal continued as if nothing had happened.

When Grotowski came it was as if Moses had paid a brief visit, bringing with him the tablets of stone.

I spent part of Grotowski's visit working with a group of understudies on a game which, we all knew, was unlikely to affect the production. They were very pleasant people, whose main concern was with which rep they might get a job afterwards. But they became, eventually, very earnest, and we tried to invent something that would make a collective comment about the Vietnam War – they talked of taking off their clothes and burning them, and then waiting to see what the other actors would do to help them get home.

But the event was never performed, and the other actors were being kept busy by Grotowski. In what amounted to a crash course, they were taught to use their bodies in ways they would not have believed possible: after a few days, Grotowski had them walking on all fours like cats while singing the *Londonderry Air* in three octaves.

Being forced to miss some of the Grotowski workshops, I found the physical and vocal extensions of the actors astonishing. But there were many aspects of the work which, temperamentally, I couldn't take, and which, looking back, should have been warning signals of the gulf that was to widen between Brook and some of us before the work was finished.

Being in a Grotowski workshop was like being in a church. He sat in a suit behind a table, chain-smoking – but the sound of a match being struck by someone else was enough to bring a look of anger into his face. At the other end of a large room, the actors would huddle together, as if for safety, waiting for his instructions. Since Grotowski spoke no English, the instructions were given in French and translated by Brook. The effect could be half-funny, half-chilling. Once, after the actors had been required to show the attributes of animals, Glenda Jackson had tried to be a tiger.

Being selected for criticism by Grotowski was a tribute, as was Glenda Jackson on this occasion. Brook had spoken to Grotowski about her on the day he arrived; she had immense talent, Brook said, but she kept it all inside her. She was never out of control. Grotowski set out to break down her control in order, as he saw it, to build her up again. One night he had her playing, without words, a scene from *Romeo and Juliet*. Juliet invites Romeo in secret to her bed. As they are making love there is a knock at the door. Romeo tries to jump up to escape, but instinctively Juliet pulls him back into an embrace. Finally, Romeo breaks away and escapes over the balcony.

The first time the scene was played, the episode on the bed was very brief, and one of the actors made the sound of the knock at the door. Grotowski (via Brook) ordered them to do it again. 'But this time', he said, 'I will give the knock at the door'. So Glenda and one of the male actors writhed unconvincingly side by side on the floor, waiting for Grotowski to give the knock. After what seemed a long time, Grotowski got up from behind his table and crossed the room. 'La position n'est pas correcte', he said, and moved the actor until he was lying on top of Glenda. 'Continuez', said Grotowski, and left them like that, while the rest of the group looked solidly on. Grotowski left them simulating sex for perhaps twenty minutes, with Glenda Jackson obviously trying to avoid being involved in passionate kisses while pretending to respond to them. They writhed together in total silence. Finally, Grotowski gave the knock. The couple separated with considerable relief – but the next move demanded that Glenda Jackson should pull him back for another embrace. It could have been very funny, but, given the tension Grotowski had created, there was a feeling of bear-baiting about it.

When the scene ended, Grotowski ordered a break for coffee. And he forbade anybody to discuss what they had seen. Glenda Jackson sat on her own in a chair with a coffee cup. I made some remark about the work being demanding, and she just shrugged. Afterwards, Grotowski asked a group of actors, including Glenda, to compose their faces into distorted masks, which they had to hold in place during the next improvisation. He took them through a story which ended, 'You go to a dance. While you are dancing, the door opens. The love of your life comes through the door. You go towards him. The mask drops. And you weep.'

Glenda Jackson went through all the moves with the same meticulousness, coolness and objectivity I'd admired in her work in the Theatre of Cruelty. But as she dropped the pretend mask she'd assumed, I didn't see any signs that Grotowski had broken through. I hoped he hadn't.

The next night – the last of Grotowski's visit – the RSC actors beat sin out of themselves by hammering fists and heads against the wall. And the day after that, we, the team, met to reappraise where the show was going. Adrian Mitchell and I had been thinking in terms of a rock band, lots of images from popular cinema and cartoon strips. Brook said that after Grotowski's visit we had to think again about form. And it was about this time that Denis Cannan was brought in to write the second act.

It says a lot about Brook's working method that even today I can't judge the extent to which Cannan's arrival was the result of manipulation or of what Brook saw as the force of circumstances. Certainly, you came to feel, working with Brook, that he always had a few cards up his sleeve that he only revealed when he thought it necessary. I always saw Cannan as one of the cards Brook produced. One interpretation could be that we non-estab-lished playwrights had failed to come up with what Brook saw as a workable script, and that in his desperation he went to someone who had at least had plays on the London stage.

An alternative explanation could be that he'd given the left-wing radicals their head up to a point and created something for a different kind of writer to bounce off, and that this is what he'd intended all along. I don't think that Brook had intended anything all along; I think he thought he was genuinely open to ideas, if the ideas were good enough. But I also think that he would never have found the ideas some of us were trying to put forward good enough, because they contradicted both his concept of what was 'good' theatre, and his political sensitivities. And I don't think it was an accident that the writer he brought into the team was a man who shared his own cultural background and his post-Second World War pessimism.

What I am certain of is that Brook wasn't at home in the cultural environment where Adrian Mitchell and others in the team belonged. We *liked* Hollywood movies, Judy Garland, Gershwin, Cole Porter, Irving Berlin and Co., jazz, rock 'n' roll, the Beatles. When Denis Cannan asked an actor what he saw when he heard the words 'burning negro', Adrian wrote to Peter that what I would see was 'a fat black man playing the piano and singing "Your feet's too big"'. Adrian Mitchell's spoken poetry connected with the genera-tion made aware of words by developments in pop music. And both the form and content of his poems were radical, but radical in a complex way. For example, at one point Adrian and myself were accused by Denis Cannan of being anti-American. I pointed out that we were, in fact, both avid fans of much that was American. (I could even respond to Barry Sadler's song *Fighting Soldiers from the Sky*, which seemed to me to express a genuine popular sentiment, even if it was one I disagreed with.) To me, much of the vitality of Adrian's songs came from his awareness of this kind of complexity. His song *My Girl Kate's Teaching in the States* catches this complexity. She pays her bills and gets her thrills by 'studying the influence of Yeats on Yeats' and what's wrong with that if it keeps her happy?

In the last verse Adrian writes:

> My son Tom writes chatty letters from
> Where they make bubonic plague.
> Scientific, it's terrific,
> Breeding germs to go into the Black Death Bomb,
> What's wrong with that? . . .
> If it makes him happy . . .

and the end of the song, he refers to himself as a poet

> What's wrong with that?
> If it makes me happy, if it keeps me happy,
> That's all that should matter to you.

The song faces unflinchingly up to ironies. But it's also got bounce, wit, a sense of mischief. I think that what both Adrian Mitchell and I were hoping for from *US* was a show which stated unequivocally that the American invasion of Vietnam had to be opposed and stopped because it was destructive of life, while at the same time celebrating the elements that make life enjoyable and worth preserving. There were two Americans in particular that Mitchell admired, in different ways: the Quaker, Norman Morrison, who poured petrol over himself and burnt himself alive outside the Pentagon; and Barry Bondhus of Minnesota, who, when summoned to the local draft board, emptied two buckets of human excrement over the papers in the office. Mitchell's song celebrating Bondhus ends:

> Walt Whitman
> Charlie Parker

Clarence Darrow
Ben Shahn
William Burroughs
Allen Ginsberg
Woody Guthrie
Tom Paine
James Baldwin
Joseph Heller
Dr Benjamin Spock
Mark Twain

Yes all of the beautiful prophets of America
Write across the Minnesota sky:
Look look look at Barry Bondhus –
That boy can fly.

Mitchell was much affected by Norman Morrison, the martyr, though temperamentally, he was closer to the 'sewer-realist child'. But it was the martyr, and the act of martyrdom, and particularly the futility of that act, that came to dominate the work on US after Cannan's arrival.

I was there during the day they spent on the benches. The exercise seemed to go on for hours. There were the six performers, standing motionless, apparently contemplating the Vietnam War. Every half-hour or so, one of them would take a step forward. It was one of the most boring theatre exercises I ever had to sit through, largely because I have never had much time for the school of acting which believes that what matters is what is going on inside the performer's head. Brook and the rest of us were sitting there watching, and it was all so solemn that I didn't have the courage to leave. Irreverently, I found myself wondering if the actors really were thinking about napalmed Vietnamese peasants, or if they were passing the time in the way I used to pass the time in silent Quaker meetings, going over the names of the players in favourite football or cricket teams, or simply counting the seconds in their minds.

Eventually, I began to entertain myself by writing a Brechtian scene about Buddhist monks planning a public burning. I based the characters on people I'd known in the Direct Action campaign against nuclear war. First of all, I thought, they'd have to decide which of them would burn himself or herself; they'd choose someone with the fewest social responsibilities, and also someone the movement could do without. Then they'd allocate jobs: one would get the petrol, another would see that the robes were well-laundered, so that it would look right, another would make sure that the press and TV were there. . . . When the tedious afternoon was over, I gave Brook the scribbled scene. He read it, said it was very funny, and gave it back to me.

I'd offered the scene as a counterpoint to all the inner meditation that was supposed to be going on. But it was after that afternoon when I came to the conclusion that, for all Brook's talk and writing about a theatre that went beyond naturalism, his theatre was, and had always been, basically naturalist in concept.

Meyerhold, Brecht, and, in Britain, Arden and Littlewood had rejected the theatre of representation, in favour of a theatre of demonstration. They had done so, not out of a wish to 'experiment', but because their need to show what they saw as the workings of society demanded different forms. Demystifying was at the centre of Brecht's work, and of Littlewood's too. Brecht wanted to show the audience the working processes of the theatre, because he didn't want the audience to be fooled by anybody, not even by himself. His approach to acting demanded that an actor should not say 'I am a king', but should say 'I am showing you how a king behaves'. Brook, on the other hand, asked his performers in *US* to look deep inside themselves and become the characters they were playing. And the characters Glenda Jackson and Mark Jones were asked to play were, as Cannan and Brook saw it, versions of themselves.

In the scene when Glenda tried to persuade Mark not to burn himself, it seemed to me that she got all the best lines. This wasn't surprising since burning yourself alive in London in 1966 would have been a pretty futile gesture. Glenda, Cannan and Brook seemed to revel in the hopelessness of protest; but perhaps that's an unfair subjective judgement on my part.

What isn't subjective is that by choosing to make this mock confrontation the centre of the second half of *US*, Brook shifted the show firmly away from being about the Vietnam War (which is what Adrian Mitchell and I had always thought it was about) and towards being about the inability of middle-class intellectuals in London to *do* anything about the war. Both of us tried to bring Vietnam back – Adrian had his songs, which broke the naturalist surface; I wrote two speeches. One offered as clear a defence of the American position as I was capable of writing; I hoped it would confront what I expected to be a converted audience with a position they would have to *think* against (this speech was included). The other was a speech which tried to say that what people in Hampstead argued about wasn't what really mattered; what really mattered was that as we sat there in the theatre, real people *were* being burnt alive, not by choice, but because anonymous American airmen were dropping napalm on them – and that this, not our feelings about it, was what the theatre should be confronting (this speech was rejected, after Glenda Jackson had said it destroyed the sense of the second half, which was probably true).

The key to the second half of *US* was the long speech, written by Cannan and spoken by Glenda Jackson, which culminated in her cry 'I WANT IT TO COME HERE ...'

It was this speech, more than anything else, which made Adrian Mitchell and me contemplate disassociating ourselves from the production. We didn't want the war to come here – we wished we could stop it. Beyond that I argued that the speech was intellectually dishonest. It presented life as being totally futile; it asked the audience to wallow in its own futility. Yet for several months, *we* had been engaged in an enthralling, all-consuming project. Even if the product was to be futile, the process had been enjoyable (as well as painful), had involved our imaginations, and most of all had engaged our minds. This enjoyment of work and engaging of minds were precisely what were left out of the Glenda Jackson speech. What the speech tried to communicate was a *feeling* of futility. It was all, in the end, about feelings – the feelings of one character generalised into a statement about Life.

When we objected to the speech, Brook invited us to find an answer to it. We spent a whole sleepless night trying to write answers. The problem was that in engaging the speech in the form in which it had been written we, too, were allowing ourselves to be dragged away from what mattered, into a discussion of *our* feelings – which we also thought were irrelevant.

In the early hours of the morning, in what must have been an all-night coffee bar, we found a joint solution. We decided that after Glenda had made her speech, one of us should walk on to the stage carrying a bunch of flowers and say, 'That was marvellous, darling. Would you do it again?'

When we suggested it to Brook, he assumed the hurt look he used to make you feel you were offending all his deepest sensibilities, and that was the end of the argument.

The Glenda Jackson speech seemed (and still seems) to me to reflect a certain confusion about the real processes involved in the making of *US*, and about the nature of Brook's relationship with actors. For weeks we were encouraged to believe that we were trying collectively to find a way of showing what was happening in Vietnam, and this is certainly what Brook wanted to happen. Yet, in the end, it was Brook the theatre magician who intervened, using all the conventional skills of a master director, to make the show work.

He virtually put together the first half of US in a morning. And there was no nonsense about the actors looking inside themselves and finding the way: he told them where to stand, where to move, which gestures to make. One actor, for example, had spent many hours studying what the Buddhist monks who burned themselves looked like as they died. He sat in contemplation, as he rehearsed, then practised falling over, slowly. But when it came to putting the show together, Brook strode forward, arranged the actor's arms and legs as he wanted them, and told the actor to remember the position. And Brook was, of course, right. What mattered was what the audience would *see*, not what was going on inside the actor's mind.

To watch Brook create stage images was to watch a master at work. Yet all the working processes had suggested that the actors must discover some deeper, inner quality which wasn't, to me at any rate, at all evident in the final performance.

Nothing was more typical of Brook's relationship with the actors than the way he presented them with the ending of the show. Throughout the summer we had been discussing American happenings, and how some kind of happening might come at the end. One night, over the usual working meal, a matter of days before the show was due to open, Brook introduced an idea: while discussing La Monte Young and John Cage, Reeves had synthesised two happenings – 'Why not burn a butterfly to Beethoven?' Brook picked up the idea, without the music. The concept was that an audience would have sat through several hours of accounts of people being burned, but that then, in front of their eyes, they would see something beautiful burned in reality. How would they react? Would they feel more strongly about the burning of a butterfly than about the burnings in Vietnam? If so, how would this affect their consciousness?

After Brook first introduced the idea, a furious argument broke out in the production team. Was it *right* to burn a butterfly? Brook's intensity made the question seem very important. We all found ourselves taking it very seriously. The general conclusion was that it wasn't right to burn a butterfly – although it was agreed that the question of how an audience would respond was intriguing. So the decision was taken that an actor would *pretend* to burn a butterfly instead.

Brook communicated the decision to the actor involved, but swore him to secrecy. The rest of the cast were not to know how the show would end until the dress rehearsal.

When, in the dress rehearsal, Bob Lloyd released live butterflies in the Aldwych and then apparently burned one, Brook called the actors together and asked them what they thought.

The same kind of earnest discussion that we had had in the restaurant broke out amongst the actors. Most of them said it wasn't right to burn the butterfly. But while the discussion was going on, one of the butterflies Bob Lloyd had released landed on the stage in front of a burly, earthy northern actor, Barry Stanton. He slammed his hand on the butterfly. Nobody seemed to notice what had happened. The discussions continued as earnestly as before. There were general sighs of relief when Brook revealed that the butterfly was only a bit of paper.

In these discussions with actors – as in the interrogations Denis Cannan had carried out – I always felt that most of the actors told Brook what he wanted to hear. They would try to gauge his mood and his feelings and say the right thing. An exception was Henry Woolf. One afternoon, before one of the final previews, Brook gathered all the actors together as he had before the first workshop began, and asked them what, after all this work, they felt about the Vietnam War. Most of them said exactly what they'd said on that first morning: the Vietnam War was terrible, it ought to be stopped, all wars were awful. But when it came to Henry Woolf, he made a long speech, beginning something like, 'If experiencing death, tragedy, torture, burning . . .' and continuing in the same rhetorical vein, until he suddenly ended, 'From now on, when I see the Vietnam War on television, I shall find it more *enjoyable*'. Neither Brook nor anybody else made any comment. Weeks later, at a party, I told Henry how much I'd liked his speech. He said, 'I didn't think anybody had noticed'.

There's no doubt that the actors were very committed to the work they'd done with Brook. Who else in British theatre could have given them such an experience in fourteen weeks' work? When I dropped in on the show after it had been running for some weeks, I was impressed by the sustained level of energy. Nobody had worked harder than Barry Stanton. But when I asked him what he thought about when he sat staring at the audience at the end of the performance he said, 'I'm hoping the last one will have left before the pubs close'. But then, of course, he might have been telling me what he thought *I* wanted him to say.

8   The first attempt at ritual: *Oedipus*

Brook on *Oedipus*:

This play, which, to all appearances is as Classical as any, seems to present the stuff of the material *most* directly. It comes straight from its time with extraordinary directness – it's as if a document were to be found in Rome which gave us the story of the Gospel at first hand without using the familiar words. It's not historical in the terms that Greek drama is – not full of references to mythologic lore. Rather in the way that *Prometheus* can communicate today through the notion of Man chained to a rock, without one's having a knowledge of the legend itself, so there's a chance that the specific quality of the Oedipus story will come over on its own: if you like, in the same way that *Godot* made an impact in San Quentin! In a way, because *Oedipus* seems so related to the theme of evasion, we're really going straight on from the Vietnam thing.

When Brook was asked to stage Seneca's *Oedipus*, the National already had contracted John Gielgud to play the lead and Kenneth Tynan had commissioned a translation from a BBC radio producer, David Anthony Turner. (In 1927 T. S. Eliot had described the play as broadcast drama.) Brook accepted because the play presented challenges both in form and content that were allied to his work at that moment, although he sometimes professed to having done it for John Gielgud. The play, while written only to be heard rather than performed on a stage, did retain the shape of its Greek model by having a major part for the chorus. This meant the destruction of the proscenium arch (or the invasion of the auditorium), begun in *US*, could be taken further; and the subject matter, in a form which strikingly exhibited less humanity than Sophocles, seemed more accurately to reflect an age in which millions had been killed in death camps. In such an enterprise Gielgud, with his natural vocal abilities and built-in stylisation, would prove an asset; however, the plodding text of a workaday translator would not. The first problem was to get a new text made, which took much time, not least because of the National's commitment legally to the one that they had commissioned. Many playwrights were discussed as possible candidates but rejected on the grounds that, although a brand new text was needed, a new play by an Arden, or a Bond, was not. A poet who could create poetic drama, rather than dramatic poetry, seemed to be what was needed, and when it was found that the most muscular and rigorous of the modern English poets also shared an enthusiasm for myth, Ted Hughes was offered the job. He wrote his own version, using his own images, but while keeping the form of the original he made radical innovations in the subject matter. Most noticeably he changed the choruses, which Seneca tended to use as showpieces for stoic philosophising and flamboyant rhetoric.

Brook went to the Brecon Beacons for a week to think about the play and came back with the idea of a box for the set. A box that opened and revealed nothing in it: the ultimate riddle, the Chinese box, the elusive solution – something that would concretely express the idea that there was no external answer to the basic questions. As the walls could fold down it would provide a platform for the play to be performed; the principals could enter up the walls, now ramps, for the main scenes, and sit outside during the rest of the action. Naturally the chorus, representing the people, would be among the people, scattered around the auditorium on the three levels of stalls, circle and gallery. The early design work was concerned with the texture and mechanical needs of the box; the model, which lived on the top of Brook's grand piano, went through many changes before gold was found to be the right colour, and that it would have to turn round and open. This apparently simple idea was then turned over to the workshops to build; it turned out to be a nightmare. The costumes also went through many stages in the search for the simple uniform which carried no overtones, the most neutral form possible without associations. The cast did not get to see the set until almost the first dress rehearsal as it took so long to solve the technical problems of building a cube which could both open and turn. When they did it gave rise to one of the best of Gielgud's *bons mots*, which had constantly lightened rehearsals: 'Oh, we should call the play *Cocks and Box*'.

Brook asked for a chorus of thirty-six, as well as the seven principals. The National Company was not large enough, it could only run to twenty-four in the chorus, but the question of size was a tactic on Brook's part. He did not believe the National Company had enough actors who could work in a flexible and physical way; by asking for so many he forced them to bring in people about whom he could have a say. Auditions, on similar lines to Theatre of Cruelty and *US*, were organised, but as these new actors would be joining the company and having to play in other productions anyone chosen by Brook then had to present themselves alone to Olivier for confirmation. Olivier settled for the standard contrasted speeches. Brook's auditions consisted of four actors, who did not know one another, working together for an hour. The basic exercise was that of playing tennis without a ball, in order to see how good they were at responding to a partner; the basic improvisations were putting characters in strange situations. One extremely experienced actor, asked to play Othello in a lift together with Macbeth and a couple of workmen, said that he really could not cope with this sort of thing, picked up his umbrella and left. Gradually a cast was formed, although there were long arguments over some of the choices, as much over members of the permanent company as over the newcomers: good speaking seemed to be the criterion for the management, whereas Brook was rather more interested in the personal dynamics exhibited by, or thought to be latent within, the actor. He finally got a chorus of twenty-nine, over half of whom were outside actors. It was finally agreed that Irene Worth would play Jocasta, although the fact that the National could not come up with another part she wanted to do proved a stumbling block for a long time – they were pursuing the concept of a company and therefore rightly reluctant to let people come in for just one part. Brook was adamant, believing her presence essential to get Gielgud over the obstacle course he was to face.

REHEARSALS

Oedipus was rehearsed for ten weeks.

The first exercise was a group attempt at 'To be or not to be': sitting or standing in a circle they attempted taking one word each with the objective of giving a unified reading of the line so that the listener would feel that one person was saying the line over and over in different ways – the character always being set by the actor who starts (ruminative, petulant, furious etc.). A line was chosen that was capable of infinite interpretation, and yet possessed a formal structure which required a certain rhythm to be followed. As a verse line it could not be broken with pauses of indefinite lengths, which would reduce it to prose. (Later, two lines from the original translation of the chorus were used, as at that time Hughes had not written his new versions: 'By fate are we driven, yield ye to fate' and 'Let me weave destiny to my own will'). It was a simple exercise which immediately produced great frustration because as the actor's ear became attuned it was quickly realised that it could not be done; yet it should have been done. It provided the basis for the chorus work in which lines and words were thrown from one side of the space to the other. It was also developed into passes, breaths and impulses which could take physical forms. The criterion was always the same: what was given had to be passed on in a living way. If it was simply passed on mechanically without anything being added then it soon became a dead impulse, a feeling of robots at work; if, on the other hand, what was given was not respected and something too strongly new was asserted then one had the feeling of being wrenched from side to side, of egos clashing. To find the precise point at which a living impulse could be truly passed around a group of people proved elusive for a long time, and took days and weeks of working away at simple exercises.

One of the cast gave an outline of the story of *Oedipus* and there followed a discussion on Tragedy, Fate, Will and Sin etc. The difference of attitudes in Ancient Greece and Modern Europe was drawn: sin was discussed with regard to Oedipus's sexual relationship to his mother and the 'Oedipus

Complex'. The question 'How much of one's life is governed by fate?' was discussed at length.

The imaginary game of tennis was played daily. The importance of making a mechanical movement into a dramatically meaningful one through the variance of pace was continually stressed. Mock fighting in pairs was practised to develop a precise response to the type and force of each imaginary blow. Brook already worked on the Japanese principle of JO – HA – Q on which he was to base the Paris work: each action must have a preparation (JO), then comes the action (HA) and then there must be a result (Q). Yoshi Oida (the Japanese actor who became a mainstay of Brook's troupe from 1968) was to comment later that so much of European acting seems simply to be the action: it is not adequately prepared for, nor is its effect fully considered and experienced. In 'the blows' exercise the immediate problem became that of actors continually anticipating what they were going to get and reacting to that instead of making themselves open to what actually happened. The control required over their physical energies seemed to make concentration much more difficult.

Work was done on sounds: actors were asked to respond to a sound the source of which they could not see; they knew the other actor was making it only with their body and clothes. They were asked to imitate it in the same rhythm, trying to make exactly the same texture of sound as before. This led to the group building up a collective sound by complementing, rather than imitating, the first until they were all involved in a jam session of natural sounds. Then the actors were given small objects to beat together (wood, tin, comic books, plastic flowers) and the importance of using rhythm as a means of communicating became clear. Strong scraping sounds might be very striking but usually precluded the actor making them from keeping in touch with the others. Rhythm again seemed of paramount importance when Hughes's first chorus, which arrived on the third day, was read: it had a relentless pounding beat to it.

The first time parts of the chorus were read in the theatre, with the actors scattered around the auditorium (this was during the first week of rehearsal), both the potential of the idea and the enormous difficulty of making it truly work, other than as a technical gimmick, became very clear.

The work in pairs developed; mock fighting gave way to mock punishment, where the receiver is prepared but cannot offer resistance or retaliation. Then one actor executed a movement or gesture that he considered as difficult as possible for his partner to imitate, the aim being to find and exploit weak spots in one another. The most difficult physical impulses produced were then practised by the group as a whole. One person would perform the gesture once, the rest would try to imitate. The actors then used this method to try to build a character, beginning with the external, physical characteristics and using rhythm as a basis for the development of movement and expressions. They then presented them to each other, doing it once quite quickly and asking the others to follow them. It showed how difficult it was to pick up someone else's idea and physical movements correctly with the same amount of energy or conviction. Brook said that 'the impact and reaction in the mock-fighting exercise when in slow motion should resemble a stone being thrown into a pool and the ripple slowly spreading over it' – the size of this 'ripple' therefore depending on the size of the stone. In most cases, however, there still seemed to be a barrier where the actions did not produce a correct reaction, but one which was almost premeditated by the recipient. The spontaneity of the exercise took a long time to achieve.

Each actor, beginning standing, was asked to deteriorate slowly into what he felt was the lowest form of life. When he reached this physically he was asked to find the sound to express the mental condition of complete 'nothing'. These positions were then frozen so each actor seemed like a robot, then slowly they came back to life, like a person recovering from a long illness.

Brook introduced an American jazz drummer who was expert in t'ai chi to the company: he taught the basic steps of the Chinese 'meditation-in-movement' science and this was then used as a daily preparation. He told the company:

t'ai chi is infinity, the absolute, it creates from 'no limit'. It contains dynamic and stoic movement, it is the mother of Yin and Yang, of everything male and female. It is the root of motion, which is division, and of stillness, which is union. It must neither be overdone nor underdone – it must be exact. Comprehension comes from growing understanding plus effort and this leads one gradually to full enlightenment.

Because of the size of the company it was divided into two groups to make the work more manageable. Both groups were put through the same exercises and improvisations, although with different results.

'The essence is the word, the word is a picture, and the picture is in you.' Work was done on images – including cats, tigers, eagles and reptiles – which expressed this. The purpose was to explore them in miniature at first and then gradually to allow physical imitation to evolve, each actor depicting the subject in different moods and situations. Then each actor presented their image to the group using the stages: relaxation, preparation, presentation, relaxation. The movement was then broken down so that each had to present it using firstly one part of the body and then sounds. Then it was presented in two rhythms, the first a walk or prowl, the second a movement or gesture – not a realistic imitation but one based on oriental theatre.

There was much reading aloud of verse, as an exercise in rhetoric; when it was Latin verse the rhetorical rhythm was easy to achieve, but with English the actors usually picked up a realistic rhythm since they understood the meaning of the words.

The first mask exercise involved each person developing a facial mask similar to the Greek model, where all the features are exaggerated. When it was fixed a mirror and a person standing at a distance of a hundred feet were used as a means of finding the limits of expression. Then various parts of the body were moved to as many positions as possible so that a character was built up. Then another mask was used, another character developed by playing to a distant watcher, and finally the actor played a scene between the two characters he/she had created.

The first eight days of rehearsal used only part of the company as *Volpone* was still in rehearsal. When the new actors arrived they were given a 'crash course' in the basic exercises. The difference between them and the first actors showed that much progress had been made. As they arrived the other basic exercise was introduced, the mirror: the attempt by two people to do the most simple basic movements at exactly the same time without either leading the other; usually done for ten to fifteen minutes it is an exercise in concentration, as eye contact has to be maintained throughout, and it brings members of the company closer together in work. It was to be replaced later in Paris with sticks.

One of the actors had been studying kendo, a Japanese martial art, and brought two of his instructors to rehearsal – one young, the other old. What was impressive was that the young instructor, extremely fit and agile, could be defeated constantly by the apparently frail and withering old one. The art of kendo is to assert oneself over one's opponent and this is achieved both with precise timing and an extraordinary voice, the technique of which is known as kyai. The voice technique develops a strong throat capable of making steel-like sounds, and some of the exercises to produce this were quickly adopted into the daily round of exercises.

(The company was solemnly told that there were two ways of attaining kyai, the slow and the quick. The slow was patient study and exercise over many years. What was the quick? asked the English actors, eager for self-improvement at a fast rate. Well, they were told, in Japan it can be acquired in a month by taking a course with a Master. What happened on such a course? Every morning those wishing to develop kyai would file in and kneel down, in a row. A bell was then placed round the neck so it rested in the middle of the chest. All the student had to do was to make a sound with a resonance so that the bell would ring. The Master walked about with a large bamboo stick occasionally hitting the shoulders of the students in order to relieve the tension. After eight hours they stopped. Apparently, the students had to be carried out as they were, by then, unable to walk. The next morning they returned and repeated the exercise. The English actors asked, would not such constant effort destroy the vocal chords? Of course, said the Japanese. What was the success rate, then, of such a technique? Oh, he said, usually thirty start and at the end of the month perhaps two have acquired kyai, the rest being apparently speechless.)

Two passages concerning the effect of plague on the body were read aloud. Several actors became 'plague-infested rats' and the rest had to get from one end of the room to the other blindfold, without touching them. Anyone who was touched had to develop, using his realistic knowledge and his imagination, the symptoms as they had been described. Slowly the rehearsal room became filled with suffering, dying, plague-ridden people. Immediately afterwards the actors sat in a tight circle and produced a sound which exemplified the suffering they had just enacted. This produced an extraordinary noise which suggested pain. Then there was a discussion of personal experience of fate, dealing with premonition and superstition. 'Is every aggressive action an act of fate or is it the aggressor's WILL? If it is an act of fate, is the responsibility there taken out of the hands of the evildoer?'

Rhetorical rhythm was further explored. Actors were asked to express personal feeling through a Latin text. Recalling a moment of intense anger each person had to express it, compromising between complete re-enactment and straight narrative. The exercise was then repeated, gradually whittling the text down from sixteen to eight, four, two and finally one line. Most actors tended to re-enact a scene and use the Latin as a means of expressing anger with an Italian accent. So the text was approached mechanically concentrating on meaning: this was evaded as the actors simply adopted a character. Only when the exercise was repeated behind masks did the realism disappear and some actors find the right tone of 're-enactment once removed'.

The description of the sacking of Troy from Marlowe's *Dido, Queen of Carthage* was read both in part and complete by each actor. Then lines were read and passed from person to person, with and without masks, standing close together and far apart, each time trying to retain the mood and rhythm of the person who began the passage. The passage, full of horrific images, seemed ineffective when read aloud, so the situation was stripped to its bare essentials and each actor concentrated on finding the one sound that would be truly expressive of the horror. Several managed to find quite remarkable ones.

During the first week it became necessary to establish certain details about the auditorium. Brook and his collaborators slipped in during a break to find the director of *Volpone*, Tyrone Guthrie, and his wife enveloped in a blanket in the middle of the stalls, sipping coffee from a thermos (it was mid-January and there was snow outside). While Brook enthusiastically embraced them both nothing seemed more contrasted than this old 'man of the theatre', in the midst of a Victorian building, directing Ben Jonson as a series of visual gags and blunting the satire so as not to disturb the equilibrium of the goodly National audience, and the *'enfant terrible'*, hell-bent on destroying that comfortable relationship with a ritual that would shock them to their very core.

After the opening of *Volpone* it became possible to work in the theatre. First the company tried to find resonating sounds within themselves which they passed around the auditorium to each other. The work of fluently passing impulses which had been built up in the rehearsal room disappeared as soon as placed in the auditorium, and it became very clear that such work could only be usefully done there.

One day was spent exploring 'the putting out of one's eyes'. Actors gave realistic and stylistic re-enactments, both of which became quite horrifying. This led to another terrifying exercise. Each actor adopted a state of being and then gradually lost the use of his/her limbs, eyes etc. and became completely lifeless. The actor then slowly returned to life, isolated in a small room, found one object upon which to focus all the attention, then reached out and grasped for life outside the room. Each person was then asked to find the personal circumstances in which they would sacrifice one or more stages of life, taking the number from life to death as seven. Each actor stood on a bench and was told to take one step each time they decided to make a sacrifice, the seventh taking him over the edge. This exercise was stopped after ten minutes because of the extreme tension that was created.

When Richard Peaslee, the musical director, arrived, more rhythmical exercises were introduced, particularly using difficult time signatures like 5/8, 7/8, 11/12 (dramatised by chants like 'Hennessy, Hennessy, Hanky Bannister' – brands of whiskey sold in the USA); and by dividing the company up into groups, he improvised harmonies and orchestral textures with their voices. Work was done on creating true echoes: five actors would repeat a line ('Fury is my strength'), each saying one word less than the person before and so decreasing and producing a tailing-off effect.

The company listened to a radio series, assembled by A. L. (Bert) Lloyd, called *The Voice of the Gods* which consisted of tribal chants from all over the world, including Shamans from Africa, Tibetan monks and the Indians of the Upper Orinoco who produce their own version of Stravinsky's *Rite of Spring*. This threw up many vocal techniques which were practised, particularly hard consonants. Also of interest and use was the belief of many of the tribes that God exists in the air and can be conjured up through breathing: the Whirling Dervishes practise this in their dancing and this was to lead Colin Blakely to perform one of his speeches turning and turning at ever increasing speed as though possessed.

Work on rhythm in the auditorium continued until it was possible for the chorus to remain in contact with each other only through sound and not, as had been necessary at the start, when they had to see each other in order to pass an impulse from one to another.

The source for the Bacchus chorus was found in the Maori haka; as the motive behind the haka is the destruction of an enemy the overall tone is one of aggression. The company contained two New Zealanders who taught it to the rest.

Much work was done on a basic exercise called the 'Hole in the road'. Brook asked the actor to walk along a road with a friend and to imagine that at a specific moment a hole opened up in the road immediately in front of them; the objective then was to find a sound which expressed the actor's own feeling of shock and danger at the precipice in front of them and yet at the same time to turn round to the friend to warn of the danger. The other basic exercise in this search was 'Chronos'. 'Chronos' is a picture by Goya which depicts a giant about to eat one of his own children. Brook asked the actors to find a way of communicating the idea of this picture to a blind Chineseman. Blind, therefore it had to be expressed in sound; a Chineseman, therefore descriptive words could not be used. Narrative was discarded as it was soon found that the least effective sounds were any to do with eating; merely touching the surface of the idea they became ultimately funny. What succeeded best were sounds which, without telling the story, set up in the listener such feelings of awe and which gave him the sense of something truly monstrous that although he might not be able to say 'Ah, that's a man eating his own children', he could say and would feel that there was something violent and monstrous happening.

The finished script arrived from Hughes after four weeks' rehearsal, which left six weeks to work on it. At once the choruses were explored in the light of techniques that had been developed and played with in the rehearsal room. Three groups were organised to find human sound accompaniments to the long speeches of Oedipus, Jocasta and Creon. The principals now were split off from the chorus and rehearsed separately. The first chorus was divided into five groups. Each actor had to find a distinctive and personal sound while being acutely aware of the other members of the group, to find the fine line between the abstract and the literal. These exercises were likened to jazz improvisations where there exists an undertone from which a 'solo' emerges when personally provoked. Each of the five groups approached the same problem differently: the idea of a city languishing under the terror of the plague.

Saturdays saw long rehearsals devoted to improvisation and the exploration of happenings; only some of the company took part: those who had experience of free improvisation and those without inhibitions. The object was to find something to present at the end of the play, something which would break the unbearable tension of the death of Jocasta and the self-blinding of

Oedipus, but which would not destroy it. The improvisations were done to try to get the actors through their natural self-indulgence towards something genuinely celebratory. Many kinds of work were done: animals, robots, nursery rhymes played by de Gaulle, Marilyn Monroe, Puss in Boots, cinema clichés (like Westerns, sci-fi, Gangsters), fairy tales. A gruesome photograph from Vietnam was taken as a basis for comedy. Many parodies were done. One scene became known as *Oedipus, A Taste of Mummy*. The workshops, with much sniggering, produced dildoes (of great beauty, clearly being made with much love) which, when strapped on, gave rise to scenes of Rabelaisian delight; within forty-eight hours of the first such improvisation reports came back from the RSC at the Aldwych, a few hundred yards across the river, of the group orgies that were taking place at the Vic. Reports of these orgies were, unfortunately, much exaggerated. Moreover, the best of this work proved impossible to recreate on stage at the end of the play, although much work was done to try to find a structure for orgiastic revelry which would be a successful compromise between a set pattern and free expression. There was also the problem of finding the proper bridge from the ending of the play to the celebration. A tape of regular rhythmic beats was played to the chorus, scattered around the auditorium, and each actor picked up the rhythm through heavy breathing, gradually developed it into laughter and then pushed it into hysteria; snake-like movements followed and they made their way on to stage carrying the rhythm continually repeating 'Oedipus, eyes, mother, prick'.

During the sixth week a mock-up of the box was set up in the rehearsal room and its final dimensions decided on. A large flat structure covered in several different shades of gold paper was used to choose the correct colour for the costumes. Without make-up and wearing identical brown costumes of slacks and jumpers the actors became merely faces and hands. Various eye-patches for Oedipus and Tiresias were tried out, plain black pieces seeming the most compelling and the least distracting.

In week seven work was in two groups: the principal speeches and the finale. Hughes arrived to make modifications in the text. At the end of the week a set pattern was established for the parodies of the birth of Oedipus, the crossroads, the Sphinx and the plague.

For the last three weeks of rehearsal, the National was on tour and although the theatre was constantly available for rehearsal it was impossible ever to get the entire company together at one time. Brook spent hours, often late into the night, closeted with the actors playing the named parts.

The chorus was placed around the auditorium and on either side of the stage. Some of those in the auditorium had to stand on pillars in the midst of the seats, for if they had been behind the audience they would not have been able to maintain contact with each other. They stood on small platforms to raise them up, but the fire authority demanded that they have safety belts holding them to the columns, in case the motion of acting should lead them to fall on top of the spectators. (Latecomers were sometimes known to ask them for programmes.) The grouping of the chorus on three levels, as well as the stage, enabled many physical effects to be achieved, as in the chorus at the beginning of Act V: when Icarus fell from the sky, the voices began in the gallery, continued in the circle and reached earth in the stalls. The effect was like Breughel's picture of the boy falling into the water.

There were many technical problems with the box, as well as with the texture of the gold covering it, which had to be completely redone after it was first seen on the stage. Such was the confusion that both the public dress rehearsals were played against a black backdrop. As the finale was frantically experimented with Brook decided to having a large golden phallus made which would be ceremonially carried on to the set and unveiled during the carnival. When the management finally saw this there was much resistance, and after the second dress rehearsal Olivier called Brook into his dressing room and told him to cut the whole end, saying it did not work and was ruining a wonderful production. The row continued until two in the morning, resulting in a smashed mirror (Olivier threw a glass) but Brook, by dint of threatening to walk out, won the right to keep the end. It was somewhat modified for the first night, but returned more graphically after that, although it never achieved what was intended: to get the audience on its feet joyously dancing and celebrating.

OEDIPUS: PERFORMANCES

Brook wanted the audience to treat *Oedipus* as one possible vehicle to answer the need for a true contact with a sacred invisibility (God?) through the theatre; but the production only seemed to underline the impossibility of making such contact now. The kind of awe it generated had more to do with being deeply respectful of actors doing technically very demanding things than getting in touch with something primal. As it never operated on the audience in the way that Sophocles' play did in the ancient Greek festivals, the Dixie band and the glistening phallus at the end seemed merely intellectual ideas. Because that true tension had not been experienced in the first place it was hardly possible to release it in an orgiastic way.

Yet the production was most successful in finding a stylisation capable of dealing with such a story and such a text: it had the feeling of being twentieth-century theatre and effectively banished those toga and fluted-pillar abominations for ever (best exemplified by the stylised delivery of Colin Blakely's speech describing his descent into hell).

The play began with a closed golden cube rotating in the middle of the stage. On either side sat actors, those who enacted the principals including the chorus leader, and throughout the auditorium at every level were the thirty members of the chorus. A low humming started which grew louder; a single note developed into harmony. As the light shining on the spinning cube became brighter, the reflections from the highly polished gold surface swirled around the auditorium dazzling the audience like a deadly sun. The actors began beating with their hands and the three principals moved towards the cube. 'Sh-sh-sh' slowly becomes 'Show'. One voice said 'Show us a simple riddle', others picked it up, played with it, broke it into fragments; it became the plague chorus. Oedipus' first speech was accompanied by vocal beats.

The chorus invoked the gods – 'Yo-o-ah Bacchus' – and was accompanied by atonal elephant horns. As the sound increased the cube opened. Creon emerged and asked not to be forced to reveal what he had discovered in Hell, but Oedipus said 'If silence is forbidden, freedom is finished. He that is silent when required to speak shakes the stability of government.' So Creon was forced to begin to tell the story of the crossing of river Dirce, the descent into Hell and the meeting with the ghost of Laius. He suddenly shifted his tone from the fear of revealing such a secret to the fear he himself felt at the meeting. He spoke the words of the oracle in a high-pitched voice over a background of chorus humming. The words conjured up Laius' ghost for the listeners and as he saw him Creon began to spin round holding out his arms, slowly at first and then gradually picking up speed until he was whirling at top speed; as he reached the lines 'Thebes will take the earth from him, His father will take the sky' he collapsed on the floor barely able to speak, repeating the whirling movement by dragging his body around and pounding his hands on the floor until he was so exhausted he could not move. What was communicated here had nothing to do with the *character* of Creon; Blakely transformed himself with the words in order to communicate the universal fear of death.

The choruses likewise were constantly being mined for sounds that would convey emotions and ideas to the audience rather than conveying frightened or plague-ridden people. The humming at the start (echoing the resonance of Tibetan monks in their ritual for the dead), the heavy rhythmic breathing which punctuated Jocasta's first speech, the groans, the dry clicking noises all gave a sense of what was happening, even if the words were sometimes blurred (as was inevitable with some of the chorus at the back of the stalls and some at the back of the gallery). What you heard depended on where you sat, but you could not fail to be caught up in what was happening. Sometimes there were suggestions of physical re-enactments. In the Icarus chorus, as Icarus fell the sound literally plunged from the top of the theatre to the bottom. Oedipus and Jocasta spoke a duologue both lying flat on separate opened ramps of the cube which suggested people sharing a nightmare in bed.

When Phorbas entered from the back of the auditorium, the house lights came on the stalls to illuminate the inevitable entrance of the person who brought the fatal message. The cube opened fully for the first time when the final truth was known. It served to enclose the unknown and ultimately was shown to be empty – at least physically. It also mirrored the revelations that were made.

Ronald Pickup played the Messenger speech with a staccato rhythm on a monotone, although the tone gradually heightened in pitch as he approached the climax. The declamation itself was flat, but agony was expressed through it so that the facts of what happened became more moving than any demonstration from the teller of his emotion alone could ever be. Although acutely aware of the significance of what he saw, and we are left in no doubt as to his own reaction emotionally to it, what comes through most clearly to us is the event itself: 'Blood came spouting out over his face and head. In a moment he was drenched.' We see what he saw rather than seeing him telling it, although his hands instinctively were raised to his face.

When the Messenger was done Gielgud simply put on two patches of black over his eyes and stood up: he had blinded himself. He moved stiffly, his head erect as if caught in some giant vice. Jocasta committed suicide by impaling herself on a sword which she thrust into her womb. This was represented by Irene Worth slowly lowering herself on to a spike, which is clearly seen to be about a foot away from her; her deep groans emitted in rhythmic gasps grate on one until she finally dies upright and open mouthed. Although not represented realistically, this was regarded by the management as a moment of pure horror of such awfulness, with its overtones of sadomasochistic sexuality, that it should not be witnessed by the girls' schools to which matinée tickets had already been sold. At that performance there was the absurdity of the directors coming on stage at the end of the fourth act to describe the rest of the play and give those teachers who felt such an image would be disturbing to their pupils a chance to leave: two groups did so. Afterwards there were mutterings about Lambs' Tales from Shakespeare and Mr Bowdler, and much wondering about what happened in the classroom when the story of Oedipus was taught: did those teachers change the end because they found if disturbing? Or perhaps they knew what Martin Esslin said:

the only sphere of primeval awe and primitive emotion left to twentieth-century mass man is sex and therefore all ritualistic theatre has to veer towards sexual shocks. Brook is no exception here.

After the tragedy came the carnival; the mighty sound of a bull-roarer reverberated through the house and a band swaggered on to the stage with a brassy

'Oh yes we have no bananas'. Coloured lights made it look like the *Folies Bergères* (the lighting designer's idea of liberating sex). Most, but not all, of the cast (for there were several dissenters who declined to take part, including the resilient Colin Blakely) donned cloaks and animal masks and danced round a giant phallus which now stood in the middle of the disintegrated cube, leading some people to believe that this was the answer to the riddle.

Ronald Pickup, on rehearsing the Messenger in *Oedipus*, recounts

Brook helped me by telling me to rehearse the speech as if I were a gargoyle, a kind of monster. 'Just envisage yourself as a strange shape from a Gothic cathedral or a monster out of a voodoo ceremony, or something like that'. I then rehearsed it in a much more grotesque way than it could be done in public. I was using the text, but he said 'Feel free about warping words'. The word *stand* didn't have to sound like *stand*. One could do anything with any of the series of words, but one was really concentrating on sound from back beyond the time words were invented; just having the words vaguely sitting on top of it. I remember that exercise most vividly because I think that was the time when I felt it really broke through. And the most ugly, awful – but for the speech real and right – sounds were coming out. And then, as time went on, it was possible to integrate them. I also went through a period when I used to do it very statically, right from the beginning. And then it started to go a bit dead. And only some two or three days before we opened, he said: 'Forget all that business about coming forward and just doing it there. Do it in slow-motion, glazed time, as if you'd been stunned by what you've seen. Or if you want a naturalistic image, think of it being like a watchman, ringing a bell, announcing the news, going along the street, telling it to the waiting population. 'So out of that came the thing of sludging through blood. Which also gave it more weight – because I'm a very lightweight actor. It made me feel more weighty than I'd ever felt before – heavier, in a good way.

Gielgud on *Oedipus*:

I'm determined not to vary in performance. I don't think I do anymore, but *Oedipus* did vary – the whole production as well as individual performances, even though we had ten weeks' rehearsal. It was a very unpredictable and variable emotional experience: almost impossible to play well, except for one or two rare performances. . . . We never quite knew what Peter Brook was driving at. He never showed us models of the set or decided till the last minute what costumes we were to wear. The management were very upset because he would not decide what we were to wear or what scenery was to be built. We had an exhausting time during the rehearsals. Peter enjoys his authority: he would walk into the rehearsal room and say curtly 'No newspapers'. It was rather like being in the army and I dreaded it; but at the same time I knew I wanted to be part of such an experiment. Peter Brook battered me down to my lowest ebb saying 'You can't do that, it's awfully false and theatrical'. He gave me extraordinary, difficult things to do. He had the shepherd come through the audience, and brought up the house lights. I used to absolutely dread it, because I had never played with the fourth wall down, never before looked at the audience. But I found that when I went into *Forty Years On* afterwards, where I had to be aware of the audience nearly all the time and speak directly to them (as if they were parents who had come to see a school play), I was able to play in a very relaxed and intimate way. This would once have terrified me, but I found it comparatively easy, to my great surprise, and I attributed my relaxation to the strict discipline of the *Oedipus* work, which had broken down many of my personal mannerisms and self-consciousness. In the big scene in *Oedipus* when I discovered what had happened – that I had killed my father and married my mother – I had to deliver a highly emotional speech kneeling on the ground, then get up quietly and go to sit at the side of the stage on a stool with the chorus, quite impassively, while the Messenger came on and described my putting my eyes out. At the end of his ten-minute monologue I had to get up and go into the voice and manner of the blinded Oedipus, trying to produce a strange strangled tone which Peter had invented at rehearsal with endless experiment. Technically that was one of the most difficult things that I have ever done in my life – very good, I suppose, for my ego. I have always been sorry that there was no record of *Oedipus*, either on disc or film, because the sound of it was so impressive.

9 Pushing the boat out: The Round House *Tempest*

By 1967 Jean-Louis Barrault, who had been given one of the two Comédie-Française salles in Paris – the Odèon – and was running it as a state theatre, had also taken over the Théâtre-des-Nations. This had existed for years at the Sarah Bernhardt as a three-month season of visiting foreign opera, ballet and theatre companies. Barrault was now presenting this during the summer at the Odéon, but he wished to capitalise on the wealth of international talent passing through and make something more interesting out of it. He formed a committee of international theatrical luminaries (Weigel, Strehler, *et al.*) and they came up with the idea of having a workshop throughout the entire festival in which the visitors could participate. They invited Brook to run it. Brook rejected the suggestion, pointing out little could be done with Japanese puppeteers for a week, or American dancers for three days, but offered to try and find a way to work with actors from different countries, providing they could all work together for a reasonable period of time. They agreed to form a group to work together for two months. Such a group could then provide a framework should any of the passers-by at the Odéon wish to join in. Brook assembled nine English actors (mainly from the RSC), five American (from the Open Theatre), seven French (from auditions) and one Japanese (who was Noh-trained). He also had three collaborating directors: English, American and Argentinian.

The space Brook found to work in was an exhibition hall in the Gobelins, the national furniture factory (Le Mobilier National) in the south-west of Paris, where the main occupation appeared to be the reupholstering of Louis Quatorze chairs for de Gaulle. It was a thirties concrete building of straight lines. The exhibition hall came close to Brook's idea of an empty space, being some 150 feet long, forty feet wide and twenty-five feet high. One of the actors called it 'a great barn'. Scattered throughout, dividing the space into bays, were large scaffolding panels fifteen feet high. Brook later had the canvas stripped off these so that the whole space became visible, they also provided a two-tiered structure on which to work.

Brook chose as raw material Shakespeare's *The Tempest*. Although he had already done it twice at Stratford-upon-Avon, he felt he had never reached the heart of the play. He said that what was extraordinary about it was that if you were to describe it to someone who did not know it then it would appear to be the greatest play in the world, as it contained all of Shakespeare's major themes which had been explored at length in other plays. However, the text itself never seemed able to deliver what it promised. Perhaps the romance form, and the long exposition of the second scene, had removed something vital from its make-up, leaving it to be wondered at by academics but failing to be ultimately a rewarding theatrical experience. He therefore regarded it as rich material for exploration, because each of the themes could be looked at and opened up without the feeling of doing violence to a perfectly formed text. Indeed the multiplicity of themes made it very inviting.

He thought the play on the stage had always seemed sentimental and pallid. He wanted to see if a free approach to the material could help the actors find the power and violence that he believed to be in the play, whether they could find new ways of performing all the other elements which were normally presented in a very artificial way, and whether these demands would extend the range of the actor's work. Most importantly, he hoped that by mixing foreign actors together he could achieve some synthesis of style which would overcome the conventional passivity of the bourgeois audience.

Brook proposed to do this by considering the story from the beginning: a deserted island occupied only by a spirit on to which comes a pregnant witch who has been cast out from Algiers. She imprisons the spirit and gives birth to a monster. Meanwhile, the donnish ruler of Milan, who prefers the library to politics, is usurped by his brother and cast out in a boat with his daughter; when he reaches the island he frees the spirit and enslaves the monster. All of this basic material, culled from Prospero's narrative in the long second scene, would be explored before arriving at the scenes of Shakespeare's play. Also, his sources would be explored, particularly five *commedia dell'arte* scenarios, including the 'echo' and 'eating spaghetti' scenes, as well as some of the 'Autos sacrimentales' of Calderón (one of the collaborating directors, Victor García, specialised in such material). The physical work to be done would be a direct continuation from *Oedipus*. This much Brook planned.

However, the Thursday before the work began Daniel Cohn-Bendit addressed a meeting of the students of the Committee of March 22 in the courtyard of the Sorbonne: they were evicted, an action which was to trigger off what became known as the students' revolt of 1968. On the first day of rehearsal actors made their way home through tear gas, past burning cars and across lines of helmeted police wielding shields and long truncheons. For a month, work continued at the Gobelins as the external situation deteriorated, it being stopped only for the company to join in marches of solidarity from the République to the Bastille. Outside the work discussions continued constantly, usually through the night, but what happened outside hardly seemed to affect, or to be fed into, what happened in rehearsals: Brook's concern was the search for essence, for basic fundamental truths; he did not want to be caught up in the day-to-day activity of what happened on the streets as he felt that that could only lead to a 'living newspaper' kind of art. His main preoccupation was to continue working, and to that end he managed to negotiate the right of the group as an international one to go on without appearing to breach the general call to strike. The French actors were particularly concerned with that, and also showed a considerable ability to spend days talking. While de Gaulle fought off the threat to the republic with comments about dogs fouling their kennels, Brook meticulously took *The Tempest* apart. Every theme, every image, every action, every relationship (actual and potential) was explored: magic, comic, tragic, politic, lyric, primitive. The shipwreck, the unholy conspiracy, the wedding, the ship of fools, the drowning man, the abysm of time, the two attempted murders, the Commonwealth, the golden age, the brave new world, love at first sight, the garden of delights, the Seven Deadly Sins, the tower of Babel – all were used as the basis for extended improvisations.

But Brook could not change the status of the workshop – it was government funded and was taking place on government property. During the second week, Barrault lost his theatre when it was occupied by the students, and as he made a speech from the stage merely asking them to respect the building and its contents, particularly the costumes (which they did not), rather than denouncing the takeover unequivocally, it was clearly only a matter of time before he was fired. (He came to London for a day during the Round-House performances and gave the actors a master-class based on the breathing exercises he had learnt from Artaud.) When that happened the international workshop went into limbo and the non-French departed catching what flights they could from darkened military airports in northern France as the country gradually came to a halt – literally, as the petrol ran out. The French contingent decided that in all conscience they could not leave to go to work in London at such a time, and remained to have endless *contestations*, so it was the English-speaking actors and the Japanese actor who sat in London for the first two weeks of June waiting for Brook to raise the money for the work to continue; he did this using the RSC as a base and getting contributions from the Arts Council and half-a-dozen theatre managers, including David Merrick. He also managed to get the Round House to work in.

The Round House was a space no less remarkable than the Mobilier National. Arnold Wesker had taken it over the year before for Centre 42, but could not raise the money necessary to turn it into a well-equipped performing space. Consequently, it had only housed art exhibitions and rock 'n' roll shows; it was to be another ten years before proper seating and acoustic panels were installed. Then it was still a nineteenth-century engine shed with a basic playing area eighty feet in diameter, beyond which were the individual engine bays and, above them, a circular gallery. In Paris, Brook had wanted to do something which would make the audience walk around – he had considered the idea of having a play in ten scenes each played continuously in its own area so that the spectators could walk on when they had seen each one. He began in the Round House by having scaffolding built similar to that of the exhibition divisions in Paris, and put each cross-shaped piece on castors. He would devise an action which flowed through the space and compelled the audience to move to keep up with it. The audience who sat on the scaffolding were moved with it. In this sense it was a natural follow-on to the spatial experiment of putting the chorus into the auditorium at the Old Vic.

There were no proper seats or benches or area designated for the spectator. They could sit or stand wherever they liked. There was a series of long, low oriental-type platforms near the outer edge of the circle on two sides, with a kind of low double runway, or hanimichi, extending from the ends of one set of the platforms. There were six movable scaffolds, some the shape of a long 'I', others the shape of a cross; they each had two levels, one at two feet and one at twelve feet. There were five musicians playing drums and percussion; the lighting was white and very bright. Five performances were given to invited audiences of about 500 people. As they entered the company was scattered around the space warming up physically and vocally; they wore the mixture of clothes they had worn in rehearsal – a karate suit, a kimono, a track suit, T-shirts and jeans.

The hour-long presentation contained various styles: songs, incantation, ritual, mime, acrobatics. Scenes were staged within the framework of the scaffolding, played with a two-dimensional framework on the one-foot wide planks; others involved the scaffoldings being moved around the space. Less than 500 lines of Shakespeare's play were used.

The limbering and ball playing gave way to the mirror exercise. Of this exercise, Brook says

> The mirror exercise is an exercise by which two actors begin to work in harmony. Then four, then six and then eight, and then twelve, until the whole group is working in harmony. This is a basis of working, the product of an actual series of exercises of many different sorts by which the group works very freely together.

The mirror exercise combined with a low hum that got louder. They then broke the mirror and ran to various parts of the set and faced the audience with archetypal masks (but made with their own faces) and equivalent characterisations; they accompanied them with animal sounds, moans, howls, whispers, grunts, gibberish. The masks had come from work on the Seven Deadly Sins and were intended to present a variety of passengers just before the shipwreck.

Some actors played the people, some the ship itself; Ariel evoked the storm, his Japanese kimono sleeves functioning as wings with which he called up the spirits, using a mixture of Japanese and non-verbal sounds. The crew shouted, 'Lost, lost, all is lost' as the storm increased. Meanwhile Miranda and Prospero were speaking in long intoned sentences, all punctuation gone.

As Irving Wardle wrote in *The Times*:

Lines, often reduced to a couple of words, were delivered in a dehumanised chant and then taken up and explored by the company in movement and choric speech: sometimes in the form of mass action, and sometimes broken down into smaller relationships. One preoccupation which ran through the programme was the question of power: how a single actor can impose his will on the rest of the company; or how a pair of actors, swapping identical lines, can match their separate strings. The other preoccupation was with isolation, shown – whenever ensemble contact broke down – by detached figures pursuing solitary ritual transformations into animals and machines.

The crew landed on the island half-dead. Miranda and Ferdinand met and touched as innocents, using the mirror exercise; they made love in a gentle rocking way. The crew woke up to explore the wonders of the island – 'Oh brave new world' – and revelled in sensuality. Caliban, one fat actor, mimed his monstrous emergence from his mother, Sycorax, another fat actress who was seemingly capable of swelling her body to gross proportions. Caliban was taught language by Prospero, beginning with 'food' and 'love', but soon progressing to 'master' and 'slave'. The word 'slave' unleashed Caliban's brutality and, escaping Prospero, he climbed the scaffolding at great speed, jumped down, raped Miranda and tyrannised the whole island. Then he was captured and thrust down into a small opening between two platforms. The chorus mocked 'How beauteous is man', and Caliban escaped and took over the island again. The islanders became monsters, Caliban became the monster-master. He and Sycorax created a wild orgy, mirrored by the company's sexual configurations. Variations on sexual positions conveyed a monster-sexuality; the Garden of Delights was transformed into Hell. An enormous pyramid was formed on the scaffolding: Caliban on top, Sycorax on the bottom, Ariel was held prisoner. 'This thing of darkness I do acknowledge mine' was echoed by the group as they prepared to kill Prospero, who had been pursued and captured, thrown to the floor as the pyramid, like dogs, leaped on and ravaged him. Caliban and Prospero were locked together in an image of homosexual rape. Ariel arrived with costumes and bright ribbons to bribe the dog-pack away from Prospero and the scene dissolved into a marriage ceremony for Ferdinand and Miranda, the rites being performed in Hebrew–Hippie–Japanese fashion. The wedding over, Prospero remembered 'I forgot the plot'. Each actor froze where he was and gradually started picking up lines from the epilogue. The verse was spoken in various rhythms, inflections and phrasings, and disappeared slowly into the distance '. . . ending . . . despair . . . relieved . . . by prayer . . .'.

Mike Stott, the house playwright on *US*, contributed some material on the idea 'If Caliban ruled the island':

All men will be splattered. I'll sprinkle their eyeballs all over the island, so I can see everything that happens. I'll build me a palace of dead men's bones, glued together with flesh and fat. I'll have carpets of human hair. I'll use their pricks to make a giant whip, with bollocks for knots. I would let Prospero live. He would be my royal bog. He'd drink my piss and eat my shit and chew my puke and gobble my snot. I'd breed off Miranda. Only daughters would live! When they got old enough to fuck, I'd get rid of Miranda. I'd have her thrown into my royal bath, my lake of sweet-smelling perfumed mud. And I'd jump in after her and fuck her deep down in the mud. She'd drown in ecstasy, and all there'd be above the surface would be my head, gazing at the moon and stars and saying: 'We are such stuff as dreams as made of, and our little life is rounded with a sleep'.

This mad fucking should be acted. 'We are such stuff' etc. should first be said to try and catch Prospero's virtuous pompous tone of voice. But as the fucking gets going it becomes more and more an orgasm.

The programme note to the Round-House performances stated:

To those who are invited to attend the open presentations of this work in progress it is important to make clear the nature of such an experimental session. Even laboratory work does not exist until it happens before a spectator. At a certain point – however it stands – work must be exposed. The spectator's interest, and thus his participation, is needed by the actors, but their aim is not to please or divert him. It is assumed that he comes to a workshop, not as he comes to a performance in a theatre, but rather because he wants to be involved in exploring questions that are concerning the theatre everywhere.

The present project is intended to bring fragments of evidence and experience to bear on these questions. The questions are: What is a theatre? What is a play? What is an actor? What is a spectator? What is the relation between them all? What conditions serve this relationship best?

Ronald Bryden, in *The Observer*, observed:

To anyone interested in the mechanics of theatre, it was fascinating, with moments as strange and effective as the best of *Oedipus*. Here was how a play looks to an actor: the private emotional scoring which he contributes to the orchestration of a dramatic text. One would give much to see the final production of *Tempest* arrived at via such rehearsal.

10   Shaking hands in the empty space: *The Dream*

In the late summer of 1970, Peter Brook produced *A Midsummer Night's Dream* at Stratford-upon-Avon. The production became one of the Royal Shakespeare Company's greatest successes ever. It played thirty-two times during what was left of the 1970 Stratford season and also played for two nights in a 'rough' version, without costumes and decor, at the Round House to 'packed and ecstatic houses'. It then toured the United States and Canada for fourteen weeks in the spring of 1971 and amassed 112 performances in six cities – it ran for six weeks on Broadway. It opened again in London at the Aldwych in June 1971, notching up another ninety-odd performances by March 1972. After that it toured in Britain and Europe and Britain again, adding more than another hundred performances to its score. It went back to the United States in January 1973, playing forty-seven times in Los Angeles and twenty-three in San Francisco en route to Japan and Australia, where it played for another 108 performances. In all, it played 535 times in thirty-six cities and towns around the world. A special acting edition of 'Peter Brook's Production of William Shakespeare's *A Midsummer Night's Dream*' was published in the United States. Amateurs wanting to stage 'this unique. . . production' were informed that 'the royalty fees are *fifty dollars* for the first amateur performance and *thirty-five dollars* for each subsequent use. . .'.

At the beginning of rehearsals on a stained canvas on the studio floor in Stratford-upon-Avon, Brook told the actors that the truth they were seeking 'has to be found by each actor'. The play would 'yield its secrets, if each individual relates himself to the whole'. He had seven weeks' rehearsal times. It was to be his last successful production for the RSC.

Some of Brook's closest collaborators were surprised by his decision to stage *The Dream*. Designer Sally Jacobs says:

My first response was that it was the play I least wanted to design. Because I . . . had this overlay of fairies and all those cliché images from productions I'd seen. I couldn't see the play at all.

Richard Peaslee, who had worked on the music for virtually all Brook's productions since the Theatre of Cruelty season, says:

This was not long after the riots and deaths at Kent State and other violent outbreaks in the US. Somehow *A Midsummer Night's Dream* seemed all very remote from all that, so I was

142

12   *A Midsummer Night's Dream,* Stratford-upon-Avon, 1970

not very interested in working on it . . . it wasn't quite where my head was at then. So, when he started rehearsing, I indicated I wasn't interested in working on it. I should have known better because he always makes projects interesting.

Peaslee was lured into the production for the last four weeks of rehearsal.

It was apparently *The Dream's* remoteness from what Peaslee called 'all that' that provided one of the attractions for Brook. Ronald Hayman, in *Playback,* quotes Brook as saying:

One of my reasons for wanting to tackle *The Dream* was that it was such a contrast with everything I had been doing since 1964. I find the material I have been working on has taken on a certain gloomy consistency. . . . If one's only inside tragic material, it's yet another false view of reality. Tragedy isn't total reality, it's a part, a version of reality and one can't but feel in the end that something is lacking within it.

But Brook concluded:

It's always the same problem – unimportant whether it's comedy or tragedy – how can you close the triangle between subject matter, the performers and the audience? It's always the same task – three points that have to be linked.

At the end of *The Marat/Sade*, Brook's actors had applauded his audience, ironically. At the end of *US* they had stared at the audience. At the end of *A Midsummer Night's Dream*, they came out into the audience and shook hands with people, establishing a physical link on Puck's line, 'Give me your hands if we be friends . . .'. The stage they left bore no traces of 'those cliché images' to which Sally Jacobs had referred.

The set was a three-sided white box; it was described by different critics as a gym, a clinic, a squash court and a circus tent. There were slits in the side walls and two doors in the back, with a catwalk around the top, used by the musicians and, sometimes, by actors. The musicians were divided into two percussion groups, playing tubular bells, bongos and bed-springs as well as zithers, autoharps and guitars. Actors watched the action from the catwalk, sometimes throwing blue and silver darts across the space or making sounds with musical saws and plastic tubes. Speeches were turned into freely improvised song, sometimes mock-operatic: 'Fair love, you faint with wandering in the wood' and 'So sorrow's heaviness doth heavier grow'.

The white box was a machine for acting in. It was lit with bright white light. The company entered to a drum roll, all wearing long white cloaks, which, when discarded, revealed the characters in primary colours. Theseus and Hippolyta became Oberon and Titania by shedding their white cloaks, which were removed as they stood in the doors at the back of the set. Philostrate became a Puck who had baggy silk breeches and a blue cap. The Fairies wore grey jogging suits.

From the catwalk, the Fairies lowered metal coils on the ends of rods – the coils were used for the trees of the forest. The Immortals descended on trapezes. Hermia had her nightmare entangled in a coiled wire. She screamed her 'O me! You juggler! You canker-blossom!' as she kicked helplessly from the trapeze on which Demetrius had dumped her. The Lovers raced and tumbled, scrambled up and down ladders, tore round the catwalk. At the end of the wood scene, Puck wore stilts: 'Up and down, Up and down . . .'. Lysander and Demetrius chased each other round the stilts.

The purple flower was a twirling plate on a juggler's stick. It was passed spinning from Puck to Oberon. Titania lusted openly for Bottom, who was carried to her bower of scarlet flowers with a Fairy's arm rising between his legs, amid a shower of confetti and streamers. Bottom's ass's head consisted of ear-muffs and a button clown's nose, which meant that the actor could still use his face.

The Mechanicals were presented as sober workmen, keen amateur actors whose play was very important to them. Pyramus' death speech was played seriously, which meant that Theseus' 'This passion and the death of a dear friend would go near to make a man look sad', and Hippolyta's 'Beshrew my heart, but I pity the man', could also be played straight. Bottom said, 'No, I assure you, the wall is down that parted their fathers' as if speaking the moral of the play.

Brook rejected stage illusion: the actors never hid the fact that they were actors performing. They frequently talked directly to the audience. The shaking of hands at the end physically brought down the wall that had parted audience from actors.

The published information we have about the rehearsing of *A Midsummer Nights's Dream* is detailed enough to allow us to construct a picture of Brook's approach to a Shakespeare text as part of an RSC season at this turning-point in his career. The process was exceptionally well documented in a book by David Selbourne, *The Making of A Midsummer Night's Dream*, in which he describes his experience of the rehearsals, and in the US Complete and Authorized Acting Edition, which contains interviews with 'Director, Designer, Composer, Cast and Crew'. The people involved do not always seem to be talking about the same process. But by putting accounts together, like pieces of a jigsaw, we can begin to discern where and what Brook was at just before he took off to Paris and his Centre International de Créations Théâtrales.

Selbourne reports that on the first day of rehearsal Brook met the actors who were to play the Mechanicals. After a warm-up, which involved Brook drumming and telling the actors to 'Find out the largest stride you can make', Brook sat the actors in a semicircle round him. They must search, he told them, for the 'immediately recognisable gesture of the experienced carpenter, joiner, weaver. . . . You must do nothing actorish, you must retain the integrity of your movements.' After which, says Selbourne, the Mechanicals read through the text, taking all the parts.

On the second day, Selbourne tells us, Brook talked to the actors about 'seeking out this mystery' in a play in which there is a 'reality beyond description', after which he asked actors to explore sounds 'unrelated to verbal equivalents'. He then took the actors into a reading, asking them to remember the sounds 'which came upon the deepest impulse'. At the end of the reading, Brook told the actors that the very last stanzas are 'the most inner portion of the whole drama', 'tantilisingly close to something secret and mysterious. We approach here whatever is behind the whole play.'

But on the third day, Selbourne reports, 'metal plates and rods have made an appearance this morning, and are being falteringly spun, clangingly dropped and spun again, by way of exercise. A technique is being learned at a director's behest, for a purpose which does not appear to be clear to the actors, and is not the subject of discussion.'

The metal plates were the result of a visit Peter Brook and designer Sally

Jacobs had paid to the Chinese Circus in Paris. Sally Jacobs says, in an interview she gave for the American Acting Edition:

We were absolutely certain that to be able to get that beautiful shock of catching your breath, we couldn't produce the magic in the way that it has always been produced. That the familiar would kill the magic. There's no such thing as the Magic Flower. We've already seen it too many times on stage. It's not magic: we know it's only a prop. So what to replace such objects with . . .? We remembered the spinning plates from the Chinese Circus – the whirling plate on the stick works very well for the Flower. Before you know it, there's that humming sound and the spinning disk. I still get a very nice feeling from that which no prop flower would ever give me.

What Selbourne, listening to Brook talk to the actors, and the actors themselves, presumably, could not at that stage know was the point Brook had already arrived at in his search for a way of making *The Dream*. Selbourne reports Brook's speeches to the actors – all is secrecy and mystery. Sally Jacobs catches the agility of the mind of a practical man of the theatre.

Brook knew that he was at Stratford-upon-Avon with what he called a 'cruel theatre'. He was not talking about Artaud but about architecture: 'One day we may hope that someone will set fire for a second time to the Stratford-upon-Avon theatre and it'll be rebuilt'. The problem was one of acoustics – to be audible on the Stratford stage actors had to shout. Brook needed what Sally Jacobs thought of as a 'contained space'. When he first talked to her about it, before he had even selected the actors, she had been in the middle of making Christmas cards.

First I showed Peter . . . dots of colour on the white cards, divided by black lines. At the time I didn't even know what the colours were – people, furniture, setting or what. They just seemed right against the pure white. And we grabbed pieces of typing paper and began folding them, trying to see how it would look. Eventually, I had a group of colours, a doll, a bit of wire, a feather – all things which seemed to fit the magic box-of-tricks that Peter was talking about.

The three-sided white box had been invented long before the actors arrived for rehearsal. And Brook had also told Sally Jacobs that he wanted a set in which the actors could remain on stage when they were not in a scene. His concept of completing the triangle between subject matter, performers and audience had already led him to decide that he wanted the actors to become part of the audience by watching and reacting with it.

Sally Jacobs:

The white space gave us a sense of distance but at the same time it was very intimate. Actors could speak very quietly if they wanted to. Acoustically, it worked quite well, especially on the large Stratford stage, where voices can get lost. But acoustics were not the main concern. Mainly, it was to create an intimate acting area, which would nevertheless give us a place where the rest of the actors who were not in the scene could surround the action and continue to watch it. So that's how the top gallery came about.

The top gallery was a practical response to a directorial decision, which had been taken before the rehearsals began. Brook brought a specific concept to rehearsal, a concept which led logically to the final physical contact with the audience. But if Brook already had this in his mind from the beginning, why didn't he reveal it to the actors when he talked about the 'secret play'?

To Brook, a part of directing has always been like conjuring – at a very late stage in the rehearsal of *The Dream*, he really did produce a rabbit, if not out of a hat, at least unexpectedly on stage. (Its owner scolded the actors for frightening it, and it did not make a second appearance.) But directing has also meant for Brook putting actors into situations and inviting them to respond. Sally Jacobs told AH:

We got a mock-up set done in scaffolding about a week after rehearsals started. . . . So much had to be explored by the performers. So we had the mock-up and the trapezes almost from the first.

The actors explored with enthusiasm.

Up and down, up and down, I will lead them up and down . . .

Puck walked about the set on stilts. At first only one trapeze had been intended, but the actors playing Oberon and Puck (Alan Howard and John Kane) developed such skills on the trapeze that a second had to be introduced. Kane asked for an extra entrance space so that he could appear suddenly on stilts in the middle of the set. Sally thought, why not more entrance spaces? Why not two more entrances on to the gallery? Things grow out of specific needs, she says, 'but, in rehearsals, the performers always experiment and find new uses for them. At least in Peter Brook productions they do.'

Selbourne, meditating about the relationship of the director to actors and playwright, barely notes the arrival of the mock set:

Second week, fifth day. . . . Metal plates are again spinning, and the actors' skills increasing. Now there have been added finger-bells, hoops, trapezes and streaming black-and-white pennants for jugglery and acrobatics. Does this mean that there will be juggling and the suggestion of orientalism (why?) in the final version? Or is this merely an actors' exercise, the development of a metaphorical balance and sleight-of-hand in which to poise the finished action?

Selbourne goes on to describe a rehearsal, the same day, of the scene in which the Mechanicals try to find a quiet place in the wood to rehearse. Brook asks the rest of the group to make the wood 'deceptively benign', so they whistle and chirp bird-calls. One of them prods Snout with a long stick – Snout brushes it away. When Bottom calls, 'A calendar, a calendar!' a fairy gives him one. Puck's entrance, says Selbourne, goes 'unremarked'. Quince corrects Thisby's pronunciation.

Selbourne noted that Bottom (David Waller) was standing close to him, 'bare to the waist, his body out of shape and aging. Can such a figure be trans-figured?' Then he describes how Brook shouts, 'The wood becomes alive' over an 'explosion of joyful fright and clamour', while Quince trembled his 'O monstrous! O strange! We are haunted!' As Bottom entered to a fiercely counter-pointed sound of rattling metal, bells and drums, Brook gave instructions – 'Distempo' and 'Cross rhythms of speech and movement'.

Selbourne goes on to describe how Titania, 'her voice heavy with a seeming desire, speaks swooningly to him . . . ("Sing", Brook tells her)' and how Titania and Bottom, 'swathed in an unrolled bale of Mechanicals' cloth in which to couple, are carried to their own transports. . . . Will these elements become fixed and settled in the production? And how do they consort with the search for the play's innermost rhythm?' Act IV, he notes, becomes 'a rude awakening into daylight. It is the dazed morning after, too bright and glaring.' Selbourne reports that at the end of the rehearsal Brook makes a speech about the 'remarkable quality' of the work done so far. The actors listen in their own silence as Brook talks about getting to the point 'where things work almost by themselves'. Selbourne concludes:

It is not clear what this means. . . . But if it means little or nothing, no one is saying, and it may not matter. For the art or technique of the director – like that of his orchestral twin, the conductor – clearly demands greater mastery of the sub- and pre-verbal than of the verbal.

By chance, we have John Kane's account of the same rehearsal. It is interesting to compare the two experiences, that of actor and that of observer.

John Kane, who played Puck, told the meeting of critics and journalists in New York:

We had no moves planned. We could move wherever we liked. The four Fairies – we called them the Audio-Visuals because they made sounds and moved things around – they could be banks, chairs, anything. And sometimes they moved actors around the stage like chess pieces. . . .

The run-through was incredible. We all had books in our hands. We really didn't know what we were doing. We were a rival gang of bricklayers. The problem that . . . the Mechanicals had was to find a quiet enough place to rehearse because we were intent on sawing our wood or tearing down walls. We did everything in our power to end the rehearsal by a group of faggot workers, and things got really heated up.

From that moment on, once people were actually concerned with doing something – they were determined to rehearse and we were determined to stop them – well, the thing took off and went at incredible speed right through to the wedding. We tore everything up . . . newspapers; we threw cushions about.

At the end, when everything quieted down and the last newspaper flicked to the floor, we stood and looked around at the incredible chaos – the debris we had created during the course of the rehearsal. We had wrecked the entire studio. Hardly a chair was left with a leg on it. It was the first glimmer we had of how a play – without thinking about it, by just going along with it – of how a play can drive you with it. How it can change you, how it can transport you. I think the majority of us were transported. We had little recollection of what

had happened. . . . Peter had talked about a parallel of savagery in the play. Yes, we understood what he was saying, but we couldn't quite see it. Then, suddenly, we had felt it,
because the savagery had moved us. We had got a hint of that 'secret play' that Peter still
talks about . . . the play that will never be found by us. . . .

Brook himself recalled that rehearsal as 'a fantastic piece of collective invention', 'an event in the sense that it could never have been repeated'. ('Will these
elements become fixed and settled in the production?' wondered Selbourne).
A number of lights had been thrown on many parts of the play, Brook said, 'just
by pure inspiration of the movement'.

The 'savagery' Brook had talked about to the actors was linked with Brook's
reading of the play as being shot through with 'Darkness'. At dusk, in his production, Theseus and Hippolyta take off their white cloaks and become
Oberon and Titania. In the darkness of the forest – always lit by a bright white
light – dark passions are unleashed. Lovers change partners, as if in a dream.
The Queen of the Fairies is coupled with a man transformed into an ass.

Selbourne describes a rehearsal at the end of the sixth week in which Titania
was trembling with desire when she told the Fairies to 'Be kind and courteous
to this gentleman', and Bottom, 'as if in heat', was hoisted on to their shoulders.
Then one of the Fairies extended his arm, with clenched fist, between Bottom's
legs, and slowly raised it to erection. As Puck and Oberon swung to and fro on
the trapezes and the rest of the cast gathered on the topmost gantry to watch, a
sardonic send-up of Mendelssohn's *Wedding March* burst forth while the transported Titania stroked the standing phallus of the exalted Bottom. 'The men',
said Brook, 'will be relating to Bottom. He is about to do it to Titania. For all of
them.'

Selbourne is describing a *tour de force* which has evolved through a complex
process. Actors have been given a magic box to play in. They have learned how
to spin plates on the ends of rods. They have practised communicating with
each other using meaningless sounds. They have read the text again and again,
trying to read it as if they have never seen the lines before, trying, as Brook sees
it, to let the lines speak through them. They have been turned loose in wild
improvisations. And they have, on occasions, to Selbourne's surprise (but not
presumably to theirs) been 'blocked' in a completely conventional way.

Fourth week, first day . . . unexpectedly, Brook is now also plotting movement in detail. . . .
He is placing characters, or steering them into his (not their) chosen positions.

And out of this process has emerged a scene which, even in rehearsal,
clearly worked as an astonishing theatrical event.

John Russell Brown complains in *Shakespeare Survey*, that the concept is very
much Brook's. He quotes Brook as having said that Oberon is 'a man taking the
wife whom he loves totally and having her fucked by the crudest sex machine

he can find. . .'. John Russell Brown argues with some justice that Oberon is not a man at all, and that Bottom is not a sex machine, and he concludes that 'The director, with his actors to help him, had discovered something which is not in the text at all. . . . ' Rereading the text (and forgetting Peter Brook's moralisings about Oberon's marital intentions) it is hard to understand how the Victorians succeeded in not finding the Titania–Bottom scenes erotic and in not seeing the bawdy in Bottom's lines ('I could munch your good dry oats', he tells Titania the morning after the night before, and she says she'll send a venturous fairy to find him 'new nuts'). As in his *Lear*, Brook has created one of those images that burns itself into the memory and makes you surprised that you ever saw it any other way.

GR writes:

There is some justice indeed in John Russell Brown's argument. If it's hard to understand how Victorians succeeded in not finding the scene erotic, it's impossible to find the Bacchanalian orgy in lines which end with Titania's instruction, 'Tie up my love's tongue, bring him silently'. John Russell Brown also has interesting criticisms to make of Brook's actors, who, he says, make comparatively poor circus performers. One of Brook's reasons for starting his Centre in Paris was his realisation that he was looking for a new kind of performer – one who combined professional acting techniques with physical skills which demanded long and sustained training. It's scarcely surprising that the RSC actors he was working with in 1970 lacked such skills. They still don't possess them twenty years on. Indeed, as the working conditions have declined since the heady days of the sixties, the actors have even lost some of those other skills Brook was able to use then.

Ironically, as the play was performed on Broadway, the sexual undertones, according to Alan Howard (Oberon), diminished. They had never been at the centre of Brook's exploration. Brook told the New York critics:

What we thought about is that the play is a celebration. It's a celebration of the theme of theatre: the play-within-the-play-within-the-play-within-the-play. One of its themes is theatre.

Sally Jocobs says he wanted to make it 'a presentation of actors performing a play'.

Three weeks into rehearsal, Selbourne tells us, Brook asked his actors to dress up for a run-through of the last act. The Courtiers were to find court costumes, 'as for a party', in a wardrobe of cast-off clothes that had been prepared for them; the Mechanicals were to put on their 'Sunday best'. The studio lights were switched off, twenty or thirty candles were lit. Act V was to be walked through by candlelight. ('When had this been arranged?' asks Selbourne. 'Did the actors know in advance about it?') One by one, in the half darkness, the Courtiers appeared – they now looked like actors in a costume drama. The Mechanicals were kept waiting, in ties and jackets, with hair slicked down.

Theseus and Hippolyta talked about the events of the night, the tricks that imagination can play. The lovers entered carrying sparklers. Theseus asked for a play, 'to ease the anguish of a torturing hour'. Selbourne comments: 'This is suddenly no arrogant prince, but a fearful ghost seeking his quietus'. While the rest try to decide which play to choose, Theseus tells old war stories: 'When I from Thebes came last a conqueror. . . '.

Pyramus and Thisby is chosen – it will be played by 'Hard-handed men that work in Athens here . . .'. Quince, the carpenter–playwright, nervously twists his hands, misreads his prologue. Selbourne writes: 'And suddenly in the court's giggles, there is only vanity . . . and in Quince a dignity to match their own'. Snout is introduced, greeted with ironic applause. 'But he has suddenly become . . . a thing of danger and terror in these uncertain shadows . . . mirth is paling.' Selbourne continues:

Fear and restless unease as well as mockery . . . now kept company with Pyramus and Thisby as their truth gained ground in darkness. But there was stress in it, and distress also. Moonshine is wan and despondent, his voice catching, when he tells the jesting court, 'All that I have to say is to tell you that the lanthorn (holding it aloft) is the moon', is saddened and disheartened at having to explain that he is himself 'the man i'th'moon', despairing of his poor props at 'this thorn bush, my thorn bush', and close to tears at 'and this dog, my dog'. . . . Hippolyta's 'Beshrew my heart, but I pity the man' is for the first time its fitting coda.

Today, Pyramus' 'Thus die I, thus, thus, thus', in such a dark and plangent mood, was in Shakespeare's major key as tragedian, not the comic minor. In turn, Thisby, played by a male actor in an aching and desperate falsetto, reached (despite it) deep into the black silence which now fell upon the Courtiers. 'Asleep, my love?' he asked, 'what, dead, my dove?' But there was only an eerie spitting and sparkling in the enclosing darkness for answer . . . it is as if the rude Mechanicals have committed *lèse-majesté* by usurping the court's pretended monopoly of truth-telling.

John Kane also describes this rehearsal from an actor's point of view.

Outrageously attired in turbans, cloaks and ostrich feathers, we sat down behind the semi-circle of candles and ran through the dialogue leading up to the entrance of Peter Quince. On cue, I left the room and ushered the Mechanicals into the presence of Theseus and his court. . . . They appeared as under-rehearsed as Bottom and his colleagues were in the text. Philip Locke as Peter Quince acted as the play's Prologue and its genuine prompter, holding the Penguin edition of *The Dream* in his hand. The court found this very funny at first, but as our jokes at their expense grew more desperate, the actual substance of their play, together with the strangeness of our environment, began to work on us and by the time we had reached the death of Pyramus and Thisby, their innocence had a weirdly moving effect on us, reducing us to silence.

Alan as Theseus thanked the Mechanicals and delivered the last speech to his court. Suddenly, at a sign from Peter, the stage-management slammed on the overhead spotlights and we got to our feet blinking in the savage brightness. 'Go on!' said Peter. 'Go on to the last speeches of the play.' I was so stunned by the shock of the lights that I began Puck's 'Now the hungry lion roars' without time to think about what was being said (which is, I suppose, exactly what Peter intended). That speech and the other three which constitute the play's Epilogue said themselves and we reached the end of the play understanding the necessary transition from the Court world to the Spirit world by experiencing it.

David Selbourne referred to 'a Chinese box of a problem' when writing about this rehearsal. 'Here was the fruition of effort, and at its heart the question "What is theatre?" burned furiously in the near-darkness.' And perhaps it was because that question was at the heart of Brook's *Dream* that the play was one of his most successful productions. For his driving obsession has always been the nature of theatre and in this play he was able to harness it to his exploration without having to allow the outside world, with its wars and madnesses and atrocities, to cloud the image. The problems to be solved were all theatrical problems. How could you show trees without showing trees? In their white Chinese box, what would the performers wear? Something timeless, Sally Jacobs says, basic functional costumes – loose pants and a blouse, a tunic dress with a bit of colour splashed on, brilliant fluorescent colours for the leading Fairies. But she found the Mechanicals' costumes more difficult:

They are actually present-day workmen. The reality of what they represent was just not to be avoided. . . . So these costumes were much more realistic than those of the other two worlds. That was Peter's idea. He was very clear about that.

So there was a 'reality' to be represented. There were questions trying to get into the Chinese box – David Selbourne hinted at some of them. Whose innocence, for example, had a 'weirdly moving effect' on John Kane? Not the innocence, surely, of David Waller and Barry Stanton. The innocence could only be that of the characters they were playing. It belonged to the world inside the Chinese box.

But there were events outside – only just outside, still inside the court theatre at Stratford-upon-Avon – that affected what went on inside. There was, for example, the opening night of *Two Gentlemen of Verona* which diverted the players' attention. There were rumours that Brook had intervened in the direction on the orders of the hierarchy. Brook was not giving any high politics away to the actors. And Selbourne also reports a stream of actors seeking an audience with Brook, wanting to join his forthcoming International Centre in Paris. Curiously enough, Selbourne, who asked himself a lot of questions about the power relationship between Brook and the actors, seems to have missed some basic realities, like the fact that, as Alan Howard casually lets slip, other work for the RSC intruded.

The rehearsals for the first, the original, production took about eight weeks. But, of course, we were playing in repertoire, so we had three matinées a week at Stratford. I was doing *Hamlet* and *Dr Faustus* at the same time. I finished *Hamlet* and started playing this. We were all in various other RSC productions.

Such incursions of social reality must have helped to encourage Brook to shake the dust of British theatre from his feet.

There are other theatrical problems, though, that Brook's *Dream* does not answer. Brook locked himself, so far as was possible, inside his Chinese box with his actors and asked them to look inside themselves to solve the 'mystery', to find their own individual rhythms, explore the limits of their own individual possibilities. Working together with them, he made this astonishing show. But the show then became a product, to be taken around the world. A new cast was hired, given a month's short-course in Paris, and then sent out, with the task of re-creating every night what the original group had created, supposedly, out of themselves.

But by then Brook had moved on. The stained canvas on the floor of the rehearsal studio in Stratford-upon-Avon was to be replaced by a carpet, which Brook would put down in remote parts of the world. His actors would travel with him to explore the limits of their possibilities by performing improvised shows on the carpet to village audiences in Persia and Africa. Working with Brook would become a way of life.

11   Persian tombs at dawn: *Orghast*

The lesson Brook learnt from the events in Paris in 1968 was that the way to avoid the work being closed down was to spread the financial sponsorship as widely as possible, so that in the event of one sponsor pulling out, for artistic or political reasons, it would still be possible to continue. So while he was directing the film of *King Lear* in 1969 he besieged foundations, governments and UNESCO until he had enough money to guarantee three years of work – without the need for any box-office contributions. In November 1970 The International Centre of Theatre Research opened in Paris, back again in the Mobilier National, which the French government were willing to make available as long as the money for the work done there came from elsewhere; which it did, mainly from the Iranian government and various American foundations. This time there were fifteen actors – from France, the United States, England, Spain, Portugal, Algeria and Japan; later in the year they were joined by two more Americans (one an American-Greek) and two Africans (from Mali and the Cameroons). There were also three other directors, from Armenia, England and Romania, and a Swiss designer.

When the group met on the first day in 1970, in a bleak room in the Cité Universitaire, Brook immediately asked them to make the place suitable for a meal and entertainment. 'Our job is to animate'. They had three hours. Some searched, some cooked, and the result was a delicious meal eaten inside a tent of coloured paper, furnished with beautiful objects. Everyone entertained each other. Afterwards the 'set' was cleared away, stripped to nothing. Brook said it was 'the essential blueprint of what we are learning about popular entertainment, the ability to assess a whole situation', and that they would need it when they reached the villages in Persia.

On the second day the work began with sticks: a development of the Chinese circus expertise striven for in the *Dream*. Holding the sticks, the group tapped out rhythms, formed bizarre mazes. The sticks became extensions of the body and voice. The actors used the sticks to contact each other, to elicit non-verbal responses, to measure their relationship to space. The sticks helped them get at pure simple impulses, and to create rich worlds of the imagination. A stick provided a straitjacket for the actor: to work inside the defined limits and make much, or try to ignore them and make little.

Brook:

The essential purpose of the exercises is to create – it takes years – an actor so organically related within himself that he can *think* with his body to the point where the exercises actually take place by themselves. It is thought and action as one, like a conductor or the brush strokes of a painter. In t'ai chi to do the exercises was to *be* it. And if the actor can produce this state of one, sensitive, responding whole, and many of the actors have, he will have developed and heightened his own natural creativity.

Language was also worked on: in 1968 much had been done with free sounds, but now it seemed more useful to use a more restricted range of syllables or words, in order to release the actor from the constant pressure of invention. So that members of the group could work together at the same level, they evolved a very simple, small vocabulary of meaningless invented words. Everyone contributed a syllable; a French actor-writer put them into shapes. 'Bash da hondo ma dai zout' etc. This became the language for improvisations.

The Japanese actor held daily classes in which simple movements and sounds from the Noh theatre were taught in the traditional way: the master demonstrated, the students imitated. Without mention of motivation or objective the Western actors approached such work as a kind of meditation, like t'ai chi. Like the sticks t'ai chi was a physical discipline whose 'meaning' was never discussed: it had to be found by the actors for themselves.

After two months Brook felt the actors' need to perform had to be assuaged. Wanting an audience without preconceptions about the theatre he decided to perform for children. He said they had a natural interest in things: without their parents' expectations – 'We've paid our money, go on and astonish us!' – they were still naïve.

Children demand that things be clear. Simple language can be a help, whereas sophisticated language is a barrier. Serious things can be done for children, provided they are done clearly. A child's fantasy and imagination make the boulevard notion of 'setting things up' irrelevant. If something is to be rich and strong enough to interest an adult audience it should, a priori, interest children.

As the raw material for the performances, which took place just before Christmas, Brook chose a story he was reading to his young son, *The Bee Man of Orme*, by the American Frank Stockton. As the actors had not been able, in a month, to make the plot clear without language, a French-speaking narrator led the children through the story between scenes; he also physically led them from one end of the space to the other. The play was performed using only sticks, balloons and ropes, and at the end the children were invited to join the actors in free improvisation which they did with great energy, picking up some of the things they had seen and going on to invent others. As they took over, inventing games, making gates and corridors, and acting people and animals, the actors withdrew and left the children to it.

After Christmas the group divided to work on Calderón's *Life is a Dream* and Handke's *Kaspar*, two plays showing a young man confronted with freedom. The Calderón was treated as a rhetorical spectacle, the Spanish text vented with great intensity; the prince, imprisoned by a tyrannical father, was usually on the top of a metal tower, or halfway up a wall, or in the middle of a cat's cradle of ropes. Handke's play, which he called torture, provided the perfect vehicle for actors trying to find truth and simplicity in language and movement without cultural overtones. Kaspar, having no memory and therefore no past, was a clean slate, a figure without a past in an empty space. Taught to speak by prompters he became imprisoned in the ideology of a language, every new word enslaving him more. The actors, although by now used to the discipline of the sticks and the precision of Noh-theatre impulses, found it almost impossible to follow Handke's very precise instructions. When Brook came to giving public performances of the play around the Paris suburbs (in community halls and schools rather than theatres) he freed up Handke's text considerably, even using music, which lessened the tone of prevailing agony that came from the first rehearsals in the cold and clinical Mobilier.

'Bash da hondo' gave way to Greek. Brook had long been interested in Aeschylus' *Prometheus Bound*. He had commissioned a new translation from Robert Lowell for Paul Scofield, which had been read in the year following *US*; there had even been discussions as to whether Scofield could manage to endure the entire performance entwined in a net which would be suspended twenty feet above the stalls of the Aldwych. But he felt the text needed more work and before that could happen *Oedipus* came along.

Calderón was rehearsed in Spanish. The group also worked on a chorus from an Armenian play, *The Chained One*, in Armenian, passages of Seneca in Latin, and the first two books of Avesta, the ceremonial language of ancient Persia, which had been used exclusively for religious incantation. The group also looked at the Greek of Aeschylus. No one apparently knew exactly how Ancient Greek was spoken, although some professors had theories. Brook took a speech and wrote it out as one long word; he gave it to the actors asking them to make dramatic sense of it by finding the form of the speech (or vice versa), so they were to explore the sounds that the letters suggested to them physically and gradually make a pattern first of words and then, if possible, of lines. After an afternoon of such individual exploration all the actors had correctly found the word divisions and one of them, a Spanish actress, had found the lines. When asked what the piece was about they all had found the emotional situation while not understanding one word of the text. Brook assumed that the true performance of Greek plays lay closer to a musical form than to modern acting, and therefore the way to approach such material was by exploratory articulation and improvisation. In addition to these dead languages Brook used a new language, Orghast, which he asked Ted Hughes to create, so that he would have blocks of sound as a basis for improvisation. If language, through its very gesture, possessed emotional overtones and meanings, then Avesta was meant to express the light, and Orghast designed to explore the dark, in the myths of Prometheus.

Brook:

Only an actor can speak a word so that, with practice, he comes to feel that he was the first to speak it. If you go into the text knowing in general what it is about and take a word, two words, a dialogue, with your imagination open to the words, the more you experience the sound the more you experience what went into making it, and hence the experience of the person who went through it. Suddenly, mysteriously, those sounds become words, words so strong, alive and vibrant, affecting our imagination through our sound and movement: suddenly we find all our feelings flowing with the words. This is true of Aeschylus and of Orghast.

Hughes:

I was interested in the possibilities of a language of tones and sounds, without specific conceptual or perpetual meaning. The idea was to build up a small range of sounds which we could then organise rhythmically. We started with a fairly complicated narrative, using several myths which we blended together into one cosmology. The Prometheus myth was one and also the mythology and cosmology of Manichaean writings. Brook wanted to open up in actors the stores of meaningful expression and feeling which ordinary language just skates over. They worked for a long time with a dozen or so set syllables that had no fixed meaning, and therefore infinitely variable potential meaning.

The point was to create a precise but open and inviting language, inviting to a lost world we wanted to explore. Music is one such language – mathematically precise, but completely mysterious and open, giving access to a deeper world, closed to direct analysis. In comparison to what we tried to do, music is very sophisticated. If you imagine music buried in the earth for a few thousand years, decayed back to its sources, not the perfectly structured thing we know as music, then that is what we tried to unearth. A language belonging below the levels where differences appear, close to the inner life of what we've chosen as our material, but expressive to all people, powerfully, truly, precisely.

My word for 'light' – *hoan* – was a completely blind invention, but it turns out to mean a ray of light in Farsi (the language of Iran); my 'Woman of Light' I called Ussa provisionally, until we discovered it meant 'dawn' in Sanskrit and is close to the old Farsi word for 'fire', now only used as a girl's name. There were quite a few coincidences of that sort. The good words are the words you invent immediately – blind, your mind completely fixed on the thing or state you want to express. Out of these root words you compound others. Some of these are good, most are not so good. After a while the words you invented blind turn out to be compounds of the first roots you established. The whole vocabulary so far must be near two thousand words, but only about fifty are the real ones.

The word 'orghast' itself is the product of two roots *org* and *ghast* – 'life' and 'spirit, flame'. So orghast is the word for 'the fire of being', 'the fire at the centre' and so, metaphorically, 'sun'. Other roots were *gr* ('eat'), *ull* ('swallow'), *kr* ('devour'), *urg* ('death'), *uss* ('light'), *bruss* ('strength') and *gra* ('fire'). At the beginning, Hughes always added rough translations as he wrote specific scenes; by the end, the actors did not need them any more. Passages were often used in performance for similar emotional situations long after the original, specific scenes had been dropped.

Words were often worked on in small groups for hours at a time. A chorus was built around the word for horror, 'hazac'; and the actors would just keep working over the *c*. Brook would say:

> Keep trying it, like a musician tuning his instrument. The last thing in music is to look for the feeling. It will come if you explore the way the voice moves through a word, finding the relationships between consonants and vowels. The voice is like a mountain with caves. Go into all the different caves there are.

This kind of exploration subtly changed the work as it progressed. Hughes switched to using blocks of sound when he discovered that constructing a language in the conventional sense did not work – 'Unless it works musically it does not work at all'. The bricks he used were tonal values like long, short, light, dark – 'assuming a western European way of speaking vowels . . . with only ten or fifteen possibilities in the musical notation of these vowel sounds'. He was always working on sounds with individual actors.

Hughes:

> In the latest phase of Orghast, which is very much the best for our purposes, there is a fixed basis: the consonants are fixed, but the vowels are free – free for me, that is. The actors stick close to what I compose but with the knowledge that if they can improve on it, the vowel is free for them too. Now that I've discovered the fixed and free basis of proceeding, it's not so important if the words aren't absolute inspirations – they're open at every new occurrence to a new and more essential kind of inspiration, as if all spelling were very, very free. There is no dialogue in the conventional sense. Wherever we approached that, the language quickly began to sound like just another language. At least it did with the earlier phrases. I think we've now got something that could manage dialogue in quite an exciting way. Early Orghast was rigid and hieroglyphic. It's still hieroglyphic but the sound sequence is becoming more free. The ideal would be a sound sequence as flexible as an electrocardiogram and an encephalogram combined. And of course actors who could operate it.
>
> The greatest satisfactions of conversation are probably musical ones. A person who has no musical talent in ordinary conversation is a bore, no matter how interesting his remarks are. What we really want from each other are these comforting or stimulating exchanges of melodies. This animal music is very different, of course, from the conventionally 'musical' voice. The real virtuosi in this line are certain animals and birds – though their ranges are pretty limited. When they speak the spirits listen. Not many human voices can make the spirits listen.

During the Easter break, Brook and the Armenian director went to Tehran to find Persian actors for a summer project commissioned by the Shiraz–

Persepolis Festival. The festival had been started in 1967 by the Persian television network, under Reza Ghotbi, a cousin of the Queen. In 1971 it was run
concurrently with a Celebration of Persia's 2,500th anniversary. The official
Persian view of the festival was that it was a modest attempt to raise the
country's cultural level by giving Persian artists a chance to see and make
contact with the best from outside. The view from outside the country tended
to see it as an expensive front to gain prestige for an authoritarian regime and
an attempt to get something else into the world press other than the adverse
comments on the Shah's brand of constitutional democracy and the (rising)
number of Tehran students being jailed. Undoubtedly some Persians benefited
from seeing the work of Grotowski, Garcia and Chaikin; and those who did
probably shared the viewpoint of politically committed foreigners. But that the
festival was out for publicity was apparent at every turn. Brook was to react
very strongly to the suggestion that he was 'bought' for publicity and allowed
himself to be paid by the Persians to obscure the political realities of the
country.

Brook:

I think this is naïve and hysterical. In thinking and speech one has to take into account the
realities of the conditions in which one works and lives, and attempt, to begin with, not to
fall foul of hypocrisy and humbug. If one wishes to take a completely purist view of money,
then one has to follow that through completely logically, and not have any relation with the
monetary system within which one lives. But one can't, for instance, work with money
from the British government, which comes into semi-nationalised theatres, make films
with money that, even in any European company, comes eventually from American dis-
tributors, work through all the different financial structures of the West, and suddenly
believe that the whole situation is transformed because one goes to the country which at
this particular moment hits the headlines and is the symbol of police brutality. It would be
completely humbug for us to work in France as though we naïvely believed that there was
no repression or police brutality there, and suddenly discover this in Iran. The desert island
in which one can work outside a complex, largely repressive social machine does not exist
and *Lord of the Flies* shows the development of that dream. Many years ago I came to the
clear position that the responsibility on each person only exists within the field over which
he has some degree of control. In the arts, the relationship with money rests entirely on
what one controls: that is, whether, having received facilities, one uses them honestly to
further whatever purpose one has set oneself, or whether one accepts to distort one's aims
to suit the purpose of the people who have given the money, or to please the box-office. We
went to Persia for a purpose: Avesta, Persepolis, *ruhozi*, the people, half way between East
and West. We gave what we could of our work to the people we were working with, and we
took away what we needed. It was made possible for us by a festival whose motives were,
to the surprise of none of us, as completely mixed up as the motives are behind any festival,
from Cannes onwards, in which commercial and political interests mix with a vague streak
of liberal affection for the arts concerned. Before leaving Tehran, I was able to have an hour
and a half alone with the Queen, when I seized the opportunity to say what had to be said
on every level of Persian life, starting with censorship, without frills, without beating
around the bush, directly to a person who, within a restricted field of movement, has got

more influence than anyone in the country. And to me the possibility of direct confrontation with certain of the powers that be, and in particular the Queen, completely balances the account. We exploited the situation given to us to draw home to them what we consider should be said at least as much as they could exploit the external aspects of our work to fit in with their general world-publicity.

When Brook arrived in Tehran, NITV told him that they had written to the hundred National-Theatre actors in the city and he could expect at least two-thirds of them to audition. But all that turned up on the morrow were two university students. When he talked to NITV they said they were not surprised as the National Theatre was run by the Ministry of Culture which was extremely jealous of the workshop Brook was doing, as it was run by television. Clearly the rumour had gone round that the auditions were rigged, that all National-Theatre actors would be humiliated by being rejected. Brook had to make contact with each of the five Ministry-run groups and persuade them to come to a meeting at which he described what he had done at the RSC. Once they heard that, there were sixty who wanted to sign up. He chose fifteen and left them with the Armenian director to work for two months doing stick exercises and learning Avesta.

Back in Paris there was a children's show at the Mobilier. When the children arrived for the first performance, whooping and rushing up the stairs, they discovered the actors scattered around the space, immobile, like waxworks. As some of the children had not the patience to wait for them to come to life and do something they decided to help them with some pinching and kicking. (The opening was changed for the second performance.) Some of *Kaspar* was performed in white masks, which scared the children already worried by the opening statues. Improvisations were done without introduction or explanation. When a battle was staged, using the shadows created by stage lights, some of the braver children leapt up to join in. The result was a complete shambles with Brook saying that the group did not know the first thing about children. Disheartened, the group set out to prepare another show, this time a highly structured series of stories: *Gawain and the Green Knight*, a ten-minute version of *Life is a Dream*, Japanese and African fairy tales. Much was in mime and in mixed languages but always with a narrator explaining what was happening. It was an improvement on the violence of its predecessor, but still low-level work; Brook felt that he had not yet found where to start with a show for children: 'It's not from an idea, not from a theme, nor is it by being locked right into a story'.

Brook worked in Paris with a Swiss designer, Jean Monod, on the set for Persepolis. Together they constructed a combination of *The Tempest* and *The Dream*. It would be a vast undertaking, a fifty-foot cube built on wheels, coloured black and silver it was open-topped, slatted-sided, constructed of steel and gauze, containing the audience seated on galleries inside. At the four corners were large cranes which could swing inside and outside the cube; railways ran through the cube so that platforms with actors and sets and fire could be shunted in and out; part of the audience could also be detached and taken 'on a quick tour of the Persepolis ruins'. Endless work went into the set because Brook did not yet know where he was going to be able to perform at Persepolis. The ruins had seen pageants and *son et lumière* but had, as he thought then, no naturally confined space with a focus suitable for a stage performance. Therefore it was going to be necessary to create one.

By now Hughes had started writing the Prometheus story, from Zeus to Hercules, in Orghast, incorporating certain scenic ideas from Calderón. By the time the group left for Tehran in June everyone had done extensive work on the first scenes written in Orghast (twelve were already working on assigned characters). Everyone also knew at least one speech in Greek, and some also knew Latin and Spanish speeches from *Hercules* and *Life is a dream*. The first work in Persia was to bring the two very different groups together, and for the Persians to learn Greek and Orghast while the Paris group mastered Avesta. After the initial getting-to-know-one-another period the work was divided up. Except for morning exercises and the Thursday-night improvisations, the company was split into four groups which rotated daily among the directors who discussed each evening what had been done and planned the work for the next day. (On *Orghast*, as previously on *US* and *The Round House Tempest*, Brook worked by assembling a group of people, with different viewpoints and talents from his own, to create a wide frame of reference in which he could find his own way.) The directors usually agreed on what was good in rehearsal, what worked, what was alive, but disagreed about why something did not work. Brook regarded the Persian project as primarily of interest to directors; but the work centred on particular actors, what they could and could not do, how their range could be extended to do more things more quickly and better.

The first attempts to get the Persian performers involved in the language were failures: despite their talents and vocal abilities, most were unable to achieve any flexibility of pitch or rhythm, or to find outlets for their emotions within the strict discipline of the work. After six weeks, only two could handle Orghast; the rest were chorus material. When this became clear, subterranean mutterings prompted Brook to hold a meeting with the Persians; as a result, three Persian actors left the company. One of them had been offered the Messenger speech from *The Persians*, but because he had no Orghast he felt humiliated. The next day Brook had to explain to the company:

The life of a group is not that everyone is equal: it's based on inequality. Some are brilliant, some are clumsy, and so on. The beginner and the clumsy actor can develop something that the skilful actor couldn't do. I do not believe in the possibility of artistic democracy. One recognises the facts head on and works to develop what one cannot do. Perhaps you will feel envious, jealous, resentful of someone else. But inside the group one recognises – one should recognise – that all natural emotions have to be kept out of the work. One shouldn't pretend to oneself but – and this is the prime discipline – one should rigorously prevent them from ever creeping into the work. Then certain traditional corrupting problems of theatre companies do not have to arise any more. For this ideal working state one needs a great sense of realism, and one must take care not to be seduced by certain dreams. For instance, exercises like those we have been doing – the sticks, t'ai chi, etc. – can make a group play rapidly and intuitively together. It's a lovely reassuring feeling: nobody at any moment stands out. Then the exercise came to an end. Now suddenly one will have a lot to do, another a little. The beautiful circle goes; the strength of mind of each of us comes into question.

These principles led to the dramatic situation here. In the honeymoon phase there was no problem. From the day that what are called 'parts' were distributed noses were being put out of joint. Last night I called together the Persian group and spoke at length about these things, the condition of our work being that everyone accepts and tackles totally whatever possibilities are offered. They had come into the work not knowing about us, perhaps they had many misunderstandings, thinking it would be something to show to their friends or improve their status. So I said that things were still in evolution and reminded them that no promises had ever been made to anyone. I said that if there was anybody not prepared to do the complex work of the chorus then this was the moment to leave. We are now going into a period requiring total concentration with no time for molly-coddling. The result was that we have lost three actors. It is disappointing but not surprising. We have come to a point of no return.

The three actors who left had to report their departure to the Ministry of Culture and give reasons. They reported a cesspool of vice and corruption. In a comic improvisation, based on a Hughes outline *Difficulties of a Bridegroom*, they said that a male and a female had been together in a large box for a few minutes. The Ministry did not take them too seriously.

Persia had two kinds of traditional theatre. One was the *Ta'zieh*, a kind of miracle play concerned with the life of the Prophet that was played in villages. The other, strongly objected to by the mullahs, was a *Ruhozi*, a kind of *commedia dell'arte* clowning by troupes of three or four, all men, using fixed characters and stories but freely improvising the dialogue. They only perform by request, usually at weddings, and always establish with the buyer of the performance (usually the bride's father) just how *risqué* the jokes can be, as they specialise in *double entendres*. The performance usually centres around a master–servant duo, the best actor playing the servant in blackface. One Thursday night Brook invited a company to play on the carpet after dinner; after they had given their own performance some of the group (most successfully the Africans) joined in undirected improvisations on the theme of prison, using a handful of words of Persian and 'bash da hondo'. This evening led Brook to arrange for the group to give a performance in a village. He told the actors:

It may give us uncomfortable moments, but it will teach us an enormous amount about what is pure and impure in communication. If this is true for the Persepolis work then it is also true for the village. What is going to play to people apparently as far as possible from ourselves in shared references? We are putting to the test the theory that communicating only goes on in the presence of the same language and references. Perhaps so. We may discover we have no communication whatsoever with them. But I personally believe, in that case, that it is because we are not free enough to make it. It is a basic acting exercise for all of us. It will quite simply question whether we can be clear and simple.

The big question is whether anything to do with a woman is tolerable. Whether it is wise to start with women present. Perhaps the women should just play instruments and sing – nothing more. We'll have to feel our way. We can have the women's parts played by men. Perhaps one woman can walk across the carpet and we'll watch, ready to rush for the bus. Having to exclude the obvious sexual themes is a fantastic, almost impossible exercise; we're putting aside the one thing we know that is common to humanity.

Brook asked NITV to find him an 'authentically rural village'. One was offered about fifty miles outside Tehran, although it was hardly isolated since it was in sight of the main road from the capital to Turkey. Uzbakhi was a large rectangular courtyard, with rooms built into the high enclosing wall of mud. About 200 people lived there. The company arrived at noon and walked round for an hour smiling at the villagers. The veiled women did not hide, just stared from the doorways. The men who were not working talked a little to the Persians. It was agreed that the company would return after lunch and siesta and play at 5 p.m. The village headman offered the schoolroom, outside the walls, for the performance. When he saw Brook's reluctance he offered the inner courtyard. The carpet was put down in the middle and one large box placed on it. As the company prepared, about a hundred children gathered round, some managing to get an impromptu game of football with the actors if they could avoid the man with a large stick who went round hitting them, to keep them quiet. By the time the show began about fifty women and forty men had joined the children. One of the Persian actors introduced the main characters and explained the story from time to time: he also persuaded the man with the stick to stop hitting the noisy children. This was then translated into Turkish, Farsi being very little understood in the village.

Hughes's scenario, *Difficulties of a Bridegroom*, concerned the trials of a shy lover. The father of the girl he loves challenges him to a gymnastic contest at which he is pathetic. Her mother and very large sister lust after him. A rival suitor is accidentally killed, and the corpse refuses to go away; even when packed into a box one arm or leg always appears at the wrong moment. A policemen arrives and is framed into believing that he himself committed the murder. The play needed only bamboo sticks and boxes. The text throughout was 'bash da hondo'.

There was great applause when one of the Persian actors entered in a dress and high heels, and at all demonstrative gags. The men laughed the most, although very few found the policeman funny. The woman giggled frequently, mainly at the hero. The children were frightened by what they took to be a Japanese magician and by the first appearance of moving boxes; but they joined in the general dance at the end. Brook thought the throwing of sweets into the audience by one of the Persian actresses was the only lapse of taste (it had been agreed that there would be no show of affluence, no crates of Coke or cameras), though she defended it by saying they were wedding sweets and the play had ended with a wedding. The actors enjoyed playing it. Afterwards they talked with the villagers, whose first question was why didn't the women play. Apparently they had all been to the cinema and had seen television, and so were hardly feudal, if not 'liberated'.

At the post-mortem the Paris group was enthusiastic about the show, and eager to talk about which parts had held the audience's attention, while the Persians were entirely negative, thought it too *Ruhozi*-like and not 'good enough art' to take to a village. They also seemed to resent foreigners invading their territory and traditions, through they never articulated it in that form.

Brook did not want to draw up rules and a pattern from the village experience, 'but be open again next time'. He thought the old convention of men playing women's parts had also added a lot to the comedy and wondered how actresses could be introduced without losing that asset. More successfully than any of the children's shows in Paris, he felt the village show had found the compromise between propositions open enough to allow a free play of energy but disciplined enough to hold the action together:

Ruhozi has been an invaluable model of improvisation. It never falls apart. At Uzbakhi I experienced something I've always believed to be true, that it is possible to communicate with anybody by finding a common language, or common forms – the circus is an obvious, universal example. The job is to reduce those fixed, common elements until you have enough to serve as bridges to the audience, but not so many as to impede the possibility of improvising totally on the tempo of the response. It is not a question of the intrinsic value of the material we use, but of the completeness of the circle we make. The village awakes memories of the very first day in Paris when the tent was built. What we found in innocence we have had to rebuild painfully in experience.

Brook's attempts to get in tune with specific locations – or, to put it another way, to make the spirits listen – was a major factor in the dramatic shaping of the two parts of *Orghast*. A reconnoitring trip to Persepolis coincided with the estimate arriving for building the set that had been designed in Paris: it was 50,000 dollars (the French construction company had a monopoly on scaffolding in Persia). As this sum was out of the question the designer was already preparing a cut-down version, with gantries instead of the cranes and without railway lines (resembling the *Dream*), when the directors visited the site to find the best place for the cube. It was soon apparent that there was no good site in the main palace, it all being very flat and open; one could only use the old ruined columns (being rapidly renovated by a team of Italian archeologists) as a cinemascope backdrop. The obvious place to play was not on the main site of the palace but in the tombs: there were two cut in the hill-side above the palace, and a row of four cut into a cliff five miles away. The smaller tombs of Artaxerxes above the palace, though difficult to work in, had a stronger feeling of being hewn out of the rock, and their small space dictated the nature of Part One – highly focused, intimate and intense with a few simple movements and a large range of sound; whereas the four tombs of Naqsh-i-Rustam, cut half way up a 200-foot cliff and spread over a quarter of a mile, implied the epic.

Brook immediately obtained verbal agreement from the festival, the Ministry of Culture and the Department of Archeology to work in the tombs, but when he arrived in Shiraz with the company six weeks later he found that no work had been done on the sites because there was no official written per-mission. A day of issuing ultimata, including a screaming row with the direc-tor-general of the festival on the tarmac at the airport, produced the necessary signatures.

The first part of *Orghast* played twice nightly on 28 and 29 August and once on 30 August. In front of the tomb was a stone shelf about fifty feet square, with a drop on one side, and on the other the face of the tomb. The audience, of between 200 and 300, sat in three rows against each of the side walls. Actors entered and exited by the edge of the shelf (two ladders on to a scaffold struc-ture just out of sight, by the door of the tomb and by a ladder up one side wall). On the sloping sides of the cliff were positioned four actors, the one playing Prometheus being chained to a ledge on the face of the top of the tomb. Most of the actors sat in two irregular lines facing each other in front of the two banks of audience, while others waited in the tomb or below the ledge. Five drummers played a variety of European, Persian and home-made instruments. The central area was lit by three spotlights. Three of the performances began at sunset and played as the darkness grew. The actors played a series of scenes based on key images, or relationships, improvising on the tight sound struc-ture of Hughes's Orghast. Speeches were used from Seneca and Aeschylus; Avesta was mainly used by the chorus. The actor playing Prometheus did in fact use the last lines of Aeschylus' play as his final speech, but he was using it as raw material to develop a relationship with a character on the ledge below who had just resisted the invitation to do something violent – in rehearsals he had used other speeches at this point.

One of the early speeches that remained in performance was:

Bullorga ombolom fror sharsaya nulbulda brarg in ombolom bullorga darkness opens its womb I hear chaos roar in the womb of darkness.

It was used by the actor above the tomb playing the godly counterpart to the king who imprisons or destroys his sons as he is fearful they will usurp him. The English actor who used it said that 'working in Orghast is more like an act of remembering than of playing a part – you search for what language was like before it became just a means of exchanging ideas and information. Once you find the key to it, its own energy, it is surprisingly free. It begins to live in its own right.'

As the sun set drums began to throb; chanting, rumbling voices broke out from different places – beneath the ledge, on the heights, inside the tomb; a woman (Light) silhouetted against the skylines intoned, *keeningly*; from the distance Man answered, *gaveh*. The chorus began making staccato noises, not in unison. Prometheus, chained on the upper ledge and Moa, inside the tomb, began to chant. Then a huge ball of Promethean fire was lowered slowly from the top of the hill, flaring over the upturned faces of the audience. Moa emerged from the tomb, set the fire in a bowl and knelt before it. God-Krogon, hidden, gave an order and King-Krogon appeared to send Sheergra (Strength) to remove the fire from man, but before he could take it away a freed slave, Furorg, lit a torch at the fireball.

Singing a lullaby, Furorg cradled a baby in his arms, and gave it to Ussa. Sheegra stamped it to death. Ussa, mad with grief, tried unsuccessfully to stab King-Krogon. Prometheus moaned as he was tortured by a screaming Vulture. The King's wife, Moasha, gave birth to Sogis, and the child was chained up in the burial chamber. As Sogis grew up Moasha taught him to speak. Furorg released Sogis from his chains by touching them with a burning torch. After a Dionysian chorus a princess sang a duet of lust with King-Krogon who became possessed. Furorg led in his family, one by one, and Krogon slew them. When made to realise what he had done Krogon blinded himself. While Sogis slept Furorg showed him, as a dream, the ghosts of Krogon's family. Moa begged Sogis for revenge. Furorg gave Sogis a knife as the blind Krogon appeared, ringing a tiny bell and feeling his way with a stick; but Sogis could not kill him. While Prometheus gave his last speech from the ledge a distant Agoluz-Hercules chanted Avesta. Sogis followed the voice out into the desert while the blind Krogon entered the burial chamber.

The audience usually sat in silence for some time before applauding, once for six minutes; although it was not quite silence. After much ado the festival had managed to get the roads around Persepolis closed for the length of the performances and the rehearsals of the centenary procession, which could have been staged by Cecil B. De Mille, temporarily halted; but it could not stop the army, who had a camp next to the ruins of the palace, from going about its business. So performances designed to take place in silence often had an audible background of cars, lorries, dogs and general carousal, to say nothing of the odd sentry patrolling the top of the tomb.

The sixth (and last scheduled) performance of *Orghast: Part One* was cancelled when the festival discovered it had not allowed any time for the Cracow Symphony Orchestra to rehearse. However, it was played again – for the Queen. No one from the directorate had come to the opening performance of *Orghast*; only when word had got out that it was 'all right', in the sense that it did not contain anything offensive about the Persian kings of the past, nor any account of the defeats of the Persian army, did any official turn up. By the time it had finished its run it was decided that the Queen would see it. So the following Saturday there would be a final Part One at Persepolis at sunset for the Queen and her party (which would have been impossible to accommodate with any general public for security reasons) and afterwards they would see the last rehearsal of Part Two at Naqsh-i-Rustam. There would then be one single performance of Part Two, at daybreak on Sunday. The festival authorities failed to tell their technical staff about the extra performance, with the result that the entire set-up at the tomb at Persepolis had been stripped down and had to be replaced. By the morning of the Queen's performances it had not been fully restored so the technical staff were divided, some to supervise the restoration of the small tomb, the rest still doing battle at the large tombs with ladders, fires and a temperamental sound system; when the technical director tried to leave Persepolis to go to Naqsh-i-Rustam in the afternoon he was stopped by the military. When the actors arrived they were stopped for thirty minutes. No one was allowed to go to the toilet. All preparations were conducted under the gaze of a dozen men with Smith and Wesson pistols in their shoulder holsters (they only put their coats on five minutes before the Queen arrived). She saw a strong and fast performance, but even she did not get silence, the army camp continuing its normal traffic.

Afterwards, the Queen departed to wait for Part Two while the technicians made a dash for the other site to finish the fires and ladders. However, they arrived to find Naqsh-i-Rustam ringed by security police: no one was to be let in until Bushehri, the festival director, arrived with the list of those cleared for security, and Bushehri had gone off with the Queen. No amount of explaining that there would be no performance for the Queen to see unless the technicians were allowed in made any difference. Brook arrived with the company. The answer again was No, not until Bushehri brought the list. Brook tried to walk in and was pushed back by a guard. He sat down on the steps, and then exploded. He asked the company to get back on the bus. They would all go to a nearby restaurant, and return only when the Queen arrived and they could get into the site. But the bus driver would not leave without the liaison officer's permission; he, trying to calm things down, would not risk Brook and the actors not being there when the Queen arrived. 'Very well', said Brook, 'we will walk'. He led the way off the bus and with Irene Worth on one arm and Natasha Parry on the other he set off, down the road, across the desert in moonlight. They blocked the road to stop cars getting past. After a few minutes a police car roared up and told them, in Farsi, to get off the road, or else. Before the 'or else' could be put into operation Bushehri and a general arrived. Brook went to speak to them. As the general became angry Brook gave him a violent shove in the chest and asked him how he liked it. 'I do not', the general replied. Brook told Bushehri that the company had come to prepare something for the Queen, they cared about what they were going to do for her, but the people who were supposed to care for her did not care at all. They were going to the restaurant, because the bus had refused to take them. 'Do you want us to go on walking', Brook asked, 'or will you get the bus to come for us?' The bus came and took the company to the restaurant. On the way they passed the Queen and her friends *en route* to the tombs.

A Persian professor of international law told Brook that the situation was extremely dangerous; a Persian journalist said it was essential to find a way out, or 'this will make every headline in the world. If the Queen is upset the Shah will close down the festival. It will mean the end of everything liberal.' At the restaurant Brook addressed the company: 'There is only one thing that matters, there is only one reason for our being here, and that is to perform. And that is what we are going to do, but in the right time and the right way.' It was 9.55. The technicians thought it might take to midnight to set up. Bushehri believed the Queen might wait an hour, but not two: he offered an apology to the company, explaining that the incident was the result of having two or three separate security networks.

When they returned to Naqsh-i-Rustam Brook was asked to talk to the Queen, sitting in a dark bus in the middle of the desert surrounded by a score of her companions. The Queen began by observing that the roles appeared to have been reversed – here the royalty was being made to wait while the artists did the entrances and exits. Brook told her, at length, about the events of the past weeks, and step by step analysed the causes of the evening's debacle, making several comments about the true state of Persian hospitality and efficiency. He concluded by saying, 'You have seen our work and you know your security people. You can believe what you choose.' After he left the court advised her to leave immediately. But she stayed. Meanwhile, under the gaze of the security guards, the technicians prepared; people who had to go to the top of the cliff to light the fires found bayonets thrust in their faces, it took twenty minutes to organise an escort.

Brook told the company:

We have only one responsibility, to our work. We must take any situation and transform its energies into the energies of our work. Now we have to put together the circle between ourselves.

The rehearsal started at 11.05. The Queen had sat in her bus for an hour and twenty minutes. Afterwards, she said it was a good thing she had not come to see the dawn performance, or it would have finished in broad daylight.

A few hours later about 1,000 people saw the only performance of Part Two of *Orghast*. The performance started in darkness and ended with the sunrise. Scaffolding ladders were erected up to two of the four tombs set fifty feet up in the stone. Facing the cliff was a series of low mounds, which created an extraordinary acoustic.

It began with fires being lit on the top of the cliffs. Behind the waiting crowd, harsh calls pierced the night air, and – wheeling around – the audience saw wild figures, holding torches, running towards one another, swarming below the tombs, sweeping through them.

The action continued from Part One; Krogon, now half dead, came to his last death, crawling blindly from a pit across the rock face, followed by Furgorg, Ussa (still seeking revenge), by Moasha and the murdered family. From the tomb of Xerxes, the Vulture shrieked. Sogis and Agoluz arrived from Persepolis, driven by the memories of the place, where old kings, armies, battles and feuds could still be felt. Darius and Xerxes appeared as in a dream. High above, from an imperial tomb, an emperor emerged, flanked by torchbearers, acclaimed by the soldiers below.

Then came a slow ritual procession: the King, his wives, his son, Strength and Violence – speaking Avesta and Orghast. The Vulture stood in the mouth of one tomb. The wild figures were the chorus, now far from static, chasing and fighting their way from side to side of the area as the procession moved along the face of the cliff. They used the text of Aeschylus' *Persians* (unbeknown to the Persian officials who spoke no Greek, although one of the translators, a schoolboy, had constantly asked whether the part about the defeat of the Persian army was being used: it was forbidden to stage *The Persians* in Persia). Although the action looked like a small-scale religious rebellion (or, in its grander moments, like an old movie spectacular) it was intended to invoke the vibration of the place itself, which the Persians called the City of the Dead.

In a fissure in the rock Moa shouted curses in Orghast at the approaching Krogon. The procession stopped. From across the plain another murdered son of Krogon called. Agoluz-Hercules became Xerxes at the moment he was completely defeated; his search centred on the Cube of Zoroaster, a fire-temple where he descended into the underworld to meet a magician. So the action criss-crossed the thirty yards between the mounds and the cliff, the audience following, and slowly moved towards the fire-temple, a building that rose forty feet from a moat. It was melodramatic and romantic – anything fire-lit tends to be both – but it dramatically explored the space. From 200 yards up the valley came the voice of the Messenger from Salamis, a transmogrified Prometheus, who slowly advanced to the temple. Agoluz spoke to the magician and cried for his father; Pramanath answered from the cliff. Agoluz, Furorg and the Vulture crossed to the cliff, slowly climbing in search of Prometheus' rock. As the sun rose the actors were spread out along both the top and the foot of the cliff, freely chanting Avesta, as a man slowly led a cow up the valley.

THE CRITICS ON *ORGHAST*

Andrew Porter, in *The Financial Times*:

Brook's knowledge of contemporary music with its spacial effects, counterpoints of random detail under large-scale control, and free juxtaposition of speech and song (a 'concert performance' of *Orghast* would grace an ISCM Festival). . . . Every musician will understand at once the enthralling interest of *Orghast* . . . the effect was overwhelming. . . . The playgoer who has entered deeply into *Orghast* has passed through fire, and can never be the same again.

Irving Wardle, in *The Times*:

It has certain obvious ties with Brook's previous work, but essentially it marks the beginning of something which is not only new for Brook but without parallel in theatre history: the creation of a form of drama comprehensible to anyone on earth. But there is a stupefying series of contradictions. Seeking a broad open public, the company played to the exclusive elite of a royal arts' festival. Seeking a non-rational form of action, they assembled a highly analytical collage of Western and Asian myth. Seeking a language accessible to everyone, they erected a verbal blockade. . . . The initial impression, in short, was that if Brook's aim had been to exclude the public he could not have done a more thorough job. . . . All the objections can be answered. The structure is defensible as an attempt to melt corresponding national myths down to universal archetype; the invented language as a method of placing the international company on an equal footing. But all such arguments, for or against, miss the point by erecting an intellectual barricade against a work intended to awaken the prelogical faculties and conjure buried music out of the earth.

    The style of performance is vigilantly attentive to the environment's demands. . . . In terms of pure sound, its effect is often thrilling: particularly in the language transitions between the long sobbing vowels of Orghast and the droning hiccoughs of Avesta. Dramatically, though, it strikes me as a crucial weakness that the performance of Part One comes most to life during the coda – when the essential action is finished, and the performers can give themselves over wholly to making music. There seems to be a deep-rooted misunderstanding of the respective properties of language and music. Music alone was not enough for the company. Every line of the Orghast has a translatable meaning; 'I didn't want to write nonsense' said Ted Hughes. So why should an audience be expected to respond to apparent nonsense, no matter how sonorously delivered? The answer, from Brook's and Hughes's point of view, would be that translation would kill the force of the original and explanation usurp the place of direct response. It is beautiful, but much of the dramatic life is rooted in the particular cultures of the actors, not in a buried, biologically shared spirit. I am dubious about the jungle of interlocking myths. As the production makes no concessions to the basic factor of human curiosity (in public debate Ted Hughes was reluctant even to disclose that the word 'orghast' means 'sun'), its effect on me was to awaken intellectual frustration more than any sense of feasting on the archetypal honeycomb.

Part One was the work of Brook the research artist, but Brook the showman took over at Naqsh-i-Rustam. . . . Where *Orghast I* had the character of a secret company for the few, *Orghast II* was grand opera. . . . *Orghast I* (like Brook's *Tempest* exercise) is evidently the first stage of a work in progress. *Orghast II* has no such future: it existed only within the special circumstances of the occasion, burning itself out in a single night like a firework display. Brook commands his audiences no less than his actors, providing an area of freedom within an unbreakable form, and directing every eye to whatever has to be seen. The associations with *Orlando Furioso* and Mnouchkine's *1789* are inescapable. The difference is that few people at Naqsh-i-Rustam had much idea of what was going on. . . . However, in obedience to its setting *Orghast II* has a far thinner texture than its predecessor; and the appropriate response is, less to its mythological or intellectual content than to its achievement as music and spectacle. Brook's evident purpose was to release the awe-inspiring presence of the place itself into dramatic expression. And it is on this ground, if any, that his work can be faulted. Naqsh-i-Rustam, as it stands, is alive. What Brook has done is to replace it to a stage set: a greater one than Reinhardt ever dreamed of, but still an artefact.

Lest there should be any misunderstanding of Brook's current line of research, it is worth quoting this disclaimer he made to an interviewer in Shiraz: 'I don't give a damn about ritual, about myth or about universal language or universal brotherhood. And I'm not trying to create a new myth theatre or a new formalised theatre or anything of that sort.' What he is in search of is a route back to the springs of drama itself: and at this stage of the work it is too soon to start slamming any critical doors.

Ernst Wendt, in *Theater Heute*:

I have never felt theatre a more decadent business than it was in this unreal setting, before a few hundred guests, guarded by military weapons. The actors were paid to obscure reality with their long-rehearsed play, which was a striking example of a movement in the theatre towards mystification. The attempt to combine stage, performance and spectator into a *unio mystica* was a highly artificial, over-perfected experiment which will serve to confuse the course of theatre. In seeking to awaken mythical powers below the detritus of civilisation, the production had gone so far beyond physical reality that it had reached the radically abstract point of 'pure theatre-craft', formalistic acting.

Brook had hoped there would be time to do a carpet show for the nomads who move across the desert near Persepolis, but Persian Television wanted to film *Orghast*. Clearly the scope of Part Two made it impossible as they did not have any sophisticated equipment capable of filming the action in the dark, but the enclosed setting of Part One was manageable. Brook stopped them filming a performance, and they had not been able to organise filming a dress rehearsal, which he had offered. Now it came to a question of time. Brook always insisted that a carpet show was 'an equal pillar of our work', that 'an act of theatre exists only as it happens' and that the presence of an audience is essential to 'complete the circle'. Yet he called a company meeting to discuss it, saying 'it is now very clear to me that it is possible and worthwhile to make a simple record of it, as far as it is ever possible in the theatre'. The majority of actors wanted to make the film. It took from dusk one evening until late morning of the following day to do it.

Brook still wanted to do another village show on the return trip to Tehran, but without any time to rerehearse *Difficulties of a Bridegroom* he decided to do the first part of *Orghast* to see whether it would stand up to the critical eye of a naïve audience. A site was found twenty miles from Isfahan: the remains of an old building – a mosque perhaps, no one knew for sure – enclosed by a wall just outside a group of small villages of 300 people; almost gothic, it seemed an ideal replacement.

Brook:

We have a responsibility of doing an interesting adaptation. The intention is to make it clearer without changing anything essential. It would be naïve, and moreover bad work, to present it unchanged. What we have to make clear is not the plot but the relationships. Anyway, as we know the story is impossible to tell. The tomb did something for us: we used its atmosphere and presence. Now we have to do it ourselves. The chorus needs to be much freer, less static and ritualistic. But be clear: we are not making it simpler for the village; they are a more exacting audience than we had at Persepolis.

The actors rehearsed for three hours in the ruins with a constant audience of children. By six o'clock about 200 men had appeared, and behind them a huddle of a dozen women. Though an introduction was made to the characters – dividing them into gods, demigods, men and heroes – there was constant, noisy discussion from the start: who, what, why? The physical placement of the audience – similar to Persepolis being bunched together with things happening all around – instead of creating a mystery, led to chatter, merriment and finally confusion. The use of the place only baffled this audience. As darkness approached the performance broke down, as there was no centre, no focus. They only enjoyed the melodrama, the fighting and moments such as the Vulture poking Prometheus in the ribs with a stick, which they found very funny as they obviously knew that situation. The actors were downcast at the shambles, but Brook thought it most useful, exposing the primarily intellectual parts of *Orghast* that the sophisticated, indulgent audiences at Persepolis had let the company get away with.

Brook:

The avant-garde can't be healthy without the total sanity of its opposite. It is the opposite of the Artaud pole. When you see all those expectant, open faces, you can't leave them unfulfilled. You have to make a circle to include them.

The response was absolutely true to the different stages of development of the material. They were held for the first ten minutes, when Man was stealing fire, but that had no connection with the next scene. We weren't in a position to take advantage of their laughter by adjusting our rhythms to the unexpected response. We saw at Uzbakhi how the comic is the only sure way of connecting. Spectacle is secondary. The Shakespearian moment between comedy and tragedy is the only form.

We should never visit a village once only. The only way to find a true form would be to keep going back to this audience and make it work from second to second. That place was a miracle for us to find, but to do it on a carpet, with nothing else, would be the true test. It is the most satisfying discipline I can think of today, seeking forms that make sense in an Asiatic village. Clear images have to be found. It is not a matter of playing up or down. The villagers are an honest audience, not like a sophisticated one, who do what's expected of them.

All the questions have been put. Theatre is the most pitilessly difficult form. It is often forgotten. In the history of formal theatre there may have been four or five flashes. Aeschylus, Shakespeare, Chekhov, Beckett . . . and of course all the thousands of moments of unsung, unscripted performances in villages across the world.

It was to those villages across the world that Brook was now heading.

12   Into the deserts: Africa and California

When he returned from Persia, Brook went to three foundations – Ford, Robert Anderson and ·Gulbenkian – and explained his artistic aims and practical needs. He then spent a year in the Mobilier working with a small group of actors, most of whom had been in *Orghast*.

The group improvised Ted Hughes pieces, turning some of his poems into sounds. They tried to develop a system using signs, syllables and silence. They worked on bird sounds. They studied Greek to absorb the hard sounds and sliding vowels. They mixed these up with improvised sounds and with elements of Japanese and African songs which required using the voice in a particular way. Brook was striving for the meaning of *sound* rather than the meaning of *words*, and for a theatrical language that was more physically expressive than English and more universal, able to be grasped emotionally anywhere in the world. The greater the physicality of the language – even to the extent that one moves one's lips and chin – the greater the emotionality. Thus, Brook contended, the hard muscular sounds of Greek offer a challenge to the contemporary English theatre's flat, colourless language that, to him, had become debased and meaningless. But could sounds and signs ever surpass language?

The group spent days trying to discover when a bird sound was not a bird sound, and when a song was not a song. (Yoshi said, 'I don't know when a song isn't a song. But I think a song begins when you wish to speak of the devil or God or fire'.) Brook was trying to find out if there was a point *beyond* song where it would lose its cultural background. He was after a form of artlessness. Hughes created a few sounds to help the actors create the artless song: KO – OOOM KA – OOOM KE – OOOM.

Throughout the year a set of exercises was developed based on boxes – corrugated cartons of various sizes.

Brook:

A box is an ordinary unpoetic object of the everyday world. But a box is also an object that has a million identities. It can be what you cherish, what you guard, what you protect, what you preserve something in, what you hide in, what protects you. It is a good test for the actors as well as the audience's imagination. A small box slowly moved from the side to the middle of the area as though by itself; in fact you couldn't tell if there was a motor inside or what. Everyone's attention was caught. When the box stopped in the middle of the space there was a moment's pause and then the box started breathing. There was a person inside it. Now when 500 people are looking at a cardboard box that is breathing, the very thing that I'm talking about is taking place. The audience is not told anything specific, nor is it told how to respond. It can sense a strangely poetic thing – it may find it funny or sad. In this case everyone was surprised and yet full of laughter.

The work was punctuated with *stages*, when the group would be joined by other people, usually for three weeks. Moshe Feldenkrais came to teach his science of body movements, working to increase awareness of the natural function of every part of the body. He taught that a transformed understanding would liberate the muscles to the point where the body could move with minimum effort and maximum efficiency, the ultimate aim being the transformed state of 'a potent state of mind and body'.

The American Theatre of the Deaf joined the work for three weeks. So did a mixed group of foreign actors. Some of them found the work difficult. During the meal break one evening an American was in tears, but Brook had not noticed it and called the group back to work. Malik defied the order and started singing African songs. Then Brook asked to see an improvisation. A Greek actress said 'Peter, I haven't got the energy'. The American, still crying, said, 'I mean, could we have something *familiar*'. Brook noticed and immediately asked Cathy Berberian to sing, and so each member of the group sang a song to entertain the others. Some had been composed during the trip to Persia, songs of love and struggle which revived memories. One was called *Essence* – 'who? what? where? why? Essence'.

When all the circle had sung Brook asked three actors to perform an improvisation for the guests of Hughes's poem, *The Rock Spirit*: 'The rock spirit, an ogre, waiting, yawning, sees one coming, retreats into the rock. Enter mother bird with child. Mother bird dances.' There was silence at the end until Hughes started to laugh uncontrollably. Brook smiled. Hughes was laughing because he had seen something complete. They knew that they had seen the *duende* (Lorca: all that has dark sounds has *duende* – the mysterious power that everyone feels but that no philosopher has explained.) Brook said to an actor who had given up after twenty minutes: 'Never stop. It's a universal truth. One always stops as soon as something is about to happen.'

At the end of one *stage*, Brook told the actors 'The point is none of you really cares about the work'. They looked shocked and he would not explain. The permanent members were given a brief holiday. Brook left for Africa, to reconnoitre.

Brook:

We're going off to Africa at the end of the year with material which will be only half formed. But we're then, with Ted Hughes, going to be developing and developing, very much influenced by the fact that if one of the villagers gets up and walks out, we're going to rewrite, we're going to restage, and we're in fact going to be evolving our material exactly according to principles I've lived through in what is something which theoretically has to be totally rejected – the awful commercial theatre.

Throughout the year, occasional performances were given in the Mobilier for various audiences: students, psychiatrists, deaf-and-dumb children, businessmen and delinquents. Playlets were performed using Ted Hughes's material and boxes. Handke's *Kaspar* was also performed, and toured around a few community halls in the suburbs. They played two versions of the play on the same evening before a small invited audience. The first was true to the strict text, the second was opened up with improvisations, and speeches were turned into songs.

For the deaf children they would make very physical performances: actors wove shapes and rhythms with long bamboo sticks, they formed a labyrinth, created images, balanced the sticks on their heads, hurled them round the room, flicked them from hand to hand, whirled them round like warriors until, after forty-five minutes, the group formed a giant which was eaten by a caterpillar when it chased a midget. Occasionally the stick went flying, an actor would fall over. The children took what they wanted, turning away when they were bored, when the actors repeated something they had already done once twenty minutes before. Afterwards, the group gathered round in a circle to watch the deaf children perform their own improvisation – a cops-and-robbers tale.

Brook (the month before leaving for Africa with the group):

There are two worlds, the world of everyday and the world of the imagination. When children play, they pass quite naturally through the two worlds all the time, so that at one moment a child can hold a stick and pretend it's a sword. At one moment you can tell him to drop that stick and he responds to that. At the same time you can tell him to drop that sword and he responds to that. The two worlds coexist. In most societies, particularly in Africa, the imaginary world and everyday world intermingle. The theatre should be the meeting place between these two worlds. But in the theatre of illusion – the theatre of curtains and scenery and seats – the curtain goes up and supposedly there is the world of imagination, and then the curtain goes down and we are all back into the everyday world, as though the everyday world has no imagination and the imaginary world has no everyday. This is both untrue and unhealthy.

The healthy relationship is the coexisting one. And the coexisting one in artistic form makes it possible for an adult to find his way back to what every child knows unaided. Which brings me to a single example: if you put a cardboard box in front of an audience and the audience can see it is a cardboard box and a poetic object, they are seeing this in a double light. They are seeing it on an imaginary plane and on a real plane, and they respond to both simultaneously, letting whatever responses they have be perfectly natural.

In Africa we hope to find such audiences – audiences that are unconcerned with 'correct' responses. In fact, in Africa, people have no conception of theatre at all, but they are very close to the everyday movement of life and imaginary world as well. A sophisticated audience in London and New York can be very easily bluffed – and that's one of the reasons we're doing experimental work elsewhere. What we want is the lively response of an audience which, if it's not satisfied with what it sees, gets up seconds later and leaves. And that is what we are going to Africa to meet. We are looking for what is really human, what is the real substance of life.

In December 1972, Brook went to Africa with eleven actors (he would return with thirty), a composer, a doctor, a stage-manager, two cooks, a French observer, an American photographer, a British journalist (John Heilpern who chronicled the trek in *Conference of the Birds*) and an African drummer. They were joined at an early stage by a French film crew. There were three English actors, three American, two French, a German, an African and a Japanese. They travelled in five Land Rovers and a Bedford truck, with a crew from Minitrek, who usually took tourists on safari. They took twenty-four bamboo canes, a trunk of musical instruments, a case of white costumes, and several empty cardboard boxes. They went from Algiers across the Sahara Desert through Niger to Cotonou, on the Atlantic coast in Nigeria, and returned through Dahomey and Mali. The journey lasted three-and-a-half months. Brook's intention was to play improvised carpet shows in villages where the inhabitants did not even have a word for theatre in their language. But Brook had also planned to develop work during the tour on what was to become a major preoccupation during the seventies: his theatre version of a twelfth-century Persian poem, *The Conference of the Birds*.

After crossing the burning desert, Brook and his flock arrived at the oasis of In Salah, an ancient fortress town, 500 miles from Algiers.

Brook:

Our first performance was the most moving moment of the whole journey. Because it was the total unknown, we didn't know what could be communicated, and what couldn't.

Somebody took off a big, heavy, dusty pair of boots that he'd worn through the desert, and put them in the middle of the carpet. This was already a very intense moment. Everybody staring at these two objects which were loaded with many sorts of meanings. And then one person after another came in and did various improvisations with them, on a really shared premise: that first of all there was the empty carpet – there was nothing – then a concrete object. Everybody, the actors and the audience, saw these boots as though for the first time. Through these boots a relationship was established with the audience, so that what developed was shared in a common language. We were playing with something that was real to everybody, and therefore the things that came out of it, the use that was made of them, was an understandable language.

All we discovered after was that nothing had ever happened resembling this before on the market. Never had there been a strolling player. There was no precedent for it.

Brook's account of what happened at In Salah is very strange. He often uses scientific terminology to describe his work, and talks about a field of research, but is curiously reticent sometimes not only about deeper meanings but also about the concrete surface. When Michael Gibson asked him to describe the improvisations on the carpet with the boots, he replied, 'You can never capture that sort of thing in a description'. Yet Heilpern managed to describe very precisely what he saw occur when the boots were put on the carpet:

The crowd stares at the boots. The actors stare at the boots. Everyone in the place is staring at a pair of army boots. It was as if we were all seeing them for the first time. Then Katsulas (who had taken them off in the first place in order to cover a pause while they thought of something to follow the first piece of action, involving a corpse, which died a death) approached the boots. What luck! To find a pair of boots in the middle of nowhere. So he put them on, for he hadn't a pair of his own. Then he's in those great boots, and he's feeling really good, and he's strutting around that carpet a new man, a powerful man, a *giant* of a man! (He is a tall, well-built actor.) Sometimes the boots won't walk where he wants them to. They kick and fight him. But Yoshi Oida decides he wants the boots, confronts the giant, grows frightened, hides in the crowd. Uproar! The giant goes after him, but grabs a child instead. Everyone's laughing now, except the child who's really scared. So the giant, who's a gentle giant, takes off one of the boots and gives it to him. The child doesn't know what to do. 'Blow', mimes the giant. Marthouret is on the carpet now, blowing into the boot for the child. No sound. Blow harder; no sound. *Harder!* The boot makes the sound of a conch. Swados is blowing her brains out on the conch at the edge of the carpet, and everyone knows this but it doesn't matter. The child's eyes are wide. The giant asks him to try. He blows and blows, and the sound comes. The child just looked at the boot and he looked at the sky, and he couldn't say a word.

Now this account may be a poor substitute for being there, but Heilpern's vivid writing certainly gives some idea of what happened on that carpet; and anyone with a television set now roughly knows what a small town in the Algerian desert might look like. What was present that Brook would think indescribable? Does the description make the work too simple, not capable of having 'significance'? Talking about the trip, Brook referred to 'the right sort of simplicity' while also using phrases like 'human contact . . . through this particular form called theatre, without a shared language'.

Brook:

Many times before going I had to explain, struggling through a whole screen of questions, why a group should want to go and do this. One would come into a village where such a thing had never happened. We'd see the chief of the village and, through some interpreter, perhaps just a child from the village, I would talk to the chief and explain in very few words the fact that a group of people, from different parts of the world, had set out to discover if a human contact could be made through this particular form called theatre, without a shared language.

It was an event that was always welcomed, and always taken directly on its own terms for what it was. And when the performance worked well, what happened was something that could only happen through such a form.

What did it do? It wasn't supposed to do anything. Certainly you can't go into a village, play for an hour, and then go away having changed their lives. But it is quite clear that the way is open to hundreds of companies. Hundreds of groups could, if they wished – very inexpensively, too – go up and down the continent, playing this way and meeting nothing but appreciation. Something very active could happen, quite different from what happens on the level of official culture.

There is something very disarming about this account. The image of him explaining his research into a shared theatre language to a chief through a child interpreter; his modest acceptance of the fact that an hour of his theatre is not going to change people's lives; his assurance that this kind of work receives 'nothing but appreciation' are all typically Brook – as is his vision of 'hundreds of groups' going up and down the continent with carpet shows. And yet we are talking about one of the world's major theatre directors. He could have been spending the seventies making his millions with Broadway musicals. How much more inventive and enterprising and entertaining to take a carpet show to In Salah! And, for that matter, to another desert town, Tamanrasset, where the second performance they gave in Africa ended in collapse, largely because Brook had put the carpet under a tree on a narrow track that led to the market (at one point an old truck came up the street and the show had to be stopped and the carpet rolled up to let the truck through). After the show, Brook told his actors that they should have taken more risks (he was not referring to the episode with the truck, but to the fact that they had gone on trying to perform material from *The Box Show* when it clearly was not working). Brook said, 'It is our whole reason for coming to Africa. Change and develop with each audience – or we're lost.'

That night, according to Heilpern, Brook was heard singing to the stars by the camp fire, 'in his amazing breathless voice', some lyrics from *The Desert Song*:

> Oh, give me that night divine,
> And let my arms in yours entwine.
> The desert song calling
> Its voice enthralling
> Will make you mine.

Brook decided to build a show around the shoes, as Andreas Katsulas had placed them on the carpet in In Salah. He asked Heilpern to write a scenario. Heilpern was not allowed to use dialogue because of the search for a universal language. He came up with a story involving an old hag, a greedy king, two ridiculous thieves, a devious merchant and a corpse – each of whom is transformed by wearing an abandoned pair of shoes.

The Shoe Show was first performed in a poor village – Brook had put the carpet down in 'a dusty wasteland surrounded by hovels'. As they sat waiting for an audience to appear, Brook put the scenario ('A scrappy piece of paper') on to the carpet ('conjuring the rabbit out of the hat' writes Heilpern, using an image that many people have found themselves using about Brook). 'You might like to try a little of this.' Most of the actors only had time to glance at the piece of paper.

After some preliminary music ('Michele Collison fights Natasha Parry in sound'), a song in English (the group's anthem, 'By the Waters, the Waters of Babylon, We lay Down and Wept') and some instrumental work ('crazy, burbling sound duets'), which apparently had the crowd in hysterics, Brook ordered: 'SHOE SHOW!' Katsulas put the shoes on the carpet. Helen Mirren (once labelled 'The Sex Queen of the RSC') entered, bent double, as an ugly hag, cursing her way round the edge of the carpet. ('And I was so proud of this', writes Heilpern, 'it's ridiculous'.) She found the shoes, stared at them, slowly put them on, taking her time, and became young. ('Oh, fantastic!') King Katsulas then entered, with a one-legged shoe collector, because the ridiculous thieves had failed to appear. Heilpern writes:

'This is what improvisation is all about', I told myself. 'It's silly to have a heart attack.' But I couldn't believe what was happening on the carpet. There seemed to be a rival Shoe Show going on. King Katsulas was merrily cartwheeling round the place in the magic shoes when lovely mad Miriam Goldschmidt suddenly decided to enter with a rival shoe, which was dangling from a stick. I know things had got a bit out of sequence. But I definitely didn't write the rival Shoe Scene. I was practically up on my feet slinging her off the carpet. Brook was helpless with laughter. King Katsulas looked stunned. There was a rival shoe dangling under his nose. But you could tell what was going on. She was a wild sorceress. All those wild sounds, she had to be. . . . She was saying, 'You give me your shoes and I'll give you mine'. . . . And people were laughing so much I was already pretending I wrote it.

Heilpern's description of what happened on the carpet during this remarkable première tells us a lot about the working methods Brook had built up with his groups since he started his 'research' in Paris. Just as the idea that he came to Shakespeare rehearsals with a completely open mind was less than accurate (he came with a concept and began to explore the possibilities from that) so the idea that the actors went on the carpet with 'nothing' was a misconception. All the hours of exercises, work with sticks, t'ai chi, acrobatics, work with Ancient Greek and Japanese, Feldenkrais movements, as well as the improvisations with cardboard boxes, shoes and (in the near future) bread – all this work had given the actors a vocabulary, resources, a store of ideas waiting to be brought out when a particular situation arose. The actors had played with shoes in Paris. Miriam Goldschmidt, in creating a rival shoe show, was calling on fragments of earlier work, which she had at her disposal. Katsulas had to find his own response, outside Heilpern's scenario. ('Well, in the end my precious script seemed to get a little lost in a thrilling tale about General Katsulas leading an army patrol through the jungle'.) But, by asking Heilpern to write his scenario, and then offering it to the actors in the form of a scrap of paper on the carpet, Brook had set up a situation in which something could take off.

They were to perform *The Shoe Show* in many different situations. In the cattle market at Agades, they played to a crowd of 500 people, 'shoving and jostling, screaming and laughing together round the carpet. . . . Nomads on camels peeped over the top. . . . *The Shoe Show* sank without trace. . . . "Do you know what's wrong with the script?" Brook whispered to me after half an hour. "We haven't got over the fact that the show is meant to be about shoes".'

In a second performance in Agades, though (in a field near a Tuareg village just outside the town), 'The show', Heilpern tells us, 'really took off.' The audience for the performance had been formed in a spectacular way. The group had arrived at the field to find a man and a boy playing drums and gourds. They were joined by women dancing. 'The women were bunched together in brightly coloured costumes, best outfits, singing and clapping for us. And they weren't stopping either. . . . And then of course it dawned on us. We weren't expected to play, but to watch. They must have thought it a bit grand to bring a carpet to sit on.'

Elizabeth Swados, the composer, edged her way towards the women and joined in their music. They helped her with the chants and the rhythms. Others from Brook's group left the carpet – some joined in the singing, some joined the drummers with their own drums.

Suddenly, 'the field was full of leaping Tuaregs'. The men had dashed into the centre of the field. 'They rammed a walking stick into the ground and jumped up and down with such force the earth vibrated. . . . It was as if they were using pogo sticks.' Then Yoshi appeared 'with a specially tiny stick he'd found somewhere and was leaping up and down on his knees. Because he was the leading midget.' Yoshi led the leaping Tuaregs back towards the carpet. Katsulas raced towards the carpet and everyone followed. 'Transformation! There's a new audience round the carpet.' Bagayogo announced the beginning of the show by holding up Katsulas's boots and shouting, 'SHOES!'

At one point in the show, Yoshi gave the shoes to a Tuareg who happened to be the village schoolmaster. He thought they were a gift and clung on to the shoes. But the show could not go on without them. 'Enter a wild sorceress with a rival show.' Sorceress and Ridiculous Thieves failed to get the shoes back – the schoolmaster, writes Heilpern, became a king on the edge of the carpet. Finally, a shoe collector, 'the one shoe collector in existence', got the shoe back by repeatedly saying please. There in space and time, says Heilpern, 'two different worlds had met and joined each other' (though he makes no comment about the reaction of the village schoolmaster when he lost the shoes he thought he had been given).

Much later, in a field near a collection of hamlets in Nigeria, the group had what Heilpern calls a 'shattering' experience with *The Shoe Show*. They had gathered an audience of more than a hundred by performing acrobatics when

Katsulas 'strode confidently on to the carpet'. But the show was greeted with bewilderment. Katsulas frightened the children. He began to babble in English. 'Anyone care to join me?' During the show, he usually tried to get rid of the boots by lobbing them into the audience – another actor would bring them back. On the spur of the moment, Brook arranged for his son, Simon, to take the boots back to Katsulas. 'Oh, no, not you!' cried Katsulas. 'Go away!' But the young child kept walking towards him and held out the shoes. And suddenly, writes Heilpern, 'the unexpected event began to go beyond mere charm. It was as if the child wasn't acting. Somehow we were compelled to watch, it was so truthful. And for the first time the silent audience responded and understood.'

Heilpern does not tell us how he knew the audience understood, and he is uncomfortably close to cliché when he goes on: 'The child in his innocence had done what all the others with their fine acting skills couldn't do. If only for a few moments he had shown us the nature of simplicity.' After the show, Brook asked the chief of the village what people had seen. After consultation, the chief said, 'We have seen something about a pair of shoes. We have seen shoes change people in some way. . . . I do not think anyone else could say more.'

The actors were unusually reflective after this performance. But Brook was fascinated by the entire disaster. 'But can't you see?' Brook knew exactly what was wrong and nailed it. In language reminiscent of Kane, describing how he felt after Brook had talked to him just before the opening night of *The Dream*, Heilpern tells us that 'at last I understood'.

Attempting to create a universal language, the show had been built round a theatre convention of the West. This is the convention which takes it for granted that shoes can transform people, bring luck and disaster, the popular folk reference on which so many children's stories are based. I'd seen too many pantomimes. But the African villagers hadn't, or any form of theatre as we know it. The audience couldn't understand what was happening because it couldn't share the convention. How simple everything seemed now!

What Heilpern does not explain, though, is why audiences at other performances had not been bewildered. Brook used the occasion to lecture Heilpern on the qualities of children.

It's extraordinary but a child can do something the adult actor finds so very difficult. It's impossible for a child to act in a complex way. Through experience and understanding the adult struggles to arrive at the same point the child reaches through innocence. In a sense there isn't such a thing as a gifted child. There are children who are in their natural state of childhood innocence. But the adult may never fully realise what he's lost or what he's become. The actor who performs in familiar territory plays before people who reflect his own state. If the group were to perform before a sophisticated city audience the actors would most likely be seen as apparently normal individuals. But the moment they're not in tune with the audience, the moment something *really* disturbs them, everything collapses in a second. We see it in Africa time and again. The moment the actor doesn't receive the sort of response he expects, his true state is revealed. In fact it's a highly dislocated and complex state. It can reach the point where two actors facing each other in a state of panic don't actually see each other. Their eyes are glazed. But the eyes of the child are alive.

The show was performed again, in an open field, without shade, near the village of Itagunmodi. Two of the actors were too sick to perform, the rest looked near exhaustion. The many children in the audience, who spoke no English, were silent.

Barbara Ann Teer, founder of the National Black Theatre in Harlem, was there. She demanded afterwards:

What do you feel now? Have you got to know anyone here? Have you entertained *one* child? Who have you touched? *Touch* those people! You hear me? *Touch them!* What are you *using* them for? What do you know of Africa? What do any of you know?

Professor Beier, their contact in Yorubaland, said,

I think you've insulted the people of this village. Brook's actors can't sing, they can't dance and it doesn't seem they can act. What does it mean? Why have you come here?

'Surprisingly', adds Heilpern, 'the villagers minded less than anyone'.

The saga of *The Shoe Show* is, in many ways, typical of what Brook and his actors experienced in Africa. Long journeys in convoys; wrangles over who did the washing-up in camp; rigorous exercises often lasting for six hours a day; negotiations between Brook and local officials about where he could put his carpet; and shows, some of which left the actors elated, while some seemed to be disasters.

At Agades, after the second performance of *The Shoe Show* – the one which 'sank without trace' – this group, which was trying to bring theatre to people who did not have a word for theatre in their language, were suddenly confronted by theatre. It was part of an Independence Day celebration, to which the local préfet invited them. In a small courtyard in the centre of Agades, 'a raised slab of concrete served as a stage. Three dim light bulbs hung by a thread. A curtain was slung perilously over a temporary line.' On this highly conventional stage, Tuaregs danced and sang, a magician slashed a sword across his bare chest and, writes Heilpern, 'the curtain opened on the new and magical world of that special group of Africans known as the Peulh'.

The Peulh rolled their eyes and flashed quick smiles on and off – but they also made music which, apparently, had Brook's composer, Swados, 'on her feet the instant she heard it'. Brook arranged for the group to meet the Peulh the next day in a hut. Later he recalled what happened:

Once we sat in Agades in a small hut all afternoon, singing. We and the African group sang, and suddenly we found that we were hitting exactly the same language of sound. Well, we understood theirs and they understood ours, and something quite electrifying happened because, out of all sorts of different songs, one suddenly came upon this common area.

Brook goes on to describe an invitation to a funeral ceremony, in a village near their overnight camp. After watching the villagers dancing and singing, they were asked to perform.

So we had to improvise a song for them. And this perhaps was one of the best works of the whole journey. Because the song that was produced for the occasion was extraordinarily moving, right and satisfying, and made a real coming together of the people and ourselves. It is impossible to say what produced it, because it was produced as much by the group that was working together in a certain way, with all the work that has gone into that, and as much by all the conditions of the moment that bore their influence – the place, the night, the feeling for the other people – so that we were actually making something for them in exchange for what they had offered us.

It was a remarkable song and, like all theatre things, something that then is gone. One doesn't, in the theatre, create things for a museum or a shop, but for the moment, in a totally expendable way. And there, an instance of that sort of theatre, of one which makes something just for that moment, actually happened. You ask: what did we leave? I think the true question is: what was shared?

Brook's description is very vivid, and clearly articulates something he himself at that minute believed. Yet at least part of him, in Africa, was looking for work that he could eventually shape and offer as a product to what was to become, in the next decade, his audience in the global village. And other statements he was to make, about the poles of improvised and prepared work, suggest that this duality was never far from his mind.

In his search for a 'universal language', Brook revived Hughes's *Orghast* in the courtyard of the Emir's mud palace in Kano, for an audience of street salesmen, giggling children, market women, intellectuals, politicians, dons, singers, dancers and rowdy townsfolk. As soon as Brook's group began to utter their primordial cries a rival group, outside the courtyard walls, began to mimic them. Ted Hughes seemed to be winning until Malik Bagayogo, playing the God of Darkness, cried the words 'Bullorga Torga', at which there were terrible snorts of laughter. Malik paused, then repeated the phrase with more emphasis: 'Bullorga Torga'. This time the audience exploded. Malik was not to be laughed down. 'Oh, Bullorga Torga!' he cried again – and then again, and again, five times in all. By this time the audience were in hysterics. The phrase invented by Ted Hughes happened to be very similar to the Hausa slang for cunt. (When asked why he did not cut the phrase Malik said 'Mais c'est dans le texte'.)

To Michael Gibson, Brook summed up the thinking behind the work in Africa as follows:

It is quite obvious that, in the total sickness of the society that we're living in, the possibility of affirmation through the theatre is virtually excluded. Positive affirmation, for example, really depends on the possibility for a poet not to be just an individual speaking from his own private world, but to be like the Greek dramatist, a recognised spokesman, heard and understood by everyone, who finds things that they feel deeply but cannot put a name to, that go through the crucible of this one individual and come out as a name. In the way that the whole world for centuries before Oedipus sensed Oedipus and this sense became concentrated by an individual into a word of three syllables.

The *Marat/Sade* production was possible on that scale because it wasn't affirming what was good and glorious in life, but something that most spectators could relate to very directly, violence and madness. . . . Disturbance is one of the lifelines in large-scale performance. The other one is the returning to roots, where affirmations can still be made, in the sense of the ethnic theatre; . . . the tiny regional group, using the local slang and local references, can rediscover all the elements of theatre. Or there is still another direction, and this is the one we're looking for. And that is not to deny the regional principle, but to complement it in a different way. And that is to say that within the human body there is another root, because the human body, in all its aspects, organically, is common ground for all of mankind.

Our work is based on the fact that some of the deepest aspects of human experience can reveal themselves through the sounds and movements of the human body in a way that strikes an identical chord in any observer, whatever his cultural and racial conditioning. And therefore one can work without roots, because the body, as such, becomes a working source.

Brook is able to define the objectives and gains of the work from the group's point of view. But when he assumes that the group has been making a real communication at a deeper level of universal consciousness to villagers in Africa, he is relying solely on his own subjective feelings. (When he has to make a genuine, specific communication, like agreeing with a village chief where the group can perform, he sometimes finds himself using a child as a translator.)

He feels a certain desperation at a general loss of 'humanness' and 'meaningfulness' in the West and he seems driven to search for these qualities in Africa and the East. But he sometimes talks about Africa in the same way that he talks about the 'natural state of childhood innocence' and 'the childhood state of oneness'.

The African who has been brought up in the traditions of the African way of life has a very highly developed understanding of the double nature of reality. The visible and invisible, and the free passage between the two, are for him, in a very concrete way, two modes of the same thing. Something which is the basis of the theatre experience – what we call make-believe – is a passing from the visible to the invisible and back again. In Africa, this is understood not as fantasy, but as two aspects of the same reality.

Brook is using 'Africa' and 'the African' as a generalised concept, an idea on which he can hang his theatrical experiments. He is clear about attempting to return to a clean beginning, where consciousness can be restructured. But he is very vague about the people and the culture he is experimenting with.

In going to Africa, Brook saw himself as engaging with what is left of an oral culture. Like a theatrical performance, the form of such a culture is ephemeral and leaves no permanent trace: all 'epics' have to be remembered, and the stories are dependent on the context in which they are told.

As Brook says, such a tradition has to take the audience into account. The storytellers act as 'first person to second person', not as 'third-person' actors offering material to be observed. Western audiences, as Brook sees it, observe forms rather than engage with meanings. His work in Africa was based on the belief that to get back to meanings it was necessary to get back to primitive, interpersonal encounters.

But to believe this is to deny the importance of social structures, institutions, politics. It is to turn one's back on the world as it exists. John Shotter, social psychologist, writes:

What Brook misses, and it is his most important omission, is that people do not just evaluate their circumstances and actions, they evaluate their evaluations, and choose between them to the extent that they accord with (or not) the kind of person they felt they want (or ought) to be. And furthermore these evaluations of evaluations are done linguistically, and involve formulations or articulations of moral, ethical, aesthetic institutions.

To give an example: *The Shoe Show*:

Everyone can appreciate, no doubt, the relief shoes bring in rough terrain (their value there); also, removing them after a while (another value); giving them up to a fellow in need (yet another). But what about the dilemma of giving them up, or retaining them? A play formulates or articulates these intuitively-felt dilemmas, and it does so in a way which attempts to coordinate their formulation with this or that total vision of things: one which exalts the collective over the individual, or vice-versa. All actual societies, modern large-scale ones, constitute one selected order from many. That there is *an* order matters, we all depend for our identity upon it, even those victimised by it. Plays question the social order, and formulate alternatives; and they rely for their force upon accessing the intuitively-felt dilemmas of their audience.

The problem is with understanding one's audience; it's perhaps the writer's problem. They are very used to writing for an anonymous, general audience, but they must write for an audience they know. Plays for a mass audience can only access what they have in common: angst and fragmentation, and a general sense of loss (of something).

Shotter is generalising himself when he writes of a 'mass audience' – he is clearly thinking about the 'mass Western theatre audience' (it would be possible to imagine a Muslim playwright writing affirmatively for a mass Islamic audience). But he is surely correct in seeing Brook's experiments in creating a 'universal language' as being divorced from the social structures of the people with whom he was trying to communicate – and therefore as communicating only in a limited way. (One of the examples Brook offers of a successful communication relates, interestingly enough, to a social event – a village funeral.)

We have to come back in the end to the real purpose of Brook's 'experiments' – the purpose that lies behind his talk of the 'body' as 'the common ground for all mankind' – and to put the question that matters: did his pilgrimage to Africa with his international flock of actors help him towards what he was really looking for – a form of 'less deadly theatre'? The serial was to be continued later that year in the very different context of the United States – which is where, in July 1973, Brook took the same eleven actors, and some of the entourage, but not the Land Rovers and crew.

They first went to California, where they shared a workshop in San Juan Bautista with El Teatro Campesino. At the first meeting Luis Valdez and the other Campesinos explained that they were not theatre people: their art came from political struggle, having started during the strike of 1965 organised by Cesar Chavez on behalf of the farmworkers. They had then performed 'actos', short pieces with political messages using slapstick, a kind of agitprop. Now they had broken from the union, in terms of formal membership, and had developed their own brand of 'cosmic comedy', which dealt not only with anti-Vietnam-War material but the whole of Chicanismo.

At this first meeting, themes came up which dominated the work of the next two months – the 'deliberate' act, death and the body, communication and energy, meaning and message; also, tensions and contradictions came up, the Paris group being concerned primarily with the theatre and the subtleties of the body, the Chicanos with 'race' consciousness and the immediacy of bare bones. The groups swapped exercises, the Campesinos doing the Serpent and Mohawk social dances; the Centre did t'ai chi, Feldenkrais, passing impulses etc.

They performed for each other, the Paris actors attempting to play Campesinos (Brook commented on a certain sentimentality). Valdez' main reason for the joint work was to learn about improvisation: the Campesinos had done much more of it in the early days on the picket lines and Valdez wanted to move again in that direction. They played an acto with a basic script (boss, labour contractor and worker) which broke down when others entered and tried to improvise. They also did part of the Seven Deadly Sins, with fantastic masks, completely choreographed.

They met Chavez; standing under a tree surrounded by children, and a ring of bodyguards, he told fables, about the twig which bends in the storm but does not break, about the cricket who jumps in the lion's ear and tickles him until he tears himself apart, about the red of the thunderbird flag representing the worker's spirit. A *padre* appeared and performed Mass under the trees. The farmworkers served a very good Mexican lunch. Chavez, vegetarian for five years since his fast destroyed his guts, ate only fruit. There was the atmosphere of a Sunday afternoon picnic.

The first joint performance for a strike-orientated audience was in a high-school playground in Salinas, where the Union was holding a meeting. The Earth and the Sun gave birth to the first Ranchero and the first Campesino. Eventually, the whole structure of injustice developed, until the third child, Huelga (which means strike in Spanish), wins the struggle against the

Teamster and his Sweetheart, Contract (the play was based on recent events – the Union had been cheated out of its contracts by the corrupt and powerful Teamsters Union). The play was well received (two of the cast were given ten dollars, 'to stop on the way back for a soda').

At Forty Acres, the original strike headquarters in Delano, they played on a decrepit old flatbed truck for a thousand people who had come to hear Chavez announce that the negotiations with the growers had failed and the Union was right back where it was eight years before. They played *The Fattest Man in the World*: A Fat Grower (stuffed with pillows) gets forcibly reduced by his pickers. After three years Fat Teamsters push their way through the crowd, up on to the truck, and convince the Grower that he looks undernourished. Together they start stealing from the farmworker, but Huelga comes on and forces a show-down in which the Fat Baddies loose their stuffing and their pants. The acto ends with a victory dance in which the Fat Grower is 'encouraged' to partici-pate.

They attended a Mass in a church which had banners on the wall reading:

WONDER BREAD   HOMEGROWN HOSTS; IF WE DIDN'T BELIEVE IN THEM WE WOULDN'T PUT OUR NAME ON THEM   COME FLY WITH ME   OK OK OK OK OK OK OK

The music was fake folk songs sung badly; the group thought it was vile, saying that the *Birds* had more meaning, more religion than the Mass which had lost all its mystery and beauty.

Brook:

Theatre and religion do not have the same purpose. It would be too easy to take advantage of a certain real hunger for mystery, for the spirit, which pervades our world, and for which the churches are failing to provide. But religion, unlike theatre, does not come from man and cannot.

The group then moved to Aspen, a ski resort cum intellectual haven in the mountains of Colorado, where they were hosted by the Institute for Humanistic Studies. Because it rained they played in the dining room of a Victorian hotel. But not, as Brook states, for 'theatregoers – sinister types who go to the theatre for pleasure'. The show ended with a candlelight procession in which all the children from the audience were recruited. Some criticised this as sentimental and bad.

They moved on to Onigum, Minnesota, to the Chippewa reservation where they spent a week with the Native American Theater Ensemble. It began with a pipe ceremony conducted by a descendant of Chief Joseph.

They worked on choruses, with sticks, and the travel dance. The groups improvised together, using a myth from Jerome Rothenberg's *Shaking the Pumpkin*, a genially obscene trickster tale called 'Coon cons coyote'.

At a water ceremony the descendant of Chief Joseph recited his sign-language poems *On a New Cradle-Board, Monument in Bone* etc. He was asked to join the Native Ensemble because they wanted to know more about ritual. Some of the Paris group had picked up sign language from the work with the National Theatre of the Deaf; they now exchanged it for the Indians' sign language.

After a week in Connecticut the group moved to New York, to the Brooklyn Academy of Music (BAM): a vast building containing an opera house and several theatres – home to Robert Wilson's School of Byrds, Whirling dervishes, Buddhist monks, Japanese rock opera, as well as hosting black fashion shows and revivalist meetings and showing Arabic movies for the population. The group worked in a newly refurbished ballroom, but had to use the upper boxes of the opera house as changing rooms.

They gave theatre days. A limited number of free tickets was distributed by the International Theater Institute. Each day was divided into three sessions: in the morning the group did exercises, first demonstrating, then inviting the visitors to participate; in the afternoon they improvised; and in the evening they played the *Birds* on a rich sensuous carpet with all-white costumes. Outside performances were also given, in the neighbourhood streets and gyms.

Sid Chapin reported, in the *Christian Science Monitor*:

Where milk trucks used to load up, Mr Brook's people found their way, effortlessly, unstagely into the lives of some teenagers. A stereo set was throbbing with The Who. Helen Mirren began trying her own thing to the music near where a boy was doing the same. They compared steps. Malik wandered over to a couple of boys working out at the basket ball hoop and lifted his hands to invite a catch. A bongo drummer, sitting on the rug that had been set down, set up a counter-rhythm and was joined by a bass, a guitar and somebody with a swanee whistle. The stereo was turned off and thirty people were drawn round the new combo. 'It is at times like this that I am happy to be an actor', said one of the group.

Brook:

The training of an actor is like that of a *samurai*: it may last for years and lead up to one sudden confrontation. The only rule is that one is *never* prepared for the situations one really meets.

They played in the basement auditorium of a community centre in Bedford-Stuyvesant; the audience comprised a few children and teenagers (all black). They made music and played games with the children, and performed a piece about a spiritualist, Mother Mary, who calls spirits to her shop in a weird neighbourhood full of charlatans and hippy musicians.

One theatre day was spent with the National Theater of the Deaf and the Native American Theater Ensemble, who had never met before; most of the morning and afternoon was spent comparing Indian sign language and deaf hand language.

In the Italiaelcome datacompn section of Cobble Garden they encountered a very negative audience of kids whose totally uncontrolled energy compared badly with the civilised black audiences they had become used to playing to.

Three hundred junior high-school students came to BAM for a matinée. Actors performed a partially prepared improvisation about a Brooklyn landlord and a house full of strange people. Malik improvised a Brooklyn–African dance. A beautiful girl from the audience joined him. Afterwards, she asked if she could join the group.

Grotowski's group came over from Philadelphia where they were holding workshops. He refused to participate in games: 'One is not obliged'. The day was non-verbal, non-active. One of the group said that it hardly seemed to happen at all.

The trip to the States ended with a week's performances of *The Conference of the Birds*.

13 Flying over the mountain: *The Conference of the Birds*

I asked Brook what he thought was his biggest fault. There was an agonisingly long pause during which he cupped his head into his hands, staring into space.

'What', he replied at long last, '*is* a fault?'

John Heilpern, *Conference of the Birds*

The work on *The Conference of the Birds* had been continuing alongside Brook's 'experiments' in both Africa and the United States. And if Brook saw himself as trying to discover a 'universal theatre language' in his work in African villages and with the Campesinos in California, we have to remember that what he was also doing during those journeys was exploring a way of staging a major production which he would offer in what was soon to be seen as a global village.

In *The Birds*, the Hoopoe bird, having encouraged the birds to journey across the world in search of the Simorg, puts himself at their head and cries 'En route!' It is not difficult to see Brook playing the role of the Hoopoe bird as he leads his flock across the deserts of Africa and California.

Both Hughes and Brook were interested in Sufism, the ideas of a mystic Muslim sect that believes in self-perfection through intuition and self-knowledge, and in the union of the mind with the Divine. They wanted to use the twelfth-century Persian poem, *The Conference of the Birds* – a religious and philosophical fable of some 5,000 verses, which is dense with images, allusions and metaphors, and considered as a Sufi classic – as a basis for work. That the poem is virtually unknown in the West (although reminiscent of the Holy Grail legends) offered Brook unlimited possibilities. It tells the story of a journey towards enlightenment. The stories within it are sensual and fierce, passionate and lyrical. There are shootings, stabbings and arguments – between fathers and sons, wives and husbands, kings and subjects, tyrants and slaves, victims and aggressors.

Work began at the Mobilier in Paris and was continued throughout the trips to Africa and America. The performances given in 1973 were always improvised. Precise information about which bits of *The Birds* were worked on is hard to come by. It was still improvised when presented at the Bouffes in 1975. It was not until 1979, when Brook wanted to stage it at the Avignon Festival, that he asked Jean-Claude Carrière to write a script. The script at least gives us some idea of the kind of material Brook had been working on.

In Carrière's version, the story is narrated by the Hoopoe bird, who speaks in the third person, establishing a form Brook was later to use extensively in *The Mahabharata*. Carrière's version begins:

One day, all the birds in the world, those which are known and those which are unknown, met in a great conference. When they had gathered, the Hoopoe bird, very moved and full of hope, placed himself in the midst of them.

The Hoopoe bird says he sees amongst the birds only disputes and wars, over crumbs of bread, scraps of territory. But in his journeyings, he has heard of a great king, the Simorg. The birds' only salvation lies in making a long and dangerous journey to see the Simorg – they will have to cross a burning desert, they will encounter many difficulties. One of the king's feathers once fell in China – the Hoopoe bird shows them a drawing of this feather, together with some Chinese characters, which, he says, mean 'Go in search of me, even, if necessary, to China'.

The Falcon says he already sits on the hand of a king. The Hoopoe tells fables about false and ridiculous kings, like:

A king heard that a beggar was telling everyone in the country of his great love for the king. The king sent for the beggar and said 'If you love me, either you leave the country immediately or have your head cut off'. When the beggar said he preferred to leave, the king had his head cut off.

The birds begin to make excuses. The Duck spends her life in water – she is purity itself. Who can compare with her in water? For the Partridge, life consists of precious stones, and they are found in the mountains – impossible to leave them. The Heron very much wants to go, but is afraid. What exactly is this king? The Hoopoe bird tells him the story of a Princess. One day when she is out walking, she sees a slave who has 'extraordinary beauty'. She falls in love with him and has him drugged and brought to her at night. All night, the slave is treated as a king. All night the Princess makes love to him, weeping. At dawn, the slave is taken back to where he came from. He wakes with a start and says, 'What I saw I saw in another body. I heard nothing although I heard everything. I saw nothing although I saw everything. . . . I don't know if I dreamed or if I was drunk. . . . I don't know where I am going. But I must leave. I must leave.'

The Hoopoe bird encourages the birds with many other fables. At last, he places himself at their head and cries, 'En route!'

The birds have to cross a long burning desert. They meet a Bat who has heard of the sun and who looks for it every night. 'Sleep if you want to', he tells them. 'I have to search for news of the sun.'

They meet a Hermit with a long beard who spends his life looking for the answer to a question. When they ask him what the question is, he tells them that all his life he has had a passion for aubergines. But something told him that if he ate aubergines, a great and terrible misfortune would strike him. He tried to think of other things – work, family, oranges, sheep – but always he came back to aubergines. Finally, he succumbed. His mother found aubergines for him, had them cooked, very well, and he began to eat them. But before he had eaten half an aubergine, there was a knock at the door. A man came in and put his son's head on the ground. So he decided to become a Hermit, and the question he is spending the rest of his life searching for an answer to is, 'What is the connection between the eating of aubergines and the beheading of his son?' But he has not yet found the answer. And what, asks an Exotic Bird, does he do in the mean time? 'I reflect, as you can see', says the Hermit, and he combs his long beard with a huge comb. The Dove laughs and tells him that he has not found the answer because he is only thinking about his beard. The Hermit says the Dove is right and tears out his beard. The Dove laughs again and tells him he is still only thinking about the beard which he has now lost.

The birds also encounter a bird who is walking alone across the desert. 'Why don't you use your wings?' asks the Falcon. The Walking Bird tells them that he made a vow that he would cross the desert on foot – he wanted to go and see the Simorg. 'And have you seen him?' asks the Sparrow. The Walking Bird says he spent fourteen years walking across the desert. When he reached the end of the desert, he decided that he had acquired 'all the perfection of which I was capable – useless to go further'. So he turned back, without seeing the Simorg, and now he is recrossing the desert, still on foot: 'I must remain faithful to my vow'.

The birds meet an Old Man who has seen the Phoenix die:

The Phoenix lives for a thousand years and knows the exact moment of his death. When that moment arrives, he gathers around himself a heap of leaves. . . . When he has only one breath of his life left, he beats his wings and waves his feathers. This movement produces fire. The fire sets the leaves alight. Soon . . . everything is reduced to ashes. But when not a single spark can be seen, a small Phoenix appears in the middle of the hot ash.

After this final encounter in the desert, they see a mountain and rejoice. But they still have to cross seven valleys. In the first valley they find a man looking for something in sand which he is sifting through a sieve. 'What are you looking for?' 'I am looking for my way.' In the Valley of Love they burn. In the Valley of Nothingness they learn that 'Everything that has been and that will be is nothing but an atom'. But, 'Even in Nothingness there is a secret. . . . If everything fell into Nothingness, from the fish to the moon, you would find at the bottom of a well the leg of a tame ant.'

They cross the Valley of Death. In the moment of death, says the Hoopoe bird, a being learns a thousand secrets he never knew before. A Butterfly burns himself on a flame and a Wise Butterfly says, 'He learned what he wanted to know'.

Many birds die on the journey. The few who survive to reach the Simorg's palace are met by a Chamberlain, who shuts the door on them. Even the Hoopoe bird loses hope: 'Like you I have been the victim of an illusion'. But the Chamberlain returns and leads them to the Simorg; 'At last they beheld the Simorg and they saw that the Simorg was themselves . . .'. They question the Simorg, without using language. And, without using language, the Simorg tells them (in Carrière's text), 'The sun in its majesty is a mirror. He who seems himself in this mirror sees his soul and his body. He sees himself in his entirety. If there were thirty or forty of you, you would see thirty or forty birds in the mirror.'

Carrière's text ends:

Then the birds lost themselves forever in the Simorg. The shadow merged into the sun and that was all. The way remains open, but there is no longer either guide or traveller.

Or, as Judy Garland might have put it,

> Birds fly over the rainbow,
> Then why, oh why, can't I?

The Conference of the Birds ran as a central strand through Brook's work in Africa. Infuriatingly, Heilpern is rarely as explicit and concrete about the work done on *The Birds* as he is about *The Shoe Show*.

He writes of improvisations, of turning sounds into bird calls, of birds gathering and following a man on a journey, diving across the carpet like flying fish. Of Katsulas sweating and cursing as he practises bird movements, 'ugly as a vulture'. 'You know the way I should be doing this, but you're not telling me', he said to Brook, who replied, 'I don't. I really don't know the way. But I know one can be found.' Heilpern does not try to describe what the bird movements were.

He tells us birds were introduced into an improvisation called *The Ogre Show*, but that the work was slack, and he quotes Brook talking to the actors:

Look! We haven't got time to waste in soft thinking. The action must be full of something that makes people WANT to watch. It's the whole core of our work. Here you are sitting in a circle. An African walks by. What does he see? Nothing very positive. How can we heighten this story? How can we develop and sustain interest? It needs to be clear and strong. But if there's no exploration, nothing will be found.

All of which sounds pretty vague. But, in an attempt to explore, Brook invented experiments with charlatans, tricksters.

From accounts of the work in the United States, later in the year, it is clear that the Hoopoe bird had not yet been fixed. Instead, two charlatans were to persuade the birds into setting out on a journey. Each member of the group was asked to play an archetypal trickster, trying to deceive the others. Brook said,

'Imagine in a truthful way something that isn't truthful'. Accounts of the work in the United States refer to characters like the 'Ridiculous King', the 'Ridiculous Princess'. Clearly the group were improvising around the fables the Hoopoe bird was to produce in the finished version.

The composer, Swados, began to write songs based on bird language. The actors are said to have taken to these, squawking with delight. In the village of Gangara, during the final performance in Niger, a bird trio improvised a story – boy bird meets girl bird, boy bird fights over girl bird – which is said to have intrigued the audience and brought applause.

Heilpern's account of Brook in Africa ends with a description of a performance of *The Birds* in Oshogbo, in an open-air theatre, 'a rough concrete stage at the back of a crumbling colonial residence'. Heilpern writes:

On top of the walls which surrounded the courtyard, and from the forest behind the concrete stage, the actors appeared as half-human birds, and called to each other, gathering for a journey. The crowd erupted as if they were at a bullfight! . . . Incredibly, it was as if the shape and form of Brook's longed-for theatre of the future was at last bursting open. And something wonderful, something more than Brook had waited years to see. For there was the unique and individual colour of a real group, sensing each other out, playing with danger and care, but performing as one, absolutely as one true group of people who have come together to share what they have to offer.

Precisely what they had to offer Heilpern, tantalisingly, does not tell us. But, whatever it was, they lost it:

Like the high-wire act that begins to wobble, up there, the actors seemed to lose their nerve. . . . But for all that, something priceless had sprung from it. It was a seed, and a beginning.

In California, they worked on *The Birds* with El Teatro Campesino, only now it was called *Los Pajaros*. The rehearsals were slow and painful.

Brook:

There's a big difference between the Huelga pieces and *The Birds*. The actos are made as much by the audiences as by the actors. In political theatre, when the audience is with you, you get back more than you put in – the actors are helped and carried – the theme is always the same: struggle. But *Birds* presents itself to a neutral audience and must be made entirely by the actors; that's why it's interesting, challenging, demanding. We haven't even got the conventional aid of a text – we're making a new play, and its power depends on each actor relating his own reality to the work and sharing it with others.

I'll tell you a secret: why I chose this piece out of all the others I could have chosen. . . . Every spiritual journey needs preparation. I wanted to make a piece which, if played right, would give everyone in it a true experience of a real journey. Thus, the whole play is just a preparation for something else. You only get as far on a journey as you want to go – and if you go all the way you get an experience one can never forget.

So *Birds* was transformed into an agitprop piece. The Simorg became the thunderbird of the Union flag; the journey became the struggle of La Causa.

Unity became Union. The death of the Ridiculous King was related to the very recent murder of two strikers. The audience seemed to follow up to a point, but afterwards many of the actors felt the spiritual message had not been synthesised with the political message.

At the end of the joint workshop, *Birds* was played in a small park in Livingston, as a benefit for some Campesinos in danger of being evicted for political reasons. The audience was very cosmopolitan: Portuguese, Chicanos, Arabs, two Sikhs. The opening routine, an argument in which everyone spoke a different language, went well as it was immediately grasped by the crowd. The Journey was described not in terms of, but only with reference to, Huelga and the Union; although there was a Grower and a Ridiculous Farmworker, and a chorus, made up of all the actors who had not individual parts. They thought the performance successful. It raised seventy-four dollars and seventy-four cents for La Causa.

In their week in Minnesota, working with the Native American Theater Ensemble, the groups both played the *Birds* one afternoon; almost no audience showed up. Brook played one of the Charlatans, for the first time. He said, 'There never can be a final structure to the play as we do it now not until it can be done with a company of thirty Sufi shaykhs'.

When they reached New York the structure of the *Birds* was further changed. It had never been clear that the birds themselves wanted to set out on the journey, that the Charlatans (who represent the Hudhud of the book, symbol of the spiritual guide) only appear in answer to an inner need of the birds themselves. Too often it had seemed as if the Charlatans were in fact little more than charlatans, conmen. As the actors began to show more clearly the need for the journey, so the idea of the play began to emerge more strongly. All the actors were now carrying a copy of the poem around with them.

The actors felt that whoever was playing the Charlatans had to convince them each night that the journey was worthwhile. The Charlatans' job was to rearrange the tales within the tale to overcome the birds' reluctance to set out on the journey. The excuses became more real, more agonised, so it became more difficult to move on to the second part of the play, the Travel Dance. A simpler transformation, involving walking and calling, was found (instead of what had been a magic potion and Bird-of-Paradise feathers). But the Travel Dance and Sticks and Valleys remained the same and never seemed as real as the start of the journey.

At the start of the week's performances of *Birds*, the stories were done as dreams: each bird dreamed the story which would free him from his hesitation, in which he himself played the dream-role of a human being in some parallel situation. Brook thought it the most honest performance ever. He told the actors that he had felt them genuinely *caring* about each other and the play. He often stressed this caring as one of the most important aspects of the work.

On the second night the transition was solved spontaneously by Natasha who began to circle around the candle in which a butterfly had just immolated itself. As the other actors followed, the movements led smoothly into the dance. The audience was a mixture of Brooklyn kids and New York theatre people which did not jell, but produced some tension.

On the third night the Charlatans took a new approach which led to much silence and abstract improvisation. Some of the audience walked out.

Brook:

The danger of such an idea is to fall into the tragedy of the avant-garde: a failure to communicate. The great potential of doing this *once* is that the bones of the play can be laid bare, the dramatic energies reached on a certain primitive incomprehensible level. So we had a play that was intensely interesting but totally impossible to understand unless you'd seen several other performances, a private commentary on the work by the workers for the workers. Yet this is what research is about. The lack of words allowed a certain energy to run through the performance from beginning to end – but the audience was left out. Through free form we return to a certain condition of Noh theatre: Noh is difficult to understand even while it communicates something – and yet it remains pure. For three years we have been seeking such a secret.

The next night there were three Charlatans. Brook and some of the actors were disturbed by the 'vulgarity' of the work. The stories almost became a series of humiliations: the dream sequence had been dropped, and the tales were arranged for an uncomprehending flock of birds led by sinister magicians, intent on destroying something in them.

Experiments with the structure were attempted: the Charlatans walking, reading from the book and carrying symbols at the opening; a new sequence for the description of the Valleys in which each Valley is given a brief powerful image acted out by one of the Charlatans. It was never done again; the new form was expected to unify the different factions in the audience, but it did not. The meeting afterwards to discuss the performance was cut short by a bomb-scare.

The last day was devoted to preparing for a marathon: three performances of *Birds*, at 8 p.m., at midnight and at dawn. Yoshi, one of the evening Charlatans, dreamed of a synthesis, an indoor performance with all the spontaneity and energy of an outside performance – human contact *and* high quality. He wanted to do *Birds* as a carpet show. So the first show began with some minutes of tootling, banging, scraping, rattling and whistling on the huge collection of toys and musical instruments. This had an exhilarating effect on the audience. Yoshi became a King and the group danced for him, as they had for the King of Dahomey in Africa. What they did went far beyond what they usually did in terms of energy and control; before it had only been individuals who achieved this level: now the whole group managed to do it.

Bruce Myers and Natasha Parry, the Charlatans at midnight, wanted to 'return' to the book. Their sense of inevitability was one of holiness, silence, seriousness; they wanted to approach some of the specifically Persian Sufi elements of the work. In the opening ceremony they used the sound of a feather and a clapperless bell, the scent of a cleansing incense, rosewater, a real white dove in a box and a magic potion made of attar, roses and wine. They recited lines from the book, calling on all their classical Shakespearian training, an aspect they had ignored all summer in deference to 'commitment and spontaneity'. Backed up by sounds of delicate and meditative intensity from a few small drums, gongs, guitar and vina, it was the opposite of the exuberant and noisy joy of the previous show. Michele, as Ridiculous Princess, found for the first time a real love for her slave, a Puerto Rican actor. Miriam was an amusing, sinister fly who got caught in honey. Lou spontaneously worked on a story from the book, of the Bat who searched for the sun. François' death, as Hallaj, and resurrection, as the Phoenix, made the transition work from the Stories into the Travel Dance.

After the Sticks, through which the birds passed to enter the Simorg's palace, all the actors sat quietly in a darkened circle around the carpet. Natasha said,

If any of you have felt any well-being through watching this play, remember the poet Farid Ud-din Attar in your prayers. Remember him well – each master teaches in his own special way, then disappears.

Brook said that despite the version's proposed emphasis on the book and on words, it had created a real silence; that people trying to explain to him afterwards what they had felt were speechless. Yoshi said it had been the most fruitful approach to the 'third position, between actor and priest', to the actual material of the poem, to a contemporary theatre.

At the dawn performance Brook and the composer were the Charlatans. The room was set up in a new way – the carpet was at one end by the door, there were seven candles in a row down the length of the hall, a sort of altar with a mirror at the end. A large audience crowded in as the show began with exercises on the carpet. Then Brook led everyone to the middle of the room where they improvised. There was a series of wild free-form solo dances, then the composer directed the actors in a song, giving them parts to develop. Brook directed a story of lonely old men in a house, in love with a woman of silk; in the end they found real love. Then Brook unveiled what was under the altar – a wooden statue of eleven birds. He said, 'the end can become a new beginning' and led everyone back to the starting point, the carpet.

Brook, at the last circle on the carpet after the show, said:

The work is about something much more important than theatre style, it's about revealing truth – and there's no way of dividing truth up into 'spiritual' truth or 'funny' truth: there's only one truth. All this has been opened for us by doing a work like the *Birds*; it took us perhaps a year of reading to realise that understanding this book necessitated *serving* it, getting inside it, grasping it. In coming to grips with this reality, one comes to grips with a work which is about theatre and about life: it has to become true in a theatre form, and yet it is about something far beyond theatre, something within each one of us. The work becomes meaningful only when all our talents and skills are to serve something, something other than the actors ego, or even the group, or good work. Imagination and humour, excitement, energy and passion must be devoted to something more: this thing which is called, on paper, *Birds*. This is when theatre takes on the promise of something real, when it becomes more than just a poor thing to get involved in.

These improvised performances of *The Birds* took place in New York in the summer of 1973. Two years later, in 1975, Brook presented more improvised performances of *The Birds* to restricted audiences at the Bouffes. But in 1979, he decided to take the performance to the Avignon Festival. And at this point he not only got Carrière to write a script, he also asked Sally Jacobs to design the show.

Until then, the actors had worn white costumes. Now Sally Jacobs gave them gorgeous raiments with swathes of silk plumage. She also designed hand puppets, but Brook felt that to allow the fast changes needed from character to character and from earth to flight they needed to use masks. He chose Ancient Chinese ones, although they were not markedly oriental in appearance. Brook saw them as denser, more essential expressions of a human truth. He believed their undistorted features to be the result of a deep naturalism created through the precise observation of psychological realities. Yet their intensification of these states through simplification took them from the specific to the universal. They were all objective and archetypal manifestations of essential types and natures, a mysterious and haunting timelessness. He also had some modern masks made, also Balinese, which were grotesque and caricatural embodiments of certain primal forces; animal-like masks of this type were used for the Thieves.

Brook said:

A mask is a two-way traffic all the time: it sends a message in, and projects a message out. It operates by the law of echoes: if the echo-chamber is perfect, the sound going in and the one coming out are reflections: there is a perfect relation between the echo-chamber and the sound; but if it isn't, it's like a distorted mirror.

The masks were used in different ways in the performance, almost entirely in the illustrative episodes before the Valleys. They were used for types – like the Warrior King, the Beautiful Princess – and to convey a change in an individual's state – like a young slave who spends a night with a princess who has drugged his wine. He is masked for the night, and removes it afterwards when he returns to earth.

Physically, the masks were manipulated in different ways. For the full imposition of a role they were worn normally. To express self-concealment behind a false image, they would be held either in contact with the face, or a few inches from it (people pretending to be kings used them in this way). They were also used as puppets, extended at the end of an arm wrapped in emblematic material, their movements conveyed through the manipulation of arm or hand. If a beggar represented in this way was executed, the wrist was suddenly bent and the mask dropped.

Traditional head masks were rejected as being too cumbersome to represent birds. The diversity of the birds' plumage was conveyed by different exotic materials draped around their arms, necks and shoulders. The Dove was hung with expanses of white silk. The Falcon was represented by the actor holding up two claw-like fingers, hooked forward. The Owl was represented by two hands wrapped around a stick in front of the neck, as if perched on the branch of a tree. The Parrot held the bamboo bars of his cage in front of his face, while his nervous head movements, twitchy facial tics and squeaky whine established his character. The Peacock had a bombastic voice and a proud strut. He held open above his head a beautiful painted fan. A sparrow walked hunched over a stick. A Bat's attempts at flight were suggested by the noisy opening and shutting of a battered umbrella. There was a Nightingale besotted by love, and a beautiful Lebanese Dove. The birds twittered and squawked, hopped and walked stiff-legged as they encountered splendidly masked figures.

The hand puppets consisted of a glove-like head of the bird with a gold, red or white beak, and rich floating silks or laces for the wings. The actors became birds so they could 'fly'. Before the journey started on the Hoopoe had been represented in this way, as he had already made part of it. At the moment of departure the birds assumed a V-formation, with the Hoopoe at the apex. They improvised sounds, building to a crescendo. Suddenly there was a blackout, a long pause in darkness. When the lights went up, the birds were in tranquil flight, supported by gentle sounds from the musicians. Flying above the desert they see far beneath them a Hermit. This was a small Balinese puppet, but as the birds circled and landed the puppet was replaced by a masked actor. These puppets were finally abandoned when the birds met an old Sage at the end of the crossing of the desert, who enacted for them the story of the death and rebirth of the Phoenix. He asked them to put their personal belongings into his black veil, symbolising the self-abandonment and annihilation marking the death of the old self.

In the Seven Valleys all masks and puppets were abandoned, as the tone of the performance changed into the abstract and the spiritual. In the First Valley an actor wearing a cloak sat painstakingly sifting sand. The Second Valley began with a whirling violin player contrasted with a croquet ball being slowly knocked across the carpet, which was intended to represent pain (the blow on the ball) and the solitude of love (the violinist). The Last Valley used the technique of shadow-play theatre. With a candle and pieces of folded material attached to the ends of pieces of bamboo, the actors told the story of three Butterflies in their flight around the flame. The one who reaches full understanding is consumed in the candle, which goes out.

The last sequence showed the arrival of the birds at the gate of the Simorg's court. First refused, the Chamberlain gave each bird a bundle of sticks. To signify the opening of the imaginary hundred curtains covering the entrance to the king, they wove abstract geometrical patterns on the air, slow and mesmeric. The actors turned to the spectators to include them in the circle. Serenely, they looked out beyond them. Slowly they advanced across the space towards the light to the accompaniment of tiny ceremonial bells. The audience was gently invited to take up and continue the challenge outside the theatre.

The Birds was performed at La Mama Annexe, New York, in 1980, with the *Ik* and *Ubu* on following evenings, and the programme stated that:

The performance has been studied in constantly changing physical circumstances in urban and country areas in Asia, Africa, Europe and both Americas.

The critics were ecstatic – 'astonishing', 'spellbinding', 'perfection', 'sublime', 'matchless', 'supremely challenging theatrical event of the season'. Even the hard-boiled Edith Oliver, who thought *The Birds* a 'tedious mess' when she had seen it in Brooklyn, now wrote, in *The New Yorker*, that it had been

transformed into a truly enchanting show, overcoming my firm prejudice against actors impersonating birds or animals (especially horses). . . . In this semi-abstract work the theatrical imagination of Peter Brook can be seen at its most astonishing.

Brook said the plays could be regarded as a trilogy:

The pure, rough, crude, energy of *Ubu* expressed the actors' celebration of energy. The heightened naturalism of the *Ik* is a celebration of detail, and the inter-cultural accessibility of the *Birds* is a celebration of the possibility of crossing barriers.

The programme notes also said,

The present New York season reflects a phase of the Centre's work that is now completed.

14   Carpet shows at the Bouffes: *Les Ik* and *Ubu*

In 1974, Brook discovered a derelict theatre in the tenth *arondissement* of Paris, behind the Gare du Nord, near a little park usually frequented by prostitutes and their Arab customers. A large, handsome, seven-storey building with elaborate cast-iron balustrades on every level, it had been constructed in 1876 as a 'théâtre à l'italienne': a proscenium arch with a horseshoe-shaped auditorium and three circles. It had not been used since 1952, when the interior had been destroyed by fire. Brook persuaded the Ministry of Culture to give 1,000,000 old francs (10,000 pounds) to pay for three-months' work of essential repairs.

What remained of the seats and the stage and equipment was completely stripped out. The stalls became the main acting space, surrounded by a semi-circle of raked wooden benches, on which 260 people could sit. The seating in the circles, for a further 250, was adjusted for sight lines so that this forward area, on which there would often be a carpet, became the focus of the audience's attention. Elizabethan-like, everyone was close to the performance, and most of them watched the actors against a background of other spectators.

Where the stage had been was now a gaping hole. For the first productions it was used for entrances and exits, with metal catwalks being installed across the back wall of the stage, but after five years Brook had it filled in, providing a stage some sixty feet in depth.

No attempt was made to restore the theatre. Crumbling decorations and engravings, pockmarked and scarred dirty white walls remained, with blotched and fire-blackened peeling surfaces. Holes were punched into the proscenium arch at the levels of the circles, for actors to poke their heads through.

Outside a simple painted sign says '*Théâtre*'. The entrance is a small doorway all but obscured by a brasserie on one side and a clown shop on the other.

From the moment Brook moved into the Bouffes, the pattern of his working life changed. In the first part of his career, his way of working had been dictated by the demands of the commercial theatre: he had been restricted to a three- or four-week rehearsal schedule. In the sixties, at the RSC and the National, he had been able to make some space for himself. But he was always restricted by the demands of the artistic directors and their institutions.

Now at last he found himself in control of his own working conditions. He was able to create a team of collaborators and a pool of international actors who understood what he was about and wanted to work with him in his way. He never created a permanent company, as Brecht had done with the Berliner Ensemble. But there were people he could draw on for particular projects. And in Jean-Claude Carrière, who had previously scripted films for Luis Buñuel, he found a lucid, laconic writer, whose unfussy, direct skills were exactly what he was looking for.

In the two decades since Brook staged his first production at the Bouffes – a French version of *Timon of Athens*, scripted by Carrière – he has allowed productions to evolve, to be dropped for a time and then brought back in a more developed form, to be reworked for English-speaking audiences, to be televised, to be taken round the world.

His work during this period may be divided into a number of areas. There were productions he and his group created during the seventies: *Les Ik*, *Ubu*, *The Conference of the Birds*. There were his Shakespeare productions, *Timon d'Athènes*, *Mesure pour mesure* (to which must be added his brief return to Stratford-upon-Avon to direct *Antony and Cleopatra* for the RSC). Then there were productions in the early eighties of two contrasting European masterpieces, *La Cérisiae* and *Carmen*. Ten years of work culminated in his production of *The Mahabharata* in 1985 (he was to continue working on versions of that for the next four years as well). He then staged *Woza Albert!* (in which two blacks gleefully contemplate the arrival of Jesus Christ in South Africa), after which he returned to Shakespeare, but again in French, and again translated by Carrière as *La Tempête*. He produced another slimline version of a French operatic masterpiece, his impressions of Debussy's *Pelléas et Mélisande*. And finally, in 1993, the perfect miniature, *L'Homme qui*, the culmination of three-years' research concerning patients with neurological disorders.

These divisions are made for convenience only. Throughout the period, Brook has been evolving work at the Bouffes and offering it to his audience in the global village, as the opportunities, also largely created by himself, arose.

In 1975, Brook produced a ninety-minute show adapted by Jean-Claude Carrière, Colin Higgins and Denis Cannan from Colin Turnbull's book, *The Mountain People*. Turnbull was an anthropologist who had gone in 1964 to study a northern Ugandan tribe, the Ik. They had been hunters until 1946 when the government had taken over their land and turned it into a National Park. They were forced to live as farmers in barren mountains. Turnbull found that the shock of relocation, coupled with drought and famine, had brought about a complete disintegration of social and family structures. He called them 'ruined pieces of nature'.

Brook saw this material as

a very rare meeting between a personal experience, objective facts, and poetic, mythic elements. The Ik survive – at a cost – and so do we. The parallels are alarming. The same sort of situation can be seen in Western urban life. For me, it's the perfect metaphor: something which exists on two levels – real in the sense of life as we know it, and real in the sense of a myth.

Brook used Turnbull's work as the point of departure. The actors improvised episodes in the book, as well as doing detailed physical work on what they saw and heard in the tapes and films. The mass of material thrown up by the actors' physical exploration and improvisation was disciplined within the constantly readapted written version, which was then translated into French by Carrière.

Brook:

What we were really interested in was trying to evoke a sense of the humanity of a very particular African people, neither by ignoring the fact that they are different from us nor by imitating. To do this, the actors do not have to impersonate or imitate completely what they are telling; they have to do something that is half way and they have to know enough about it, feel it deeply enough and then find the minimum suggestion that evokes that. We worked there on a very particular technique which was taken directly from photographs: the actors imitated photographs of Iks so that they tried to get exactly, in every physical detail, into the posture of the starving Ik that the photograph showed and then find the action five seconds before, five seconds after it – very different from any other sort of improvisation we have done. It has enabled the actor watching and each one correcting the other to discover, gradually, the reality of the hunger, not from an emotion, but from an exact sense inside himself of what it meant to be standing in that position with that part of your body sagging, with that part of your mouth open. The whole of our research work has been to try to make the quality of acting less of a communication through imitation and more a form of natural language, moving towards an Elizabethan model where many different people of different ages, cultures, classes, can respond together.

The Ik were played by actors who had been on the African journey. Brook claimed that through that experience they had come to 'sense the emotions underlying unfamiliar gestures. Even the way people carried objects around had a meaning'. The external physical manifestations were copied rigorously so that each actor could uncover his own Ik-ness and thereby understand the inner state of the tribe.

Various Brechtian devices were used in performance. The house lights were left on throughout. Short dramatised episodes were constantly punctuated by direct narrative to the audience: either by Turnbull himself, using the voice-over technique, or by one of the actors playing the Ik dropping his role to read directly from Turnbull's book. But the wide social statements of the book were omitted. The actors performed in their own clothes, without make-up or any attempt to act African. The form was understated, sparse and flat – a series of

13   *Les Ik*, Yoshi Oida, Bruce Myers, Andreas Katsulas, Bouffes du Nord, 1975

simple images with all externals removed. But they were stark and haunting images. At the Bouffes there was still the cavernous hole where the stage used to be. Rungs on the back wall were used for climbing up the mountain, the ascent to another, promised land.

It began with the actors slowly spreading soil about the playing area, and then carefully placing stones here and there. Turnbull's precarious car ride to meet the Ik was represented by two actors sitting on a trunk while others rattled pots and pans and scraped cans on the floor.

There were simple rituals: an Englishman making early-morning tea, with his pre-heated pot, packet of Earl Grey and biscuits on a plate; an Ik ceremoniously placing a dead body in the proper position. Turnbull's modern paraphernalia – mosquito net, tape recorder and camera – was contrasted with the objects used to symbolise the Ik's elemental existence – sticks, rocks, fire, earth.

The Ik barricaded themselves in so as to eat alone. They threw out their children at the age of three. Under their amiably smiling masks they were lying and ruthless. A boy ferretted in the earth and sucked pebbles for nourishment. Later he was lured close to a fire by his mother who proffered food, but then pulled it away so that her son burned his hand. She laughed, like all the Ik, at the misfortunes of others. But the scene was played in a flat unemotional way. All the time one had the feeling of watching people who might at any moment roll over and die.

One wordless scene showed a group lying round a fire and picking up a four-note melody, each adding his or her own variations and rhythms. Using voices and stick percussion, they created a gentle and very private nocturne.

Two Victorian missionaries tried to buy the Ik by promising them food in exchange for recognising Christ. They taught the Ik 'Rock of Ages'. In the funniest scene in the show they roared out the hymn, absurdly grotesque and discordant. (In London it became quieter: perhaps it had been too entertaining.) When no food arrived the Ik chanted their own version of the song straight at the audience: they used the same tune, but their own words, pleading for food and tobacco.

Turnbull watched two young Ik mutually masturbating off stage, all the while still looking for food. As Atum (Yoshi) told Turnbull, 'le sexe, c'est exactement comme chien'.

A despairing woman pulled apart a roughly made hut. Malik, as an old man turned out by his daughter to die, performed a prolonged circular exit to the accompaniment of a distant piping lament which you gradually realised he was making himself.

When government sent famine-relief again, the Ik gulped huge mouthfuls of it down, only to immediately vomit it up, whereupon they crammed more grain down, again and again. For the Ik considered a good man to be one with a full stomach.

At the end the remaining Iks shuffled slowly on their haunches away from the audience into the chasms where the old stage had been. They vanished into it one by one.

AH writes:

The Ik was the first show I'd seen at the Bouffes. Brook had first told me about the theatre a couple of years earlier. I'd been in Paris briefly that summer and he'd invited me round to his flat in Montparnasse for a drink. A lot of people were there.

At one point I found myself talking to him about The Gulag Archipelago. I made some flippant remark about the book having made Solzhenitsyn a lot of money. Brook turned on me very seriously as he had done the night during the US rehearsals when Adrian Mitchell and I had briefly celebrated the stabbing of Verwoerd. What mattered, said Brook, was that the gulags were there. The book reported their existence, which had to be recognised. For Brook, they seemed to confirm his perception of the human condition as unrelentingly bleak.

It was, perhaps, an hour later that he told me he'd just got hold of this theatre, up by the Gare du Nord. A ruin of a theatre, he said, all burned out, just the shell of the stage left. 'You'd love it', he said. 'You must go and see it.' But I was leaving the next day, and I only finally saw it when I went to see *Les Ik*.

The show seemed to me to belong perfectly to Brook's bleak landscape. In writing about it, I naturally saw it from the perspective of *The Marat/Sade* ten years earlier. *The Mahabharata* was still ten years in the future. This is the review I wrote:

The *Marat/Sade* and *The Ik*, ten years apart, mark the twin peaks of Brook's attempt to invent, virtually single-handed, a genuinely contemporary theatre. They also reflect the cultural assumptions on which that attempt has been based. I believe that it's important to examine those assumptions with some care. They demonstrate the difficulties facing any individual in our society who is struggling consciously to create new artistic forms.

In *The Ik* the ultimate in human experience is represented by the mountain people described by Colin Turnbull. He found them to be a people living at the extreme limits of anything that could be described as humanity, for whom the only good is food; who, when they find food, gobble it down secretly in order not to have to share it with members of their own family; who build stockades to protect themselves from each other; who drive their children out to fend for themselves at the age of three; who see giving food to the old and dying as criminal waste; who will gorge themselves sick on relief grain rather than distribute it to those in need; and whose only pleasure is to laugh at the misfortunes of the weak and helpless. In the preface to his book, Turnbull tells us how he was driven to say repeatedly, 'How inhuman' – then adds that to say 'How inhuman' is to presuppose 'that there are certain standards common to all humanity'. His book is largely about how he was driven to question that presupposition.

It's not difficult to see why Brook, in search of the ultimate, should be attracted by such material. But there's a further point of affinity between himself and Turnbull, which Brook referred to specifically:

As in anthropology there are two schools. Certain researchers prefer to go into a far country knowing nothing about it, while others leave only with documentation and after deep study. For me, with Shakespeare, the questions only become strong, hard, interesting when you're inside them. You can approach a Shakespeare text without knowing anything outside.

Turnbull, in his own first chapter, describes how, for him, the Ik were in the beginning a completely unknown quantity. He didn't even know their correct name. And he sees this as good. 'In this case', he writes, 'there was all the advantage of an almost completely clean slate'. His approach to this anthropological task was that of Brook's to Shakespeare: both would like to come at their subjects with virgin minds.

But, of course, neither Turnbull nor Brook can do this. Turnbull doesn't bring a 'clean slate' to the Ik. He brings a discipline and a whole set of values and assumptions. But at least these values are openly stated, and the importance of the book lies in the way they're thrown into question by what he observes.

Brook also brings to the subject a discipline and a set of values and assumptions. But in Brook's case, the assumptions *aren't* openly stated. In *The Marat/Sade* Brook asked his actors not to perform madmen, but to become mad. In *The Ik*, after ten further years of experiment, Brook has carried the possibilities of 'being', rather than 'acting', to an even more complex level. While rehearsing the play, the actors representing the Iks themselves built and lived in an Ik stockade, and played out episodes in Turnbull's book which were never to appear in the script. The result is that, throughout the two hours of the play, they become Iks.

This 'being' is achieved without the aid of any surface naturalism. They make no attempt, for example, to look like Iks, by appearing naked, or painting their faces in a uniform colour (there are people of many different races and hues in the cast). They wear their rehearsal clothes and keep their own physical appearances. And they don't create, for the most part, any specific characters. They're able to move at will from being young children to very old people. Brook even establishes a non-naturalistic use of language (reminiscent of the invented language of Orghast). The actors speak gibberish to each other, but offer explanations in French when necessary.

What they do create consistently is the quality of being Ik. The 'being' is revealed in the way the actors behave – in how an old woman falls over shrieking with laughter when she shakes hands with the actor playing Turnbull (she's so weak with hunger, she explains, that the gesture pulls her from her seat); in how a stockade is built and later destroyed; in how an idiot child picks up a berry from the ground, contemplates it with delight, and puts it into her mouth, only to have it snatched away by another child; in how a man whittles away endlessly at a block of wood. Though the actors show different characters, they always remain *inside* the Iks, throughout the performance (as Brook wishes to remain *inside* a Shakespeare text). Look at this, says Brook. *This* is human experience.

In a universe where all is madness, Sade becomes comparatively normal. And in a universe where all is degradation, Turnbull becomes the image of futile action. Both these interpretations arise directly from Brook's despairing vision of the human condition. But both, significantly, distort the material he is working with.

In *The Marat/Sade* Brook overwhelmed Weiss's contradictions with the reality of madness. Turnbull is similarly reduced in *The Ik*. The Turnbull of *The Mountain People* brings to his research that set of cultural assumptions about the nature of 'humanity'. He finds these assumptions withering away. He even begins to lose his own 'humanity'. But what he retains to the end is his active intelligence. In a final chapter, he uses this intelligence to turn our responses to the material back on ourselves, to ask us to analyse our own society, to become aware of the Ik qualities in our welfare state. And to become aware of them, not simply in order to throw up our hands and say in horror, 'Well, that's life, and there's nothing to be done' – but in order that we may use *our* intelligence to make a rational effort to change direction.

None of this emerges from Brook's play. Since the central reality of *The Ik* is the Iks themselves, Turnbull is seen, not as an active intelligence, but as a victim. He exists only in relation to the situation he too finds himself *inside*. This is established in one of the first scenes, in which four creatures stare at Turnbull who is in a sleeping bag behind a mosquito net. Presently, he emerges from the bag, takes out a folding table and chair, which he sets up, lights a primus stove, fills a kettle with water from a plastic container, warms the teapot with water from the container, and is on the point of throwing the water from the teapot on the floor, when he glances at the staring creatures and carefully pours the water back into the plastic container.

In such a scene, Brook seems to me to achieve his aim of a 'super-naturalistic' theatre. All Turnbull's actions are totally natural: he boils a real kettle on a real stove. But since they're seen through the eyes of the staring creatures, they take on the quality of a strange, absurd ritual. Our 'normal' actions are judged against a situation in which a drop of water means the perpetuating of a life.

But the actions that are so judged are, in the end, only the superficial, surface actions. Brook has, in this particular scene, found an adequate image to represent the thoughtless waste of the 'civilised' societies. But as the play develops, we're not presented with the kind of analysis of those societies that Turnbull himself sketches out. We're offered instead a picture of Turnbull's personal moral despair. We see him only through his reactions to the creatures who are around him. Our attention is focused, not on our society, but on Turnbull's sensibility.

How painful it must have been for him to have his water delivered daily from the police bore hole! When all around him people were dying because a polluted pool had dried up! How terrible it must have been to realise that your efforts to save one here and there were so futile! No wonder he felt such anger against the universe! And how morally corrupting to find yourself developing Ik-like qualities, in self-defence – hiding away when you eat your provisions, forcing yourself to feel no pity or human sympathy!

Turnbull's book ends with an appeal to us to *choose*, and adds a warning: 'It is difficult to say how long the choice will be open to us before we are irrevocably committed'. He's pessimistic – but he does still recognise the possibility of choice, and therefore of action.

Brook's play ends with a positive statement that all action is impossible. Turnbull's last speech in the play is one which offers his own final solution: to round up the Iks like cattle and disperse them in small groups amongst other tribes far away. 'No need to say', says an administrator in a final line, 'that your proposition is not acceptable'. It would be impossible to imagine a more direct assertion of the total futility of human action.

In both *The Marat/Sade* and *The Ik*, then, Brook presents powerful images which deny the usefulness, and even the possibility, of rational action. In doing so, he reflects, as an artist, the despair of a society which accepts that we are caught in a situation that we are completely powerless to change.

There are two paradoxes in the position Brook takes up. The first is that this man, who wants to question everything, and who asks audiences to question their own most cherished values, who believes in approaching experience naked and entirely without either illusion or faith, holds himself with a stubborn tenacity to his own faith in the futility of human action based on intelligence. He does so in the face of the evidence of the texts with which he is working – evidence left by such an intelligence as Shakespeare himself, whom Brook prefers to see as an anonymous, ambiguous figure, existing outside historical time and place. In *The Mountain People*, Turnbull's faith in his own values was questioned by the evidence offered by the Iks. Brook's faith in futility is not in any way questioned by Turnbull's intelligence. This seems to me to represent the other side of the coin from the 'facile optimism' Brook wants to challenge. In place of such optimism he offers an equally facile despair.

And this leads to the second paradox. For, because the despair is facile, the result is that, though Brook is trying to disturb, shock and assault the consciousness of his audiences, the despair joins hands with the optimism and, in the end, only succeeds in bringing an easy comfort. For if all rational action is futile, then the most we can do is to contemplate, with compassion, the sufferings of others. We can, in fact, feel righteous for spending an evening doing this instead of watching those old entertaining movies on telly. [After *US* one of the actors, Henry Woolf, had said that the experience of the show would mean that 'When I turn on my television set, I shall find the Vietnam War more *enjoyable*'.] Listening to the applause that burst out in the crowded theatre after the last Ik had vomited up in front of the audience his last sack of relief grain, I couldn't help thinking that Brook, the miracle worker, had pulled it off again. He'd made the Iks enjoyable.

The next year *The Ik* came to London, and Turnbull's own words were used. The reviews were mixed, respectful, but slightly puzzled from critics who mostly had seen nothing from Brook since the *Dream* six years before, but knew he had been travelling.

Irving Wardle, in *The Times*, thought it was a 'small' event that trembled on the brink of obscenity (like *US* and *Orghast*)!

It is a study of total human degradation rehearsed in conditions of subsidised security and imported from Paris as the intellectual treat of the month.

Others found it 'spare, dour, drab: a workshop specialising in sackcloth and ashes . . . rather dull', spoke of its 'sheer feebleness . . . fragmentary and clumsy', while Tynan's reaction was one of 'great baffled sorrow'!

It seemed to me that he had discarded all the immense technical skills that he had used previously to dazzle, startle, amaze and stun audiences by appealing to their sensibilities, which was his great power.

The quality of acting and the style in the performances certainly proved that he can make actors transform themselves into African tribesmen with considerable skill. I couldn't help reflecting how much more effectively a BBC2 film documentary could have done exactly the same job – not just a parallel job, but the same job, done better. There seemed to be no specifically theatrical excitement in the show – it was just a series of short, realistic scenes linked by straight 'voice-over' narration.

When it got to New York, Robert Brustein also said Brook needed a playwright (a point made earlier by Tynan), and continued:

I found myself just a little troubled about his parade of human misery before an audience helpless to do anything about it. . . . Ultimately Brook cannot shake off his inheritance, no matter how much he may despise it. Even his belief that he can is a Western idea, which dates from Rousseau. . . . He is in the grip of a powerful Romantic delusion at the moment, but anything one holds obsessively and long enough takes on its own validity. Brook is trying to make a point about the international roots of primitive theatre; I don't think he has proved it yet. But the effort, if not the result, compels respect, and it brings the theater just a little closer to the serious purpose for which it was first conceived.

Brook rejected the dogmatism of his socialist-realist critics, defending his production as an honest attempt to confront a splintered and confused reality. He believed that the other side of the coin was inferred within the pessimism concerning that particular reality. He described the play as 'the image of a world that is betraying its possibilities'. He believed it offered a rare challenge to the limitations of a strictly Marxist analysis. The old unity of the Ik did not have an economic basis: the collapse resulted from the removal of cohesive spiritual traditions. He saw any interpretation of the situation purely in terms of the imposition of capitalist oppressors as naïve. In this situation, it would be simplistic to suggest that economic intervention could be effective.

In *The Empty Space*, Brook had written, 'Along with serious, committed and probing work, there must be irresponsibility'. Perhaps as a reaction to the seri-

14 *Ubu*, Andreas Katsulas, Jean-Claude Perrin, Alain Maratrat, Bouffes du Nord,
1977

ousness of *The Ik* he now decided to be irresponsible. In 1977 he finally staged Jarry's absurd masterpiece, *Ubu*.

Brook had wanted to do it at LAMDA in 1964, but felt he had not the right actors. He had commissioned Spike Milligan to do a version for C.I.C.T., but they could not agree on the tone (it would finally be staged by Marowitz in London in 1980). Now he did it in French, trying to capture the brutal energy which he said came off the page at you. It was a splendid example of 'rough' theatre.

In *The Empty Space* Brook recalls a Czech production he had seen on German television, which had turned the play into a comic strip:

This production disregarded every one of Jarry's images and indications; it invented an up-to-the-minute pop-art style of its own, made out of dustbins, garbage and ancient iron bedsteads. Ubu himself no longer the pear-headed 'masque' figure, with Jarry's own spiral design highlighting his inflated 'gribouille'. This was no masked Humpty Dumpty, but a recognisable and shifty slob, while Mère Ubu was a sleazy attractive whore. In this way the audience's belief was caught because it accepted the primitive situation and characters on their own terms.

Brook worked with Carrière and the actors on all four of Jarry's *Ubu* plays in order to make a composite text. The first half was mainly from *Ubu Roi*; after the bear scene it followed *Ubu sur la Butte*. The second part was taken from *Ubu Echaîné*. Some of Jarry's original songs were inserted, principally 'La chanson du décervellage' from *Ubu Cocu*. So Ubu as king became Ubu as slave.

Jarry's plays desecrate the French sacred concepts of glory and freedom. Brook's production also gleefully assaulted, in the first part, common notions of authority, justice and order, while, in the second, making a determined effort to maintain that freedom and slavery are the same thing.

The staging consisted of physical clowning, impressive acrobatics and the most resourceful invention. It was raucous and noisy, coarse and fast. The actors sweated and spat and roared. Apart from Père and Mère Ubu, every actor played many roles, but the characters were always clear. The performance was filled with macabre knockabout humour and demented sight gags, all done in the most economical way. The overall effect was of a highly disciplined circus troupe improvising a farce. The tone was that of a silent film, or music hall.

The set could have been lifted from a building site. It consisted of two old cable drums and a few bricks. Piled on top of each other the drums became a throne; rolled along they were carriages and chariots, bulldozers and juggernauts. The old bricks represented money, weapons, food, and the perilous edge of the death-trap into which the tyrant shoved his foes; the actors jumped from brick to brick while crossing a river in flood. A brick was a chicken, then it was roasted and eaten, right down to the bone. There was also some real food, which was really eaten (the detritus – orange peel, banana skins, Vichy bottles – being thrown into the audience). Ubu held court with a toilet brush. In a scene needing snow, he simply threw some confetti into the air and chattered his teeth as it descended on him. There were all-purpose sticks and some wooden pantomine swords, and an old shaggy rug, variously used as King Ubu's cloak, a bedspread and a bear; when a general had to be eaten by one, it ate him all, throwing back only his hat and a bone.

At one moment, a family, played by three actors, huddled around the bricks, which represented a small fire on which food is supposed to be cooking. The space occupied by the scene was miniscule. Then the grotesque dictator Ubu entered and with one kick obliterated the entire household.

Courtiers and aristocrats were condemned to death by being ordered to run into a wall. The actors hurled themselves against it. Then a blind man entered. He raced in every direction except towards the wall. The battlefield was bombarded with golf-ball missiles flung from the circle.

Ubu and his Monster Spouse were comic giants, indestructably alive no matter what regrettable incidents befell them, and always in the certainty that they would survive. They underwent manifold transformations of Rabelaisian greed, lust, bestiality and physical terror while maintaining their playful and direct contact with the audience. Their confident French postures strikingly were continually being undercut by hard-hat, street-wise derision. This Ubu was an apocalyptic slob, a roaring grasping 'man of the people', with a protruding stomach and rasping voice, who had slurped and belched his way to the top. His wife was a gross brute.

Captain Bordure was played as an awkward hunchbacked clown. The same actor played the battlefield Tsar as a cigar-smoking Movie Mogul.

The performance was played with house lights on. When Mère Ubu went looking for treasure in the crypt, she blundered about with her candle and asked someone in the front row to help her shift a paving stone. There was audience contact of the most natural and unaffected kind.

Throughout, there was a percussion accompaniment, provided by a remarkable Japanese multi-instrumentalist, which was as subtle and witty as the action was raucous and demonic. While Mère Ubu crept through the vaults, the sound suggested slamming doors and flying bats.

Brook began with two pairs of Père and Mère Ubu, the second being black. Throughout the fortnight of previews they alternated with the two, larger, white actors. But he found that this changed the rhythm of the evening and emphasised unfavourably the change of tone between the plays. The sardonic variations on liberty and slavery became something else when masterminded by the blacks. He decided to drop them. Only later when the white actress playing Mère Ubu left the company did the black Miriam Goldschmidt get to play the part again. But now she was married to a gargantuan racist, so the meaning was not altered.

The next year the production came to London. Now it was a multi-lingual performance: still basically in French, but interspersed with English in a very comic way. Sometimes there were asides to the audience, like subtitles in a movie, sometimes as a kind of narrative, and sometimes it was mixed ('Je suis King of Poland') as well as straight ('who will sew up the seat of your knickers?')

In 1980, *Ubu* was presented at La Mama in New York. By now Miriam Goldschmidt had taken over as Mère Ubu. She played her, cross-eyed and rubber-faced, as a shrewd and lewd pussycat, a gutter-talking Lady Macbeth who goaded her husband with 'If I were you I'd stick that ass of yours on a throne'.

The American critics enjoyed it. The *New York Times* called it 'an absurdist cartoon', and *Time* a 'scatological bourgeois baiting nineteenth-century travesty of Macbeth'. Richard Watt, in the *Daily News*, said it was 'So broadly performed on the almost bare playing area it could be comprehended in some remote tribal village'.

Robert Brustein tended to agree with the English reviewers, who generally found it lovable and harmless:

the goofiness occasionally falls into silliness, and the spirit of adolescent clowning occasionally palls, but there are some very funny images in the production. . . . But for all its primitiveness *Ubu* is the product of a highly sophisticated sensibility and for all its rejection of European culture it could only have been produced by the West. The same might be said of its director.

15 Popular Shakespeare: *Timon d'Athènes*, *Mesure pour Mesure* and *Antony and Cleopatra*

In between *The Ik*, *Ubu* and the various productions of *The Birds*, Brook returned to Shakespeare. His first production at the Bouffes, in October 1974, was *Timon of Athens*. In the programme he asked:

Why Shakespeare?

At the time of moving to public expression of our work it was natural that we should turn to the best example of a complete theatre, the Elizabethan theatre. Shakespeare has shown in an astonishing way that the theatre could be at the same time popular and aristocratic, obscene and poetic, truculent and metaphysical, that the noble thought could exist with the joke. Moreover, the Elizabethan theatre was always played in the open air, in a sort of forum, a place where all the currents met.

Why *Timon*?

Because I like the play. There are moments when certain themes are closer to us. That's why in certain countries at certain times one plays certain plays rather than others. *Timon* today is a play of the moment: it deals with money and inflation. Certainly they are not the only themes, as no play of Shakespeare is built on a single subject. But waste, credit, consumption, prices and affluence are there. It puts the finger on problems which touch us. The story of Timon is that of a man who, living above his means, thought he could buy joy. He created a universe – a sort of paradise – which had nothing to do with the one in which he lived. The Athens invented by Shakespeare is imaginary. It strangely resembles the Athens under the colonels, a town of corruption. But that's by chance, for Timon's Athens is finally as symbolic as Ubu's Poland, it could be anywhere.

Moreover, the protagonists behave like Greeks, Romans, Londoners. At that time make-believe was natural: in religious painting you can see in Holland a Christ confronted with a Burgomeister and, in Italy, the good citizens of Venice. That's not anachronism. It's what you would call the naïve imagination. To return to the plot: in this town there's a man who instead of facing the crisis makes a lot of noise and creates mirages. Exactly like today when most of the Western countries are faced with the oil crisis: they turn a deaf ear, continuing to consume more daily, and behave as if the illusion can last for ever. For Timon the dream is stronger than the reality. Now one fine day he is forced to pass from the dream to reality. The experience is terrifying. It's at that moment that the development of the play reaches its crucial point and poses the question that concerns us all: how to behave in the face of disaster?

The main line of the play is the destruction of the known. Timon, and with him the audience, find themselves in front of the unknown. Towards the end of the play several actions overlap; the death of Timon, his relations with other characters, the return of the conqueror Alcibiades are like electric wires which short. For each spectator faced with Timon's ransacked world and Alcibiades' burgeoning world a vital question is asked: who will be destroyed? Who will be saved? That's the reality. Shakespeare doesn't give an answer.

215

In another interview he puts a different emphasis on Timon:

> Timon tries to do good. When his naïve, even quixotic, approach to free-handed altruism fails, Timon rejects activism and becomes like those who adopt an oriental religion in order to retreat from society, or who resort to alcohol or to drugs to escape their problems. Timon is like people who retreat to a wooden house in the trees, men who pull out of the rat race. He dies in confusion. He has not reached any point of *transcendent understanding*.

TEXT

Jean-Claude Carrière provided a clean and witty text. Shakespeare's elaborate Jacobean rhetoric was translated into simple modern French prose. Carrière concentrated on conveying the story with the utmost clarity. Shakespeare's sentences were broken down into shorter phrases of concentrated force.

There were few cuts. The only scene to go was that between Apemantus and the Fool (II.ii. 51–134) which, although possibly by Shakespeare (as opposed to his collaborator, Middleton), does seem to be implausible and spurious. The treatment clarified literal meaning at expense of the irrational and the emotional. So a phrase like 'religion to the gods' (IV.i.16) became 'devotion'. Two lines later

> Degrees, observances, customs and laws
> Decline to your confounding contraries;
> And let confusion live!

became

> Ordre, rituels, coutumes, lois, à la trappe. Vive le chaos!

Down the hole is very laconic: the loss in language, meaning and effect is obvious. 'Raise me this beggar and demit that lord' (IV.iii.9) became 'Ce mendiant, au pinacle. Ce noble, à la rue', and later in the speech

> Therefore be abhorr'd
> All feasts, societies, and throngs of men!
> His semblable, yea, himself, Timon disdains.
> Destruction fang mankind. Earth yield me roots.
> Who seeks for better of thee, sauce his palate
> With thy most operant poison

became

> Fêtes, foules, horreur, adieu. Timon méprise son semblable, lui-même. Qu'une griffe éventre la race humaine. Terre, donne des racines. Si quelqu'un te réclame mieux, badigeonne sa bouche de ton meilleur.

Much of the original English meaning may be lost in archaism, but its effect is resounding; in French the meaning is clear, but the effect flat. Of course, this is the best speech in the play, but it is clear that even here Brook was not interested in the thunder of the language (after all Beaudelaire or Verlaine might have made a reasonable effort at Timon's invective). He wanted contemporary work, one that would speak directly to our times, not something situated in a historical past, whether Greek or English (or French).

Instead of hearing the play begin with

> Good day, sir
> I am glad y'are well
> I have not seen you long; how goes the world?
> It wears, sir, as it grows.
> Ay, that's well known

at the Bouffes we heard

> Bonjour, Monsieur
> Je suis content de vous voir
> Je ne vous ai vu de longtemps. Comment va le monde?
> Il s'use, monsieur, à mesure qu'il grandit.
> Oh, c'est bien connu.

No wonder the *lycée* to which the cast took the play thought it had been written yesterday.

This straightforward text drove home the reading of the play as the dramatic confrontation of an idealistic man with the realities of a self-serving world.

Brook said:

Of course in the great Shakespearian masterpieces, as in Greek tragedy, the content is inseparable from the series of syllables. When you change one vowel you change the musical structure. It's not for nothing that I chose to mount *Timon* in French and not *King Lear*. In *Timon* in English the musical values are not very important.

For all its modernity of theme – Marx had commented on the speeches about money long before the price of oil provoked such a crisis in the world economy – there were sound reasons for *Timon* being one of Shakespeare's least performed plays, mainly to do with the unfinished state of the existing English text (an uneasy collaboration with Middleton in 1604 which failed to get on to the stage), rather than its bristling misanthropy, or broken-backed structure (the incredible reversals mid-way have not prevented *Coriolanus* or *The Winter's Tale* being continually in the repertoire). Doing the play in French removed many of the problems and provided Brook with a neutral text on which he could project his own vision. This he did in a most effective and theatrical manner.

Nothing fixed the play in time, place or style. There was an informal atmosphere as the actors wore their ordinary clothes which generally remained visible beneath their costumes. What they put on served as a simplified guide to character, externalising the moral nature or function as in the medieval theatre. As a whole they formed a non-specific jumble of stereotypes. No stylistic unity was imposed. Many costumes were a satirical caricature consistent with the Jonsonian nature of the minor characters. It was a miscellaneous ragbag of bellbottoms, beads, whatever, which enabled the play to be seen as an abstract fable.

Timon wore impressive clothes: a cloth of gold shirt and dazzling white suit made him into a golden boy. For the first party he added a gold neck chain and a white and gold robe. He looked like, and possessed all the assurance of, a young Kennedy. For the second half the gold had gone and the same suit was in shreds.

Alcibiades was the cartoon of a Greek general or South American dictator with a black and gold uniform – all epaulettes, medals and shining buttons – and a red cloak. The thieves looked like Middle Eastern brigands: all were clad in black leather jackets and flat black caps sporting heavy dark moustaches. The painter had a symbolic Bohemian neckerchief. Apemantus was a tramp.

The flattering friends wore light floating robes of plain materials over their ordinary clothes and, for the banquets, donned flowing gilded cloaks, smacking of cheap ostentation and degraded aristocratic pomp. The senators first appeared with flapping black academic capes, suggesting crows; visiting Timon in the second act they became grotesques, wearing tailcoats and top hats and carrying tightly rolled umbrellas. The debt collectors sported tight suits and gangster Borsalinos. The predatory creditors carried outsize surreal account books.

The actors entered at the same time as the audience, mingling with them. The poet and painter conducted the opening dialogue from the hole burst high in the wall on either side of the proscenium arch at the level of second balcony. Timon emerged gloriously from the abyss (where the stage used to be); at the end of the play he would painfully and slowly redescend into it.

When the creditors began to doubt Timon's solvency, action broke out all around the building. One creditor appeared like a distressed angel out of one of the high openings. Another appeared in a crag high on the other side. Still others came down the aisles. One walked from the rear of the theatre, stepping from bench to bench through the sitting audience to get to the central space.

At the end, Alcibiades stood on the metal catwalk at the back like an avenging angel towering over the quaking senators. In an earlier scene, while the senators had discussed the errant soldier's punishment, the victim stood motionless in the same place on the catwalk.

The performance was essentially the telling of a story by a group of actors to an assembled ring of spectators. Initially, the actors consciously adopted a narrator's stance, maintaining a certain distance between themselves and their roles. The only scenic props were sack-like cushions arranged in a circle, so it looked like a carpet show. When the play began the actors not performing sat on the cushions to form an inner circle of focus; they listened and watched, so there was very little separation between actor and spectator. This continued throughout the first half. During the interval the spectators were invited on to the playing area.

In the first half the back wall became a screen on to which ominous shadows were projected when actors used the stairs up from the abyss. The lighting was almost uniform for the whole performance. It grew dark at the end of the first part as the lonely Timon cursed mankind, and it became a bright oppressive glare in the second act.

The masque of the first banquet became something out of the Thousand and One Nights; the frenzy of a Whirling-Dervish dance and floating, glittering capes conveyed a sense of debauchery, waste and excess. The guests crouched down, chanting like Arabs praying; but inside this framework of some North African city or a Middle Eastern harem, Cupid appeared in mock-Kabuki style, played by the Japanese actor, Yoshi Oida. Two flattering lords lay with their heads in Timon's lap and he fondled them. But at the second banquet he drenched and stoned the same guests and drove them off the stage.

Apemantus was played with bitter cynicism and great anger by Malik Bagayogo. He was always to be found outside or on the fringes of the circle, observing and judging like the spectators with whom he allied himself; he would rasp his savage barbs directly to the audience around him. At the party he hovered like an uninvited guest. It was impossible not to see here a comment on colonialism in the casting of the only black actor in the company in the part of the prophetic, choric 'fool', especially in the middle of the oil crisis.

With all the mystique stripped away, and such detached presentation of feeling, precise, economic signalling of behaviour, there was little of what traditionally might be expected: the epic grandeur of Timon's universal despair. Instead, Brook emphasised the materialistic causes of Timon's tragedy, thus making other causes seem either remote or implausible. The images were of a society in which human behaviour turned wholly on the possession or lack of money and gold.

We saw a rich young prodigal, barely past his adolescence, dispensing wealth with abandon. Looking like everyone's memory of Gérard Philippe, François Marthouret was a handsome poised creature of casual grace, smiling like a Parisian playboy, whose habitual stance was a hesitant half-step forward. Until the moment at which he realised he had been betrayed, he was superlatively sunny. Then the smile became a snarl and by the last act he was bellowing with unforgiving rage. The money he found in the fourth act was not coin but gold dust which he blew out of his hand at all who came to visit him.

It was a moral fable on the waste and crime of living beyond one's means. But whereas Shakespeare was observing at first hand the beginnings of the consumer society, and, like Jonson, noting the effect of money on people, Brook believed it was even more of a play about 'commitment'; the question, for him, was how does a man conduct himself when confronted with disaster? Does he, like Timon, write his own epitaph, give up and descend into the grave?

Timon is the only Shakespeare play mentioned by Marx. He saw the acquisition of the power of money as the instrument of universal division, which in a capitalist society would become a god-like force alienating man from his fellows and from himself as a social animal. Brook saw a universal fable of man alienated from an unnatural society, in search of natural values. For him, the tragedy of a man who when thrown into harsh confrontation with reality would withdraw from society.

Brook believed that the inner motivation in Shakespeare was to be found in the music, rhythms and imagery of the text. The actor's task was to stimulate a response by freeing the spectator's imagination. But there was a mixture of styles, traditions, races and accents. Some of the French text was lost even though performed so close to the audience. Seven of the actors had done the African trip and were highly proficient in free and improvisatory forms, but they were African, American, English, Japanese: only one was French and he played Timon. Carrière's lines gave the others some problems. This basic dilemma was to stay with Brook in his work at the Bouffes. He replied to criticism by saying that it was characteristic of Shakespeare to revel in amalgams; and that a rich strangeness in him was better than consistency in someone else.

Brook's premise – that today we are one world, that narrow nationalisms should be broken down – implies a multi-national company. But audiences are normally only fluent in one language, and plays are written in that one language. An actor who cannot handle the text finds his expression in such a form severely limited. The play may well become international at the cost of sometimes being incomprehensible or simplistic.

Although John Higgins, in *The Times*, thought it was 'a remarkable personal vision of an impossible play', other English critics were less enthusiastic. Robert Cushman, in *The Observer*, said it was not 'from moment to moment, amazingly inventive', – what the production could not do was 'to establish the play as a unity'. While John Peter, in *The Sunday Times*, thought Marthouret gave a cool performance that showed that Brook was not interested in exploring

this tantalisingly unfinished study of a deeply insecure man driven first to insane generosity and then to furious self-abasement. . . . There are, of course, memorable scenes of haunting theatrical imagination. But they are few. We are left with the strange spectacle of one of the greatest of English directors, who could draw on the resources of a great English company, doing an intellectual exercise with a mediocre Shakespeare play, in French, with just competent actors, in a Paris suburb. Why?

The French had no such reservations. They gave the production two Prix, as the best of the year. The 112 performances were sold out to predominantly young audiences, many of whom, like the *lycée* pupils, obviously thought they were seeing a new play.

The *New York Times* called it 'a living emblem of the West brutally awakened from its paradisial consumer's dreams by the oil crisis'. Tynan did not see it, but thought the choice significant:

I think the connection with Beckett and the philosophy behind him gave Peter a justification for the world view which was later to become dominant in his work: that human beings, left to themselves, stripped of social restraints, are animals and are inherently rotten and destructive. You might almost call it a ritualistic misanthropy; and it has been the driving force behind Brook's work from the early sixties onwards.

It was significant that he should choose another deeply misanthropic play which further demonstrates and underlines this view of human nature which begins to dominate his work.

For his next foray into Shakespeare Brook returned to a play he had staged with great success at Stratford-upon-Avon in 1950, *Measure for Measure*. That wildly inventive production had catapulted the play into a central position in the classical repertoire. It had been filled with grotesque details in the prison and brothel scenes, and with stupendous visual gags – Pompey had been dragged across the stage at top speed and down a trap at the end of a rope. In *The Empty Space* Brook wrote of

A base world . . . the disgusting, stinking world of medieval Vienna . . . we must animate all this stretch of the play as the roughest comedy we can make . . . the rough is in prose, the rest in the verse. . . . If we iron Shakespeare into any one typography of theatre we lose the real meaning of the play.

Jean-Claude Carrière's French text was in prose and kept only what was vital to the plot. The production lasted two hours. There was no interval. All changes of place were eliminated as well as characters. Most of the action took place on a tiled hexagon in the centre of the space; each scene flowed into the next without a break. There was no scenic contrast between public and private places. The naturally ruined texture of the Bouffes easily looked like a castle gate, prison, fairground, city street.

The costumes were a casual mixture of ancient and modern, Lucio having a hint of Elvis Presley, and Isabella, close cropped, looking like Joan of Arc. There was no scenery except three small benches – Claudio had a token bed of straw. The house lights were unvaryingly on, except for one brief episode. There was no music.

The Duke appeared neither as a vehicle of providence nor as a manipulator, but, as played by François Marthouret, as a young man of charm and authority. Having nowhere to hide, he openly watched the action from among the spectators. He seemed bound on a search for a perfect form of order, which would fall somewhere between the individualistic anarchy of Lucio and the unremitting Puritanism of Angelo. He would periodically fix his eyes on a visionary horizon; he still kept on his monk's habit after revealing himself in the last act.

The most complex performance came from Bruce Myers, playing Angelo with some comic wit and little natural pomposity, although strongly suggesting the ram-rod-backed Puritanism, with all its attendant hypocrisies. When aroused by Isabella he sat by himself, trying to justify and rationalise his lust by focusing on each word. His monologues became the mad, very human, battles of physical demands and psychological self-control. He clearly delineated the shift from self-satisfaction to self-hatred.

Isabella was played by a young actress, Clémentine Amouroux, who had never appeared on stage before, only on television (perhaps Brook was influenced in the casting by the fact that he was later to film the production for television). Being ideally young she was free of sexual inhibition and with her boyish build strongly projected youthful idealism; but she lacked spiritual pride and her militant purity lacked punch. She was sensitive and warm, but lacked the necessary element of fanaticism, thus diminishing the importance of the central debate. So when she, like her predecessor at Stratford-upon-Avon, paused long before agreeing to beg for her brother's life, the hesitation lacked the explosive effect it had had in 1950. She made a stone-faced final exit, giving no indication as to how she would respond to the Duke's proposal. The casting also raised questions as to why Angelo should prefer this Isabella to Mariana. For while playing all the sadness and gentleness of a lonely woman, Mareille Maalouf had a dark-eyed powerful theatrical presence beside which Mlle Amouroux's pallid frailty seemed curiously characterless. In this company she looked, understandably, at sea.

Maurice Bénichou, an experienced exponent of deflationary comedy, played Lucio, the quintessential rake, as an anarchic free spirit, on nodding and winking terms with the audience. Convivially sleek and chic he could also be vicious, the smile always bordering on a snarl. He lolled against the wall, quite without fear, after the return of the Duke in the last act.

Andreas Katsulas made Pompey an ingratiating hulk. Although he always seemed comparatively harmless, there was a moment when the apprentice executioner put a frightened white hamster on a chopping block in the middle of the stage and crouched over it with an axe. For a moment he managed to convince the audience he really was going to do it.

Mistress Overdone was a motherly black straight out of an Algerian whorehouse, and Escalus was a grave African judge – even if they only had passable French accents. Although one of the most powerful images consisted of the three judges – Duke, Angelo and Escalus – standing side by side, it was the marvellous clowns who dominated the production, with the feeling that the rest had a natural flair for comedy but were strenuously trying to play straight. Complex characters were created without becoming stereotypes, but the ingrained comic instinct and natural affability kept undermining the emotional undertow of an ambiguous play which thrives on shifting moral sands, and which was already weakened by the neutral playing of the Duke and the underpowered Isabella. So Bernadine's refusal to be beheaded came over with explosive power, but there was little sense of Claudio's life really being in danger.

Yet the comedians did not create the reeking work so present in the first production, and noted by Brook in *The Empty Space*. The teeming invention of *Ubu* was not used in *Mesure*. Even the comedy was battened down, austere, so that Overdone and Angelo seemed to inhabit the same world. But it was not a complete world (in the sense of the decadent Vienna of state apartments, festering streets and dark corners), rather a neutral battleground for the collisions of abstract principles. The ideas and principles emerged very clearly, as did the shifts of motive, even if the emotions that accompanied them were not so strongly delineated. The achievement of the production was that, without lighting, costume, decor or make-up, Brook made the dark and baffling comedy emerge as the work of a popular dramatist.

Robert Cushman, in *The Observer*, thought that although the play was no longer a confusion it remained a puzzle. 'There are no glaring contradictions in it . . . but there is no overriding coherence either.'

Eric Shorter, in *Drama*, said he felt cheated,

Cheated because Brook seemed so anxious to exaggerate his love of austerity and dread of luxury. Isn't there something Peer Gyntish about this peeling away of orthodox surface effects to discover the nature of theatrical pleasure? It is as if he were trying to find out just how little the spectator needs before he no longer considers a play worth watching.

Irving Wardle, in *The Times*, said the production was designed for a Paris audience

to convince them that Shakespeare could write like Racine. By concentrating the action the show achieves a perfect consistency between the life-and-death drama and the low comedy, so that the old question of how to classify the work simply does not arise. . . . The play is diminished by being presented as an ironic fable. The tragic possibilities are blocked off. . . . Not all of the play is dragged into the light.

And Brook's Stratford *Antony and Cleopatra* appears a tradition-encrusted revival compared with the clean sweep he has made of *Measure for Measure* in this blitzed pleasure dome.

15   *Antony and Cleopatra*, Stratford-upon-Avon, 1979

Although Brook started rehearsing *Mesure pour Mesure* in Paris in the spring of 1978, by the middle of July he was back in Stratford-upon-Avon for the first time in eight years, to stage what would be his last English production, *Antony and Cleopatra*. Only after it opened at the beginning of October did he return to finish *Mesure pour Mesure*, which then had its first night three weeks later.

Brook:

All my life I've been drawn to undiscovered Shakespeare. *Antony and Cleopatra* has been smothered by images superimposed by the Victorian era and by the cinema. It is forty-five short scenes of intimate behaviour. There is no pageantry. Everything concerns personal relationships. People, including those with famous names, are introduced in close-up as they were in, say, *Holocaust*. It is only through them that the trappings have been invented. Shakespeare didn't decorate the play. The Empire may be towering but he keeps it out of sight.

Sally Jacobs:

We knew we could perform any Shakespeare play without sets. Everybody had got into a terrible sort of dead end, over-pictorialising everything. One actually started again with that over-made element of pictorialisation which is associated with Cleopatra. One was stuck with that in one's hand. We had to get rid of that in order to release the play. Liz Taylor and Richard Burton; Cecil B. De Mille and Claudette Colbert and the Victorians – and just sheer spectacle. The barge – and the treasures of Tutankhamun. And the way I did it was – I went completely in the other direction.

It was a necessity to create the right sort of intimate space for the play to happen against an ambiguous background. A place where one could always be aware of the outside world affecting the domestic space – and to relate these. Which is why it's a half-seen world, semi-transparent, anchored by the carpet area. There was no obligation to set the difference between Alexandria and Rome. It should be a place which everything can flow through, and the people come and bring their world with them and take it off with them.

There were two opposite ways of using space. There was a way of arranging the enclosure which was more domestic, and another way which was more archetypal, noble, architectural: so that one gave us the grandeur, and the other gave us the domesticity.

Brook rehearsed for ten weeks. He began with six actors: Antony, Cleopatra, Octavius, Enobarbus, Charmian and Octavia. They spent the first two days reading the text, talking about language. Then they spent a month on the carpet: exercises, physical work, sounds, freeing of the imagination, improvisations, rhythm. Brook asked them to make the connection, to carry this experience over into the work with text.

Four weeks later another four actors joined the work. Brook only had the whole cast (twenty-six) for the last four weeks. The first day the whole cast was present the play was read, sitting in a circle, with one copy being passed from hand to hand. Actors did not read their own parts: at the beginning of each scene, or the entrance of each new character it would be picked up by the next actor. The copy went round the circle several times. After the first dress rehearsal, the entire day was spent discussing the performance. Everyone was asked to make a contribution, to watch and talk about scenes they were not in.

The production lasted three-and-a-half hours. There was, finally, one interval, after Octavia's return to Rome in the middle of the third act; during the previews it had been moved around, at one time there had been two (the second coming after Antony's death). Two small scenes were cut: II.iv, a ten-line scene between Lepidus, Maecenas and Agrippa (Patrick Stewart said, 'we never could understand why it was there'); and III.v, the Eros–Enobarbus twenty-five lines which ties up the plot about Pompey, although it was rehearsed for six weeks.

Brook and Sally Jacobs found a wonderfully simple solution to both the sprawling layout of the play, and the problem of doing a chamber piece in the vastness of the Memorial Theatre at Stratford-upon-Avon.

The set was a semicircle of four opaque plastic panels, with wide gaps between them to allow for entrances and exists. Above they were connected by other sections which sloped inwards, dome-like. It divided the stage so the down-stage area could become an enclosed acting space; on the floor was a large rush carpet. Beyond the glass the empty stage stretched out to white walls. The translucent panels made figures beyond seem like shadows. Down stage there were three more panels on each side, smaller ones which could be brought in to enclose the action (for the Athens scenes at the end of the first part and for the monument at the end). Up against each panel was a bench. The benches were brought down stage for the Roman scenes. On the carpet were four striped cushions, more being added for Pompey's galley. During this scene, the carpet was suddenly flown, like a great sail, dropping Antony to the stage from its upper edge. A smaller, pale carpet was used as the playing area for the fourth act, being used to drag the dead Antony off stage. During that scene another large, bright red carpet was slowly flown in. Having suggested Cleopatra's monument it was lowered to the floor. There were two round brass stools. The cast did all the scene changes, except for clearing up the mess after the drinking scene and the laying of the monument.

All this enabled the play to be staged with great fluidity. As there was no upper level for the monument, the dragging of Antony to Cleopatra along the floor, wrapped in her women's scarves, seemed easy and natural. Usually this is a cumbersome proceeding, involving ropes and winches, like the messy, deliberately unheroic, suicide before it.

The long running time was due to the almost uncut text and the slow and emphasised nature of some of the speaking, not because of armies marching on and off and elaborate changes of scenery which had afflicted productions since the discovery of authentic costumes in 1825 (Shakespeare's text had often been chopped in half in order to accommodate such spectacle). There was barely a beat between the end of one scene and the next. Twice the actors remained on stage during another scene: Antony and Scarus stood still at the end of IV.x, while Octavius spoke four lines (the sum total of IV.xi), the two High Commands on the eve of the battle, back to back, making their dispositions; at the end of the next scene Antony remained down stage, prostrated in grief, his outstretched arms on the two brass stools, while Cleopatra and her entourage played IV.xiii up stage, beyond the screens. Antony's shame at losing the first battle – 'Hark the land bids me tread no more upon it' (III.xi) – was expressed down stage in little light while his attendants waited in the obscurity beyond the screens. Enobarbus watched the sea battle at Actium standing far up stage, his back to the audience, while music, discordant noise of fighting, and the lights rose and fell three times. There was one visual shock: at the moment of Antony's victory – (IV.vii) blood-soaked sponges were thrown at the four screens from up stage, staining them for the rest of the performance.

The costumes gave an overall feeling of a timeless Mediterranean world – both Roman and Egyptian, they could have belonged to a distant period, they could have been almost contemporary. Instead of togas, notoriously restricting to the actor's movement, there were the large loose robes of the Middle East, which suggested important men in a hot climate. Antony's followers wore red,

Caesar's blue with white stripes in various patterns. Pompey wore black, his followers browns and greys. Antony had a striped dressing gown in the first act, and a light leather armour with a Tartar helmet for Act IV.

Cleopatra's variety was reflected in a chameleon-like succession of robes (more than the rest put together) moving from androgynous glamour to hieroglyphic formality, from North African kaftans to regal splendour. The only ornament she wore was the pearl she received from Antony. She and her woman had short cropped hair; they wore Arab headdresses for III.xi, the scene after the first defeat.

Octavia was played coolly and wore yellow, the only one on stage to do so.

Although the production seemed to emphasise Antony's age – all his lieutenants were grizzled, balding old troopers and the arming scene was played by candlelight as an insomniac obsession in the small hours – Alan Howard seemed too young, even dashing in the first part of the play. Only after the shame of defeat did he audibly darken and visibly stumble into the 'noble ruin' that Scarus has already called him. Howard got Antony's madness, being frantically suicidal in his determination to fight 'by sea, by sea', but there was no god-like magnanimity. There seemed no serious resolve to break the 'strong Egyptian fetters'.

He was a loner, looked upon by Octavius and Pompey as a senior partner by whom they had always felt far outclassed. Antony shared this belief: there was incredulity on both sides when he met his first defeat. Howard collapsed and covered his eyes, unable to contemplate the unbelievable humiliation. Antony, in defeat, 'valiant and dejected by turns', ranted and swaggered until he could regain his dignity.

'Oh, my fortunes have corrupted honest men' came out as wry, rather than anguished, and he spoke 'All is lost' with a broad smile on his face. The single combat challenge to Octavius was a wild, self-consciously absurd boast. The euphoria at the prospect of Cleopatra's birthday party was decidedly forced.

He sat cross-legged with hands folded for the fatal sword stroke that never came and committed his own hari-kari in a ritualistic, stylised way, although the death was shown as an ignoble mess. Antony's grim patience while Eros delayed and finally evaded killing him was even comic. He was embarrassed about his botched suicide. There was nothing heroic about the way he stumbled towards the monument in an unbelieving and painwracked daze. 'Now my spirit is going' he told Cleopatra at last with restrained irritation, and 'I am dying, Egypt' became a complaint against Cleopatra's continued appetite for his body.

Glenda Jackson's Cleopatra was not the skittish girl who could hop through the public street, nor the erratic pettish woman variously described as 'whore', 'strumpet', 'trull' and 'Egyptian dish'. A more accurate image to describe her character than 'storms and tempests' would have been plagues of locusts. She was self-aware, icily observant, sardonic to the point of contempt, and far more self-sufficiently ruthless than the Cleopatra suggested in the text. She had the snap of natural command and a sustained interest in power.

One mood was meticulously established before moving to the next: there was little that was mercurial or volatile. One moment, Cleopatra would be gesturing with her hands and arms in writhing slow-motion, like an Indian dancer (the analogy with the Sphinx became almost literal as there were hieratic arm and hand movements and formal poses), the next she would be kicking the messenger around the floor and pulling his hair out. Glenda Jackson did not find a natural bridge between such moments of the double-sidedness so central to the character, so it just seemed like an actress playing two kinds of woman – although the scene became very funny with much thunder and lightening and Cleopatra throwing a knife at the fleeing messenger.

The curt astringent delivery was most effective in monosyllabic lines like 'See where he is', or the reflective 'Then Antony, but now'. As Brook said, her performance emphasised the point that Shakespeare makes her speak in the most direct way. An edged disembodied voice delivered even the catalogue of her forthcoming humiliations as Caesar's captive in tones of amused indifference. But she made 'O my oblivion is a very Antony and I am all forgotten' deeply erotic and sensuous.

She came into her own in the last act, playing a superb final scene. Glazed into trance-like grief by the death of Antony, she was transformed from the moment she entered the monument and went on to relish her defeat of Caesar's triumph with light-hearted and malicious ridicule.

The tone, even in defeat, was humorous rather than solemn or heroic. At the beginning of the play their relationship was restrained – almost arrogant and formal. But they were both exhilarated by the news of Fulvia's death and by the prospect of battle. They seemed to have an increasing mutual dependence in the trauma of defeat. Separately shattered, they gradually patched each other up for another gaudy night. Towards the end the lovers tried to generate some mutual intensity by clutching and grabbing at each other as if finding a last refuge from the world that has failed them. There was much howling at each other's presumed suicides.

Patrick Stewart was an impeccably detailed, resilient and warmly sympathetic Enobarbus, having his master's cynicism but a heart to break as well. He was a mellow, genial voluptuary who died with a smile thinking of those gaudy nights with Antony. Their male bonding relationship was very strong. Antony's reaction to Fulvia's death, 'There's a great spirit gone', was spoken with hollow irony, one caustic eye being fixed on the audience. He threw away

> What our contempts doth often hurl from us
> We wish it ours again.

So 'She's good, being gone' became a piece of crude truth and

> Fulvia is dead
> Sir?
> Fulvia is dead.
> Fulvia?
> Dead

had the neat comic timing of a double act. Enobarbus greeting the news with an explosion of incredulous laughter and Antony was surprised into joining in, so they ended up in an outbreak of wild embracing which destroyed any wry implication that might have been found in Enobarbus's

Why, sir, give the gods a thankful sacrifice.

They were really glad to be shot of her.

The episode showed Enobarbus, not as the usual keeper of his general's conscience, but as his junior partner in dissipation. 'Now he'll outstare the lightning' was spoken in admiration even though followed by the realistic plan for desertion. This conflict eventually and graphically killed him.

Jonathan Pryce's Octavius was a slightly gawky, shy, smiling man, with no knife beneath the cloak; he was neither cynic nor ambitious plotter. At the beginning he was patently sincere, as if rather immature and vulnerable. His hero-worship of Antony was manifest, especially after the reconciliation. He was nervously thrilled to be able to marry him off to Octavia, his beloved sister, with whom he had a complicated, part-sexual relationship: he tended to fondle her whenever he had the opportunity. Constantly looking to his allies for reassurance at the peace conference, he seemed a serious almost priest-like figure, taking the cue from his later lines

> You shall see
> How hardly I was drawn into this war
> How calm and gentle I proceeded still
> In all my writings.

But when challenged he scampered on stage triumphantly yelling 'he calls me boy', and made the message into a paper kite. The gawkiness went as he gained authority and learned the political realities of life, developing into the icy calculating demi-god of the later scenes; but the *naïveté* remained in his overt and enthusiastic curiosity when he encountered Cleopatra. The play ended with him taking a prolonged backward look at her before his final departure.

His senators were similarly restrained and kindly seeming; but they were also shrewd. Their conversation with Enobarbus after the *rapprochement* was played as a skilled piece of diplomatic investigation about the real likelihood of a change in Antony. The Rome–Egypt contrast was made far subtler than in most readings, which made it hard to understand Antony's attraction to Egypt.

The attachment between Antony and Octavius became straightforward human love between the veteran and the younger man; after first parley, each side put his point with the slow vigilance of a chess player. The reconciliation was sealed with a delighted embrace. Pompey began with loudly self-confident blustering and then seized Antony's patronising hand of friendship with intense relief.

Pompey clearly gave way to his own generosity and died of it. David Suchet played him as a dark, impulsive, emotional Corsican, a man with an eye for the main chance destroyed by his own impressionable weakness. The Bacchanal on his galley was splendidly done, being first funny then orgiastic – as the drunk Lepidus was passed round like a ball – and finally sinister. It was a flight from intoxication into the wilder realms of imagination. The discussion on transmigration was played with great emphasis and comic brilliance. At the climax of the dance Enobarbus fell off a bench, pulling it on top of him and embracing it; it fed Octavius his line 'Enobarbus is weaker than the wine'.

Instead of taking the usual interval after this upbeat explosion of energy Brook went straight on to the Parthian war scene (which is usually cut). It erupted through the gaps in the screen. In the text Pacorus is already dead, but Brook had him butchered on stage.

The clown (Richard Griffiths) who brought the asp was a real comedian. He wore a red nose and slippers. There was even a hint of harlequin about his costume. He tentatively approached the glass-bound sanctuary and removed his slippers, which he then wore on his hands; he even conjured the asps out of the air rather than from the basket, which proved to be empty; and he delayed Cleopatra's grand departure from the world with a series of false exits leaving through one gap in the panels as she said 'farewell' only to show up at another to add a further hilarious afterthought – 'I wish you joy of the worm'. This farcical scene kept the play down to earth. It was a complete success, not only because it was so expertly played, but because of the effect it had on Cleopatra. She seemed to establish a relationship with him, paradoxically as she had not with anyone else, including Antony; she seemed genuinely interested in what he had to say. And far from imperilling the death scene, by playing up the humour it intensified it by contrast.

The production was not well received. Several critics thought it was a case of Coriolanus having an affair with Elizabeth I., these being recent successes of the respective actors. The RSC press office seems to have put out a misinformation campaign to combat any suggestions that it might have been the casting that was wrong with the production (to head off the press getting any whiff of the truth about the rehearsals: that only the principals had been fully engaged in the play; Brook had been amazed at the lackadaisical time-serving attitude of the rest of the company – he clearly had been away from the average English actor for too long). *The New Statesman* was fed with 'According to the RSC Deep Throat, Peter Brook was so delighted by the initial rehearsals with his five or six leading actors that he rang head office suggesting the remaining thirty or forty parts be cut'; and Brook gave interviews saying he had deliberately waited until Alan Howard was available, and that Glenda Jackson had been in his mind since she played Madame Ngu in *US*. The latter may be true, though he made no mention of the six months he spent reading the play with Jeanne Moreau before they both decided that, although bilingual, she could not play the part in English. But the hype about Howard made no comment on the first choice to play Antony, the American Stacy Keach, a powerhouse of an actor who might indeed have got sparks off the formidable Jackson.

Irving Wardle noted that although 'Brook's approach to Shakespeare has always given more from moment to moment than any other dramatist', this production stood in

austerely muted contrast to *Lear* and the *Dream*. The antiseptic setting is in ironic contrast to the form and content of the play. Brook points up all the things that do *not* conform to the myth of a world well lost. . . . Direct human affection of the Roman kind is the one thing he cannot get from Glenda Jackson's inexhaustibly various Cleopatra. They make a stupendous and utterly unmoving pair. Plainly victims of a *folie à deux*, the production shows in merciless detail the price they pay for it.

This reaction was characteristic of the reviews, most of whom criticised the starkness of the production, the coolness and objectivity of Glenda Jackson's performance or the purely intellectual response engendered. Bernard Levin complained, in *The Sunday Times*, that what was lacking amid the irony was 'the racing of the blood'.

Clearly the production was ahead of its time. Had it been eleven-and-a-half years later the portrait of the lady dictator would have wrung true: Antony might even have been seen as an errant Minister of Transport. But by then Glenda Jackson was to have political ambitions of her own, successfully using her Egyptian experience to command the good people of Hampstead to vote for her.

Brook responded, in *The Times*, to the criticisms of Glenda Jackson as being too prosaic.

I feel Glenda has been unjustly attacked. Cleopatra in the flesh has nothing to do with the Cleopatra Enobarbus describes. Shakespeare was not covering her in mystery. The reverse is the case. Because he makes her speak in the most direct way. She is even described as a gypsy, which today would be rather like calling her a wog. The death of Antony transforms Cleopatra. The shit drops off her and she becomes simpler and purer. She is almost like one of those dissolute fourteenth-century popes who has a ball until the very end of his term and then suddenly discovers religion on his death-bed. Finally she enters into the Egyptian tradition; her own death is not a tragedy but a transfiguration.

Antony has also been misconceived as a tired man. He isn't. His words explode with vitality. He takes on Cleopatra because she is a legend, a kind of Evita, but there is nothing about her at this point which suggests the mysticism or mantels of the East, whatever Enobarbus may say. And so Antony dies having lived well by his own lights but never having achieved a higher level of existence. That is left to Cleopatra.

Patrick Stewart, who played Enobarbus, gave an interview two days after the first night:

There's almost nothing that is 'worked out'. Pompey's galley *is* the one scene which was built up of pure improvisation. It is not Brook's way to take any scene and to place the actors and to ask them to move here and there, so that at rehearsal things would change constantly, every rehearsal, in a search to find the happiest solution to a particular problem. That scene was given no formal shape until a few days before we appeared in front of an audience. He knew that he wanted it to have initially, not a sort of boisterous rugby-club feeling, but something which was to do with liquor and food, which had not brought men into a beery, boisterous state, but rather to something which was elevated and very refined – where wits were sharpened. A little like – I suppose – being slightly stoned. This was the way we rehearsed it one time, and out of that, delicately, the Egyptian Bacchanal would begin to grow. And what happens there is entirely improvised – and indeed is every night; it never repeats itself.

The picking up of the singer was finally worked out, when he passes from one character to the other. But all the things that happen on the fringe, the moving around, the wildness, the tumbling on to the carpet, when the carpet goes up – all that is improvised.

GR writes:

It is interesting to note Stewart's assertion that the scene was improvised. On being questioned he admits that the main moves and business were fixed; the order of the lines was certainly fixed. But for an actor who was used to having everything fixed at an early stage in rehearsals, all the externals of blocking, the fact that it had come so much later, after weeks of improvising, had clearly left him with the feeling that he was playing the scene far more freely than he was used to; he was, in fact, playing a totally unchanging script.

It was a production of great intelligence: the overall shape of Acts III and IV became crystal clear, in itself a major feat of staging. The reading broke decisively with the received idea of the play and the voluptuous tradition of the past: that it was a tragic love affair of two doomed great-hearted principals ranged against a cold-blooded political adversary. Brook's rejection of visual elaboration may have diminished the play's military and imperial themes, but it focused on the generous acceptance of the humanity of every character in the play. Brook's use of almost all the text also jarred with the two-hour traffic of the stage he was currently making in Paris. Although it may be a great text, it comes from the Folio and certainly doesn't bear the imprint of how Shakespeare and Burbage would have adapted it for their stage. They certainly didn't play it all, and it's hard to see how a complete text would square with the idea of popular Elizabethan theatre.

It also bravely tried to allow the audience to make an imaginative response by closing down the space to confront us directly with the central relationships, the battles and the pomp belonging to the world elsewhere – beyond the glass dome. But such a presentation needs remarkable performances from everyone individually, as well as the ability to work together; the main stage at Stratford was not designed for a chamber piece. There are only four real characters in the story. For the rest they come and go, Shakespeare deliberately ringing the changes on the retinue so that the god-like figures at the centre will seem even larger than life. Here there was no doubting the quality of the individual work of the supporting actors, but few of them were integrated with anyone else. Finally, one had an impression of a whole so well drilled and ordered that the actors had no room to breathe. I suspect it was forced on Brook as a way of dealing with a company which was not a company and which could not bring the give-and-take of living impulses to their work.

The larger failure took place at the centre, on the carpet itself. One would have thought that after the brilliant Beckettian staging of Gloucester on the cliff, the shame following the first defeat at sea (III.xi), with both protagonists agonising separately side by side on the stage, would be shattering. But it was not. With a mis-cast Antony and a hyper-defensive Cleopatra who had little going on between them the scene appeared to be a demonstration of petulance. They had not opened themselves up to each other, so there was no underbelly to the agony, no vulnerability and life to the suffering.

Since Tynan said Edith Evans's Cleopatra was 'Lady Bracknell cruelly starved of cucumber sandwiches' the line of pretenders to the crown of Egypt had been consistently mauled by critics: Peggy Ashcroft had been seen as a 'ravenous famine victim'; Margaret Leighton was a 'neurotic society hostess zonked out on tranquillisers and Martinis'; Vanessa Redgrave a 'half-crazed flapper'; Janet Suzman a precursor of Christabel Pankhurst; Dorothy Tutin a pedigree cat; and Judy Dench the suburban housewife. To this list could be added Glenda Jackson's dictator. As an interpretation it could be justified in the text, but what proved fatal to the performance was the complete absence of the wantonness that is at the heart of Cleopatra, and which distinguishes her from the upright Octavia, as well as the absence of the passion that forms an umbilical cord with Antony throughout the play, which is taken for granted and cannot be broken. Taken for granted because in such a many-scened play the two characters have so few together (and are hardly ever alone), and in those few they are usually quarrelling. Shakespeare has turned the commonplace perception of two of the world's great lovers on its head. But if something strong and unbreakable, some almost indefinable chemistry, is not present, then all too easily the play degenerates to the level of *Who's Afraid of Virginia Woolf?*, and the audience spend the evening doubting the veracity of the story, by asking constantly, 'Why?' For the play to truly work there must be some sense of the kingdoms that have been kissed away, both internal as well as external, otherwise there is no tragedy. *King Lear* had been scalding hot as a performance. *Antony and Cleopatra* was barely lukewarm. It was to be to the last original production Brook would stage in England.

16 No samovars in Paris and New York: *La Cérisaie* and *The Cherry Orchard*

Brook:

It must be approached as a theatrical movement purely played. A false Chekhovian manner that is not in the text, and sentimentality, must be avoided. . . . *The Cherry Orchard* is not gloomy, romantic, long and slow but a comic play about real life.

The reason *The Cherry Orchard* touches people in extraordinary ways is because, as in any great work, behind it is a myth. This is a poem about life and death and transition and change. Chekhov was writing about it when he was dying. Knowing that he had a short time left, he felt a theme emerging: something loved has to be relinquished, disappointment has to be accepted. And he wrote it in a language that he forged for himself; it was not the language of Shakespeare or of Pushkin.

Brook assembled an entirely new company, with the exception of his wife, Natasha Parry, who played Lyubov (Madame Ranevskaya). He said:

The very basis of the international company is that anyone can play anything. Blacks play whites and young play old. But there are degrees of obligation, correspondence and physique in Chekhov. Every actor has a different background, but they have several things in common: a degree of aptness physically and a level of competence with Chekhov. They are experienced professionals who have not lost their innocence, their knowledge of what first brought them into the theatre. But I could not advertise: open call for innocent actors.

He had some trouble, certain actors turning down the offer because they thought the part was too small, although he persuaded Michel Piccoli to play Gaev. Brook gave his own version of Stanislavsky's 'There are no small parts only . . .':

The audience has no way of telling who has the biggest part. It's like a family on Christmas day. After the day is over, one can ask, who spoke most and who spoke least?

After the great Jean Dasté declined Firs, Brook found an old comic actor, Robert Murzeau, who was in retirement; he said he had been waiting for nearly sixty years to do Chekhov and gratefully accepted. (Dasté, having run his own company for thirty years, had had plenty of experience with the classics.)

Nothing was cut from the Russian text: Carrière translated it together with Brook's Russian-born mother-in-law. As in the versions of Shakespeare, they aimed for directness and simplicity. Brook was consciously trying to avoid any poetic charm, reflective sentimentality or aristocratic langour that characterised Western productions: there would be no dying falls, no glowing sunsets.

16   *La Cérisaie*, Joseph Blatchley, Anne Consigny, Natasha Parry, Natalie Nell, Bouffes
du Nord, 1981

The production was rehearsed for ten weeks. On the first day there was a
lavish Russian dinner.

It was played without an interval; it lasted two hours and a quarter. Against
the peeling walls, shabby proscenium and undecorated balconies of the
Bouffes were set some splendid Persian carpets on which the action took place.
The costumes were true to the period, being designed by Chloé Obolensky –
who had written a book about Russia at the turn of the century – so the refine-
ment of the dresses, the parasoles etc., reflected the reality of the time of the
play, without being slavish re-creations. There was a minimum of furniture.
Until the third act there were no chairs or sofas for anyone to sit on except for
the odd hump contrived in a carpet. Then came a high-backed chair (wooden
in Paris, upholstered in New York). In the second act a carpet was rolled up to
suggest a fallen tree for the governess to balance on. The carpets were rolled up
again just before the family is forced to leave the estate at the end of Act IV.
Dust-sheets were placed over the minimal furniture. The elegant decay was

simply suggested by an old bookcase. Screens were used in the third act to mask the up-stage party, so one only had the occasional glimpse of the dancers rotating in the far distance, as the violinist in the little Jewish band played a high, sentimental melody. The most breathtaking moment came at the climax of the scene as Lopakhin staggered into the screens and knocked them down (in the text he knocks into a small table): the dance suddenly stopped and a very private scene had become embarrassingly public.

One critic thought the running time had come down simply by removing

what many might regard as one of the key elements of any Chekhov play – the samovar: how many minutes are spent in preparing and sipping tea or eating herring and drinking vodka. The menu here is a bottle of champagne, a cup of coffee and a single cucumber; in doing so he must have saved at least a half-hour of running time.

The performance was light and fast, strongly characterised and very funny, with mercurial changes of mood. The narrative line was very clear, the tone often trivial and frivolous. Yet there was a constant undercurrent of a sense of loss, of frustrated hopes, that could be plugged into at any time. No one was allowed any emotional indulgence, there were many moments of self-pity but no wallowing. Notes were struck, and then we passed on. Yet that performance had great warmth and depth of feeling. All the characters were trapped in private dreams which they revealed as direct confidences to the audience.

Characters rushed on and off the carpet exuberantly, pursued each other round the screens in the third act, rolled about on the floor and lolled as at a picnic and very often just squatted down, with legs crossed. Entrances and exits were made through the audience, and both the circles were used. People called goodnight from the gaping holes in the proscenium arch and galoshes were flung down from the top circle.

Maurice Bénichou, Brook's co-director, gave an example of the rhythmic structure they consciously worked for:

Take the arrival at the house. Everyone is happy, congratulating themselves, talking, joking, laughing. Then the tutor of the dead child appears. A leaden silence embraces all: suddenly emotion and tears replace the carefree frivolity of a few moments before. Then all of a sudden Ranevskaya looks at Trofimov, and asks him why he has become so old and ugly. It's over, the pain is dissipated. It's ridiculous for her to continue crying in front of everyone else, so Chekhov finds her an escape route. They move on to other things. A trace lingers in her heart, and in the spectator's imagination: we now know she retains a deep scar inside her. And we have learnt this much as if by chance: nothing is prepared – which is what gives theatre that illusion of the unpredictability and movement that dominates reality.

These shifts became the very texture of the production.

When Lopakhin, a little drunk and very excited, both sorry and triumphant, returned towards the end of the third act to announce that he has bought the orchard, Lyubov reacted to his news by clutching herself as if in physical pain, bending in an odd curve to one side and, as in the stage direction, catching the furniture to keep from falling. Firs and Gaev stood back to back listening. Lopakhin's half-jig of victory, celebrating his purchase, was slowly tempered by the realisation that he has forfeited any chance of affection from the aristocratic woman he has bought out. He ended up throwing himself prostrate on the floor behind her chair at Lyubov's feet, tugging ineffectually at her hem. You caught for a moment the emotion he felt for Lyubov – the memory of the young girl who bathed the bleeding nose of the 'little peasant' – and the despair at not being able to save the estate for her.

There was very little business that was not specifically mentioned in the script. Charlotta performed an elaborate trick with ribbons in Act I and in the second act the inept Yepikhodov fired a gun.

The acting was uniformly impressive. Although the characters were passing each other by, there was little doubt that the actors were responding to each other. There was a delicacy, a quality of filigree work about many of the exchanges. Natasha Parry, in a series of beautiful dresses – smart black and white lace and sequin – caught the emotional vulnerability of woman to perfection, giving orders without being quite able to command. The character was played neither for charm nor as a star part. She had a marvellous ability to convey pain in a very moving way, as when sitting in the chair quietly crying as Lopakhin tells how he has bought the estate. Returning from Paris, she swept into the nursery of her bankrupt estate, her dark eyes brimming with tears as she looked out nostalgically at the orchard (a single sweeping glance of the auditorium). The memory of her son's drowning years before was deeply touching, yet it was immediately dispelled by the brash strains of the distant band, and she rapidly recovered her equilibrium. She was kittenish, seductive and disillusioned, but not drained of faith – and as much out of touch with reality as her brother.

Piccoli's Gaev was as child-like as his sister and equally emotional, brimming with avuncular charm and his abiding love for billiards. Not played as an old fossil, but a well-intentioned man who is powerless to alter the course of his life. His long-winded ode to the century-old bookcase was a high point of absurd comedy. The hilarity of his futility was matched by the poignance of his entrance after the sale of the orchard like an old-age pensioner shambling back from the market with his dinner. He stood, sad and exhausted, dangling a bundle of anchovy and herring tins, trying to find the courage to announce the estate's sale to his sister well before Lopakhin arrived. The relationship between brother and sister was noticeably close.

Arestrup's solid, kindly but baffled Lopakhin, sweatily trying to persuade these dreamers that their style of life is done for and that they must at least try to be serious, made sense of a problematic character. Here was a picture of a man of considerable, if misguided, sensitivity, although gruff and unpolished. Brook obviously believed that when Trofimov says Lopakhin has the hands of an artist the remark is not meant ironically (he also describes him as a 'beast of prey' and 'a fine sensitive soul'). He was in his own way just as dreamy as Lyubov whom he constantly upbraided for her impracticality. She ignored the impending auction of her home because any available means to 'save it' would change and therefore destroy it. But when Lopakhin could not recruit her to his scheme he plunged ahead, basing his gamble less on business acumen than on an incoherent belief in the benefits of universal home ownership. This portrayal also made their implausible relationship both credible and moving.

Trofimov was seen as a rounded character, a sometimes foolish but basically idealistic young man whose opinions changed wildly. When upbrading Lyubov or Lopakhin he looked immature, but his vision of a happier future, at the end of Act II, was thrilling; while proclaiming it he prompted the moon to rise – 'I can feel my happiness coming – I can see it'.

While Firs was an impish, bearded figure in formal black stooping over a cane and seemingly rooted to the soil, Charlotta Yepikhodov and a gouty Pishchik were all broadly conceived roles, sometimes clown-like to the point of farce.

The production was greatly praised, although certain critics, as usual, had trouble in liberating their imaginations. They found it impossible not to regard the playing space at the Bouffes as a set which related to the play rather than simply an empty space in which they would collaborate in a performance. Eric Shorter, in *Drama*, thought it

not altogether an artistic triumph since Chekhov did not come out of the association altogether unscathed. But it was a triumph of tone over tradition, of emotional excitement over a ruminative text, of inventive staging over limited resources, and of theatrical exhilaration over textual melancholy.

BROOKLYN

While *The Mahabharata* was playing at the Majestic, Brook rehearsed *The Cherry Orchard* in English with a new cast. Only Natasha Parry repeated her role from *La Cérisaie* in Paris seven years before.

The Majestic was a large theatre in Brooklyn. Built in 1904 it had been a vaudeville house before becoming a cinema. It had closed in 1968. It had been restored for *The Mahabharata* at a cost of 5,000,000 dollars. The first thirteen rows of the orchestra were ripped out and the stage raised six-and-a-half feet to meet the front row of the new stalls: the stage was now sixty-two-feet deep. The boxes were chopped off leaving arched alcoves for entrances and exists.

Scenic artists painted the alcoves to resemble decaying archways. The front five rows of the balcony were eliminated, which helped the sight lines, although the new seats were stools with backs and the rows became progressively higher as they went back. The theatre used to seat 1800; now it held 900.

Where the original plaster on the walls resisted removal it was left alone, so creating layers that looked as if they were growing over one another, like scales. Paint still crumbled from the walls, fragments of friezes were chipped and mottled. Ducts were exposed. Decades of dirt around the proscenium arch was left. Nothing in the restoration was made too nice. It looked like a theatre in decay.

For *The Cherry Orchard* a large and beautiful Persian carpet was placed in the middle of the stage. Another was hung on the back wall.

Most of the American critics liked it. Frank Rich, in *The New York Times*, thought

> On this director's magic carpet *The Cherry Orchard* flies . . . (it) pauses for breath only when life does, for people to recoup after dying a little. . . . Mr Brook has give us the Chekhov production that every theatergoer fantasises about but in my experience almost never finds.

Time said it was a 'splendid insightful version' and *The Nation* mentioned that 'Brook's production clears the dust off the play'. But not all the notices were good. Edith Oliver, in *The New Yorker* said it was 'scattered and shallow . . . a major disappointment', and Weales, in the *Commonweal*, thought the production formless and short of illumination.

> The performers rattled around the immense playing area, unanchored in place or time. I had no sense of a 'group' at the Majestic – not even a disintegrating group.

Robert Brustein, in *The New Republic*, was as acerbic as ever:

> Brook's Chekhov must have suffered a sea change during its ocean voyage: I found it a singularly colorless ordeal. No doubt my response is influenced by having had to sit for two-and-a-half intermission-less hours in those padded benches with which the Majestic (otherwise a marvelous theater) has been uncomfortably equipped. Perhaps the puritanical Brook wants his affluent BAM audiences to share the same hardship as his audiences in Iran and Africa. Still, his production scheme for *The Cherry Orchard* is equally spartan. We may sit on benches, but the cast usually sits on the floor, like Turkish beys at supper, protected from lumbago only by the warp and woof of a Persian carpet.
>
> Brook is a daring director with a high intelligence. What accounts for the flatness of this interpretation? Well by having us concentrate on language and action he also makes us concentrate on acting, and the acting is plagued by serious casting errors – not to mention the director's inability to coax consistently textured work from a majority of his company. The absence of a company is a root problem. The actors fail to create a unified world. . . . I'm afraid the most disappointing thing to be said about this production is that it provokes no argument. . . . It's neutral and that's why we end up feeling neutral about the play and the characters.

GR writes:

I sympathise with Brustein's disappointment. Sitting in the balcony at the Majestic was a strange experience. One felt that what one was seeing both 'is and is not' Brook's *Cherry Orchard*. 'Is' in the sense that one was looking at a production which looked almost exactly the same as that in Paris, with the same shape and rhythm to it, the same grouping, the same timbre. 'Is not' in the sense that it had almost none of the quality of the ebb and flow of life, the light and shade of emotion, the joy of watching actors work together that had made *La Cérisaie* so memorable. What one saw was a marvellously organised piece of theatre which in Paris had revealed a complex structure of relationships, in which feelings and emotions collided. In Brooklyn, the actors were unable to communicate with each other, so the truths they imparted to the audience were very partial ones.

As many critics pointed out the space was vast, far too vast for this kind of production. What had been an intimate, yet animated, affair, played almost in the round in Paris, became a noisy set of isolated turns in Brooklyn. Natasha Parry's delicate qualities did not project far enough. Even Josephson, perfect casting for Gaev, with a pale face across which emotion flitted like a shadow, and an actor with a long history of playing in large national theatres, seemed to be diminished by his surroundings. If the famous daughters, of Arthur Miller and Norman Mailer, had the right qualities for their parts they certainly had not the technique to act them. One longed for Stephanie Roth, far too sleek for Varya, to play either of the other parts. Under the circumstances I was very grateful for Brian Dennehy's strong Lopakhin, a man whose frustration and bewilderment reached me in the circle. As did Linda Hunt's evil puppeteer of a Charlotte. The Yugoslav Trofimov also came through loudly, but by no means clearly.

In Paris there had been a Scandinavian Lopakhin as well as two English actors – Lyubov and Trofimov – but you would not have known it from listening to the text. It may not have been a naturalistic representation, but what happened on the carpet had a unity, of sound as well as of performing style. In New York everyone seemed to be acting in a different style: noisy American jostled with refined Europeans, here the English classical actor, there someone from the Actors Studio, first a soap cameo, then a vaudeville turn. In Paris the disparate, and sharply defined, parts seemed part of the whole; now they grated and looked competitive. The loudest usually won; although Gaev and Ranevskaya had some fine moments, they were unable to sustain the emotional line in a predominantly circus atmosphere created by the other actors. Harshness and cruelty, subtly interwoven into the structure in Paris, were now the dominant notes.

An in-the-round production had moved to a proscenium arch, a situation which implied a visual picture which it could not deliver; and so the English lady, the Swedish gentleman and the Yugoslav student inhabited the same space as a mixture of Americans. In such a play the sound of the voice is an essential part of the character, as much as the clothes and the walk. Brook seemed to have thrown overboard the reasoning which had resulted in the new company being formed in Paris. Was this a return to internationalism? In that case where were the black actors?

17 Destined to die free: *La Tragédie de Carmen*

For two years at the end of the forties, Brook was a director of productions at the Royal Opera House, Covent Garden; he did five productions before being fired in the scandal over *Salome*. Lord Harwood benignly summed it up:

The consensus of opinion was that this was not only an ill-conceived approach to *Salome*, but that it was the climax of a series of more or less unmusical productions. What would be sad would be if the objects of these attacks were to look on them as modern equivalents of the scandals which attended the premières of *Pelléas* or the Stravinsky ballet scores: this production was no avant-garde affair, but thoroughly retrograde in its 'twenty-ish' search for something new and startling. Anyone who saw *The Dark of the Moon* will know that Peter Brook's early promise has not gone unfulfilled and that his talents are very considerable; but his next production will have to break all records by its strict adherence to the implications of the music if he is to begin the long process of breaking down the prejudice against him and his works which he has so effectively built up at Covent Garden.

There was no next production at Covent Garden. Brook had done an over-lavish *Boris Godunov* (as Charles Stuart said in *The Observer*: 'Boris has been got up regardless. Nothing is left undone'); a moving *La Bohème* (although *The Times* commented that 'Excitement is not an unmixed boon to an opera'); an inelegant *Marriage of Figaro* (Desmond Shaw Taylor in *The New Statesman* said it veered from 'undistinguished to downright illiterate'); a feeble *Olympians* (Eric Blom in *The Observer* called the production a 'hotch-potch of good details and sadly ineffectual patches'); and then he came to *Salome*, with designs by Salvador Dali, which was called 'deplorable', 'idiotic', 'exasperating', 'hideous'. Desmond Shaw Taylor launched into it:

the minor characters were turned into a set of Alice-in-Wonderland playing cards, and Herodias bobbed in and out of a headdress which might have been invented in an off moment by the White Knight. Four miniature umbrella frames rose and fell over Herod's pavilion until the electricians were tired of working the switches. Like most of the 'special effects' this proved an ideal distraction from the music. The switchboard is rarely left alone for five minutes altogether. The sun rises, night falls, the moon appears and disappears (sometimes several moons at the same time) and within one short scene and in no natural sort of order. As for spotlights they could not behave more vulgarly and intrusively in a music hall than they do nowadays at Covent Garden. Deplorable lapses again and again reveal a slighting attitude towards music. The boos that greeted Peter Brook at the end . . . were an indication that the public has by now had enough of the 'Crazy-Gang' technique of opera production of which Mr Brook is the leading English exponent.

A large part of Brook's reputation as an *enfant terrible* came from what happened at Covent Garden: his theatre productions might be controversial, but

17   *La Tragédie de Carmen*, Helene Delavault, Howard Hensel, Peter Brook, Bouffes du
Nord, 1982

they were never booed; not even *Scobie Prilt* was booed. It is not surprising that
after a couple of shows at the Metropolitan in New York in the fifties, under-
taken, one suspects, to consolidate his American reputation, he left the form
well alone until he was able to return to it on his own terms. This he did triumphantly with his production of *Carmen* in Paris.

In 1978, Bernard Lefort, who had been selected as future Administrator
General of the Opéra in Paris, went to see Peter Brook. Brook thought that
Lefort was going to invite him to direct an opera already chosen by Lefort for
production in the Palais Garnier. To Brook's surprise, Lefort wanted to talk to
him about a possible production in Brook's own theatre, the Bouffes du Nord.
Lefort's suggestion was either Jañécek's *The House of the Dead* or Britten's *The
Turn of the Screw.*

Brook asked for time to think. Lefort himself was surprised when Brook
came back to him with the suggestion of staging *Carmen.* Lefort had already

planned a 'popular' *Carmen* at the Palais des Sports, but had not decided who was going to produce it. He unhesitatingly accepted Brook's suggestion because, as he put it, the two projects did not seem in any way incompatible with each other. Brook brought in Jean-Claude Carrière as writer. Lefort gave the musical direction to Marius Constant.

Brook was delighted by Lefort's approach to him. He tells us that when he and Michelle Rozan had gone into the Bouffes for the first time seven years earlier, they had said to each other, 'These walls must sing'. Since then, Brook had used music in his productions when it seemed right to do so. He had often thought of following the use of music to its logical conclusion and staging a work entirely in song.

There were clearly constraints. There was no possibility of having a huge orchestra, a vast crowd of singers. It would be necessary to search for a way of using the surroundings. Lefort's suggestion made such a project possible.

Brook wrote in his introduction to the published text:

> The production of *Carmen* in the Bouffes took place in the continuity of our work, because it involved an attempt to bring a musical work to life in radically different conditions. The difference sprang above all from a relationship of a different kind between the singers and the audience. The physical arrangements themselves in the classical music theatre – the stage, the pit, the huge orchestra, the size of the theatre – lead to a certain kind of relationship, which is well known. What we are trying to create at the Bouffes depends on the concentration, the truth and the intimacy of direct theatre.

Transforming Bizet's huge melodramatic musical spectacular into a form of chamber opera was clearly the kind of challenge that the Brook of the late seventies relished.

Bizet's *Carmen* was adapted from a short novel written by Prosper Mérimée in 1847. In the annals of French literary history, Mérimée is seen to have had two particular qualities. He is defined as a concise writer – the French literary historian, Emile Faguet, says that, written by the kind of nineteenth-century novelist who goes about his work accumulating details and exploring all the possibilities in a situation, the material in *Carmen* could have provided five volumes. Mérimée, says Faguet, concentrates on the central element in a situation – presumably what Brecht was to call 'the gestus'.

He is also defined as 'unreservedly pessimistic'. But his pessimism, says Faguet, is without anger – to show anger would be to lose your deportment. 'A discreet and quiet bitterness', is how Faguet describes Mérimée's characteristic 'gestus'. So he writes short works 'in which the inattentive might see only "histoires piquantes"', but which in fact offer 'an elixir of pessimism and misanthropy: wild, sensual and stupid men, fantastic, cruel, lying and treacherous women'. Misfortune is always present – 'all these adventures end in an atrocious way. Murder upon murder in *Carmen*. . . .'

Mérimée set his *Carmen* in 1832, a period when, Carrière points out, Spain was still, in the eyes of Europe, a savage country. Goya had only died four years earlier. The French remembered the atrocities of a guerilla war – which was when the term 'guerilla' was invented. The bandits of the Sierra Morena were a reality.

But in 1852, five years after Mérimée had written his novel, twenty-three years before Bizet was to compose his opera, Napoleon III had married into a great Spanish family. Spain was transformed from the country of the monstrosities of Goya to the country of dancers who stamped their feet in café concerts. Bizet's *Carmen* belongs to this later Spain, the Spain of boleros and castanets. Everybody agrees about this, says Carrière. The problems arise if you go back to the Mérimée original, which

… without saying a word about a folklore which didn't yet exist, tells a precise story, which claims to be close to reality . . . and which touches us today with a certain dryness, a coldness, minutely detailed, far from romanticism.

Carrière examined what Bizet had done to make Mérimée acceptable to the opera-going public of the 1870s. He could not present in a legitimate theatre the 'thief–prostitute–witch' of the original, but he did succeed in putting on stage a character who seemed scandalous to the 1875 spectators. And he created a new character, Micaela, who represented the village past of Don José, his roots, his love for his mother. He turned a simple picador, Escamillo, into a heroic matador, 'the incarnation of all the men Carmen might have known'. And he weakened the character of Don José himself. In the Mérimée, Don José had been a real bandit. He had seriously wounded a man in his Basque village, which was why he had become a soldier. Later, he had met Carmen's husband, provoked him to a duel and killed him – an episode which had been left out of the opera.

On the other hand, says Carrière, if Carmen had inevitably lost in Bizet most of her young sensuality and lack of scruples, she owes to the opera her dimension of great tragic heroine. Bizet created the classic contradictions of Carmen – that on the one hand, she submits herself to what she accepts as her 'implacable' destiny, and on the other hand, she declares herself free, will wildly affirm her freedom, even if it costs her her life.

In his adaptation, Carrière uses the parts of the Bizet score that he can accommodate in a version that tries to recapture some of the dryness and sharpness of the Mérimée. But he hangs on to Micaela and to the image of the matador.

In the Bouffes, Brook used fifteen musicians to represent an entire symphony orchestra – each instrument took on the role of a section of the orchestra. (But at one point he brought in the sound of a full orchestra on tape. His reasoning was cheerfully practical: the audience needed a lift at that point.)

The musicians were divided into two groups, with one group at each side of the playing area, partly visible to the audience. Brook objected to the fact that, in operas as they are conventionally produced, the singers have to face front and bellow across the musicians. Brook wanted his performers to play as actors, who happened to be singing as well as speaking. He used only six actors in a performance, but he rehearsed three casts, so that during a long run the performers would be able to stay rested and relaxed.

Brook and Carrière removed the scenic extravagances of Bizet – the spectacular crowd scene outside the cigarette factory, with which Bizet opened, the dancing with the smugglers in the mountains, the fiesta surrounding the bullfight. In this *Carmen*, Escamillo shows us the bullfight in a solo rehearsal. The opera is staged, as the American academic Jim Carmody noted, in a landscape of clay that

provides an almost naturalistic milieu in which actors perform an old story shorn of its nineteenth-century romantic fatalism. . . . The clay floor creates a space in which the characters regain their origin and achieve a new kind of theatrical authenticity, cut free from a tradition of stage-gypsies and stage-peasants that has been inseparable from the opera's history on stage. . . .

The walls of the theatre, the rough wooden audience benches, and the earthen floor of the aisles all echo the texture of the stage floor. It is first of all at the architectural level that we begin to become aware of the decor for *Carmen* taking on a symbolic dimension. . . .

Turning away from the kind of spectacle we normally expect to find in opera houses, Brook takes his characters out from behind the proscenium and away from any location whose reality depends on the laws of perspective and the designer's ability to copy or create self-sufficient worlds. At the Bouffes du Nord, the actor alone suggests the spatial realities that surround him. In *Carmen*, changes from an exterior to an interior space are effected by throwing down an old Persian carpet or piling some beaten grey cushions together; at times a change in the intensity of the lighting adds to our sense of a shift from one kind of space to another. . . .

Throughout the production, the actors take extended walks across the landscape, following a circular or oval path around the perimeter of the stage area. Usually, the walk represents a journey from one place to the next with the music giving an emotional colouring to the circumstances of the walk. (The image of walking . . . reminds us of the constant travelling that is an important aspect of Mérimée's story: his characters are essentially nomadic. Indeed, nomadism is a defining trait of the gitanes. The scenic and dramaturgic conventions of Bizet's period were unable to represent the element of travelling in Mérimée, so the exoticism of travel had to be transposed to its static pictorial equivalent.) . . .

Brook keeps the number of props to a functional minimum, never using them as set dressing. In the tavern scene, the actors actually drink the wine and eat the fruit; Escamillo cuts a fruit in half with his knife and holds it over Carmen's mouth, letting the juice drip slowly down her throat. Moments later, Carmen smashes a small plate against the proscenium arch and uses the shards to improvise castanets, at the same time providing a musical accompaniment to her dance. . . . The emphasis is on the texture of these objects, on their brittle, expendable reality. Used, marked, and broken by the characters, the plate fragments and the squeezed dry fruit cannot be returned to the prop table to be used again in the following performance . . .

Brook . . . omits the traditional representation of a tavern filled with customers in order to evoke an interior space differentiated only by the activities performed there. Instead of watching a picturesque crowd scene, we are invited to share Don José's perception of an episode in which Carmen herself is the only source of entertainment. No longer part of the scenic reality of the tavern, her dance is for Don José alone; the scene becomes more erotic by becoming more private. Because the tavern is not physically represented, we transpose the scene to a more intimate setting in our imaginations, a setting readily supported by the carpet and the cushions that initially suggested the tavern. . . .

Most of the props function simultaneously on both a real and symbolic level. The rope provides a simple example. Early in the opera, Carmen is bound in order to be escorted to prison by Don José. On the way to prison, however, Don José becomes Carmen's 'prisoner'. She transforms the rope into a kind of fishing line and reels him closer to her while both actors 'play' the change in the rope's function. This much larger rope also reminds us of the small piece of rope that Carmen placed in a circle on the ground at the beginning of the opera, in which she arranged her cards, bones, shells and other fortune-telling equipment. The ropes are thus part of a group of images that suggest Carmen and Don José's mutual enslavement as well as the patterns of fate that encircle them.

While Don José and Carmen sleep, an old bent figure shuffles on stage to light three fires. As with the carpet, the fires have a multiple function. They provide a fairly realistic campfire lighting for the scene (the stage lighting is barely used in this section of the play) and they function as what seems to be a magical sign that the old woman inscribes around the sleeping lovers. After she has finished lighting the fires, she sprinkles a circle of orange-red dust taken from a small leather bag very like the old one Carmen kept her cards in at the beginning of the opera. The triangle of fires intersects the circle of dust to complete the magical emblem as we associate this circle of dust with the circle of rope we have already seen. The magical functions of the rope, fires and dust, together with the circular blocking patterns, create a hieratic image of the fate that encircles the two lovers. The quantities of chemicals and wood used to light three fires were carefully measured to burn only as long as the scene lasted. As the stage was rearranged for the following scene, the remnants of the fires and the circle of orange-red dust were covered with clay along with all the footprints and other traces left by the scene.

Although the gestures and movements of the actors are grounded in realistic characterisation, the blocking patterns strongly suggest the ritual and the hieratic. . . . Circular patterns of movement are introduced and variations of them are composed in an almost musical manner. The quick pirouettes of Escamillo, the languid curling gestures of Carmen, and the long circular journeys around the stage amplify the circles of rope and dust without departing from the realities of character and event. . . .

The integrity and honesty of the actors also serves to authenticate the world of the opera. There is a paradox here that Peter Brook has very ably crafted. The actors wear no make-up or period hairstyles and the costumes seem roughly correct as far as period is concerned, but they are obviously costumes and look as if they were dug out of storage rather than specially designed for this production. In short, the presence of the actor is not at all dissimulated despite the realistic physicalisation and characterisation. Partly because the actor is so clearly one of us, the exoticism of Carmen's work becomes so authentic and enigmatic.

Brook's work on *Carmen* extends beyond a simple adaptation. He has not brought the opera up to date, nor has he written an original opera using Bizet's familiar work as a point of departure. Although he has greatly reduced the running time (to eighty minutes), this *Carmen* is not just a digest of the original: the tragic scheme of Bizet's original is left intact and highlighted. The power of Brook's adaptation stems from the transposition of the original material into a different aesthetic that draws its nourishment from the mainstream of twentieth-century performance.

Brook's *Carmen* clearly made a strong impression on Carmody, and the account he gives of the performance at the Bouffes is very vivid. What is missing, though, is any precise description of how Brook made the Bizet music work.

The style is simply and directly established in the opening scene. On the stage is a heap of rags. As Don José walks past, a hand emerges from the rags and gives him a playing card. He takes the card, looks at it, gives it back and leaves. Enter a young peasant girl, Micaela. The hand, which apparently belongs to an old beggar woman, seizes hers and holds it. Micaela sings: 'Moi, je cherche un brigadier. Ce brigadier ami s'appelle Don José. Le connaissez-vous? Répondez-moi, je vous prie. Alors, il n'est pas la?' Don José re-enters. Micaela recognises him, takes her hand away from the beggar woman's and sings, 'José!'

Micaela has brought Don José a letter, a little money, and a kiss from his mother. But from the heap of rags the beggar woman throws Don José a rose. He looks at the rose and sings, 'Qui sait de quels démons je vais être proie?' The reply comes in the familiar Bizet refrain, 'L'amour, l'amour . . .'. A figure emerges from under the rags. What we thought was a beggar woman turns out to be Carmen.

Brook, Carrière, Constant and the performers have created a miracle of freshness out of the hackneyed tunes. In this *Carmen*, the performers will sing the well-known songs. But the words of the songs will sound like dialogue. The actors will talk to each other in song. What is more, they will talk to each other in song while performing physical actions.

In the tavern scene, Carmen is about to dance for Don José when the bugles sound the retreat. She sings in reply, mocking the bugles:

> Bravo! J'avais beau faire. . . . Il est mélancolique
> De danser sans orchestre. Et vive la musique
> Qui nous tombe du ciel!
> La, la, la, la, la, la. . . .

Angrily, she throws him his equipment and taunts him:

Taratata mon Dieu . . . c'est la retraite. . . .

He throws back his equipment. But at this moment, his officer enters. Don José strangles him. Escamillo knocks, announcing himself. Don José and Carmen disguise the corpse as a drunk client. As Escamillo sings of the bravery of soldiers and bullfighters, Lillas Pasta, the tavern-keeper, signals to Don José that they should take advantage of the song to get rid of the body, which they do, leaving Escamillo to sing the Toreador song to Carmen.

Brook's handling of the music is at its best in these earlier scenes – light, witty, ironic, matching the action. It is only later, when the music has to carry more weighty emotions, that the 'naturalness' of the style encounters problems.

Carmody does not seem to notice now many changes Brook and Carrière made in Bizet's plot. There are several more deaths in Brook's version than in Bizet's. In Bizet, Don José does not kill his officer and Carmen's husband. Above all, in the Bizet, the Matador emerges from the arena in triumph as Don José stabs Carmen in the back. In Brook's version, fate deals the losing hand to the Matador as well – and Carmen knowingly accepts her fate: 'C'est ici', she sings to Don José. They kneel side by side and Don José kills her.

Brook's production provoked extravagantly varied reactions, mostly positive from theatre critics and negative from music critics. Jan Kott thought it was 'Perfect. No one has ever shown a romantic Carmen who is tragic. Except for Brook.' Michael Billington, in *The Guardian*, said it was 'powerful' and wrote of its 'mastery of mood':

Brook has not superseded Bizet's opera: what he has done in a production of luminous simplicity, is to disinter the doom-laden story concealed inside it. . . . In this production you get the chilling feeling that you have, for once, seen the sinews of tragedy beneath the flesh of Bizet's masterpiece.

This opinion was not shared by his colleague, Gerald Larner, *The Guardian*'s music critic, who said it had been done 'at immense cost to Bizet's *Carmen*', and called it a 'hideous distortion'. The use of recorded orchestral music made it even worse

partly because it admits theoretical defeat, and partly because it involves the piano in an out of tune and out of time embarrassment when the live instruments take over again. This has to be said because the very brilliance of this performance of a new *Carmen* could create a dangerous demand for more now that it can be seen in this country.

AH writes:

Larner makes it sound as if Brook – whose rough edges, another critic said, had been 'smoothed out in middle age' – was still threatening the 'riparian' delights of insular old England. If he could get away with such brilliance, what on earth might happen next to opera in Britain?

I didn't see Brook's *Carmen* in the theatre, only in a filmed version on the small screen. I found much of what I saw a delight. Brook had actually made dialogue in song entertaining! I liked Carmen's sung trickery when she seduced Don José into setting her free, and her mocking parody of the bugles sounding the retreat. I liked the suddenness of some of the deaths (which reminded me of the films of Carrière's former collaborator, Buñuel), and the macabre comedy of carrying out a dead body during an aria. I liked the joke with the Bizet overture, which reminded me of the gag Brook pulled in *The Dream* with the Mendelssohn *Wedding March*. I liked the simple use of props – the way, for example, Carmen uses the rope Don José is leading her with to pull him back as if he's a hooked fish. I particularly liked the way Escamillo, in the tavern scene, cuts an orange in half and squeezes the juice into Carmen's mouth. (What was the significance of the oranges? a serious German professor asked Brook. Were they related to the cannon balls that were rolled in *Ubu*? Brook replied that the play was set in Seville so naturally there would be oranges.)

The fact that Brook messed Bizet about didn't worry me at all. When he distorted Dürrenmatt and Arden, I'd complained, because it seemed to me that those authors had been trying to use particular forms of theatre to make precise political statements, and that Brook had muddied what they were trying to say. I didn't think Bizet had been trying to use opera to make a statement, political or otherwise.

While Brook remained playful and practical in *Carmen*, I enjoyed what he'd done. But it seemed to me that even he couldn't make the impassioned appeals and rejections of the closing scenes anything but absurd. Precisely because he'd made the rest seem 'natural', his version invited us to ask questions that we'd never asked with Bizet. Why the sudden change in Carmen? Why does she suddenly declare in song her love for the bullfighter? Why does the woman who mocked the bugles turn into a tragic figure, who kneels and accepts her death? Are we supposed to take seriously the dialectics of Destiny and Free Will? These questions can only have arisen in my mind because I found that what had, in the early scenes, been entirely enjoyable, had finally become ponderous and boring, and a bit ridiculous. (Though, of course, if I'd seen it in the theatre I might still have been captivated by the magic of the occasion.)

The reasons why Brook and Carrière went back to Mérimée are completely understandable. And Brook's approach to the practical problems of de-mystifying opera seemed to me admirable. But he couldn't resist his own received mystifications in the end.

An underlying theme in much of Brook's work is that, when you're confronted with implacable destiny, all you can do is lie back and enjoy it. So it was with Carmen. Freely she lived and freely she died – knowing that a gal's gotta do what a gal's gotta do.

In 1992, Brook returned to opera: *Impressions de Pelléas*, his and Marius Constant's version of Debussy's *Pelléas et Melisande*. Brook said:

With *Carmen* one could take much greater liberties. Not that one takes liberties for their own sake, but Debussy is much more exacting in every way. Two works coexist here. For me, the orchestral version is a symphonic poem, and if the orchestra part is played for all its worth, it's legitimate for it to swamp the words. That's why it's so great on records.

The performance lasted ninety minutes without an interval, Constant and Brook having cut an hour of Debussy's music. Debussy's own original piano version was used as accompaniment, divided into two parts for two pianists, since it is so dense as to be almost unplayable by merely two hands. (When

Brook can work out how to fit an orchestra of twenty-four into the Bouffes, the usual limit being fourteen, he says he will do *The Magic Flute*.) As with *Carmen*, there were three rotating casts again, Melisande always played by an Asian soprano, dressed in a blood-red kimono. Brook wanted this to be an allusion to the oriental kitsch of the time, but also an anachronism. 'It becomes a sort of surrealism, the imagination begins to work on two levels at once.'

The performance was an intimate series of hushed dialogues rising only at the climaxes to fully projected operatic passion, set in a stripped-down *fin-de-siècle* living room with the characters gathering round a piano.

Brook:

One is always looking to find the compatible image. In the nineteenth century, gauze and fairies, as in *La Sylphide*, genuinely touched the imagination. But today one has to accept that that simply doesn't wash. If I made it 100 per cent German medieval, the words and the performance of the music and the psychology wouldn't set well together.

There's a funny overlapping of two worlds in Debussy, those of myth and a kind of nineteenth-century hothouse. The hypersensitivity of Proust was as much in my mind as Debussy. *Incredible* passions were stifled by this closed world, and only a few artists were able to discover the finest shadings of emotions.

The mysterious, mythic triangle of innocent love and raging jealousy was played almost as a drawing-room charade, but one in which the intensity and immediacy of singing actors in a space far smaller than an opera house gave the action what John Rockwell in *The New York Times* described as 'a primal power'.

Impressions de Pelléas fared far better with music critics than *Carmen*, probably because more of the score was left intact, although the editor of *Opera Today*, predictably, found it 'dismal'. It was the theatre critics who were less impressed, feeling that Brook's quest for purity had produced something too abstract and remote. Joyce McMillan, in *The Guardian*, found it 'exquisite', but thought the deep, vulgar, 'human-interest' quality had been stripped out of it.

The characters appear as simple, highly refined outlines . . . this shifting pattern of sound, light and physical expression is made utterly absorbing. . . . But for me, it remains to be seen whether a performance so smooth, so fine, so polished, so perfect, has the power to lodge and hook in the memory; or whether it simply slips through the mind without leaving a trace, all form, no content, too rarified to make us care.

Brook:

There is no distinction for me between working with actors and opera singers, or in the balance between natural dramatic expression and the artifice of an ornate form like opera. Debussy himself constantly sought a natural style of declamation from his singers. I have carried that quest for true human expression to the limits that Debussy's opera allows.

I don't believe there is such a thing as a true but artificial form. In decadent art, the form takes over, and that has its admirers, as in kitsch today. But it's inherently superficial and it's dangerous to accept and applaud artificiality as something in its own right. Japanese Noh, Kathakali, opera and ballet are particular forms that true artists can make real. I can cite my own experience; when I first saw Margot Fonteyn dance Giselle, or Ulanova as Juliet, I could believe that this was a real woman going mad, or a real fourteen-year-old. Even if one takes a photograph as being real, these were 100 per cent convincing. With *Carmen*, when the performances were good, when the audiences were involved, it was more real than a lot of movies one sees. For me, any convention can be enlivened by a conviction that makes it real at the moment it happens.

18   Nirvana at last: *The Mahabharata*

Peter Brook's production of *The Mahabharata* was first presented in French at the Avignon Festival in July 1985. It was performed in the Jacques Callet limestone quarry between Barbentane and Boulbon, near the meeting of the Durance and the Rhone, eight miles south of Avignon. It was performed either as three separate three-hour plays on three successive evenings, or as a dusk-to-dawn marathon. The all-night version was timed to end with a meal in paradise being lit by the rising sun.

Later, Brook took the French version to his Bouffes du Nord theatre in Paris, where it was also played, either as three separate plays, or as a marathon, though sometimes the marathon began at 1.00 p.m. and ended at 11.00 p.m., with lengthy intervals between the separate parts. David Williams wrote a detailed

18   *Le Mahabharata*, Bouffes du Nord, 1985

descriptive account of one such performance at the Bouffes in March 1986.

Brook then worked on an English version, which he first presented at Zurich in August 1987. It was performed through the night in a boathouse on the edge of the lake. Michael Billington wrote in *The Guardian*: 'It ended sensationally ... with the revelation that the back-wall of the boathouse was like a large movable blind which was slowly lowered to reveal a dazzling morning sun. Even Nature now appears to be directed by Peter Brook.' Brook took his English version to the United States (Geoffrey Reeves saw it in New York in 1988 in a marathon version that began at 1.00 p.m.), and to Glasgow (Albert Hunt saw it there, also in the marathon version that began at 1.00 p.m., in June 1989). *The Mahabharata* went to Glasgow because London could not come up with the money. Brook converted the Old Museum of Transport in Glasgow into a suitable performance space and left Glasgow with a theatre. Since he also took the English version round the world, and made a film from it in 1989, it can be said that Peter Brook spent four years fully engaged with *The Mahabharata* in one form or another. But the work of preparation had begun long before that.

According to Brook himself, he first encountered a section of *The Mahabharata*, *The Bhagavad-Gita*, when he was beginning to think about *US* in late 1965. A young Indian had talked to him about *Bhagavad-Gita*, an abridged version of which is confided by Krishna to one of the main participants in the war which takes place in the third part of Brook's epic. But in 1965 Brook had not known that *The Bhagavad-Gita* only formed a small part of an enormous poem. In his introduction to the English text, published in 1985, he describes how he became aware of the existence of the work:

The day I first saw a demonstration of Kathakali, I heard a work completely new to me – *The Mahabharata*. A dancer was presenting a scene from this work and his sudden first appearance from behind a curtain was an unforgettable shock. His costume was red and gold, his face was red and green, his nose was like a white billiard ball, his fingernails were like knives; in place of beard and moustache, two white crescent moons thrust forward from his lips, his eyebrows shot up and down like drumsticks and his fingers spelled out strange coded messages. Through the magnificent ferocity of the movements I could see that a story was unfolding. But what story? I could only guess at something mythical and remote, from another culture, nothing to do with my life. . . . After the interval the dancer returned without his make-up, no longer a demigod, just a likeable Indian in a shirt and jeans. He described the scene he had been playing and repeated the dance. The hieratic gestures passed through the man of today. The superb, but impenetrable image had given way to an ordinary, more accessible one and I realised that I preferred it this way.

Brook's next encounter with *The Mahabharata* occurred in Paris in 1975. Jean-Claude Carrière, author of Brook's French version, writes:

One evening in 1975 Philippe Lavastine, a remarkable professor of Sanskrit, began telling the first stories of *The Mahabharata* to Peter Brook and me. We were completely enchanted. For five years we met regularly, Peter and I listening to the poem without reading it.

Carrière began his first version of the play in 1976. Since the original Sanskrit poem is, according to Carrière, about fifteen times the length of the Bible, this was a considerable undertaking. Both Carrière and Brook made several journeys to India. Later, all those involved in the project – actors, musicians, designers – went to India with Brook. One Indian dancer, Mallika Sarabhai, was recruited in 1984 – she had met Brook a year earlier at Ahmedabad, where she and her mother were preparing a version of *The Mahabharata* from the point of view of two women, Gandhari and Draupadi. (She was shocked, she says, when in the final version Gandhari was made to say, 'Draupadi, like all women, made no distinction between her husband and herself. She was part of him. She was him.' 'Never would an Indian woman impregnated by *The Mahabharata* speak like that!', she exclaimed.) Carrière writes:

I began the final draft in autumn 1982. I continued throughout 1983 as well as 1984, when research began with the actors, as well as the music composition. When rehearsals began, in September 1984, the play was written, but there was as yet no definitive structure. Throughout the nine months of rehearsal, incessant changes were made. For a long time, we had no idea how lengthy the play would be, how many playing hours we would need, or how many plays were involved....

Eventually a clear line began to appear, which led from a mythical tale of demigods told by a storyteller, to characters who became more and more human and who brought with them the theatre as we understand it.

Since Peter Brook spent so many years of his life working on *The Mahabharata*, we can only conclude that it had a particular importance for him. What, then, was the 'clear line' that finally emerged in the French text written by Carrière and translated into English by Brook himself?

Brook's staged version takes the form of a story told by one of the characters, Vyasa, to a Boy. The story is written down by Ganesha, who has a man's body with an elephant's head. The actor who plays Ganesha later discards the elephant's head and becomes a central character, Krishna. The entire epic is performed by twenty-two actors and six musicians – the musicians become part of the action.

The three plays tell the story of two sets of cousins, the Kauravas and the Pandavas. They are all descended from the gods and have heroic stature. In the original poem there were, apparently, 100 Kauravas, but they are represented in the plays by two central figures, Duryodhana and the eldest of his ninety-nine brothers, Dushasna. There are five Pandavas, all brothers – we are introduced to them near the beginning of the first play, *The Game of Dice*.

The Game of Dice sets a style of storytelling. It consists largely of third-person narrative, accompanied by images created by the actors, and by musical sounds. The narrative style is very fluid – 'Twenty years went by', says Vyasa, and Ganesha simply draws a line across the page of his book. As in the original poem, there are many digressions. At one point a king dies without descendants. But without children, as Ganesha says, 'This story cannot go on'. Only Vyasa himself can 'do the necessary'. So the storyteller becomes part of the story: he makes love to three princesses.

The Game of Dice ends with a scene in which the oldest of the Pandavas, Yudhishthira, loses his possessions, his brothers, himself and Draupadi (the wife all five of them share) in a dice game, which is rigged. They are exiled in a forest for twelve years and are required to spend a thirteenth year in disguise. The second play, called *Exile in the Forest*, covers this period. It includes a section in which one of the brothers, Arjuna, the best archer in the world, travels to the Himalayas to acquire from Shiva 'an absolute weapon' – 'It can destroy the world'. Towards the end of the second play, we see the Pandavas farcically disguised in the Kauravas's court, but in the closing scenes, as the text says, 'The masks fall', and the scene is set for the war which gives its name to the third play, in which 18,000,000 people, including the main protagonists, die. But Brook, the theatre magician, has one last trick to play.

The aged Yudhishthira, who has survived the war, is apparently shown heaven and hell – his enemies, the Kauravas, are in heaven, his brothers, the Pandavas, are in hell. Yudhishthira cries, 'Go and tell the gods I'm outraged. That I despise them.' But Vyasa goes to him, 'gently', while Ganesha reappears with his writing materials.

VYASA: Then the keeper of the last dwelling said to Yudhishthira: 'Stop shouting. You've known neither paradise nor hell. Here, there is no happiness, no punishment, no family, no enemies. Rise in tranquillity. This was the last illusion.'

Ganesha repeats, as he finishes his writing, 'This was the last illusion'. The published text concludes:

Yudhishthira looks around him in astonishment. He sees his brothers, Drapaudi and Kunti, smiling, intact. The other characters reappear, calm and relaxed. . . . For an instant they wash in the river, then sit beside the musicians, who play as the story comes to its end. Refreshments are handed round. They are slowly enveloped by the night.

Or, if you happened to see the plays through the night, in the quarry, outside Avignon, or in the boathouse at Zurich, they were bathed in the rising sun.

The above brief story outline gives very little idea of what happens in a performance of *The Mahabharata* that lasts something approaching nine hours. Two of the main characters have been omitted. When Vyasa intervenes in the story to make love to the three princesses, the first princess closes her eyes because Vyasa's body is 'caked in mud', his beard 'yellow with age'. Vyasa tells her: 'I have given you my sperm and you will have a son. He will be called

Dhritarashtra and he will be king. But as you closed your eyes on seeing me, he will be born blind.' David Williams describes what happened in the performance he saw at the Bouffes du Nord:

To signal the moment of birth . . . three rush mats are held up by figures concealed behind. . . . As Vyasa describes him, Dhritarashtra (Ryszard Cieslak) slowly lowers his screen to reveal himself. . . . His blindness is conveyed immediately and minimally: he fumbles for the top lip of the screen, an onlooker passes a hand in front of his unseeing eyes.

Cieslak, who was the actor Grotowski brought with him to the US rehearsals, played the blind king in both the French and English versions. In the entire performance he is only allowed two moments when he can see. The first moment comes towards the end of the second play, just before the war breaks out, when Krishna appears to make the Kauvaras a final peace offer. Krishna is described with rays of light streaming from his skin, and the blind king cries, 'Lighten my eyes for a moment, I beg you, let me see you!' 'Yes, here are your eyes', says Krishna. David Williams writes:

In this performance, Cieslak rarely demonstrates, nothing is explicit; it is a performance of tiny economical nuances. An almost imperceptible increase in the brightness of the light on his face, a tiny hand gesture, a sense of focus in his eyes, a real tear: and then he returns to darkness. Cieslak's face is now ravaged, the radiant purity of *The Constant Prince* has crumbled with the passage of time; his face records his experience, like a map or a weathered stone. Here he creates for us an immensely tragic figure, wavering on the brink of decrepitude, disintering echoes of Oedipus, Lear, Gloucester, Prima. He saws and spits his way through the text with a voice of rock and glass. Words become bitter balls of phlegm to be spat, blows from a rusty hammer. . . .

(Williams was, of course, writing about the French version. The less tolerant American critic, Robert Brustein, was to write in New York of Cieslak's 'losing struggle between the English language and his gutteral plosives'.)

The only other time Cieslak is allowed to see is in the final meal, when he has regained his sight.

Alongside the Polish actor, Mireille Maalouf, born in Paris but brought up in the Lebanon, played the blind king's queen, Ghandari. David Williams describes her first entrance as Ghandari:

Great pomp, celebration, acclamation in movement and music; a spectacularly majestic public procession created with sublime simplicity. A stately queen, draped in luxurious trappings, borne in on the shoulders of her attendants: Indian or African parasols lend height to the image. . . . The reveller-celebrants carry huge curling Indian brass instruments: an elephant's trunk at the front, the swaying rhythm of its progress rippling back through the body of the bearers. Somehow more evocative than a dozen real elephants. The image is established instantly and with economy, then just as quickly dispersed as joyful illusion evaporates: for Ghandari's husband is blind, a state she determines to share. She ties a simple black band around her eyes, from now on the absence of light and colour will be her lot. . . .

Ghandari's black band is only taken off again for the meal at the end. (Mireille Maalouf has said, 'The band allows stronger concentration, and at the same time isolates me from the others. It is ultimately a very Brookian paradox: to find yourself isolated and to project your feelings in "rapport" with the other actors and with the audience'.)

The other main character left out of the story outline is Drona, the master warrior-brahmin, played by a Brook veteran, Yoshi Oida. He wears the black robes of a martial-arts master and when he first arrives he sets up a test of archery skills: Arjuna wins – as he fires an arrow into the sky, Vyasa lobs an impaled dead bird into the space. (Tricks with bows and arrows offer a lot of entertainment in *The Mahabharata*. In *The War* arrows seem to be caught in mid-flight, in hands or mouth, to be tossed aside or snapped. When Arjuna fires an arrow at Bhisma – who has the right to decide when he will die – Krishna carries the arrow across stage, slowly twisting it through the air towards Bhisma's heart.)

Soon after his first appearance, Yoshi becomes a statue of himself. A pupil has sculpted the statue so that he can learn from Drona even though Drona has refused to teach him. He proves to Drona that he will be more skilful than Arjuna. But Drona has promised to make Arjuna the best archer. He keeps his promise by ordering the pupil to cut off his own thumb, which the pupil willingly does. (The story is one of the many stories within a story which *The Mahabharata*'s style allows.)

Brook once described how Yoshi dropped in on a rehearsal of *A Midsummer Night's Dream* and showed the actors how to make night. What Yoshi was doing, said Brook, was 'dazzling but not very human'. In *The Mahabharata* Yoshi plays his warrior-brahmin with a very light touch. But he is, ironically, at his most human when, briefly, he is playing, not Drona, but a general called Kichaka, at the Kauravas's court. The Pandavas are in disguise, and Kichaka makes an assignation with the five brothers' wife, Draupadi. A haunting melody is played on a wooden flute, Yoshi scatters powders and rice on the floor and on the bed, lingers over a shape concealed in a sheet, then slides under the sheet, leaving his face visible. His hands wander, and his face registers that they have not found Draupadi. They have found Bhima, the strongest of the Pandavas.

The Senegalese Mamadou Dioume, playing Bhima, drags Yoshi out of sight, wraps him in the sheet, rolls the sheet into a ball and then kicks the ball off stage. It is one of the more entertaining stories within the story.

What comes through the nine or so hours of this everyday story of superfolk is the combination of spectacular theatrical magic and simplicity of playing. It comes across, for example, in yet another digression, when the storyteller, Vyasa, describes how one of the supermen, Karna, was born, after Kunti has invoked the sun:

SUN:	I am here, Kunti. I am the sun. You conjured me and I have come. What is your wish, young lady?
KUNTI:	Oh, excuse me. I wanted to try out a mantra, that's all.
SUN:	Oh, no, Kunti, it's not all. You can't have brought me down here just for that. It's unthinkable. You must come into my arms and I'll give you a son.
KUNTI:	A son! I can't, I'm a virgin, I am only fifteen. You must always protect women, even when they're guilty.
SUN:	I know all that, but one doesn't disturb the sun for nothing.
KUNTI:	Go back to the sky. Forget what I did. I'm only a child. Forgive me.
SUN:	I'll say again: it's impossible. The sun is going to be your lover, the sun will give you a son, and I can reassure you, your virginity will remain intact. Abandon all your fears and come into my arms. (*Kunti allows herself to be loved by the Sun.*)

The English text is both coy and ponderous. But when played by Miriam Goldschmidt, as Kunti, and Mavuso Mavuso, as the Sun, the scene takes on another dimension. Miriam Goldschmidt plays Kunti as anything but a virginal schoolgirl. When Mavuso Mavuso appears, from behind the held-up cloth Brook uses throughout as a theatrical curtain, Miriam's expression and her eyes say, 'Well, what have we here?' She looks at Mavuso and then looks in complicity at the audience, inviting the audience to share her obvious delight. Mavuso eyes Miriam as if he cannot believe his luck – 'Well, well, look what I've found!' He too invites the audience to join in the fun. Miriam and Mavuso throw the lines lightly to each other. They flirt with the words. Sleep with the Sun? Of course she can't, she's only fifteen and a virgin! She plays mockingly at being demure. That's all right, says Mavuso, she'll still be a virgin when it's all over. He doesn't actually wink at the audience, nothing so gross – but he invites us to enjoy the irony. When the two of them withdraw discreetly behind the cloth, they are like lovers eager for bed. The audience is included in the game – we become part of the circle.

The digression is over, we are suddenly plunged back into the epic. They must stop the brothers fighting, says the Boy, but Vyasa replies, 'No, I forbid it' – he is the storyteller. And Karna declares, 'Arjuna, wherever you look, I'll always be ahead. Why are you waiting? Take up your arms. I am ready.' The two of them will eventually confront each other in the war that ends the world. But it is the story within the story that has given us immediate pleasure.

The nine-hour performance contains enough moments like this and enough displays of spectacle to keep the audience generally entertained. Geoffrey Reeves noted that very few people left the marathon performance in New York before the end and that the American audience seemed to watch attentively. (Some of the actors in Glasgow, though, told Albert Hunt that around 4.00 a.m. during the all-nighters they sometimes got the feeling that there was nobody out there. One actor would begin to pitch the level up a bit, the others would match him, and for a time they would all be competing with each other to win perceptible attention. After such performances, the meal in paradise was even more welcome than usual.)

At Avignon, Geoffrey Reeves points out, the atmosphere must have been even more magical. (At one point in Avignon, there was a blinding flash, like a nuclear explosion, which apparently stayed for some time on the spectator's retina.) In his theatre at the Bouffes, and all the other theatres *The Mahabharata* was performed in, Brook reassembled as many of the physical elements he had used in the quarry as he could. He had a pool at the front of the stage and a river at the back, with sand on the space in between. The wall at the back was high and flaking, worn with hollows scraped out. It looked like a cliff. David Williams describes how at one point the Kauravas appeared, hanging from rungs at different heights, 'watching, immobile, horrified vultures . . .'. Brook used this space with complete mastery, sometimes opening it out to give the sense of a Hollywood epic, sometimes using lighting, focus or simple props to create a very close intimacy between a single performer and the audience. A woman stands by the pool. She catches a fold in her Indian dress and in one movement she turns it into a baby which she is cradling in her arms. The death of a young king is created, visually, by a corner of a vivid scarlet cloth being dipped into a river. The two-years' pregnant Gandhari orders a servant to strike her distended stomach with an iron bar: 'Harder! Harder, I tell you'. A huge, black iron ball drops from her skirts and rolls across the stage. The image is so powerful that we scarcely hear Vyasa telling the servant to cut the ball into a hundred pieces and put them into a hundred earthenware pots – out of them will come the hundred sons of the Kauvaras.

When the performance is over, images remain in the mind. A scarlet-faced figure of death dances in slow motion with tiny steps around his opponent. The power of Shiva is suggested by two yellow flags (borrowed from Chinese opera). The actors openly toss powder into the air to create the dust and smoke of battle. Sticks and bamboo screens are used as bows and arrows, shields, tents, shelters, beds, war machines. Drona's secret defence weapon, the disc, is created by twenty-foot long scaling ladders which whirl like the giant spokes of a wheel, while a single actor slips like a Houdini between them. A huge wheel whipped across the sand becomes an army of chariots. When the wheel sticks in the mud, Karna is killed. The dying Drona picks up an earthenware pot, as if to drink water. From the pot he pours blood over himself (an echo from *The Marat/Sade*). Bhishma dies upright on a bed of arrows.

One of the most spectacular scenes is the one in which Arjuna travels to the Himalayas in search of the ultimate weapon – Brook uses the full depth of the stage. As Duryodhana lobs petals into the water of the pool, a circle of fire is created round the pool and traps him. At the same time a trail of fire snakes across the sand and seems to ignite the river at the back. The scars along the back wall are caught in the flickering lights. In the next scene, there is a blackened circle around the pool.

David Williams notes the fluidity with which Brook uses the space. This is how he describes the creation of the Kauvalas's court:

A new world once again established with clarity, economy, speed. . . . Ropes at least sixty feet in length are attached to the domed base of the cupola, the theatre's ceiling; two on each side suggest the dimensions of the palace . . . they are used to suspend a pair of swinging benches. . . . The musicians move to a carpet centre stage behind and between these benches to enact 'musicians' within the fiction; as they begin to play, the perfect image of a court at ease . . . blossoms before our eyes. A number of oil lamps, as well as tiny candles floating on silver bases in the pool. Tapa Sudana performs a short Balinese puppet entertainment for the court's delight: the comic tale of a king losing his head, which culminates with Tapa pursuing one of the puppets off into the 'audience' on stage. . . . Mats with bolsters form a circle . . . around an inner central space, lit more sharply than its surrounds. An empty space . . . waiting to be filled. . . .

Michael Kustow, who had joined the team working with Brook on *US* back in 1966, and who has also written a long essay on what he calls 'Brook's great theatre of the world', uses this scene as an example of what he calls Brook's 'surreal plasticity of storytelling'. He writes, describing the performance at Avignon:

Carpets are unrolled and cushions piled high on the stone and sand of the quarry. A king and his entourage loll back, enjoying a puppet show produced from behind a multi-coloured cloth. The puppet seems to run amok, stealing kisses from the ladies. It's all very relaxed. . . . The exiled king Yudishthira and his family appear at court disguised as beggars, servants and eunuchs. They are ordered to tell a story. They begin the tale of Hanuman, the monkey-god, and how he prevented Bhima from following the path to heaven by barring the way with his thick heavy tail. The disguised Bhima does a clown show miming the difficulty of the obstacle. Three speeches later Yudishthira is spellbinding the audience on stage and in the quarry with a fierce description of our dark era of destruction, a foretaste of cataclysmic conflicts ahead and a fable which assumes that in some central sense the world is already destroyed.

Kustow provides his own English version of this speech:

It's the age of Kali, the dark-time, the fields turn to desert, crime stalks the city, blood-eating animals sleep in the main streets, droughts, famine, the sky swallows up all the water, dead, hot earth, then fire swells, swept by the wind, fire pierces the earth, destroys the underworld, wind and fire turn the world to a crust, huge clouds appear, blue, yellow, red, clouds like sea-monsters, like shattered circles, with garlands of lightning, water falls, water pours down and drowns the earth, twelve years of storms, mountains tear the water. I can't see the world any more, and then the first god, when nothing is left but a grey sea without man, without beast, without tree, the creator drinks up the terrible wind and falls asleep.

Kustow adds:

As Yudishthira speaks these words (part of a tale which he began as entertainment and has turned apocalyptic) the silence in the house is almost unbearable. A vision of destruction imagined two thousand years ago dredges our worst nightmares now.

Or, as Peter Brook himself puts it:

In *The Mahabharata* the descriptions of ultimate war are in exactly the same terms as the descriptions of Hiroshima, of Bhopal, and the way that nuclear war is described. In a way it is not surprising – what was invented by the poetic imagination is now reinvented by the scientific imagination. Neither Jean-Claude Carrière nor myself have stretched or pushed the parallel. It is there. If you read the original, it is terrifyingly there.

Not even the most hostile critic would deny that Brook's version of *The Mahabharata* has plenty of theatrical invention (though some would say that the invention is spread rather thin over the nine hours). Most of the countless people around the world who have seen the performance would probably agree that the international actors often achieve an immediate relationship with the spectators, what Brook calls completing the circle. But Brook himself implies that *The Mahabharata* is bringing some kind of truth: 'We're dealing with what's true for us in the late twentieth century'. He writes:

In a dishonourable age it is challenging and stimulating to be reminded of finer attitudes. Each person can measure himself and see what he would most essentially respect when he is faced by a level of behaviour that is more dedicated, goes further than his own. In *The Mahabharata* the word appears from a person with a different value depending on the quality of the person – so exactly the same statement coming out of the mouth of a dishonourable man has a different value coming out of the mouth of an honourable man. When somebody reaches a certain very high level he becomes so close to truth that he is incapable of speaking anything other than the truth. This is very, very deeply rooted in *The Mahabharata*.

Brook himself has referred more than once to what he clearly regards as a key scene. It takes place near the beginning of the third play, *The War*.

At the end of the second play, *Exile in the Forest*, Krishna has made what David Williams calls his 'final attempt at peace' (what President Bush would have called 'going the extra mile').

The dispute that has arisen between the Kauravas and the Pandavas is about whether or not the Pandavas have kept to the terms that were laid on them when they lost the game of dice. The Kauravas say that the Pandavas showed themselves before their twelve years in the forest were up. The blind king has pardoned them for that – let them give up all claim to the kingdom and stay free. The Pandavas are asking for the kingdom as their 'unshakeable right'.

In his final peace attempt, Krishna reveals that the Pandavas are willing to settle for five villages. Duryodhana replies on behalf of the Kauravas:

A king does not stake his kingdom. A king does not stoop to ask for five villages. I will not give five villages. I will not give one village. I will not give the point of a needle of earth.

After this, apparently, war becomes inevitable.

Before the war begins, Krishna has made an offer: one side can have the mass of his armies, the other side can have him, 'alone, unarmed, taking no part in the battle.' Arjuna, on behalf of the Pandavas, chooses Krishna alone. So it is that when the war begins, Krishna is on hand to give private advice to Arjuna – and this is the scene that Brook quotes as being particularly important.

As the text describes it, the warriors take their positions for the battle. Arjuna, led by Krishna, is advancing between the two armies. He grasps his conch to begin the battle. Then, on the other side, 'he sees Bhima, he sees Drona, his cousins, his friends'.

ARJUNA: Krishna, my legs go weak, my mouth is dry, my body trembles, my bow slips from my hands, my skin burns. I can no longer stand. What good can come from this battle? My family will be massacred. If this is the price, who can wish for victory, or pleasure, or even life? Uncles, cousins, nephews, and Drona, my teacher – they are all there. I can't bring death to my own family. How could I dare to be happy again? No, I prefer not to defend myself. I will wait here for death.

He throws down his bow and arrows – and Krishna says: 'What is this mad and shameful weakness? Stand up.' There follows an exchange of aphorisms.

KRISHNA: You must rise up free from hope and throw yourself into the battle.
ARJUNA: . . . The mind is capricious, unstable; it's evasive, feverish, turbulent, tenacious. It's harder to subdue than taming the wind.
KRISHNA: You must learn to see with the same eye a mound of earth and a heap of gold, a cow and a sage, a dog and the man who eats the dog. The mind is greater than the senses.

Arjuna says that he feels his illusions vanish and adds, 'Show me your universal form'. Krishna does so, adding, for good measure, more explanations.

KRISHNA: Matter changes, but I am all that you say, all you think. Everything rests on me like pearls on a thread. I am the earth's scent and the fire's heat. I am appearance and disappearance. I am the trickster's hoax. I am the radiance of all that shines. All beings fall in the night and all beings are brought back to daylight. I have already defeated all these warriors, but he who thinks he can kill and he who thinks he can be killed are both mistaken. No weapon can pierce the life that informs you. No fire can burn it; no water can drench it; no wind can make it dry. Have no fear and rise up, because I love you.
ARJUNA: Thank you, my understanding has returned.

Duryodhana asks, 'When will they stop talking?' Arjuna blows on his conch and the battle begins.

AH writes:

If Brook himself points us to this scene, we must assume that he takes it seriously. This is the part of *The Mahabharata* Brook first encountered when the Indian came and talked to him about *The Bhagavad-Gita* at the time of *US*. Brook, who has often talked about a theatre that goes beyond words, and who demonstrates such a theatre at times in *The Mahabharata*, here obviously feels the need of words – one has some sympathy with Duryodhana's 'When will they stop talking?'

The words have been adapted from an ancient Sanskrit poem, into French, by Jean-Claude Carrière. Brook himself has translated them into English – the director who has in the past sometimes shown himself willing to use the writer for his own needs has now turned writer himself. (It is ironic that in his search for new forms, Brook has used verbal narrative in whole sections of *The Mahabharata* to the exclusion of what is normally thought of as 'drama'. He has written the words, and then he has asked members of his company who are not native speakers of English to find their own 'truth', as he always does. The effect can be revelatory – but it can also be limiting, as Brustein pointed out in his comments about Cieslak's losing struggle with English.)

In most of the narrative sequences, the flatness (and sometimes absurdity) of the language is hidden by the richness of the visual invention. But in this scene we have only the words, and they are supposed to carry some earth-shattering meaning – literally, because the words persuade Arjuna to blow his conch and launch the war that will kill 18,000,000 people and destroy a world.

In the French version of the play, Krishna was played by Maurice Bénichou. Brook gave the role in the English version to one of his veteran British actors, Bruce Myers. It was not difficult to see Myers playing Brook in this scene, as Magee played him in *The Marat/Sade*. Krishna is confronted by an actor who has hesitations about playing the part he has been given. Krishna shows Arjuna 'the deepest movements of his being and his true battlefield'. It is what Brook has seen himself doing with actors for many decades. (He even has Krishna say, 'I am the trickster's hoax', so including in the catalogue of goodies Krishna embodies the right to deceive in the search for truth.)

The language of Krishna is supposed to reverberate across 3,000 years of orally transmitted Eastern culture. But it sounds very like the language of a Hollywood epic in which a producer has allowed a scriptwriter to indulge himself with a bit of philosophising: 'Through your body I see the stars, I see life and death, I see silence . . .'. Krishna's 'Act as you must act' could well be translated into 'A man's gotta do what a man's gotta do'. As Bruce Myers put it, in a television interview, 'Krishna says, "Get up, you're weak and cowardly, get up and fight"'. The line could well have been spoken by John Wayne – but we must remember what Brook says about the quality of a word depending on the quality of a person. Krishna, we must assume, has reached such a 'very high level' that he is 'incapable of speaking anything other than the truth'.

But what is this 'truth' that Krishna is speaking? Kenneth Tynan once pointed out that when Brook produced *The Ik* in 1975, the programme said, 'As far as anyone knows, the Ik still exist'. Tynan wrote, 'Here we are, invited to feel compassion and horror at their plight, but nobody in the production had even bothered to find out whether they still existed!'

In the same way, Brook associates *The Mahabharata* with a real place, India – 'The Mahabharata is like India itself, you can put any number of adjectives and definitions on it and it is always beyond them'. But the India he speaks and writes about is very much the India of his own imagination.

'We visited India: after we'd been there a week I got everyone together in a forest and I said, 'Everybody try to capture his most essential impression up to now of India in one word'. There were thirty people, three rounds and about ninety words emerged – 'chaotic, calm, luminous, dark' – every sort of contradiction one can imagine.'

The suggestion that Brook's actors tell him what they think he wants to hear has been made more than once. Here, Brook has selected, from what they told him, what he has chosen to remember. But Sotigui Kouyata, who came from the Upper Volta to play Bhisma, lets slip another impression India made on some of the members of Brook's group. He told *Théâtre en Europe* (October 1985), 'For my part, I wasn't very shocked, as some Westerners were, by the great poverty of India: an African doesn't feel out of place over there'. He went on to say that what impressed him was the presence everywhere of Hinduism, 'the deep respect, the attachment Indians have to their religion, which truly forms a part of their life'. But when Brook asked his actors to give their first impression of India in one word, why did all the words Brook remembered confirm his own impressions? Did none of the Western actors offer the word 'poverty'?

Would it have mattered if they had? The only explicable meaning that can be discerned in Krishna's digest of *The Bhagavad-Gita* is that worlds come and go: 'All beings fall in the night and all beings are brought back to daylight'. What does a bit of poverty or the occasional destruction of a world matter, as long as you follow your dharma? (Having accepted that war is inevitable, Krishna, in following his dharma, breaks all the rules in order to win it. 'No lily-livered humanist, him', comments David Williams approvingly when Krishna tells Bhima how to kill Duryodhana by shattering his thigh, against all the agreed rules of engagement.)

It would be absurd to criticise Brook for failing to confront poverty in India when he is telling a story about demigods. But he himself calls attention to the parallel between the destruction described in *The Mahabharata* and the threat of a nuclear holocaust. And he appears to detach himself as much from that threat as he does from the fate of the Ik or from poverty in India.

But *The Mahabharata* was not made in a vacuum. At the time he was working on it with his actors, there was a campaign in Europe against the installation of a new generation of nuclear weapons, just as there had been an anti-Vietnam War campaign at the time Brook was workng on *US* (and learning about *The Bhagavad-Gita* from the Indian who came and talked to him). His response to the threat of a nuclear nightmare in *The Mahabharata* was precisely the same as his response to the Vietnam War in *US* – that it is of little consequence in the long run, that there is nothing we can do about it, and that all we can be responsible for is exploring the 'deepest movements' of our being and following our dharma. Brook's dharma led him to make *The Mahabharata*.

While he was working on it, though, he had an uncomfortable encounter in India. He described it in a television interview:

I don't think any intelligent being can think that this great story is to be taken literally, as saying we must go to war. But I did have a frightening experience. At the very beginning of the Falklands War, I was in Delhi. I went to a cocktail party, and a lady came up to me and said, Ah, your Mrs Thatcher has followed Krishna's advice. And I said, No, in *The Mahabharata*, every single human possibility is explored both by the human characters and by the god to avoid war. Krishna, who is shown as an all-powerful god, uses his power. He goes and argues, he goes and tries to touch every button of human understanding in the adversaries to bring them not to go to war. And when every conceivable process is exhausted, in a story which is still symbolic, because it's as much about an inner as an outer struggle, you see that conflict can't be avoided.

But this, of course, is the point where detachment itself becomes a political attitude. Those who were opposed to the Falklands War argued that every conceivable process had not been exhausted. Mrs Thatcher would have found it useful to say she was following her dharma.

While *The Mahabharata* was being performed around the world, a war of catastrophic dimension was being fought between Iraq and Iran. The West helped to arm Iraq. As I wrote these comments, the most destructive forces ever marshalled in history were unleashed against Iraq, led by the West. Mallika Sarabhai, Drapaudi in Brook's play, says 'As for this terrible war which is the main subject of *The Mahabharata*. . . . For me it's very clear: you have to cut off a gangrened limb. When evil reigns you have to struggle to put an end to it.'

But when do you decide that what reigns is evil? When it threatens your oil interests?

Mireille Maalouf, who played Gandhari in *The Mahabharata*, studied in Beirut. She told *Théâtre en Europe*:

If I agreed to play in *The Mahabharata*, it's above all because there is this theme of war. . . . Some people reproach Gandhari for being submissive, which I reject absolutely: she sees the injustice in the world, hurls herself ceaselessly against it, suffers it, revolts against it, but can only cry out when she thinks, even if she has no effect, because she has no power. It's the same in Lebanon – I can cry out, but that changes nothing.

When the war in *The Mahabharata* is over, Gandhari is allowed to curse Krishna:

GANDHARI: Krishna, I curse you: one day, all that you are building will crumble: your friends will be massacred by your friends; dried blood will coat the walls of your dead city where only vultures reign; your shattered heart will mourn; you will leave, solitary; a passerby will kill you.

But Krishna/Brook is given the right to reply:

KRISHNA: Yes, Gandhari, what you see is true. I know. But even if you can't see it, a light has been saved.

Brook makes it all right in the end. In paradise, the blind king regains his sight and Gandhari takes off the band she has worn as a blindfold. But it is only in the theatre that Brook can make it all right.

Mireille Maalouf says, 'I'd suggested to Peter that after the journey to India we should go to the Lebanon so that everyone could feel what war was really like, what happens in families. . . . But you can't expose an entire troupe to bombardments just for the sake of theatre.'

Mireille Maalouf ends her interview in *Théâtre en Europe* by saying, 'For me, work in the theatre is always strongly linked with life'. Work in the theatre is clearly strongly linked with Peter Brook's life. But the work he produces sometimes has very tenuous links with life outside itself.

Robert Brustein, writing about *The Mahabharata* in New York, refers to Brook's efforts to develop a 'universal language for the stage' as 'informed by honourable, sometimes even heroic motives. They were also sad evidence', he adds, 'of how firmly rooted our theatrical messiahs were in their own cultural topsoil'.

Brustein continues:

The Mahabharata, at least in its New York incarnation, carries this melancholy message throughout its entire nine-hour length. It may be one thing to see it outdoors in Avignon, at ten dollars a ticket, watching the sun rise over the concluding rites. But at 96 dollars a seat in a production estimated at 6,000,000 dollars and in a Brooklyn theater renovated at a cost of 5,000,000 dollars in order to replicate the battered and unpatched conditions at Brook's Bouffes du Nord, this costly 'poor theater' begins to take on some of the bourgeois grandiosity (despite the atmosphere of feigned seediness) that made Nietzsche rage so rabidly against Wagnerian opera. . . . Exquisitely transformed into an Etruscan ruin . . . the Majestic has essentially become an expensive colonial outpost for Peter Brook, created and outfitted for his personal use.

Unlike Brustein, some of the critics who have vividly described *The Mahabharata* have allowed themselves to be colonised. Michael Kustow, who once praised Brecht for his 'materialist poetry', describes *The Mahabharata* as 'a fierce theatrical and spiritual torch'. David Williams describes the final scene as

therapeutic, a gentle shared act of reintegration and celebration at the culmination of a story told, the collective bringing into life of a resplendent *Teatro Mundi*. We have come to taste directly what the Indians refer to as *Lila*: the world as cosmic illusion and play, man's celebration of his humanity.

But Williams has the honesty to add a postscript:

Back home on the Metro, feeling revivified, fully alive, the scales lifted from my eyes and heart. A hiss and a shout behind me, a knife fight has broken out in the compartment. An Algerian and a drunken Frenchman, snarling for blood: the battle spills over. Do I act, try to break up the fight? What is the difference between theatre and life?

Vittorio Mezzorgiorno, who played Arjuna in Brook's *The Mahabharata*,, says: 'Another day he [Brook] said, "The only difference between theatre and life" . . . (I waited) . . . "is that the theatre is always true".'

The word Brook used was 'vrai'.

19 Farewell to Shakespeare? *La Tempête*

A Saturday in early December 1990 – in Paris it has been a bright, sunny day. At the Hotel Salé, a huge exhibition of work collected by Picasso throughout his life has drawn the crowds. Picasso's range continues to astonish. Can it really be thirty years since Peter Brook began to say that twentieth-century theatre needed to learn from what Picasso has done to painting?

In the evening, outside the Bouffes, a crowd spills over the pavement waiting for the doors to open. On offer is Brook's latest production, yet another effort at *The Tempest*, in French, scripted by Jean-Claude Carrière: *La Tempête*. It has already been to Brook's now-regular British venue, in Glasgow, a city which has helped to finance the production. The British critics have had their

19   *La Tempête*, Bakary Sangaré, Sotigui Kouyaté, Bouffes du Nord, 1990

say: John Peter – 'the distillation of Brook's lifelong interest in the way we co-exist with the brute world in servility and enchantment'; Martin Hoyle – '. . . the magic comes off. . . . The pace slackens with the comic scenes. . . . The production almost founders on Prospero's tortured French vowels. . . . Its strength lies in the universal, fairytale quality of its pageantry and ritual.' And Michael Billington, in *The Guardian*,

It becomes a poetic fable about the dream-like nature of human existence, with magical, translucent simplicity . . . we are offered a multi-layered Shakespearian fable about power, freedom, responsibility and charity. If the production achieves a rich dream-like mystery, it is because Brook has been wrestling with this conundrum of a play for over thirty years. . . .

Twenty-two years ago, Brook gave us a rough *Tempest* at the Round House in which actors simulated a sexual orgy when Caliban's rebellious powers erupted against Miranda. But now Brook has told a BBC interviewer on television that *The Tempest* speaks to us, in our present time, of chastity and virginity. No surprises in this apparent contradiction – the metaphysical Brook has often said that Shakespeare is so rich that his voice speaks of different visions to different ages. And the practical Brook has always had his finger on the pulse of his audience – in the sixties, sexual orgies were in; the eighties are reported to have rediscovered chaste virtues.

In the Bouffes, little has changed since the mid-seventies. There is still the enthusiastic scramble for tickets at the table which serves as a box office. There is one price for the whole house, 70 francs, but the benches are now numbered. Some spectators still sit on cushions on the floor around the playing area. When the show is due to start, there are still plenty of empty seats. The performers are happy to wait until they have all been taken.

The back wall behind the playing area is white. The holes in the proscenium, which used to offer additional entrances, have been filled in. A huge marked out rectangle of sand, jutting out through the proscenium from the back wall to the spectators on cushions, forms the main playing area. Up stage, slightly off centre, is a solitary rock. Two musicians enter and sit to one side against the proscenium arch – one is a Japanese percussionist (Toshi Tsudirtori); the other, an Iranian (Mahmoud Tabrizi-Zadeh), plays various stringed instruments, dulcimers and kamantches.

A tall black actor, with knotted hair, dressed in white, enters. He is balancing on his head a long thick decorated staff. He stops and takes it off. He slowly moves it up and down like a see-saw. Containing small stones, it makes a gentle sound, like waves. The drummer joins in.

Other actors enter. Quickly and lightly they make the outline of a rocking boat with their sticks. The actors sway from side to side, the sound goes up and down, the poles undulate. The boat comes apart as they spin off, leaving the aged Gonzalo, played by Yoshi, Brook's only survivor from the Round House *Tempest*. Yoshi uses a stick to give us a drowning man. He holds it horizontally in front of his body and we recognise it at once as the surface of the ocean. He raises it to his shoulders, then to his chin, eyes it warily, raises it above his head, brings it down again to his chin, shows us his mouth gasping for breath as he goes under again.

There has been much talk of Brook's Prospero, played by Sotigui Kouyate, a black African. The metaphysical Brook has said:

In other cultures, in the societies we call traditional, images of gods, magicians, sorcerers and ghosts evoke deep human realities. So an actor from such a culture can touch them without embarrassment. Mature African actors simply have a different quality from white actors – a kind of effortless transparency, an organic presence beyond self, mind or body, such as great musicians attain when they pass beyond virtuosity.

Sotigui Kouyate's French is far from 'effortless', but at least he is dealing with a text by Carrière and not by Shakespeare. Brook gives him a blue cloak, which he takes off when he lays aside his art, and a small stone which he holds, black-magic style, over Miranda's head, when he tries to get her to remember 'the dark backward and abysm of time'. (Miranda is played, in a full-length white gown, by a beautiful young Indian woman, Shantala Malhar-Shivalingappa.)

The African actor may be able to touch deep human realities evoked by images of gods and magicians, but the practical theatre magician, Brook, is not taking any chances. He has been here before – he knows that the long expository second scene of *The Tempest* has defied his powers more than once. And so he falls back on skills he once seemed to have put aside – wasn't it Heilpern, as long ago as 1973, who said he could never imagine Brook using lights again? Brook uses lights to help out this scene. As Prospero talks about the 'gentleness' of the 'noble Neapolitan, Gonzalo', we see Yoshi walking wearily across the back of the stage to sit on the solitary rock. And as Prospero continues his explanation, the other three noblemen also walk wearily across the stage (Brook has cut Adrian and Francisco, leaving Gonzalo as the only courtier accompanying the King of Naples and the usurping Duke). As they leave the stage, Yoshi slowly gets up and follows them. Miranda goes and sits on the rock and is quickly hypnotised to sleep.

When Ariel enters, he wears a model ship on his head as a hat. He is also played by a black actor – Bakary Sangaré – and he has a heavy, menacing presence. He is assisted throughout the play by two very material spirits dressed in green, who help to stage manage the magic. When Ariel describes the effects of the storm to Prospero, he takes the boat off his head and uses it to demonstrate what happened. When asked 'the time of day', he rapidly ascends the side of the proscenium arch, on metal rungs.

On this particular evening, Caliban is not being played by David Bennent (whose performance has been much praised), but by a small white actor, Pierre Lacan, who normally plays one of the spirits. He enters with an old cardboard box which he sits in while he eats his dinner – which consists of a yam, which he apparently dislikes, as he spits it out. He runs up a rope on the opposite side of the proscenium arch from that scaled by Ariel. Brook not only uses lighting changes but physical movement and a running soundtrack to help him through this second scene – the story of the usurpation has a relentless drum beat under it.

The spirits come into their own in the scene in which the noblemen explore the island – the spirits wave green palm leaves in front of them while making bird noises. They make a circle of sandcastles for Gonzalo; and make a butterfly, on a stick, land on Ferdinand. Ferdinand is played as a teenage youth by Ken Higelin. Brook may have felt driven to make a play about chastity, but he clearly has little faith in the subject's entertainment value. As Ferdinand is forced to prove his love for Miranda by piling up logs, the spirits steal the logs from the pile and put them back for him to pile again – it's an old silent movie gag.

Brook, in fact, seems to distrust spirits which are not material. When Prospero puts on an entertainment for the virtuous young lovers, he invites them to look in the air and follow the movements of spirits he says he has conjured up – but there are no spirits to see. And when Iris, Ceres and Juno do materialise (they look like Armenian figures with masks, though Billington identified them as Kabuki) they are allowed only four lines of the 'honour, riches, marriage' blessing before Prospero waves them impatiently away – he has suddenly remembered the 'foul conspiracy', through which Caliban, Stephano and Trinculo plan to kill him – but by this time the evening has taken off into another, genuinely theatrical, magical dimension.

'The pace slackens with the comic scenes . . .', John Peter has written. But not tonight. Stephano and Trinculo are played as a double act by the white Frenchman, Alain Maratrat, and the white Englishman, Bruce Myers. From the moment they enter, on this particular occasion, they run away with the show. Suddenly recognising each other as Neapolitan gentlemen, they go off into a torrent of mock Italian which ends in operatic song. When Stephano, playing the king to Caliban, imperiously orders Trinculo to stand further off, Bruce Myers wanders away to the back wall of the stage. 'Plus loin', cries Maratrat, and Myers tries to walk through the wall. On their way to murder Prospero, they are distracted by bright clothes, thrown pantomine-style from the wings. Maratrat dresses himself up as a ridiculous king: red robes, green breeches tied round his neck, a silly hat. Behind him the spirits swiftly form bamboo sticks into a mirror frame, and as Maratrat turns, Bakary Sangaré / Ariel appears in the mirror. White French Stephano and black African Ariel do their own version of the mirror sequence from the Marx Brothers' *Duck Soup*, which exists on a rarefied plane of experience indeed. In the final redemption scene, in which Caliban calls Trinculo, 'Ce pauvre idiot', Bruce Myers burns, not with repentance, but with blank disbelief. How could anybody possibly see him as an idiot? The magic circle Brook looks for between actors and audience is joined in celebratory mirth.

Do Maratrat and Myers run away with the show when Bennent is playing Caliban? Did they suddenly take off on this particular evening, as jazz musicians sometimes do? What the joy of the evening makes clear is that Peter Brook, at the Bouffes, has, over the years, created a space in which theatre magic can happen. (Who would ever have imagined a British actor making such surreal poetry out of farce?) Even Brook's attempt to make Ariel's final departure heavily 'significant' – given his freedom at last, he pauses as he leaves and looks soulfully at Prospero, as if feeling nostalgia for his enslavement – does not destroy the sense of celebration. Nor does Prospero's equally dramatic farewell. The actors receive the kind of 'prayer' one suspects Shakespeare himself was referring to when they are given a spontaneously warm ovation by the very mixed audience.

The audience could not express its feeling, though, by rushing on to the playing area. As soon as the actors left, the stage management came forward and guarded the precious sand. We had to exit carefully.

Epilogue

So where, at this point in Brook's astonishing career, has the search led him? Almost certainly not to the end. Those critics who rather romantically see his return to *The Tempest* as a hint that he is thinking of saying a long goodbye to the theatre, as Shakespeare is said to have done after writing Prospero's farewell, are underestimating his capacity for survival. More than thirty years ago, Tynan wrote of him as a man approaching the summit of his powers, when he directed his first *Measure for Measure*. We can see now that, for Brook, the search had scarcely begun. There are no signs that it is yet nearing its end.

The search has certainly taken him away from the confines of a British theatre that is no less deadly now than it was when Brook made his first entrance. In most British theatre, the old treadmill is back: *Macbeth* is rehearsed in a leading regional company for three weeks with six actors. The emptiness at the centre of British theatre can't be hidden by the lavish displays of hi-tech in the new buildings to which artistic directors have become the new slaves.

Tynan once accused Brook of being politically naïve: and when it came to trying to handle on stage political issues, like the Vietnam War, he was – his resigned acceptance of the inevitability of global destruction in the last play of *The Mahabharata* becomes far from mystical and abstract in the context of a real US led war in the Gulf. We are back where we were in 1966 and the political objections remain.

But in theatre politics, in the arena where he was in a position to act – and he said at the time of his visit to the Shah's Persia that he only believed in personal responsibility in matters the individual could affect – he was far from politically naïve. As long ago as 1968, he recognised what he wanted to escape from. He set about creating his own working conditions and for more than twenty years he has had freedom. One brief return to the RSC to direct *Anthony and Cleopatra* in 1978 seems to have reminded him, dramatically, of the world he had escaped from – he has never, (at least so far), shown any inclination to repeat the experience. (Throughout Peter Hall's tenure at the National, there was much talk of a project but Brook always managed to avoid one by saying that anything they discussed could be done better at the Bouffes.)

Those who have argued that Brook should never have left and that he is partly responsible, by his absence, for the current state of British theatre, have ignored the extent to which the RSC and the National always remained impervious to his presence – willing to take acclaim from his successes, but never willing to listen and learn or treat him as anything other than a maverick genius, sometimes to be humoured. Can we blame *Carrie*, *Jean* or *Starlight Express* on Brook? There are other reasons for the almost total decline of British theatre in the last twenty years, apart from the mediocrities leading it.

The problems of running the theatre buildings, which house such institutions as the National and the RSC and which have always been crucially underfunded by successive philistine governments from Harold Wilson's onwards, have eaten into whatever creative talent the artistic directors had so that their individual work has tended to decline. We have no wish to criticise Brook for refusing to be caught in the treadmill. Brook is not in Paris running a national theatre for the French with the responsibility for producing a spectrum of plays, so why should anyone think he ought to be performing a function like that in England? As Robert Brustein says, no other British director has proved so daring and original – certainly not over so long a period. Who would presume to tell someone of Brook's artistic stature that he should be working in Britain rather than France?

Brook has had to create his own workng conditions to make possible that relaxed continuity which extended work with trusted collaborators has given him since he went to Paris. This hasn't led to the formation of a permanent group, of the kind Brecht was able to form in East Berlin after the war, but to the establishing of a way of working, a discipline of creating in a situation where people could come and go. For *La Cerisaie*, he was able, virtually, to bring together a new performing group and make it part of his working situation (though, significantly, this didn't work when he tried to repeat the experience in New York, away from his Bouffes structure). But although a masterpiece, *La Cerisaie* was not a company show. Brook may have needed to go to Persia and Africa to find the style of doing it, but the actors he worked with certainly didn't. Natasha Parry would have been (in GR's words) as 'breathtakingly marvellous' had she spent the 70's at the RSC or the National, and no-one else in the Chekhov cast had been where she had been with Brook.

Brook won his freedom, but he has had to pay a price for it. Part of the price has been the taking of work developed for one environment – normally the Bouffes – to other less suitable environments, like that in Brooklyn. Brook has often insisted on the importance of process – and some of his more intriguing 'experiments' have led him to remote villages in Africa and to work with Campesinos in California. But he has always insisted that process is not everything – that a piece of work has to be put before an audience before it can be seen even as a completed experiment. This inevitably leads Brook into contradictions. Can every performance of *The Mahabharata* at Brooklyn be seen as a unique experience? Where does process end and a packaged produce take its place? (Brustein's comments are particularly apt). At the same time one has to say that a part of Brook – a part of Brook that we find to be completely admirable – wants his work to be seen on a world stage. This part of Brook belongs to the practical world of showbiz. He may have spent years 'researching' the spiritual truth that is hidden in *The Conference of the Birds*, but when he wants to stage the show at Avignon he asks Carrière for a script and sends for Sally Jacobs.

Brook seems not to have had any difficulty in living with this limitation on his freedom, (if that is, indeed, what it is). But another limitation raises more questions. When talking about theatre, Brook has always come back to Shakespeare, again and again. But the working conditions he has created for himself cut him off from what most people would regard as central in Shakespeare – the language.

Since his experience at Stratford in 1978, he has been faced with an unavoidable choice. Most of the international actors he works with in Paris are not capable of handling Shakespeare in English: they can just about handle the, in many ways, admirably laconic texts provided by Carrière. So what might have been a central area for 'experiment' – how can an actor working with Brook's disciplines for decades develop as concrete a way of handling Shakespeare's words as he or she now handles bamboo sticks? – remains crucially unexplored.

In the earlier part of Brook's career, around the time he was directing *Lear*, and, a few years later, *The Dream*, one of his preoccupations was how this verse could be spoken. He never got very far beyond throwing away the old tricks of rhetoric, trying to get closer to 'everyday speech', Scofield no longer playing the Lord's anointed, but giving us an old man. For a time, in his search for verbal expression as concrete (or abstract?) as the work with sticks was to become, Brook experimented with ancient languages and Ted Hughes's invented language. It was an experiment which, happily, he discarded – but he came back, not to Shakespeare, but to Carrière. So in twenty years, Brook's work on Shakespeare in Paris has been limited to Carrière versions of *Timon*, *Measure for Measure* and *The Tempest*. *Timon*, philosophically, clearly relates to the bleak visions Brook was offering us in *Titus Andronicus* and *Lear*, as does *Measure*. One suspects, though, that his return to *The Tempest*, in spite of the talk of chastity and dark African gods, had more to do with the fact that he thought he'd never successfully mastered a difficult text, and that he wanted to take it on again.

It has to be on Brook's own terms – the life of the performance in the theatre itself, the marriage of form and content – that one takes issue with some of the work since 1970. In the 50s and 60s, one went to a Brook production to connect with a more intense kind of reality (as in the *Marat/Sade*). One went to be 'linked'. Some 'links' were stronger than others, and at that time you could still get them elsewhere in British theatre – Joan Littlewood was still working. The problem is that, in Brook's case, the occasions have grown fewer and fewer. If you had one a year, that would be something. But what has the 80s produced at the highest level? *La Cerisaie* (but not *The Cherry Orchard*), *Carmen* and *La Tempête*. While we were watching *The Mahabharata*, we could have seen all three and still had time left over for *King Lear*. Perhaps Brook needed the discipline of having to deliver one play a year with a scratch company so that he could spend the other nine months developing his dharma. Would he have found that intolerable? Would that have forced him to look at the two-thirds of his beloved Shakespeare he has so far avoided? Since he went to the Bouffes, he has found a style and a place for presenting Shakespeare in the most popular and dynamic way (though still not in his own language). But Shakespeare hasn't been prominent in his researches.

It's difficult to avoid the criticism that Brook's freedom has given him the opportunity for indulging some of his private spiritual fantasies. The final version he produced of *The Birds* extended the range of practical possibilities in the theatre by its bold and inventive use of puppets to change scale and move through different physical dimensions. It offered new and exciting theatre experiences. But it hardly offered that new spiritual experience Brook had told his actors they were wrestling with over the years. Its originality lay in its form: its final message looked suspiciously like Judy Garland's 'Birds fly over the rainbow, why, then, oh why can't I?'

In the same way, the message in the final episode of *The Mahabharata* looked very much like Hollywood's 'A man's gotta do what a man's gotta do.'

The fact that these texts invite such comments is a measure of their limitations. One has only to compare them with the Shakespeare Brook admires. (What's the message of *Lear*: 'Don't give the kids anything while you're still alive'?)

Brook spent years on both these projects. Yet the man who sees Shakespeare as a touchstone has never, in more than forty years, engaged with work that could fall well within his vision (such as *Troilus and Cressida* or *Coriolanus*), spent only three weeks at Birmingham in the 40s putting together *King John*, and has never faced up to the dark forces of *Macbeth*.

Brook now says that he no longer feels able to stage Shakespeare – which can only leave his admirers rueing what might have been. But he has spoken of plans to deliver a ten hour epic – an exploration of the entire history of world theatre. Is the suggestion a promise or a threat? It was something of a relief when, in March 1993, the result of his latest research, on which he had been working intermittently for three years, turned out to be a small-scale masterpiece which once again extended the concrete possibilities of theatre experience – and which distilled that experience into only one hour and three quarters.

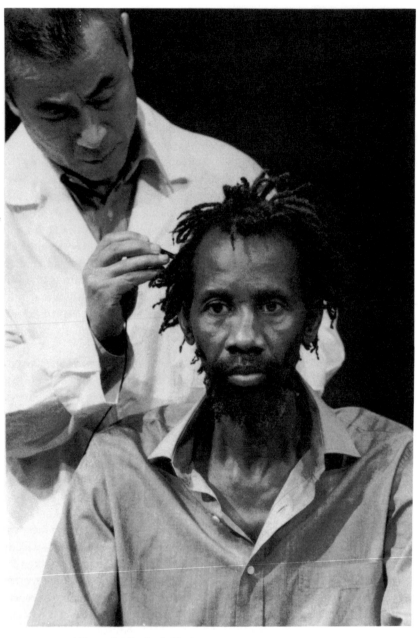

20   *L'Homme Qui*, Bouffes du Nord, 1993

L'Homme Qui grew out of Brook's interest in a book by a doctor, Oliver Sacks, called *The Man who Mistook his Wife for a Hat*. Sacks's book chronicled his experiences with some two dozen patients who had neurological disorders. Brook began by asking his group of actors to improvise, using the text of the book. But he found that they could never succeed in making the material rise above the level of soap opera.

Brook then invited Sacks to come and look at the improvisations, hoping that the author himself might find a way into the inner life of the book which the actors seemed unable to tap. But Sacks only sat and smiled, saying how wonderful he thought it looked. Not knowing how to proceed, Brook put the project aside and embarked on *La Tempête*.

It wasn't until Brook went to talk to another eminent British neurologist that he realised that the form of the book, while making it enlivening to read, was itself the barrier. The neurologist discussed the various diseases Sacks dealt with, saying that all of them except one were fairly common so that doctors had well-known clinical tests to deal with the symptoms. As an example, he talked about the first story, (about the man who mistook his wife for his hat), in which the man is taken to meet the doctor and talks to him quite normally. In Sacks's version, it's only at the end of the interview, when the man bends down to tie up his shoe-lace and gets it wrong, that Sacks realises the man is misfunctioning. The neurologist told Brook that there were standard tests which would be done in five minutes if one suspected a patient of having such a disease. Brook then realised that the problem with the Sacks material was that it was already 'dramatised' – that Sacks had 'written it up' to make it more engaging for the reader, and that this was why the acting group was finding it impenetrable.

So Brook selected four of the actors, (it would have been impossible for a larger number to gain regular access to the hospital), and they spent months studying patients before returning to the text of Sacks's book. Now that they had their own experience to draw from, they found their work with the text extremely rewarding.

The performance takes place on a bare rectangular stage on which there are four white chairs, tables, a small television camera, and two TV monitors. Four actors – one French, one German, one African and one Japanese – continually change roles in order to enact the experiences of some two dozen patients. They also take it in turns to be the doctors – as doctors they always wear white coats.

A man looks into a mirror and fails to recognise himself.

A music professor mistakes a hat for one of his students.

Yoshi gazes at a rose in total bafflement.

A patient makes a tape recording of himself reading a poem. When he hears it played back, he weeps at his own inability to read it properly.

The hour and three quarters ends with beautiful technicolour images of the brain appearing on the screen for two minutes as the actors sit and watch.

What is extraordinary about this achievement is the way it resolves, through simple concrete images, problems Brook has been engaged with for many years.

The content of the show takes us back to the Beckett of *Happy Days*. Traditionally drama shows us human beings in conflict with each other. Beckett offered us the image of a woman whose own perception of herself and her condition was in direct conflict, not with other characters in the play, but with the way we in the audience perceived her. We saw that she was buried, first up to her breasts and later up to her neck, in a grassy mound, her existence narrowed down to a handful of everyday objects – a toothbrush, toothpaste, spectacles, a hand mirror – which she kept in a bag, and which she couldn't even reach in the second act. Yet she ended the play by insisting, 'Oh, this is a happy day. Will have been a happy day. So far', and by humming a snatch of a well-known romantic song. Beckett used external objects to make concrete an internal state of mind.

In the same way, Brook uses external images – and particularly images on a TV monitor – to objectify an inner struggle. Paradoxically, this emphasis on an internal struggle also takes us back to Brecht – the Brecht who wrote, 'Closely examine the behaviour of these people. Consider it strange, although familiar . . .' Brecht wanted his audiences to see the familiar as strange – and this is precisely what Yoshi does when he contemplates a rose with disbelief.

Brook also realises, in this astonishing piece, his aim of connecting the theatre experience with the experience of the abstract art of the century – but in an entirely clear and comprehensible way. The technicolour images that appear on the screen at the end of *L'Homme Qui* are beautiful examples of abstract art – but they are also scientific diagrams of the brain. Brook has achieved a synthesis of the kind he was writing about in the 6os, which is at the same time both mysterious and lucid.

Brook could not have achieved the clarities of *L'Homme Qui* without the freedom to research which he has created for himself over the years. If that freedom has sometimes led him into grandiose projects which take us into realms of mysticism into which some of us find it hard to follow him, it has also given him a way into a precise and sharp theatrical language which is still waiting to be explored and extended.

The next ten hour epic either beckons or threatens. In the mean time, we can only look forward in eager anticipation to the many more pieces of magic – like *La Tempête* and *L'Homme Qui* – which Brook, the practical man of the theatre, is going to produce from his voluminous conjuror's sleeves.

Select bibliography

(This does not include first reviews which appeared in newspapers or periodicals, nor material not directly quoted which appears in *The Shifting Point* or *Peter Brook: a Theatrical Casebook*.)

Books

Attar, Farid Ud-din. *La Conférence des Oiseaux*, adaptation by Jean-Claude Carrière (Paris: C.I.C.T., 1979)
The Conference of the Birds, adaptation by Jean-Claude Carrière and Peter Brook (Connecticut: The Dramatic Publishing Co., 1982)
Berry, Ralph. *On Directing Shakespeare* (London: Croom Helm, 1977)
Brook, Peter. *The Birthday Present: a Play in One Act* (BBC TV 1955) (Chicago: The Dramatic Publishing Co., 1966)
—. *The Empty Space* (Harmondsworth: Penguin, 1968)
—. *The Shifting Point: Theatre, Film, Opera, 1946–1987* (New York: Harper and Row, 1987)
Cannan, Denis and Higgins, Colin. *Les Iks*, adaptation of Colin Turnbull's *The Mountain People*, trans. Jean-Claude Carrière (Paris: C.I.C.T., 1975)
—. *The Ik*, with introduction by Colin Turnbull (Connecticut: The Dramatic Publishing Co., 1982)
Chekhov, Anton. *La Cérisaie*, French version by Peter Brook, Jean-Claude Carrière and Lusia Lavrova (Paris: C.I.C.T., 1981)
—. *La Cérisaie*, Collection 'Théâtre et Mise-en-Scène' (Paris: Hatier, 1985)
Constant, Marius, Brook, Peter and Carrière, Jean-Claude. *La Tragédie de Carmen*, from Bizet, Mérimée, Meilhac and Halévy (Paris: C.I.C.T., 1981)
Cook, Judith. *Director's Theatre* (London: Harrap, 1974)
Curti, Lidia. *Peter Brook e Shakespeare* (Naples: Istituto Universitario Orientale, 1984)
Esslin, Martin. *Artaud* (London: Fontana/Collins, 1976)
—. *Brief Chronicles* (London: Temple-Smith, 1970)
Grotowski, Jerzy, *Towards a Poor Theatre* (London: Methuen, 1969)
Harwood, Ronald. *The Ages of Geilgud* (London: Hodder and Stoughton, 1984)
Hayman, Ronald. *Artaud and After* (Oxford University Press, 1977)
—. *British Theatre since 1955* (Oxford University Press, 1979)
—. *Playback* (London: Davis-Poynter, 1973)
—. *Techniques of Acting* (London: Methuen, 1969)
—. *Theatre and Anti-Theatre* (London: Secker and Warburg, 1979)
Heilpern, John. *Conference of the Birds: The Story of Peter Brook in Africa* (London: Faber and Faber, 1979)
Hughes, Ted. *Oedipus*, adapted from Seneca (London: Faber and Faber, 1969)
Hunt, Albert. *The Theatre of John Arden* (London: Methuen, 1974)
Innes, Christopher. *Holy Theatre* (Cambridge University Press, 1981)
Jarry, Alfred. *Ubu aux Bouffes* (Paris: C.I.C.T., 1977)
Kott, Jan. *Shakespeare our Contemporary* (London: Methuen, 1965)
Kozintsev, Grigori. *King Lear: The Space of Tragedy* (London: Heinemann, 1978)
Marowitz, Charles. *Confessions of a Counterfeit Critic* (London: Eyre Methuen, 1973)
—. *The Act of Being* (London: Secker and Warburg, 1978)

—. *Prospero's Staff* (Indiana University Press, 1986)

Montassier, Gérard. *Le Fait culturel* (Editions Fayard, 1980)

Oida, Yoshi. *An Actor Adrift* (London: Methuen, 1992)

Selbourne, David. *The Making of A Midsummer Night's Dream* (London: Methuen, 1982)

Shakespeare, William. *A Midsummer Night's Dream*, RSC acting version (Chicago: The Dramatic Publishing Co., 1974)

—. *As You Like It* (London: Folio Society, 1953)

—. *Timon d'Athènes*, adapted by Jean-Claude Carrière (Paris: C.I.C.T. 1976)

—. *Mesure pour Mesure*, adapted by Jean-Claude Carrière (Paris: C.I.C.T., 1978)

—. *La Tempête*, adapted by Jean-Claude Carrière (Paris: C.I.C.T., 1990)

Smith, A. C. H. *Orghast at Persepolis* (London: Eyre Methuen, 1972)

Styan, J. L. *The Shakespeare Revolution* (Cambridge University Press, 1977)

Trewin, John C. *Peter Brook: a Biography* (London: Macdonald, 1971)

Turnbull, Colin. *The Mountain People* (London: Picador, 1974)

US. Script of Aldwych production, ed. Albert Hunt, Michael Kustow and Geoffrey Reeves (London: Calder and Boyars, 1968)

Weiss, Peter. *The Persecution and Assassination of Marat as Performed by the Inmates of the Asylum of Charenton under the direction of Marquis de Sade*, adapted by Adrian Mitchell (London: John Calder, 1965)

Williams, David. *Peter Brook: A Theatrical Casebook* (London: Methuen, 1988)

Interviews with Brook

Adair, Gilbert. 'A meeting with Peter Brook', *Sight and Sound*, 49/1 (Winter 1979–80)

Albera, Philippe. 'Attentat à l'Opéra', *Révolution*, 136 (1982)

Ansorge, Peter, 'Interview with Brook', *Plays and Players*, 18/1 (October 1970)

Bablet, Denis. 'Rencontre avec Peter Brook', *Travail Théâtral*, 10 (October 1972/January 1973)

Barber, John. 'Down to the bare boards', *Daily Telegraph* (10 February 1977)

Billington, Michael. 'Written on the wind – the dramatic art of Peter Brook', *The Listener* (21 and 28 December 1978)

Cott, Jonathan. 'Interview with Brook', *New Age Journal* (December 1984)

Cox, Frank. 'Interview with Brook', *Plays and Players*, 15/7 (April 1968)

Gibson, Michael. 'Brook's Africa', *The Drama Review*, 17/3 (September 1973)

Godard, Colette. '*La Cérisaie*', *Comédie Française Review*, 96 (February 1981)

Greer, Herb. 'Credo Quia Contra-Courant est' *Transatlantic Review*, 57 (October 1976)

Hayman, Ronald. 'Life and joy' *The Times* (29 August 1970)

Hentoff, Nat. 'Brook: Yes, let's be emotional about Vietnam', *New York Times* (25 February 1968)

Labeille, Daniel. 'The formless hunch', *Modern Drama*, 23/3 (September 1980)

Lahr, John. 'Knowing what to celebrate', *Plays and Players*, 23/6 (March 1976)

Lawson, Stephen R. 'Interview with Brook', *Yale/Theater*, 7/1 (Fall 1975)

Liehm, A. J. 'The Politics of sclerosis: Stalin and Lear', *Theatre Quarterly*, 3/10 (April/June 1973)

Levin, Bernard. 'Interview with Brook', BBC 2 (April 1982)

Million, Martine. 'Le Sens d'une recherche: entrien avec Peter Brook', *Travail Théâtral*, 18–19 (January/June 1975)

More, Shelia. 'Interview with Brook', *The Observer* (5 April 1964)

Mossman, James. 'Throwing out the cobwebs', BBC 2 (27 July 1971)

Munk, Erika. 'Looking for a new language', *Performance*, 1/1 (New York: Shakespeare Public Theatre, 1971)

Oakes, Philip. 'Something new out of Africa', *Sunday Times* (4 January 1976)

Parabola. 'Leaning on the moment: a conversation with Peter Brook', *Parabola* 4/2 (Spring 1979)

—. 'Lie and glorious adjective', *Parabola*, 6/3 (August 1981)

Ronconi, Luca. 'Interview with Brook', *Cahiers Renaud-Barrault*, 79 (1972)

Seymour, Alan. 'Interview with Kenneth Tynan', *The London Magazine* (August 1965)

Sutter, Arthur. 'Shakespeare isn't a bore', *New Theatre* (June 1947)

Théâtre en Europe. 'Shakespeare and *The Mahabharata*', *Théâtre en Europe*, 7 (June 1985)

'*The Mahabharata*', *Théâtre en Europe*, 8 (October 1985)

Trussler, Simon. 'Private experiment – in public', *Plays and Players*, 11 (February 1964)

Wada, Yutaka. 'Interview with Brook', *sogetsu*, 142 (June 1982)

Articles

Bernard, Kenneth. 'Some observations on the theatre of Peter Brook', *Yale/Theater*, 12 (Fall/Winter 1980)

Billington, Michael. 'RSC in *US*, *Plays and Players*, 14 (December 1966)

—. 'From Artaud to Brook, and back again', *The Guardian* (6 January 1976)

—. 'A sandwich course by the signpost man', *The Guardian* (22 January 1982)

—. 'A fire snake in the sand', *Théâtre en Europe*, 8 (October 1985)

—. 'Close encounter of the Brook kind', *The Guardian* (12 May 1989)

Bishop of Woolwich. 'The Aldwych liturgy' (*US*), *The Guardian* (November 1966)

Brook, Peter. 'Style in Shakespeare production', *Orpheus*, 1 (1948)

—. 'Salome', *The Observer* (4 December 1949)

—. 'To Moscow to put on "Hamlet"', *Vogue* (15 April 1956)

—. 'The influence of Gordon Craig in theory and practice', *Drama*, 5/37 (Summer 1955)

—. 'Gordon Craig', *Sunday Times* (17 July 1956)

—. 'An open letter to William Shakespeare, Or, As I Don't Like It', *Sunday Times* (1 September 1957)

—. 'Faust', New York Times (27 October 1957)

—. 'Oh for empty seats', *Encore* (January 1959)

—. 'From Zero to the infinite', *Encore* (November 1960)

—. 'The Cuban enterprise', *Sight and Sound* (Spring 1961)

—. 'A search for a hunger', *Encore* (July/August 1961)

—. 'Happy Days and Marienbad', *Encore* (January 1962)

—. Contribution to discussion: 'Are critics any good?', *Encore* (November/December 1962)

—˘ Contribution to discussion: 'Artaud for Artaud's sake', *Encore* (May/June 1964)

—. 'What about real life?' *The Crucial Years*, RSC (1963)

—. 'The road to *Marat/Sade*', *New York Herald Tribune* (26 December 1964)

—. 'False Gods', *Flourish* (Winter 1965)

—. 'Endgame as King Lear: or how to stop worrying and love Beckett', *Encore* (1965)

—. 'Finding Shakespeare on film', *The Drama Review*, 11/1 (Fall 1966)

—. 'Is MacBird pro-American?' *New York Times* (19 March 1967)

—. '*Tell me Lies* in America', *The Times* (17 February 1968)

—. 'La merde et le ciel', *Le Théâtre Baroque I* (Cahiers dirigés par Fernando Arrabel) (Paris: Christian Bourgois, 1968)

—. 'Eighth world theatre day: international message', *Le Théâtre en Pologne*, 6/3 (1969)

—. 'Les lieux du spectacle', *Architecture d'Aujourd'hui*, 152 (October/November 1970)

—. 'Le Théâtre sans Fard', *La Nouvelle Critique*, 33 (April 1970) (from an ORTF interview in the series 'Un certain regard')

—. 'In a sense' (re *Orghast*) (Paris: C.I.R.T., 1972)

—. Brook at the Brooklyn Academy of Music (workshop sessions recorded and transcribed by Sally Gardner) (September/October 1973) (unpublished)

—. 'The world as a can opener', *New York Times* (5 November 1973)

—. 'Lettre à une étudiante Anglaise', *Timon d'Athènes* (Paris: C.I.C.T., 1974)

—. 'The complete truth is global', *New York Times* (20 January 1974)

—. 'The three cultures of modern man', *Cultures*, The UNESCO Press, 3/4 (1976)

—. 'Théâtre Populaire, Théâtre Immédiat', *Le Monde* (24 November 1977)

—. 'Filming a play' (contribution to symposium at Ivry 1977), *Cahiers Théâtre Louvain* 46 (1981)

—. 'Les Espaces indefinis', *Techniques et Architecture* ('Ruptures dans l'architecture du spectacle' special edition), 310 (1978)

—. 'The living theatre of the Outback', *Sunday Times* (17 August 1980)

—. 'Espaces pour un théâtre, *Le Scarabée International*, 2 (Summer 1982)

—. 'A world in relief', *10 Ans du Festival d'Automne* (Paris, 1982)

—. 'Message pour Santarcangelo': conference devoted to Peter Brook and Jerzy Grotowski, Santarcangelo di Romagna (9–11 June 1983); transcription in *Les Voies de La Création Théâtre XIII* (1985)

Brook, Peter and Marowitz, Charles. 'A theatre of nerve-ends', *Sunday Times* (12 January 1964)

Brook, Peter and Reeves, Geoffrey. 'Shakespeare on three screens', *Sight and Sound*, 34/2 (Spring 1965)

Esslin, Martin. 'The Theatre of Cruelty', *New York Times* (6 March 1966)

—. 'Are we to blame for *US*?' *New York Times* (6 October 1966)

Heilpern, John. 'Session based on voice' (Paris: C.I.R.T., 1972)

—. 'Peter Brook: the grand inquisitor', *Observer* (18 January 1976)

Hughes, Ted. '*Orghast*: talking without words', *Vogue* (December 1971)

Hunt, Albert. 'On Joan Littlewood and Peter Brook', *International Theatre Information* (Summer 1973)

—. 'Acting and being', *New Society* (20 February 1975)

—. 'The trials of working with a master magician', *New Society* (26 August 1982)

Johns, Eric. 'Wonder boy', *Theatre World* (June 1949)

Kane, John. 'When my cue comes, call me and I will answer', *Sunday Times* (13 June 1971)

—. 'The actor as acrobat', *Plays and Players*, 18 (August 1971)

Kott, Jan. 'After Grotowski: the end of the impossible theatre', *Theatre Quarterly* 10/38 (1980)

—. 'The theater of essence: Kantor and Brook', *Yale/Theater* (Fall/Winter 1982)

Levin, Bernard. 'The seeds of genius: watch them grow', *The Times* (3 April 1980)

—. 'Two men on remarkable journeys', *The Times* (26 June 1980)

Marowitz, Charles. 'Lear Log' *Encore* (January/February 1963)

—. 'Notes on the Theatre of Cruelty', *Drama Review*, 34 (Winter 1966)

—. 'From prodigy to professional, as written, directed and acted by Peter Brook', *New York Times* (24 October 1968)

—. 'Brook: from *Marat/Sade* to *Midsummer Night's Dream*', *New York Times* (13 September 1970)

Morley, Sheridan. 'Peter Brook: quarrying theatre in Australia', *The Times* (7 April 1980)

Munk, Erika. 'The way's the thing', *Village Voice* (12 May 1980)

Oida, Yoshi, 'Shinto training of the actor', *Dartington Theatre Papers*, Third Series, no. 3

Read, Bill. 'Peter Brook: from Stratford-on-Avon to the Gare du Nord', *Boston University Journal*, 24/3 (1975)

Rogoff, Gordon. 'Mr. Duerrenmatt buys new shoes', *Encore* (March/April 1959)

Reeves, Geoffrey. 'The Persepolis Folies of 1971', *Performance*, 1/1 (1971)

Schechner, Richard (ed.). '*Marat/Sade* forum', *The Drama Review*, 10/4 (Summer 1966)

—. '*The Mahabharata*', *The Drama Review*, 30/1 (October 1985)

Selbourne, David. 'Brook's *Dream, Culture and Agitation – Theatre Documents* (Action Books, 1972)

Serban, Audrei. 'The life in a sound', *The Drama Review*, 20/4) December 1976)

Shorter, Eric. 'Lost man of British theatre', *Daily Telegraph* (17 October 1974)

—. 'Off the cuff, with Peter Brook and Company', *Drama*, 129 (Summer 1978)

—. 'False prophet?' *Daily Telegraph* (12 February 1979)

Tynan, Kenneth. 'Director as misanthropist: on the moral neutrality of Peter Brook', *Theatre Quarterly*,
        7/25 (Spring 1977)
Wardle, Irving. 'The saint and the sabyrite', *The Times* (14 September 1968)
—. 'The Indian pilgrimage of Peter Brook', *The Times* (5 May 1982)
Williams, David. '"A place marked by life": Peter Brook at the Bouffes du Nord', *New Theatre Quarterly*,
        1/1 (February 1985)
Wilson, Peter. *Sessions in USA: A Chronicle* (Paris: C.I.C.T., 1973)

Index